2nd Edition

HERB GARDENING IN TEXAS

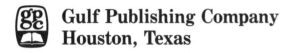

Gulf Publishing Company
Houston, Texas

2nd Edition

HERB GARDENING IN TEXAS

◆ SOL MELTZER ◆

◼ 2nd Edition ◼

HERB GARDENING IN TEXAS

Illustrated by Terry J. Moore

10 9 8 7 6 5 4 3 2 1

Gulf Publishing Company
Book Division
P.O. Box 2608 ☐ Houston, Texas 77252-2608

Library of Congress Cataloging-in-Publication Data
Meltzer, Sol.
    Herb gardening in Texas / Sol Meltzer.—2nd ed.
        p. cm.
    Includes index.
    ISBN 0-88415-043-7
    1. Herb gardening—Texas. 2. Herbs—Texas. I. Title.
SB351.H5M358 1992
635′.7′09764—dc20   91-46083
                                                          CIP

With love to my wife Thelma; to my children Melinda, John, Nancy, Tim, and grandchildren Luken, Zachary, Sarah Grace; and last, but not least, to my herb garden.

Contents

of special interest...

Acknowledgments

Special credits are due Taylor's Herb Garden Inc., Vista, California for providing many of the color photographs.

Additional photo credits are due Barry Henderson, B. J. Lowe, Greg Lorfing, Marc Nekhom, Jon and Riley Newhouse, Kent Taylor, and Sol Meltzer. Gael Thompson was kind enough to do some of the drafts of my illustrations. Linda Samson deciphered my scribbling and did a fine job typing the manuscript. And thanks to Linda Mullinax for additional typing. I'm grateful to Bill Adams (Harris County Extension horticulturist) for reviewing the book and, more important, for encouraging me to write it. Thanks also to Madeline Hill for her valuable criticism, and to Bill Basham of the Houston Arboretum and Botanical Gardens.

Finally, appreciation to my wife Thelma, who furnished some of the photos, read the manuscript, and supported my efforts with encouragement and constructive criticism.

Preface

To my knowledge, this is the only book on growing and caring for herbs in Texas. Our growing conditions are completely different from those in other parts of the country. What does or doesn't do well in California, or up north, may not be appropriate for Texas. Many of the perennial herbs are grown as annuals in the North; in most of Texas they are perennial. Marjoram, lemon verbena, lemon grass, and rosemary are some examples. There are a few herbs, such as sweet woodruff and French tarragon, that are difficult to grow in most areas of Texas. They do well in the higher, cooler, shady areas of the state.

In Texas we have ample rain, particularly along the coast. I've taken that into consideration by suggesting soil mixtures that drain well and the use of raised beds for some herbs. I discuss and have sketches of inexpensive methods by which to propagate additional herbs from your plants. Some of the other sections cover drying and storing herbs, extracting essential oils, insecticidal properties of some of the herbs, how to make herbal insecticidal sprays, and companion plantings of herbs and vegetables to repel certain harmful insects.

With the exception of one or two, I have grown all the herbs mentioned. My herb garden is 60 by 100 feet, with approximately 100 different varieties of herbs. I wouldn't discuss certain methods of propagation, making a soil mix, growing under lights, etc., if I didn't use them myself. I consider myself a knowledgeable grower; whether I'm a worthy author is for you to judge.

Writing this book was fun. I'm sure you'll find several good ideas, have a laugh or two, and agree with me when I say that herbs make scents in Texas.

Sol Meltzer
Houston, Texas

Herb Hardiness Zone Map

The term *hardy* means the ability of a plant to survive the lowest average winter temperature for that particular zone. If (WP) follows an herb, it means winter protect in that zone. Some herbs do well in certain zones, but within that zone, variations in temperatures, rainfall, soil, etc., can mean success or failure with a particular herb. Many of the herbs, particularly the mints, may die back in zones 6, 7, and 8, but the root system remains alive and new growth is produced in the spring.

An herb listed in zone 6 is hardy in all zones. Herbs listed in zones 7 and 8 are hardy in 9 and 10 also. Those listed in zone 9 are hardy in 10.

Regardless of what zone you're in, all the herbs need to be planted early in the spring to establish a good root system for the following winter. In zones 6 and 7, herbs that need winter protection must be set out several months before the first anticipated cold weather.

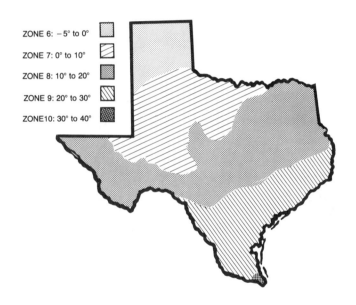

ZONE 6: −5° to 0°
ZONE 7: 0° to 10°
ZONE 8: 10° to 20°
ZONE 9: 20° to 30°
ZONE 10: 30° to 40°

Zones 6 and 7			Zone 8	Zone 9	Zone 10
Angelica	Horehound	Salad Burnet	Dittany of Crete	Aloe Vera (WP)	Aloe Vera
Camomile (P)	Horseradish	Santolina	Garlic Chives	Cayenne (WP)	Cayenne
Caraway	Hyssop	Sassafras	Greek Oregano	Ginger	Ginger
Catnip	Lambs Ear	Shallots	Mexican Marigold	Lemon Grass (WP)	Lemon Grass
Chives	Lavender	Southernwood	Mint (WP)	Lemon Tree	Lemon Tree
Comfrey	Lemon Balm	Sweet Flag	Pineapple Sage (WP)	Lemon Verbena (WP)	Lemon Verbena
Costmary	Mint	Sweet Woodruff	Rosemary, upright	Pennyroyal (WP)	Pennyroyal
Elecampane	Mugwort	Tansy	Sweet Marjoram (WP)	Rosemary, prostrate	Rosemary, prostrate
Fennel (P)	Oregano	Tarragon		Scented Geraniums	Scented Geraniums
Foxglove	Parsley	Thyme		(WP)	Sweet Bay
Garlic	Pyrethrum	Winter Savory		Sweet Bay	
Germander	Rue	Wintergreen			
Ginseng	Sage	Wormwood			
		Yarrow			

Average Dates of First and Last Frosts

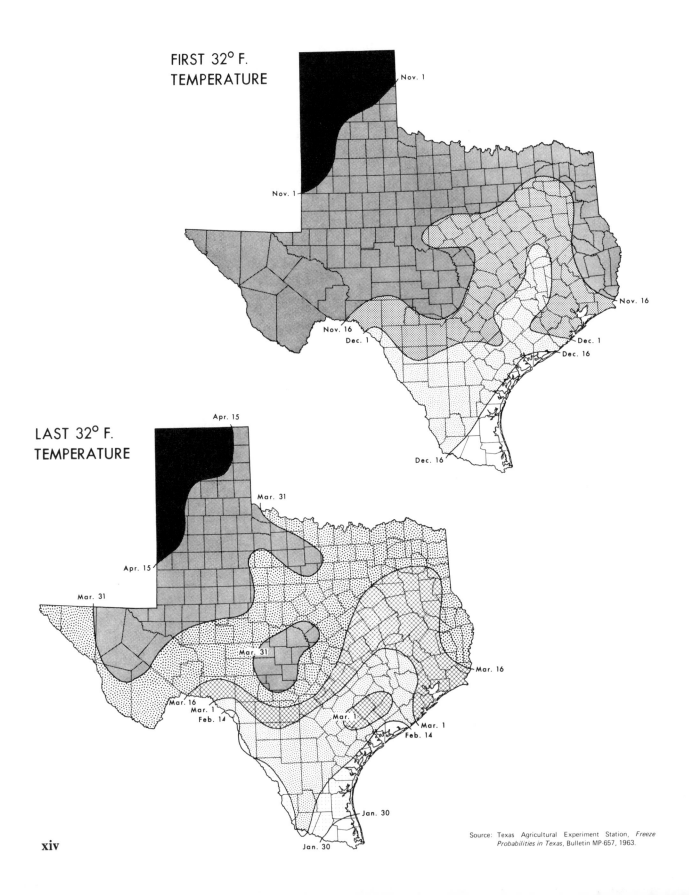

FIRST 32° F. TEMPERATURE

LAST 32° F. TEMPERATURE

Source: Texas Agricultural Experiment Station, *Freeze Probabilities in Texas*, Bulletin MP-657, 1963.

Station	Mean date of last spring freeze	Mean date of first fall freeze	Mean growing season
Abilene	Mar. 26	Nov. 12	231
Albany	Apr. 3	Nov. 5	216
Alice	Feb. 20	Dec. 4	287
Alpine	Mar. 30	Nov. 10	225
Amarillo	Apr. 20	Oct. 28	191
Angleton	Mar. 2	Nov. 30	273
Austin	Mar. 7	Nov. 22	260
Ballinger	Mar. 30	Nov. 10	225
Balmorhea	Mar. 30	Nov. 11	226
Beaumont	Feb. 18	Nov. 24	279
Beeville	Feb. 20	Dec. 5	288
Big Spring	Mar. 29	Nov. 11	227
Blanco	Mar. 25	Nov. 3	223
Boerne	Mar. 25	Nov. 9	229
Bonham	Mar. 30	Nov. 7	222
Borger	Apr. 17	Oct. 28	194
Brady	Mar. 29	Nov. 11	227
Brenham	Feb. 25	Dec. 2	280
Bridgeport	Mar. 30	Nov. 5	220
Bronson	Mar. 24	Nov. 8	229
Brownsville			365
Brownwood	Mar. 20	Nov. 18	243
Cameron	Mar. 15	Nov. 21	251
Canadian	Apr. 9	Oct. 30	204
Canyon	Apr. 19	Oct. 28	192
Carrizo Springs	Feb. 22	Nov. 26	277
Center	Mar. 17	Nov. 6	234
Centerville	Mar. 14	Nov. 9	240
Childress	Apr. 1	Nov. 7	220
Clarksville	Mar. 30	Nov. 5	224
Cleburne	Mar. 26	Nov. 10	229
Coleman	Mar. 28	Nov. 5	222
College Station	Mar. 6	Nov. 27	266
Colorado City	Apr. 5	Nov. 3	212
Conroe	Mar. 6	Nov. 23	262
Corpus Christi	Feb. 9	Dec. 12	306
Corsicana	Mar. 13	Nov. 20	252
Cotulla	Feb. 24	Nov. 25	274
Crockett	Mar. 16	Nov. 9	238
Crosbyton	Apr. 11	Nov. 2	205
Crystal City	Mar. 2	Nov. 27	270
Cuero	Mar. 8	Nov. 27	264
Dalhart	Apr. 23	Oct. 25	185
Dallas	Mar. 18	Nov. 12	239
Danevang	Feb. 23	Dec. 5	285
Del Rio	Feb. 10	Dec. 10	303
Denison Dam	Mar. 26	Nov. 10	229
Dilley	Feb. 25	Dec. 2	280
Dublin	Mar. 26	Nov. 17	236
Eagle Pass	Feb. 20	Dec. 3	286
Eastland	Mar. 29	Nov. 9	225
Eden	Apr. 3	Nov. 7	218
El Campo	Feb. 17	Dec. 2	288
El Paso	Mar. 14	Nov. 12	243
Encinal	Feb. 14	Dec. 8	297
Falfurrias	Feb. 10	Dec. 10	303
Flatonia	Mar. 4	Dec. 4	275
Flint	Mar. 8	Nov. 22	259
Follett	Apr. 20	Oct. 28	191
Ft. Stockton	Apr. 2	Nov. 10	222
Fort Worth	Mar. 20	Nov. 15	240
Fredericksburg	Mar. 27	Nov. 3	221
Gainesville	Mar. 29	Nov. 6	222
Galveston	Jan. 27	Dec. 24	331
Gatesville	Mar. 24	Nov. 9	230
Goliad	Feb. 22	Dec. 1	282
Graham	Apr. 3	Nov. 2	213
Greenville	Mar. 20	Nov. 12	237
Hallettsville	Mar. 8	Nov. 15	252
Harlingen	Jan. 24	Dec. 26	336
Haskell	Mar. 31	Nov. 12	226
Henderson	Mar. 11	Nov. 13	247
Henrietta	Mar. 28	Nov. 11	228
Hereford	Apr. 23	Oct. 24	184
Hico	Mar. 29	Nov. 2	218
Hondo	Mar. 3	Nov. 21	263
Houston	Feb. 4	Dec. 10	309
Huntsville	Mar. 9	Nov. 27	263
Iowa Park	Apr. 1	Nov. 2	215
Jacksboro	Apr. 2	Nov. 10	222
Junction	Apr. 2	Nov. 2	214
Karnack	Mar. 18	Nov. 4	231
Kaufman	Mar. 21	Nov. 15	239
Kenedy	Mar. 5	Nov. 26	266
Kerrville	Apr. 4	Nov. 6	216
Kirbyville	Mar. 22	Nov. 7	230
Knox City	Apr. 1	Nov. 9	222
Lampasas	Mar. 30	Nov. 8	223
Laredo	Jan. 31	Dec. 19	322
Levelland	Apr. 13	Oct. 30	200
Liberty	Mar. 1	Nov. 15	259
Lindale	Mar. 12	Nov. 11	244
Livingston	Mar. 14	Nov. 17	248
Llano	Mar. 27	Nov. 10	228
Longview	Mar. 15	Nov. 12	242
Lubbock	Apr. 11	Nov. 1	204
Lufkin	Mar. 18	Nov. 4	231
Luling	Mar. 3	Nov. 24	266
Madisonville	Mar. 9	Nov. 12	248
Marathon	Apr. 5	Nov. 1	210
Marshall	Mar. 14	Nov. 13	244
Matagorda	Feb. 13	Dec. 14	304
Maurbo	Feb. 23	Dec. 2	282
McAllen	Jan. 30	Dec. 10	314
McCamey	Mar. 26	Nov. 11	230
McCook	Feb. 5	Dec. 8	306
McKinney	Apr. 1	Nov. 5	218
Memphis	Apr. 5	Nov. 2	211
Mexia	Mar. 16	Nov. 21	250
Miami	Apr. 19	Oct. 23	187
Midland	Mar. 28	Nov. 15	232
Mineral Wells	Mar. 25	Nov. 6	226
Mission	Jan. 26	Dec. 18	326
Montague	Mar. 29	Nov. 6	222
Mount Locke	Apr. 23	Oct. 26	186
Mount Pleasant	Mar. 25	Nov. 9	229
Muleshoe	Apr. 20	Oct. 20	183
Munday	Apr. 6	Nov. 7	215
Nacogdoches	Mar. 16	Nov. 10	239
New Braunfels	Mar. 11	Nov. 26	260
Palacios	Feb. 12	Dec. 4	295
Palestine	Mar. 14	Nov. 15	246
Paris	Mar. 27	Nov. 10	228
Pecos	Mar. 31	Nov. 8	222
Pierce	Mar. 6	Nov. 27	266
Plainview	Apr. 11	Nov. 4	207
Port Arthur	Jan. 30	Dec. 8	312
Port Isabel			365
Port Lavaca	Feb. 18	Dec. 8	293
Port O'Connor	Feb. 6	Dec. 20	317
Poteet	Mar. 6	Nov. 19	258
Presidio	Mar. 18	Nov. 13	240
Quanah	Apr. 3	Nov. 4	215
Raymondville	Jan. 25	Dec. 22	331
Rio Grande City	Feb. 11	Dec. 13	305
Rising Star	Mar. 28	Nov. 6	223
Rocksprings	Mar. 28	Nov. 17	234
Roscoe	Apr. 6	Nov. 6	214
Rusk	Mar. 16	Nov. 8	237
San Angelo	Mar. 25	Nov. 13	233
San Antonio	Mar. 3	Nov. 26	268
San Benito	Jan. 13	Dec. 26	347
San Marcos	Mar. 13	Nov. 19	251
Sealy	Feb. 27	Dec. 2	278
Seminole	Apr. 10	Nov. 2	206
Seymour	Apr. 4	Oct. 31	210
Sherman	Mar. 20	Nov. 7	232
Smithville	Mar. 11	Nov. 15	249
Snyder	Apr. 5	Nov. 4	213
Spearman	Apr. 22	Oct. 24	185
Spur	Apr. 17	Oct. 28	194
Sugar Land	Feb. 14	Nov. 29	288
Sulphur Springs	Mar. 24	Nov. 3	224
Tahoka	Apr. 6	Nov. 5	213
Taylor	Mar. 14	Nov. 18	249
Temple	Mar. 10	Nov. 24	259
Throckmorton	Apr. 4	Nov. 7	217
Uvalde	Mar. 9	Nov. 18	254
Van Horn	Mar. 31	Nov. 5	219
Vega	Apr. 21	Oct. 21	183
Victoria	Feb. 6	Dec. 8	305
Waco	Mar. 16	Nov. 18	247
Waxahachie	Mar. 25	Nov. 5	225
Weatherford	Mar. 28	Nov. 7	224
Weslaco	Jan. 22	Dec. 13	325
Whitney Dam	Mar. 18	Nov. 10	237
Wichita Falls	Apr. 4	Nov. 6	216
Wink	Mar. 26	Nov. 9	228
Ysleta	Apr. 3	Nov. 1	212

Source: U.S. Department of Commerce, *Climates of the States, Texas*.

Herbs: Mysterious, Medicinal & Marvelous

To a botanist, a herb, or an "erb" (either pronunication is correct), is a plant which does not develop a woody stem and whose leaves and stem die down entirely sometime after flowering. Herbs may be annual, biennial or perennial. To most people, the name "herb" refers to plants, shrubs, and even some trees, whose leaves, flowers, seeds, and other parts are used for flavoring, fragrance, or medicinal purposes. It's a very general classification, and in this book I've taken the liberty of incorporating some trees that I've never seen classified as herbs.

The terms *spices* and *herbs* mean the same to many people. I prefer to classify spices as pungent or aromatic products derived from the bark, roots, fruit, or berries of certain vegetable plants, including: cinnamon, ginger, nutmeg and sassafras among others. Sassafras is both an herb and a spice, for the roots and young shoots make a tea and the leaves are used to thicken gumbo.

Most of the familiar herbs are native to the Mediterranean area, but some are native to North and South America.

Historically, the most important use of herbs was medicinal. The study and use of herbs dates back well over 5,000 years to the Sumerians, who described uses for laurel, thyme, and many other herbs. Over 2,500 years ago the Chinese had an herb book that described over 300 medicinal plants and how to use them. The Egyptians used many herbs, too. Some of their favorites were garlic, coriander, the mints, and indigo (the latter for dyeing their cloth). Both the Old and New Testaments of the Bible contain numerous references to herbs.

In the fourth century B.C. the first book on botany, *Historia Plantarum*, was complied by the Greek botanist Theophrastus. The first book on herbs by a European, describing over 500 plants, was written by a Greek physician, Discorides, in the first century A.D.

From early in the fourth century through the Middle Ages, the monasteries became the hub of herb gardening, dispensing of the many medicinal herbs. The monks also preserved and updated all the herbal manuscripts.

The best known herbals (writings about herbs) in English were *The Herball*, by John Gerard in about 1600, and the *English Physician Enlarged* by Nicholas Culpeper in about 1650. Culpeper's book combined herb uses, folklore, medicine, astrology, and magic. It was a number one book in those days, and it's still a good one today.

Years ago, if an herb looked like a part of the human anatomy or organ, it was assumed that it had medicinal value for that part. The leaves of lungwort, for example, were taken to resemble diseased lungs and so were thought to cure chest ailments and breathing difficulties. I have several books on herb potions and remedies in vogue three to four centuries ago. Some of these concoctions appear on pages 31-32.

Yet, many herbs *are* important sources of medicine: Foxglove yields digitalis, a heart stimulant. *Rauwolfia serpentina* from India is a source of the tranquilizer reserpine; morphine is a sedative derived from the opium poppy; quinine

People have grown, studied, and used herbs for over 5,000 years. Pictured here are costmary (top left), hyssop (top right), peppermint (bottom left), and French thyme (bottom right).

comes from cinchona bark; and curare, from South America, is a poison that is used as a muscle relaxant. And one we are all familiar with is the aloe vera leaf, which is very beneficial for burns, sunburn, minor cuts, bruises, and abrasions.

Herb Gardens

Herb gardens have a peculiar charm. Many of the plants have an almost fairy-tale appearance. Walking through an herb garden, with its exotic fragrances and rainbow colors, can really be a spiritual experience. Some people think of herbs as dull, green, unattractive plants. But just explore an herb garden; you'll find it a sensual delight. And there is entertaining diversity in plant characteristics: leaf colors range from the gilt of variegated golden mint to the gray-greens of lavender and wormwood; the greens are exquisite—parsley is a soft green, while pineapple sage is a rich, dark green. Interplant these two for a lush, verdant effect. Leaf textures are quite varied—lamb's ear, with its soft, furry leaves, makes a striking contrast with the coarse leaves of comfrey and borage. Your herb garden can be redolent with many unusual and delightful fragrances, from lemon verbena to peppermint-scented geranium.

Herbs make practical and versatile gardens; they can be planted as formal or informal gardens, in a rock garden, as ground covers, or as a culinary garden. These are just a few possibilities to stir your imagination. There are many situations for an herb garden—as many as you can imagine.

When most herbs reach half their mature size, they aren't bothered by the bugs. Fertilizing requirements are minimal; a light application of fer-

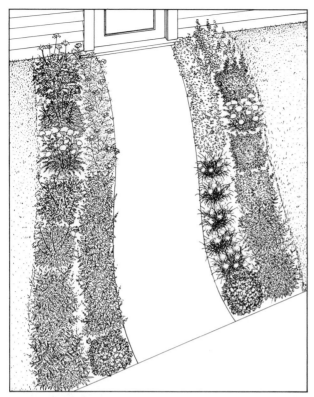

Herbs planted along the walk from the house to the driveway make leaving and returning home a little more interesting. Outer left row (from back): coriander, anise, yarrow, coriander, anise, and lemon verbena. Inner left row: English camomile, Corsican mint, and curled parsley. Outer right row: wintergreen, sweet marjoram, yarrow, sweet marjoram, wintergreen, and lemon verbena. Inner right row: pennyroyal, chives, and curled parsley.

tilizer after pruning is all that is necessary. The mints require additional watering, but most herbs manage very well with minimum water.

Informal plantings require less care than a formal garden. Both types of gardens have their place around the home. A delicate border of moss-curled parsley, with its lovely shades of soft green, is both practical and decorative. Compact green bush basil reaches a height of 8 or 10 inches and makes an excellent low border plant along a walk or driveway. Its natural compact shape makes pruning unnecessary. Some of the dwarf varieties of opal basil are a few inches taller than the compact green basil. A planting of both opal and green basil makes a striking color combination. My variegated opal basil has an unusual color variation, with variegated purple and green leaves. I grew it from seeds I collected from my green and opal basil which had grown side by side and cross-pollinated. Grow some green and opal basil yourself, collect the

seeds, and see what happens when you plant them in the spring.

Common thyme, with its small gray-green leaf and delicate small white flowers, makes a fine low hedge along a driveway or walk. Thyme may require a little pruning for shape. Silver, green, and lemon thyme make an unusual hedge or edge border.

I have several germanders randomly planted in my garden. The plants are 1 foot high and 2 feet wide, with small waxy green leaves similar to oak leaves and make a lovely hedge. The flowers bloom for several weeks and are a beautiful salmon color. Prostrate rosemary, hardy in Zones 9 and 10, has delicate blue flowers and is a most attractive, unusual low hedge. Don't prune any hedges until after they flower or you'll miss a good part of their beauty. Prostrate rosemary plants should be spaced 18 inches apart for a nice tight hedge and 4 feet apart if you want to interplant with other herbs. They flower from late May to July, depending on what zone you're in. Lavender is also a striking border, with its soft gray foliage and delicate blue blossoms.

A combination of hyssop and rue, two more herbs less than 2 feet tall, makes an unusual hedge. There are three varieties of hyssop: white, blue, and pink. Rue has blue-gray leaves and small yellow flowers which make a sharp contrast when interplanted with hyssop. Chives form lovely lilac-colored seed heads and are great borders for your herb bed. Try interplanting these with garlic chives, which have pretty white flowers and are in perfect contrast to the flowering chives.

Several of the thymes are well adapted to rock garden culture. Mother of thyme (creeping thyme) fills the rock crevices and spills out over the rocks. Caraway-scented thyme, with its pink flowers, is lovely interplanted among unusual rocks. Prostrate rosemary, lemon, silver, and garden thyme blend very well in the rock garden. The compact bush basils (opal and green) are two more herbs to interplant.

Camomile and pennyroyal make excellent ground covers. Pennyroyal will cover a large area in one growing season. Sweet woodruff, another ground cover, needs lots of shade. It does best in the eastern portions of Zones 7 and 8.

Most of the herbs make unusual individual plantings. The santolinas, grey or green, are coral-like in appearance and require very little care. They reach up to 3 feet across and 1 foot tall.

Scatter larger herbs throughout the garden or as plantings around your home. Pineapple sage reaches 4 feet across and has lovely little red

Many herbs are excellent for rock gardens. Formal plantings like these always arouse interest and add an elegant touch to the landscape. The herbs illustrated here are all sandy soil plants and will tolerate a partial-to-full sun exposure. From front: creeping thyme spills out over rocks, hyssop, lavender, dittany of Crete, sage, English camomile, santolina, garlic, and pineapple sage.

flowers that cover most of the bush during the summer. Mexican marigold mint has yellow button-like flowers and makes a fine planting against the house or as an individual plant. Catnip and lemon balm can get out of hand and need pruning to keep them in bounds. Upright rosemary, which reaches a height of 3 feet, is great in combination with golden and variegated sage.

White yarrow, with its fern-like leaves and large white flower head, is an asset in any garden. The pink variety is smaller than the white, the yellow variety is taller. White yarrow can cover a large growing area during one growing season. It does not require any care, but by midsummer you'll need to cut back on the size of the bed so that it doesn't take over the entire garden.

Want to bring bees around to help pollinate your growing plants? Bees like lemon balm, borage, marjoram, thyme, lavender, hyssop and many more.

You don't need a large culinary herb garden to supply herbs for flavoring. A 4- by 8-foot garden near your back door will easily manage a few basil, three or four shallot clumps, two clumps of chives, three or four summer savory, a restricted mint bed, a few parsley and one each of tarragon, rosemary, sage, marjoram, and thyme. Scatter some dill seeds throughout the garden and thin to a dozen plants. Dill reaches a height of 4 feet and does well among the other herbs.

Formal herb gardens require more attention than informal ones. There are unlimited shapes and sizes for a formal garden. You can design one for a triangle, square, circle, half circle, etc. You may want to close it in with a hedge of rosemary, santolina, pineapple sage, lavender or germander. You can plant sections of herbs with the same shades of green or gray. A formal garden planted around a sundial with spokes of scented geraniums radiating out from the center is quite impressive. A design like this also offers many possibilities for herb combinations. Plan your formal garden, allocating space for the herbs you wish to plant (see the chart on pages 78–79). Should you incorporate mint, remember to restrict the root system (otherwise, mint can take over the whole garden). If your garden is suitable for a ground cover, try Dittany of Crete—its foliage forms a thick mat of leaves and does well in sunny locations. Woolly thyme is another excellent ground cover. Remember to keep your tall herbs in the back of your garden; smaller herbs that require some shade can be planted in front of the tall ones. Check the chart on pages 68-69 for herb sizes and plan your formal garden accordingly.

Growing Herbs in Texas

Most of the herb books in my library are slanted to growing either on the West Coast or in the North and Northeast. Texas has different growing conditions, requirements, and insects larger and more destructive than in other parts of the country. We have a longer growing season, and herbs grown as annuals up north are perennial here in Texas. Rosemary, marjoram, sweet bay, lemon verbena, and other tender perennials can be grown outdoors all year in most of Texas. Some need winter protection such as a mulch, or, if a hard freeze is predicted, a substantial cover. A few of the herbs are difficult to grow, especially along the Gulf Coast. French tarragon and sweet woodruff for example need shade as well as cooler weather than our 90° plus.

As natives of the Mediterranean, several authors have described most herbs as growing best in poor soil and in full sun, which helps them generate their essential oils. They also write that too much water, fertilizer, and shade results in herbs with less oil but lush foilage. It has been my experience that few of the herbs will survive in poor soil. I don't recommend a regular program of fertilizing and watering your herb plants, but they do need some attention.

I'm sure that the herb seeds we purchase or collect are quite different in culture from their Mediterranean ancestors. Their growing requirements have changed considerably over the years. Several of the herbs requiring minimum water include: lavender, sage, santolina, thyme, and rosemary.

Herbs are fun to grow. Start off with half a dozen, either from seeds or live plants, and keep adding new ones.

All the annuals and most of the perennials are started from seed; parsley, sage, marjoram, chives, basil, dill and thyme are examples. Nurseries throughout Texas usually have a good selection of herb seeds and plants. If you can't find what you want, check the section on "Sources" (page 83) for seed companies from which you can mail-order herb seeds and/or plants.

Live plants that are mail-ordered are smaller than those purchased locally. In a short period of time, and with minimum care, the plant will be vigorous and healthy. Before you order live plants, check with your friends and neighbors—they may have herbs from which you can take cuttings.

Propagating herbs from cuttings is easy. (See pages 12-15 for details.) In three to four weeks most of the cuttings develop vigorous root systems and are suitable for potting. It doesn't hurt a plant when you take cuttings; it is beneficial—proper pruning stimulates additional growth.

Getting Started

Some herbs to purchase as starter plants or propagate from cuttings are sweet bay, comfrey, costmary, French tarragon, lemon grass, lemon verbena, scented geraniums (some seeds are available), rosemary (seeds are slow germinating), southernwood, unusual thymes (lemon, golden, silver, etc.), wormwood, and yarrow. The other herbs can be grown from seed (for details on seed propagation see pages 11-12).

Plant seeds directly in the garden or start them indoors, whichever you prefer. I recommend starting lavender seeds indoors; I've never had much luck with them outside. Until recently, I wasn't successful indoors or out with lavender seeds. A friend grew some for me and showed me how: Plant the seeds in a container of moist vermiculite, barely covering the seed. You can keep the container on a window sill and the seeds will sprout in 10 to 20 days. Although it is usually recommended that you wait until the seedlings have at least four leaves before transplanting to individual containers, if you are as impatient as I am, with a little care you can transplant when the

Hotcaps, fabricated from anything handy, help protect new transplants from the strong summer sun. New plants may wilt the first few days; if they do, spray with water several times a day.

seedlings have a pair of leaves. I have grown and transplanted thousands of seedlings with one set of leaves and have lost very few.

Remember, any time you set out a plant in your garden, whether the plant was purchased from a nursery, mail-ordered, or even one you've grown indoors, transplanting is going to shock it. But, though it has been grown in a controlled environment, it can easily be adapted to its new home. In cool weather this isn't much of a problem. When the weather is warm, transplant late in the day, water well, and mulch. Put a box, a piece of cardboard, or any container on the west side of the plant to provide some shade. You may see some

sun and/or prevailing wind

Another simple way to protect transplants: Stick a piece of cardboard or wood in the direction of the sun and/or prevailing wind.

wilt the first few days. If you do, spray the leaves with water a few times a day. You can plant herbs or any plant during hot weather if you'll water, mulch, and provide shade for a few days.

A Little Pruning Helps

As your herbs grow and the weather gets hot, some, such as catnip, lemon balm, and particularly the mints, will tend to get scraggly. Don't hesitate to prune—even severely. I have some large mint beds and prune several times a year with my lawnmower. People come from miles away to smell my mint-scented lawnmower! Pruning, (It's not necessary to use a lawnmower), encourages new growth which results in bushier plants. You can extend the life of some of your annuals by continual light pruning to keep them from flowering. When annuals flower and set seed, they've reached the end of their life cycle. My wife has a few sweet basil plants outside the back door that she uses for cooking. She keeps them well pruned, and her plants last much longer than the ones I have out in my garden and don't prune.

Many of the annuals and perennials will drop seed. I have volunteer seedlings of basil, catnip, lemon balm, and dill scattered throughout the garden. Here in Houston I haven't had to plant dill in a few years. I've seen dill make it through winters as cold as 12°.

A Few Things To Remember, and a Few You Should Try

Plan your plantings by checking the chart (pages 78-79) to see how large the herbs will be at maturity. If your herb is a perennial, plant in an area where it will enjoy living for several years.

Comfrey and horseradish should be off in a corner of the garden. Horseradish roots reach a considerable distance horizontally and vertically. When you harvest the roots, it's difficult to dig up every bit of root, and even a small piece of root means another plant. Comfrey roots do not have the range of horseradish roots, but they can be a problem if you don't dig up every piece.

I'm assuming that everyone has a garden with plenty of room for herbs, but you *don't* need a lot of growing space. Herbs can be tucked in among your bushes, flowers, and vegetables. Perhaps you live in an apartment and don't have a garden: containers and hanging baskets of herbs do very well on the patio. Even if all you have is a sunny window, you can still grow quite a few varieties. If you live in a closet, herbs do great under gro-lights.

In fact, I grow quite a few herb seedlings under lights in my garage, which is offset from my home and backs up to a large field. One year when my basil was a few inches high, the field mice got into the garage and cleaned me out. But I found a great deterrent: a cat!

Herbs do well as border plants. A row of flowering chives adds beauty to the yard. The bush, opal, and sacred basils are unusual and striking border plants. A permanent low hedge of prostrate and upright rosemary is lovely. Germander, lavender, winter savory and many others also make lovely hedges. In zones 9 and 10, rosemary can be planted directly in the ground. It should be planted in early spring so it will develop a good root system before the first freeze. In other zones, large pots of rosemary can be buried in the ground. They should be brought indoors before the first freeze, though.

Insects attack many of the herbs, but damage is minimal. It's different when a vegetable plant is attacked by insects: if the fruit is severely damaged, the plant is of little value. With most herbs the leaf is usually the flavoring portion. If there are a few holes in some of the leaves, or if several are totally destroyed, it's no real problem. Young basil plants are chewed on, and so is sage. The mints also get their share of gnawing. Red spiders like rosemary in containers but don't seem to care for it out of the garden.

Many of the herbs have natural insecticidal properties and attract harmful insects away from vegetables and onto themselves. The odor of some herbs actually deters some destructive insects: garlic repels aphids, and French marigold exudes a natural chemical that kills or repels some nematodes. This eel-like worm attacks the roots of tomato plants and many other vegetables. Marigolds planted around your tomato plants will help eliminate this pest. Nasturtiums repel the squash bug. Companion-planting vegetables and herbs is something I've done for years. (Charts on companion plantings of herbs and vegetables, and herbs that repel insects, appear on page 29.)

Grow Your Own

Although seeds are not expensive, it's fun to collect your own. If you're growing several varieties of herbs, collecting for next year will mean a savings. The basils are easy to collect. When the long seed pod turns brown, collect and store in a large sack in a dry place. In about a month, you can screen the seeds through a household kitchen strainer. Seeds should be stored in a dry cool area in metal or plastic containers. Bugs and mice will chew through paper envelopes. I mention basil, but most herbs seeds are easy to collect. They are all gathered in the same manner. Dill is a bit different. Cut the seed head when it first turns brown. If you let the seeds completely dry on the plant, the wind will blow most of them away.

Soil

If you are one of the fortunate few who have excellent soil, skip this chapter. If your soil can be improved, keep reading. Most herbs do well in average garden soil. If you have a heavy soil, I suggest that you work in some sand to improve porosity and permeability. What are porosity and permeability? A sponge has holes throughout, the holes mean the sponge is porous. If all these holes are interconnected, it is permeable. Porous, permeable soil can absorb large quantities of water, releasing it slowly to plant roots; this also allows better air circulation for the roots of growing plants, which encourages root extension, increasing the plant's feeding area and providing additional moisture when needed.

Potting Mix for Container Herbs

You can buy good potting soil mixtures, and I would suggest doing this for a few small containers. But if you plan to grow more than a few herbs, and especially if you'll be using larger containers, here's a mixture you can make for a fourth of the retail cost. To 8 parts of screened soil add 2 parts of sharp sand, 2 parts of moistened peat moss, 2 parts of perlite or vermiculite, and 1 part

If your soil is tight and heavy, add some sand to improve porosity and permeability.

Screen soil for potted plants prior to sowing seed. This makes the soil friable and helps the seedling root easier.

of screened compost or composted cow manure. These materials should be mixed thoroughly. If you have sandy soil, exclude the sand from the mix. The soil in my area is tight and heavy, and I have had good results for the past several years with the soil mix I'm recommending. With this mix, you may want to vary some of the proportions of the different materials. Use a mixture that meets the needs in your particular area.

Several commercial soilless mixtures are available. I use a product called Redi-Earth. It is a mixture of vermiculite, peat moss and minerals. Although it's best to use your own mix for containers that are gallon-size and larger, the commercial mix is great for smaller containers because it works well and is easy to mix up. I pour the mix into a large, clean garbage can, add water and mix throughly until it's the consistency of mud. A large quantity can be mixed up in a few minutes. There are enough nutrients in a 3-inch pot of this mix to sustain an herb for approximately 90 days, and because the mix retains water well, the plants require less watering in hot weather. It is an excellent growing medium and helps plants develop good root systems in a short time. It's more expensive than my own mix, but it's worth it.

Compost

The greatest additive for your soil is compost. Heavy clay soils are made fluffy and porous by incorporating large amounts of compost. It also adds "body" to sandy soils, increasing their capacity to hold moisture. Compost is the most complete and natural fertilizer.

Compost, in its simplest form, amounts to piling up refuse, covering it with soil and allowing it to decompose for six months to a year and then incorporating it into the soil. I have made compost for years, and it's neither difficult or expensive.

A compost pile should be 3 to 4 feet wide, 5 feet high, and as long as you want it to be. It can be closed in with cinder blocks, a wire enclosure, a pit can be dug (that's tough work) or simply layered material on the surface (dig up the sod first) as I do. Any and all organic materials can go into the compost. Materials available in Texas include: all your garbage (no bones, meat or fat), seaweed (rich in the trace elements), grass cuttings that your neighbors set out in neat plastic bags for you; leaves and pine needles (also rich in trace elements); manure from horses, cattle, poultry, pigs and rabbits; rice hulls, peanut shells, cotton seed hulls, sawdust, weeds, wood ashes from your fireplace (rich in potash), hay and straw; if you're a fisherman, fish scraps and shrimp waste contains many of the trace

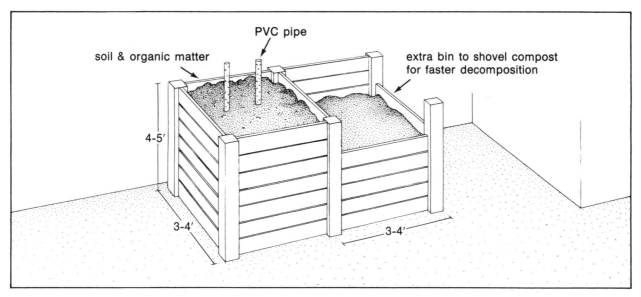

Your compost pile should be 3 to 4' wide, 5' high, and as long as you like. Perforated PVC pipe inserted into the pile will help furnish oxygen, which speeds up decomposition and reduces the strong odor.

elements. I carry several plastic bags with me when I'm at the beach or in the woods and bring back many treasures for the compost pile.

A good mix of table scraps (excluding meat, bones, and fat) will assure inclusion of calcium, magnesium, iron, boron, copper, zinc, etc. I add green sand or granite dust for potash and rock phosphate for phosphorus. Rock phosphate contains many valuable trace elements, including: calcium, iron, boron and iodine. Fifty-pound sacks of these fertilizers can be purchased at local nurseries and stores specializing in organic gardening supplies. Before I discuss building the compost, which can be done anytime of year, let's look at the basics.

(A) *The proper proportion of raw materials.* If you have enough garbage and/or grass clippings, you may not need manure, fresh or composted, to supply the necessary nitrogen. The nitrogen furnishes the heat to break down and literally cook the material.

(B) *The particles should be about an inch in size.* If they are larger, it slows the process. If the particles are too fine, they can solidify and not much will happen. Your lawnmower can be used for chopping up some of the materials.

(C) *Proper dimensions.* The compost pile should be 3 to 4 feet wide, 4 to 5 feet high, and as long as you care to make it.

(D) *Proper moisture and air.* These are absolute necessities. The consistency of a wet sponge squeezed out describes the proper moisture con-

tent. Heavy wire set on a few bricks, as a base for your compost, will provide a good source of air. A few 2 x 4s or a couple of pipes set into the pile and pulled out when it reaches proper height will also furnish air to the organic furnace.

Layers of alternate material should be 2 to 4 inches thick of soil, garbage, grass cuttings, manure and whatever you have on hand. It may take you a few weeks to reach the proper size. Wet each layer as you add to the pile. Always top off with soil; never, I mean *never* end up with garbage on top. You'll attract every critter in the neighborhood. To avoid this, some gardeners keep the completed pile covered with black plastic until it is composted.

With proper material, particle size, moisture, air, and pile size, the compost will heat up to 160° in a few days. My compost may take six months to decompose, I rarely turn the pile. It can be made in two to three weeks by turning every three to four days to bring the finished material from the center to the outside and vice-versa. When the compost cools enough you'll probably see a number of worms. They help compost the pile and are beneficial to the soil.

Finished compost is sweet-smelling, spongy, dark brown material and much of what you used is probably recognizable. The compost is as rich in nutrients as the variety of the raw materials used. Compost will improve the texture, porosity and permeability of the soil and its rich nutrients will be released very slowly to the plants. In heavy soils, compost improves friability and allows water to penetrate better; in light sandy soils it works the other way, making them spongier and better able to retain moisture.

When your compost pile is finished, mix it into the top 4 inches of your soil; by itself, it's a bit rich to grow herbs.

Some manufacturers claim compost "activators" will hasten the breakdown of organic material. In a number of carefully controlled tests by the University of California, assorted compost activators were added to raw material in the recommended amounts with no observable effects. Those piles that were injected decomposed no faster than piles without activators.

A word of caution on grass clippings: don't pile them in a large heap or load up your garbage can with them and forget about it. A study by the Health Department of Santa Clara County, California, found that there are as many as 3,000 house fly larvae (maggots) in one pint of decomposing grass. If you don't compost your grass clip-pings, you can use them as a mulch for your herbs, trees, and shrubs. An inch-thick layer of grass will dry very quickly. You can add to the mulch when additional clippings are available. They will decompose, enrich the soil, help retain moisture. As a result, mulched areas require less watering. Mulching is excellent for everything that grows: herbs, flowers, shrubs, vegetable gardens, and trees.

I don't think there is a homeowner in Texas who needs to set out grass clippings for the local sanitation department to pick up. They can be put to good use right in your own yard. It amuses me to see all those sacks of grass set out on the curb to be taken away (I wind up with most of them). The next day, here comes the man from the local nursery with sacks of commercial fertilizer that probably cost several dollars per sack and have the same nutrients as the clippings the garbage man picked up yesterday.

Propagating the Herbs

There are several ways to propagate herbs. The most common practice is to plant seeds directly in the ground. Herbs can also be grown from seed indoors and, when the seedlings are large enough, transplanted to the garden. Cuttings from the herbs can be rooted in a rooting medium just as you'd do with ornamentals. Another technique is plant division, or propagation from a piece of root. The slowest method, and that which requires the least care, is ground or air layering.

Seeds

Most of the herbs—annual, biennial, and perennial—can be grown from seed. In the spring the seeds can be sown in the garden. In two to three weeks, with adequate moisture and warm weather, the seedlings will sprout. When they're a few inches tall, thin out plants to the proper spacing for mature plants (see the chart on pages 78–79). Surplus plants can be transplanted to other growing areas. This works fine for basil, savory, dill, and a few other herbs. But I recommend starting most of your herb seedlings indoors and transplanting when plants are large enough and the weather is mild.

Seeds can be started either in a sterile soil mix, a commercial soilless mix, or vermiculite or perlite. If you use vermiculite or perlite, the sprouted seedlings need to be fertilized weekly. Use a good all-purpose fertilizer, I use a fish emulsion, for any plant.

The soil mix as described on pages 7-8 should be screened and sterilized prior to seeding. Soil can be sterilized by baking in the oven (a shallow cake pan is fine) at 200° for an hour. When the soil is cool, the seeds can be sown. Perlite and vermiculite are sterile; if you start seeds in either of these, the oven cycle is not necessary.

When seeds are planted directly in the ground, the sun's rays neutralize all of the harmful soil bacteria. If unsterilized soil is used for growing seeds indoors, however, seeds as well as young seedlings can experience damping-off. Some of the seeds won't sprout, and when seedlings are a few inches tall, fungi attack the tender stems at the soil level and they literally keel over.

Any kind of container that provides adequate drainage can be used to grow seeds. The clear plastic shoe boxes you get at most of the discount stores make excellent containers. The shoe box does not have drainage, but minimum-size 3-inch containers can be filled with soil and seeded and will do beautifully in this plastic greenhouse.

Fill the clean containers with soil or growing medium and soak thoroughly, allowing the excess moisture to drain off. Plant the seeds; if they're small, press firmly into the soil. The bottom of an extra container works very well for tamping the seeds. Larger seeds should be covered with moist soil and tamped down. A good rule of thumb for planting seeds is to cover the seed with an amount of soil three times the diameter of the seed. Thus, if the seed is ⅓ of an inch in diameter, cover with an inch of soil. If you plant your seeds at the proper depth, you'll find that germination percent increases appreciably.

Each container of seeds in the shoe box greenhouse should be labeled with date and the plant variety. Put the top on, and in seven to ten days most herb seeds will sprout. This little greenhouse can be set on a windowsill, on a table, or anyplace, for it doesn't need sun. It must, however, be inspected daily. When the first green sprouts appear, place the box in a sunny location. The best growing environment would be under grolux lights for 12-14 hours a day.

It isn't necessary to remove the cover until the seedlings almost touch the top. When the top is

Growing Herbs from Seed

(1) Place seeds in styrofoam cups with holes punctured in the bottom for drainage, then place cups in a tray of water and let them soak; seal off the tray in a plastic bag.

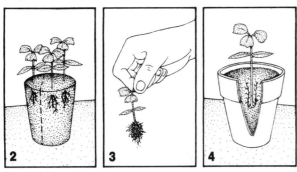

(2) When the first set of true leaves appears, tap the soil out of the container and gently pick up all of the seedlings, grasping them by the leaves, not the roots (3); (4) when transplanting each seedling to its own pot, be sure to avoid jamming the roots in an upright position, as shown.

When your seedlings are large enough (as shown here), and the danger of frost has passed, they can be transplanted out in your garden.

removed, the seedlings should not be watered for a few days. Watering is one of the main determinants of success or failure with seeds and seedlings. The soil should be moist but not wet when the seeds are planted. A temperature of about 75° should also be maintained. The small greenhouse will maintain both conditions during the germination period; as the seedlings grow, you'll have to moisten the soil slightly. Small plants dry out very quickly, and young seedlings can be lost. Plant roots must have air as well as water, so, if the soil is kept too wet, the plant can die. On bright sunny days, you may need to water the plants a few times; on cloudy days perhaps not at all. When the seedlings are large enough, with two or four leaves, they can be planted in individual containers.

Removing the seedlings and soil from the container is a simple matter. Turn the pot on its side, hold it in one hand and tap the bottom sharply with the palm of the other hand. This should be done over some paper. Gently pick apart each seedling, retaining some soil around the roots. Plant each seedling slightly deeper in its own container and water gently. Sterile soil should be used to fill the pots for the individual seedlings.

When the herb seedlings are large enough and the danger of frost has passed, they can be transplanted to the garden. They should be hardened-off prior to planting outdoors. This process gradually acclimates the plant to a new environment. To harden-off, set plants outside in the shade for a few hours. Gradually increase the time outdoors as well as exposure to the sun, and in five to seven days the herb plants will be ready for the garden. If the weather is 70° or less, the new plants do not need to be shaded. If the weather is warm, provide some shade for a few days. In a brief period, the seedlings will adjust to their new home and manage beautifully. Refer to the herb chart (pages 78–79) for the mature size of the herbs, and space accordingly.

Cuttings

Propagation by cuttings, slips, or sprigs (they're one and the same) is an inexpensive way to reproduce identical offspring from a parent plant. Several varieties of herbs can be rooted in a glass or jar filled with water. Most of the mints can be rooted in this manner. Take a 5-inch cutting, stripping off the leaves on the bottom 2 inches. Place this in the container of water and set it on a window sill. During the rooting period, water may have to be added to the container because of evaporation. In three to four weeks there will be a large enough root mass to pot the mint in its own container. The new plant needs to be indoors for a few weeks to develop a good root system. Harden-off before transplanting outdoors.

Propagating of a cutting in its own container, or of several cuttings in a larger container, is done in the same manner. A 3-inch container is adequate for a single cutting. A plastic food container, or the plastic shoe box mentioned earlier, works very well for several cuttings. Good rooting mediums are ½ sharp sand, perlite, or vermiculite and ½ peat moss. They can be kept uniformly moist and provide good drainage and aeration. I'll discuss a single cutting, but the procedure is the same for several cuttings in a larger container.

Green, soft cuttings are the best to root. Woody cuttings are difficult: the leaves can rot before the stem forms roots. Strip the leaves off the bottom third of a 3- to 6-inch cutting. Moisten the stem and dust with a rooting powder. There are several brands of rooting powder. These powders contain root-producing hormones and are available for green softwoods and hardwoods. If you are in doubt as to the procedure, follow the manufacturer's directions. With your finger, poke a hole in a container filled with moist rooting medium and gently insert the stem. Firm the rooting medium around the stem and set the container in a small, clear plastic bag. The bag that a loaf of bread is packed in works fine. Secure the top with a wire twist, rubber band, or string and put the little greenhouse on a window sill. This little greenhouse does not need direct sun or any watering. It will stay moist for several weeks. In three to four

Rooting a Cutting

Strip leaves off bottom one-third of a 3 to 6" cutting.

Dip cutting in rooting powder.

Poke a hole in the rooting medium with your finger and gently insert the stem.

Set the container in a small plastic bag and seal with a twist-tie (moisten the inside of the bag slightly).

You can put your house plants in these bags and leave for a week or two without worrying about watering.

weeks the plant will develop a strong enough root system and can be potted in its own container. The new roots should be at least ½ inch long. After a few weeks, harden-off the new plant and it can be planted in the garden.

When you leave on vacation and have a problem watering house plants, try the plastic bag method. Water your plants, let the excess drain off, and put each plant in its own plastic bag. They stay moist for several weeks.

A Propagating Greenhouse

Bench

I have a propagating misting system which is great for a small grower or hobbyist who wants to propagate cuttings all year long. My waist-high propagating bench is 2 feet wide, 8 feet long, with sides 5 inches high. The bench holds approximately 300 cuttings. The wooden bottom of the bench provides good drainage and aeration. The bench needs bottom heat in cool weather, which I provide via a watertight heating cable stapled to the bottom of the bench. The cable operates on 110 volts with a built-in waterproof thermostat preset at 70°.

It's not necessary to close in the bench. I have to because most of the time my greenhouse is open, and the wind can play havoc with my cuttings. The bench is protected with plastic. Along the length is a large piece of plastic stapled to the top. I roll up the plastic, fastening it to the top and out of the way when I'm either putting in or taking out cuttings.

Misting

My propagating greenhouse is built on the west side of the garage. I have cut a door from the back of the garage into the greenhouse. The bench has an 8-foot length of ½-inch PVC pipe with four equally spaced misters. The brass misters screw into plastic saddles that are glued to the PVC pipe. A plastic cap is glued to the far end of the PVC pipe, and a ½-inch plastic coupling is glued on the other end. From this latter connection, copper tubing is run to one end of a standard ¼″ solenoid valve. The water source is on the other end of the valve.

The time clock is wired to the solenoid valve. The time clock can be a 10, 15, or even 60 minute cycle. Enclosed with the clock are small metal tabs and you can mist at the interval that suits you best. The valve has ample capacity for a much greater span than my 8 feet. A screen from the water source to the mister is a big help in eliminating fine sand grains that can plug up the brass misters. Should they plug—and I've had it happen only a few times—a needle inserted in the spray opening cleans out any obstruction.

Misting is necessary only during daylight hours. I use an inexpensive 24-hour appliance timer that starts and turns off the mister. I mist for 10 hours during the summer and 8 hours in the winter.

Rooting

I use two types of rooting powders, a number one for softwood cuttings and number three for semi-hardwood. I've had the misting system for over 15 years with absolutely no problems (unless someone inadvertently turns off my water source). In addition to 50 or 60 varieties of herbs, I have rooted grapevine cuttings, which take six weeks. Citrus need about eight weeks for a good root system. I've been told by an expert that you can't root citrus. This was after I had rooted and given away a few dozen orange trees. I've had fair luck with sweet bay. Year-old wood roots best, and I have had about 70 percent success. There are always two or three that root in eight weeks, but most woody cuttings take four to five months. Rooted cuttings are handled in the same manner as a single cutting in a container. In 90° plus weather, when the cuttings come out of the propagator and are potted, they go underneath the bench. It's a cool humid area, and in about five days I set them outside under the shade of my trees and shrubs.

I use a propagating medium called calcined clay that gives excellent results. I have used vermiculite and perlite, but for extended periods I've found the clay works best. It has a texture and characteristics of a medium-grained sand, having good porosity and permeability. It can be purchased in 50 lb. sacks at auto parts stores. They use it on driveways to soak up oil drips from cars.

Expenses

How much does all this cost? The prices below are based on 1992 costs. Most hardware stores carry PVC pipe and fittings. Brass misters and saddles can be purchased through some of the seed companies. If you have any problems, contact me and I'll put you in touch with a source.

When I decided I wanted a misting system, I didn't have several hundred dollars to invest; I had a friend design the first mister to my specifications. It's one of the best investments I've ever made.

I've noted where some of these items can be purchased. Everything else is available at hardware stores.

If you want a better bottom heat system but at a greater cost, here's an alternate. In place of the heating cable, a 22 × 60 inch rubber mat heating

Simple misting system for propagating cuttings. Bench is filled with calcined clay and holds up to 3,000 cuttings. PVC pipe suspended above the bench has brass misters inserted.

Misting is controlled by a time clock, which you can set to any interval. Five seconds every 10 minutes on the time clock works fine.

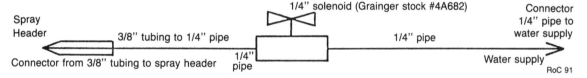

Spray Header
3/8" tubing to 1/4" pipe
1/4" solenoid (Grainger stock #4A682)
1/4" pipe
Connector 1/4" pipe to water supply
Connector from 3/8" tubing to spray header
1/4" pipe
Water supply
RoC 91

Misting system. This system is a modification of mine. It does not have as many connectors as you can see in the photograph. The solenoid is 1/4" NPT on inlet and outlet with a 3/32" orifice similar to ASCO #83417. (ASCO makes most of the valves.) A 3/32" orifice will be adequate for twice the header demands of this system.

system is available for $97.00. You need a thermostat costing $35.00. If you do this you don't need the $16.00 heating cable, so additional cost would be $116.00. This is the system I now use. There is uniform bottom heat with the mat, and with the thermostat you have a wider range of heat. These two items are available at Park Seed.

Item	Price
Time Clock (Grainger)	$ 70.00
Timer (24 hours)	8.00
Solenoid Valve (Grainger Stock #4A692)	25.00
Heating cable 48 feet (Park Seed)	16.00
8'—½" PVC pipe	1.50
½" Plastic cap	.75
3' Copper tubing—3/8"	2.50
4—Plastic saddles @ 50¢ each (Park Seed)	2.00
4—Brass misters @ $1.25 each (Park Seed)	5.00
Connector—¼" pipe to water source	2.00
Connector—¼" pipe to 3/8" tubing	2.00
Connector—3/8" tubing to spray header	2.00
3—¼" pipes	2.00
Glue (PVC pipe)	2.00
Propagating medium	10.00
Total	**$150.00 ±**

Cuttings root readily in calcined clay with regular misting.

Pineapple sage is one herb that roots readily in a simple glass of water.

A simple, inexpensive propagator: ½" cedar or redwood frame, approximately 4" high by 12" wide by 18" long. Drill small holes and insert wire arches (coathangers will do). Insert dusted cuttings, mist, and wrap in plastic.

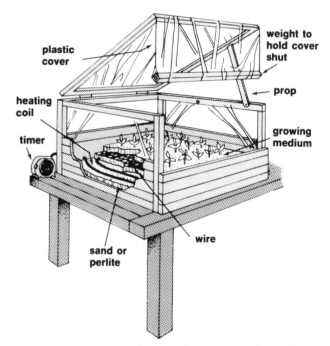

Mini electric hotbed for growing starter plants from seed.

A very simple inexpensive table-top greenhouse can be built to root 30 to 50 cuttings. Several years ago I built one to handle a number of cuttings. It works very well in temperatures ranging from 65 to 80°. The box, made of ½-inch thick redwood or cedar, is 4 inches high and 12 x 18 inches. The box should not be watertight. Drill holes in the top, two at each end of the box to accommodate bent coat hanger wire as shown in the sketch. Several cuttings are handled in the same manner as a single cutting, i.e. strip the leaves from the bottom third of the slip, moisten, and dust with rooting powder. Insert the cuttings so that there is some space between the leaves of each cutting. When the box is filled with cuttings, date and label the different varieties and place it on a large piece of plastic. Wrap the plastic around the box and tie both ends. This is a larger greenhouse than the shoe-box type, but it functions in the same manner. Remember to harden-off the cuttings before putting them outside. As with seedlings, a single container or this little box shouldn't be in direct sun, but in an open area that has good indirect light. I've had excellent results using this box-type greenhouse on a picnic table on the patio beneath the overhang of our home.

Scented Geraniums

Seeds are available for some of the scenteds, but propagation of cuttings is easy. The mother plant should not be fertilized ten days prior to taking cuttings. Fertilizing changes the nitrogen-carbohydrate ratio and retards formation of new roots. Cut several slips up to 6 inches long and remove the leaves on the bottom third of the stem. Don't plant for at least 30 minutes; this allows the ends to seal and improves the rooting process: cuttings develop roots in a shorter period of time, and a higher percentage will root. Insert the cutting in the medium and firm the soil or medium around the stem.

Scented cuttings can be rooted in any of the media. I use a moist soilless mix, but a container of soil with a sand center works very well. The latter method is a container of soil with a hole in the middle filled with moist sand. When the cutting has rooted in either of these, it's not necessary to transplant to another container.

Rooting powders are not necessary. They seem to hinder rather than help root formation with geraniums. I suggest rooting each cutting in its own container. You don't need to put pots inside a plastic sack, but leaves should be misted every few days, and soil should not be allowed to dry out. The cutting should root in two to three weeks. Gently tug at the slip. Resistance means the roots are forming. It usually takes four to six weeks from initial rooting time for an adequate root system to develop. Some of the leaves may yellow during this time, but as long as there are some green leaves the cutting is healthy. Scenteds need to be hardened-off prior to outdoor planting. I'm able to root scenteds from a temperature range of 60 to 85°. My greenhouse gets pretty warm, but scenteds continue to root.

When taking a cutting, I strip off approximately a third of the leaves. Because of their short, stocky stems, some of the scented geraniums may not fit that requirement: Peppermint, for example, may only have a ½- to 1-inch stem and four to five leaves. I have found peppermint-scented geraniums one of the easiest to root, but the way I propagate the coconut-scented geraniums is easiest of all. I have four hanging baskets under an overhang of my house. Coconut geranium is a trailing variety, and it flowers and drops seeds below to a prepared soil bed. When the plants have three or four leaves, I dig them up and plant in their own containers. I average 300 plants a year from the four baskets. They hang on a north exposure, and the small plants in the ground are hardy to at least 20°.

Trailing coconut-scented geraniums (above) flower and drop seeds. (Below) volunteer seedlings sprout in prepared soil bed beneath hanging baskets.

Layering

Layering is a method of rooting shoots while they are still attached to the mother plant. Unlike a cutting, which you detach from the parent plant and root, here the shoot is not detached until it has developed a good set of roots. Most hybrid plants do not reproduce true from seed, and layering is a good method for producing an herb identical to its parent.

Simple layering involves bending a lower branch and covering a portion of it with a light soil mix. It's a good idea to improve the soil in the area of layering. You can make a knife cut on a portion of the branch that is to be buried and dust with the appropriate rooting powder to speed up the rooting process. Most herbs will root in six to ten weeks. This varies with the type of herb, its age, and conditions during the rooting period. I rooted rosemary in a container this way and it took about six weeks.

One branch can be rooted several times, each buried portion being handled in the same manner. It may be necessary to hold or peg down the branch you're going to try to root. The branch can be held down with a fork made of wood or with wooden stakes on either side of the branch and a small piece of wire or wood over the branch secured to the top of the stakes.

Air layering is used to reproduce an offspring from a plant when this cannot be done with simple layering because the branches of the shrub or tree are too high to bend to the ground. There are not many herbs that require air layering: sassafras, sweet bay, lemon tree, and a few others may. I'll describe the technique, for it can be used to reproduce any shrub or tree.

Air layers are made in the spring on wood of the previous season's growth, or in the late summer on partially hardened shoots. The first step is to girdle or cut the bark about 12 inches from the tip end. Then remove a strip of bark an inch wide from around the stem. The exposed surface should be scraped clean to retard healing. Another procedure is to make a slanting cut a few inches long along the length of the shoot. The two surfaces are kept apart with a pebble or piece of wood. Rooting powder is dusted on the exposed surfaces. Sphagnum moss, slightly moistened, is placed around the exposed cut surfaces. If the moss is too wet, decay of the wood tissue can occur. A piece of plastic is wrapped around the shoot so that the sphagnum moss is completely covered. The ends must be sealed around the branch so that water

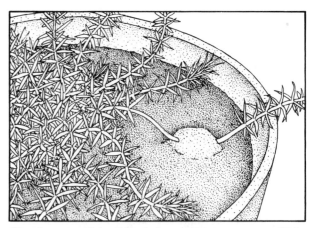

Simple ground layering of prostrate rosemary. Strip leaves of a 3 to 4" section and cover with soil. The section will root in 6 or 7 weeks. Tug gently; resistance means roots have developed. Before transplanting, brush away soil to see if enough roots have grown, then cut from mother plant.

Sprig of rosemary with roots grown by ground layering.

cannot seep inside. Waterproof tape works well for wrapping the ends. Start above the plastic to be sure the ends are tight.

Root formation can be observed through the transparent plastic. Two or three months may be required for adequate root development to support the new plant, and top pruning may be necessary to balance leaf and root system. When the offspring is severed from the parent, pot it in its own container. After several weeks of hardening-off, the plant can be set out in the garden.

Air Layering

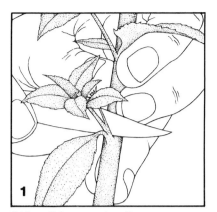

1

Strip off leaves at axil

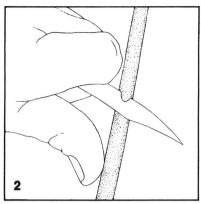

2

Make a sloped cut to expose cambium, insert a small pebble or stick to keep the wound open, and dust wound with rooting powder.

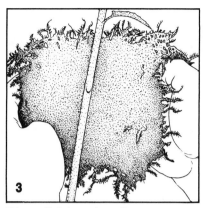

3

Wrap slightly moist sphagnum moss around exposed surface

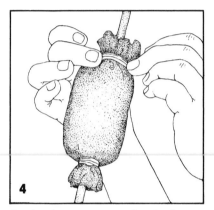

4

Seal sphagnum moss in plastic

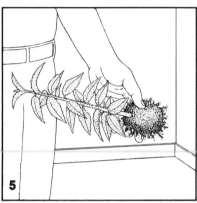

5

Adequate roots will develop in 8 to 12 weeks; sever the shoot from the mother plant and pot in its own container.

6

Herbs Indoors

The great thing about herbs is that most of them can be grown indoors. The potting mixture discussed on page 7 is the same for any containerized herb, whether it's grown on the windowsill, patio, or under lights. A window with south exposure is best, but east or west exposures are fine, too.

Plants grown indoors should be grown in at least 6-inch clay pots. Smaller-size pots dry out faster, and your herb needs more root system than a 3- or 4-inch pot can accommodate. If you don't purchase pots but use older ones instead, scrub them clean then soak in a 10 percent chlorox and water solution. An hour or so in the solution, a few hours of drying in the sun, and the pot is ready for use. Any containerized plant needs good drainage. A few inches of gravel or small pieces of clay pots in the bottom of the container will do the job.

Factors important to growing herbs indoors include adequate moisture, periodic fertilizing, well drained soil, and at least four hours of sun. Most plants die from overwatering. I'm asked constantly, How often should I water? When the plants need it. That's not as flippant as it sounds. There's a compulsion that every day, each and every plant has to be soaked throughly. Some days even twice. Wrong! Prior to watering, poke your finger an inch or so down into the soil. If you feel the slightest bit of moisture, it doesn't need watering. A good investment is a moisture meter. There are several brands on the market. Prices range from $10 to $20. It will pay for itself in a short time. The moisture tester usually has a metal probe 6 to 10 inches long. The probe is inserted in the soil, and the meter at the top of the probe gives a reading advising whether you need to water. Use the moisture tester for a few months and you'll develop a sense for knowing the moisture content without the tester.

There are several approaches to watering. I prefer to water from the top one time and the next time from the bottom up by setting the pot in a saucer filled with water. If you always water from the top, you wash the nutrients out of the soil. Continual bottom watering brings the salts to the soil surface. That's not healthy for your plants.

Indoor plants should be fertilized on a monthly basis. Fish emulsion is a good all purpose fertilizer. Set a date: the 15th, the first of the month, whatever suits you. As long as you do it on a regular basis. Manure is another good fertilizer for your plants. A sack of composted cow manure makes a lot of tea. A cup of manure in a cloth sack, steeped in a gallon of water for an hour, makes an excellent fertilizer for any growing plant. There is no odor from composted cow manure.

Herbs grown on window sills will reach 8 to 10 inches in height. As your herbs grow, turn them

You can grow culinary herbs right in the kitchen for convenience. Place some potted herbs in a box and situate near a window. Rotate the plants to promote balanced growth.

every day so that the entire plant gets the benefit of the sun. If you don't turn the plant, it will get leggy and spindly. When the plant is four to five inches tall, pinch off the top. Side shoots will develop, and pinching back of some of these will make the plant bushy.

A plastic or brass mister is always helpful. Misting the leaves not only keeps them clean, but makes for a healthier plant. A small amount of mild detergent in a quart of water used as a spray on your herbs will help reduce insect problems. Don't wait till you see leaf damage to spray. Remember, no poison sprays. You will be using these herbs to flavor your food. Organic sprays are listed on pages 20-29.

Refer to the general herb chart (pages 78–79) for herbs that can be grown indoors. Some familiar ones are parsley, rosemary, thyme, chives, marjoram, oregano, sage, basil, savory, and the scented geraniums.

Artificial Lighting

Gardening under lights is the best method for growing herbs indoors. Wide-spectrum fluorescent tubes are available in many lengths, ranging from 12 to 96 inches. Indoor light gardens can be put under cabinets in the kitchen, in bookcases, on tables, in the cellar, the attic, or the garage. You can purchase free-standing, multi-tiered metal stands, equipped with casters to provide mobility. Single-fixture units for table tops are also available.

If you're handy, you can build a two-tube fixture for under $25.00, half the retail cost. The effective growing space for a dual-tube 36-inch fixture is 3 square feet. This will accommodate a dozen herbs in 6-inch pots. You'll need to hook up a timer which will turn the lights on and off at specified times to control the length of day. The timer is plugged into a wall socket, and the electrical plug of the light fixture is inserted in the timer. I use about 14 hours to grow my seedlings to about 6 inches tall and then decrease to 12 hours. When your plants are small, the lights should be a few inches away from the tops of the plants. When the lights are that close to the plants, the heat of the lamps will raise the temperature about 8°. The light fixtures should be suspended by chains so they can be adjusted to fit the height of your herbs. A general rule of thumb: set the lights the same distance from the plant as that plant's height. If the plant is 3 inches tall, the tube should be 3 inches above the top of the plant; for a 6-inch plant, the tube should be 6 inches above the top of the plant, and so on. Herbs grown under lights are cared for in the same

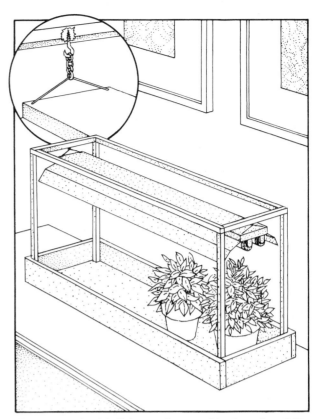

You can make this little gro-lite stand for less than $15. The 24'' fixture is housed in a frame of ½'' thick lumber, 26'' long, 18'' tall, and 12'' wide. Suspend the light fixture on chains slipped over screw hooks set into the top of the frame (this allows you to vary the height of the lighting). A 24'' fixture on sale retails for $10–$12.

manner as window sill plants except that it isn't necessary to rotate the containers.

Containerized Herbs (Indoors and Out)

I'm writing this chapter in our backyard, enjoying the variety of herbs we have in containers and hanging baskets: One-, three-, and five-gallon containers of sweet bay, chives, catnip, lemon balm, lemon verbena, lemon grass, lavender, rosemary, sage, thyme, several of the mints, and scented geraniums. Baskets of prostrate rosemary, mint, mixed culinary herbs, and scented geraniums hang under the overhang of our home and from the limbs of the trees. What herbs do well outdoors in containers? All of them!

Containers from 1-gallon to 40-gallon are useable. If perennials are planted in large containers, be sure they are winter hardy. If 5-gallon containers are used for tender perennials, keep them close to the front or back door. When a freeze is anticipated, they are easier to bring indoors.

Be creative with your containers—the characteristics of the herbs are diverse, and your containers should be, too. On shelf (left to right): *oregano, tarragon, nasturtium*. Clockwise from front: *mint, lemon grass, prostrate rosemary, basil, anise, parsley, bay, lemon verbena, lavender. Sage, thyme, marjoram,* and *chives* grow in crock; *dittany of Crete* spills out of hanging basket.

A redwood planter box is an attractive way to containerize compatible herbs. This box, 4' long, 1½' wide, and 2' high, contains chives, thyme, parsley, and tarragon.

Large strawberry pots are ideal for miscellaneous herbs. Plant upright herbs on top and those that trail in the pockets.

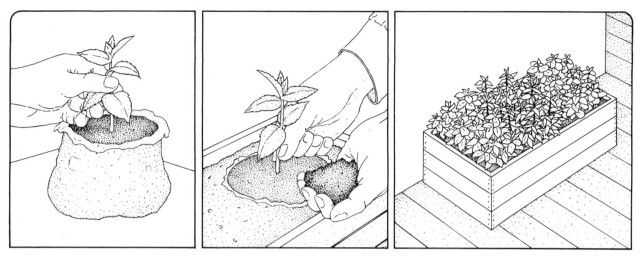

To plant mints in a container with other herbs, set the plant in a plastic bag filled with soil and then plant the bag; otherwise, the mints will make short work of their neighbors.

(Somehow, my largest containers invariably wind up the greatest distance from my garage or back door.) A planter of redwood or cedar makes an excellent container for several herbs. The planter can be divided and several herbs with similar cultural requirements can be planted together. Strawberry pots are perfect for many of the herbs. Plant the upright herbs on top and those that trail in the pockets. For hanging baskets, the upright herbs go in the middle (parsley, chives, or garlic chives), and trailing or semi-trailing varieties go around the edge (mints, prostrate rosemary, oregano, marjoram, catnip, lemon balm, savory, or whatever suits you). A large shallow clay pot is attractive and useful for several of the herbs.

Regardless of what type of container you use, there are a few basic requirements. Good drainage—whether the container is clay, plastic, or an unusual material—is a must. A few inches of gravel or broken bits of clay pots at the bottom of the container will provide good drainage. You'll want your herbs to get four or five hours of sun. They'll grow in full sun, but will dry out very quickly in the hot summer. Daily care is required. By daily care I mean checking your containers every day. Herbs in gallon size containers need to be watered every day in the summer; 3- and 5-gallon containers require water every second or third day. All containerized herbs need to be fertilized on a regular monthly basis.

If you want to make some hanging baskets, here are a few tips. Soak adequate sphagnum moss in a large bucket of water for 15 minutes. Squeeze out the excess water and layer the moss in the wire basket. There should be at least a 2- to 3-inch thickness of moss. Add the proper amount of soil, and plant the herbs.

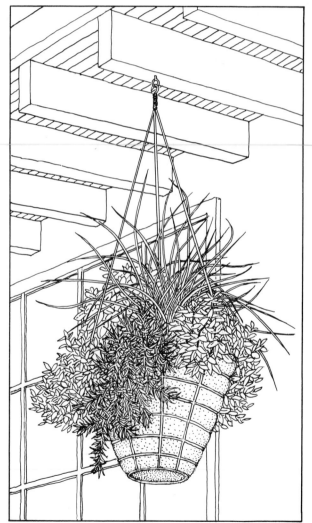

They'll grow in hanging baskets, too. Line the baskets with 2-3" of moist sphagnum moss, fill the remainder with soil, and plant. Prostrate rosemary, oregano, mints, thyme, geraniums, dittany, and chives are all good candidates.

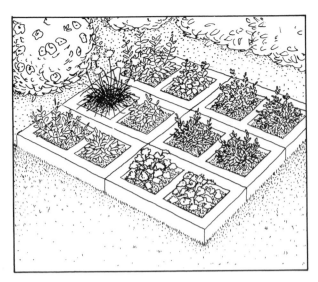

Cinderblocks make interesting dividers for outdoor herb plantings. They can be set above ground to line a walk or patio or to border a raised bed; buried in the ground, they make attractive designs and facilitate culture of herbs with different requirements. They are especially good for planting mints in with other herbs because the roots of mint will strangle out other herbs in the garden.

My first few baskets were frustrating. I had trouble fastening the wire to the outside rim of the basket so it would hang straight. I'd fasten one wire, but then the other two required adjusting and readjusting. After half a dozen baskets, it came to me. It's very easy. Hold the end with the closed loop in one hand and, get this, bend all three wires at the other end at the same time. A three- or four-inch bend is adequate to fasten the wires securely.

Be creative with your containers. I have seen commodes, chests of drawers, iron kettles, old watering cans, and many other unusual pots. As long as the container has a hole or holes in the bottom and is at least 6 inches deep, it can grow herbs. A sectioned cinder block setting on the patio, or buried in the ground, makes a fine container for several of the mints. The root system of mints can take over the garden. Mints can be planted in a plastic bag of soil and then set in a large container with other herbs. The bag will restrict the root system but should be open so the mint can be watered.

Harvesting, Drying & Storing

Most of the herbs can be used fresh to flavor your food. In zones, 6, 7, and 8, you may want to dry some for use during the winter. The herbs are simple to harvest, dry, and store. Herbs should be harvested just prior to flowering, when they contain the maximum amount of essential oil on which fragrance and flavor depend. The mints, however, have their richest oil content when they flower. In Texas, most herbs yield several crops a growing season.

You can prune approximately a third of the plant without interfering with continual production. Stop pruning early enough to allow growth prior to the first frost. If you prune right up to frost time, plants can suffer winterkill. In zones 9 and 10, winters are mild enough to allow pruning of most of the perennials for almost 12 months of the year. Harvest a quantity that you can manage for that day. If you gather too much, the leaves can rot. Mid morning is a good time to harvest the leaves. Prune a third of the plant, and if it's not quite dry or if the leaves were dirty and you hosed them off, hang in the open shade to dry.

I'll discuss several methods of drying; choose the method that suits you. The drying process requires good ventilation, heat and absence of dust. I've hung stalks and leaves in my garage, but it's too dusty and I had to discard what I tried to dry. Label what you're drying—dried leaves all look alike and some fragrances are similar. You don't want to flavor a roasting chicken with catnip instead of basil.

The quickest way to dry herbs is in the oven. The clean leaves should be stripped from the stalks, put on a cookie sheet or pan and set in the oven. The door should be open an inch or so, with temperature set at 100°. A single layer of leaves

The simplest and quickest way to dry herbs is in the oven. Set the temperature at 100° and leave the oven door open slightly. Allow 45-90 minutes, depending on the amount of leaves.

will dry in about 90 minutes. If you have several layers of leaves stacked in one pan, it takes forever to dry. A word of caution on oven drying. The fragrance of some of the herbs will permeate the entire house. When I dry basil in the oven I do it when my wife is out for a few hours. It really bothers her.

During the hot summer, herb leaves can be dried in the back of your car. Spread newspapers on the back seat and the floor and place a single layer of leaves on the newspaper. Keep the car closed up when you're not driving, and in three or four days the leaves will dry.

An attic is a good area to dry stalks of leaves, if it has cross ventilation, is free of dust, and over 90 degrees, leaves can be dried in a week. Hanging herbs outdoors is not a particularly efficient way. If it rains and you don't protect them in time, you have to start over. I have dried stalks and leaves in a large paper sack. The stalks and leaves are placed in the sack, with the top of the stalks near the bottom of the bag. The bundle is tied with string at the opening of the bag. This is labeled and hung in a warm area. It takes several weeks to dry herb leaves in such a manner. Regardless of what method of drying you use, the herbs should be dried as quickly as possible, in very little sun, so that the volatile oils and original green color are retained.

A friend who lived in Italy for a number of years told me how Italians dried basil. Leaves are placed in large crocks, alternating a layer of leaves and a layer of salt. When the basil leaves are to be used, the salt is shaken off the required amount of leaves needed.

When the herb leaves are dry, shred them between your hands or through a coarse sieve. Whole leaves, for tea, can be stored without shredding. The stems of the herbs contain essential oils, too, and you can put leaves and stalks through a vegetable chopper. This method applies to small-leaf herbs such as savory, thyme, marjoram, and compact bush basil.

Store your dried herbs in clean, opaque, tightly capped bottles. If clear bottles are used, store them in the pantry or cupboard. Examine the bottle of dried leaves in a few days. If there is any moisture on the inside of the bottle, they need additional drying. Low heat in the oven, with the door open a few inches, should completely dry the herbs in 30 to 60 minutes. Let them cool, place them in the bottle, and check for moisture in a few days.

Seeds collected for storage are harvested and dried in a manner similar to the method used for leaves. The seed heads should be cut when the seeds first turn brown. If you wait too long, the wind will get most of the seeds. I cut the entire seed head and drop it into a large paper sack. I label the bag and hang it in my garage. They're dry in about six weeks. Screen the seeds through a large sieve. Save some in a metal or plastic container for next year, and enjoy the rest. Caraway,

This dried basil has just been chopped and is ready for storing in a small apothecary jar.

dill, fennel, anise, and cumin are some of the seeds you can collect. If you dry seeds in the oven, they can't be used in the garden next spring.

Dig up the roots of comfrey, horseradish, etc., and wash thoroughly, removing all dirt. Large roots can be split or sliced and placed on a screen. The screens can be placed outdoors in the shade and brought indoors in the evening. The root sections need to be turned every few days, and in three or four weeks should be partially dry. Place the roots in the oven, at low heat, with the door open a few inches to complete the drying. Roots should be stored in airtight containers. (Large mason jars make excellent storage jars.) Don't store leaves, seeds, or roots in paper envelopes or cardboard boxes. If dampness doesn't cause mold, the bugs will chew through these containers and help themselves to your delicious dried herbs.

Many of the herbs can be frozen. Some of these are: chives, garlic chives, dill, basil, garlic, and tarragon. Cut the stems with adequate foliage, washing the dust and soil from the leaves. Tie some string around several stems and dip in boiling water for about 60 seconds. Remove and either cool the herbs under the tap or dip in a pan of cold water for a minute or two. Pick off the leaves and place them either in foil or freezer bags, labeling each bag for storage in the freezer. Garlic cloves should be cleaned and frozen in "freezer jars"; otherwise, their strong flavor will affect other foods in the freezer.

Potpourri

A potpourri is simply a collection of dried fragrant leaves and stems that one keeps in pretty jars. When you want to turn on your olfactory senses, take off the top and breathe the exotic fragrance. They are easy to make, and here are a few basics. Early in the morning, pick the leaves and petals of your fragrant herbs and/or flowers, discarding the brown blossoms. Collect a lot more than you think you'll need because there's quite a loss in volume when they dry.

Place the leaves, stems, and petals on a clean paper or cloth in a warm place and out of bright sunlight. Stir the mix a few times a day to allow all material access to air so it can dry. Just as you dried herbs for storage, you can hang small bunches of stems with leaves and flowers in a warm, clean airy garage or attic. Some people like to dry orange or lemon peel for their potpourri. Make sure you scrape and clean off all the pulp.

Potpourri needs a fixative added to retard evaporation of the essential oils. Orris root and gum benzoin are used for this purpose and can be purchased at drug stores or health food stores. Use ½ ounce of fixative for each quart of potpourri. I would suggest you use gum benzoin, for orris root can irritate the skin.

When your herbs are completely dry, mix them with the fixative in a large wooden bowl. When you mix or store herbs, never use a metal container. Wood, ceramic, plastic, glass or enamel are fine. Put your ingredients in a large container with a tight cap and store in a cool place. Every four or five days, take a wooden spoon and stir the contents. If you see any moisture, place the herbs on papers again to dry (if your mix isn't completely dry, it will mold). In six to eight weeks you can put the potpourri in smaller attractive containers.

Using Your Herbs

Herbal Sprays, Powders & Companion Plantings

In most of Texas we have longer growing seasons, which means larger harmful insects and more of them. Some of the herbs are effective organic insecticidal sprays and do not leave a harmful residue. Here's how to prepare a good garlic spray: Take 5 ounces of chopped garlic cloves and let them soak in 4 teaspoons of mineral oil for 24 hours. Then slowly add a quart of water in which ½ ounce of oil-base soap (Palmolive is good) has been dissolved and stir well. Strain the liquid through fine gauze, and store in a china or glass container (garlic reacts with metals). Try it against your worst pests, starting with a dilution of 1 part insecticide to 25 parts of water. Continue diluting until you reach the proper proportions to control the insects. I would estimate that approximately one part garlic concentrate diluted with 50 parts of water is a good mix.

Cayenne (hot pepper) is effective against several of the garden pests, namely ants, caterpillars, cabbage worms and tomato worms. Mix a cup each of peppers and water, straining the mix through gauze to eliminate the solids. Add half a teaspoon of soap powder or mild detergent and the spray is ready to use. Dry cayenne dust can be used as a deterrent for insects on several of the garden vegetables. Shred and dry the pods of cayenne. Low heat in the oven for a brief period will hasten the drying process. The dust will adhere better to the foliage if it is wet. You will need to re-dust after a rain. Wash your hands thoroughly, several times, after handling hot peppers. If you don't, and inadvertently rub your eye, it can be very painful.

Herbal teas are fairly effective against garden pests. Steep equal amounts of herb leaves and water for 24 hours. Strain the mixture through gauze or cheesecloth. Chive tea is used to control leaf and fruit scab, horseradish against fungi, hyssop against bacterial diseases, and wormwood tea is used to control aphids and caterpillars that attack the leaves of fruit trees.

Essential oils of many herbs are known to have insecticidal properties. A 2 percent emulsion spray of the oil of lemon grass was found to be highly effective on red spider and aphids. Sprays of mint, coriander, sage, and savory had moderate success against these pests. Oil sprays of a number of herbs work on mosquitoes. Elecampane is the most effective, but oils of basil, sage, marjoram, and rosemary will work, too. Insects have been repelled with oils of pennyroyal, thyme, lavender, bay, sassafras, and other herbs. Leaves of mint, lavender, sage, and wormwood can be used in the closet to protect woolens from the moths. Sprinkle liberal quantities of leaves among the clothing. This smells better than mothballs, and you'll probably attract members of the opposite sex when you wear these fragrant garments.

I don't use any poison sprays in my garden, but when I see the first signs of insect damage I use an organic powder called rotenone. It is effective for all sucking insects that attack vegetables. This powder, marketed by several manufacturers, is derived from the roots of several species of trees in the genus *Lonchocarpus*, including cube from Peru and timbó of Brazil. This insecticide can be used to control aphids, spider mites, chinch bugs, cabbage worms, mosquitoes, and even flies. Rotenone, used in normal concentrations, is not considered harmful and can be used up to 24 hours before harvest.

Another herb that is a very effective dust for destructive insects is pyrethrum, a perennial chrysanthemum (for details on the plant, see page 65). It is a short-term dust, breaking down quickly in sunlight. It is used to control cabbage worms, leaf hoppers, spider mites, and aphids as well as many household pests. Nicotine can be used against white flies, thrips, spider mites and aphids. I have read that Mexican marigold *(Tagetes*

Herbs that Get the Bugs Out

Pest	Helpful Herb	Remarks
Ants	Pennyroyal, mints, tansy	Plant near entries and around perimeter of house.
Aphids	Garlic, nasturtiums	Garlic should be planted close to rose bushes so that the garlic leaves touch the bushes. Plant both herbs near brocoli. Random plant garlic throughout garden.
Carrot Fly	Onion family (onions, chives, garlic chives, shallots, leeks), rosemary, sage, wormwood	In and about the carrot patch.
Cucumber Beetle	Radishes	Not an herb, but deters this pest. Scatter seeds in cuke patch. Eat some radishes, but leave some to help cucumbers.
Flies	Tansy	Plants should be near entries to the house.
Flea Beetle	Wormwood, mint	Interplant with lettuce.
Fleas (on your pet)	Pennyroyal	Rub leaves thoroughly on coat of your pet.
Japanese Beetle	White geranium	Plant near plants bothered by this pest.
Mosquitoes	Sassafras	Rub leaves on exposed skin.
Nematodes	French marigold	Plant around main stalk of tomato plants.
Squash Bugs	Nasturtiums	Plant several around the main roots of the squash plants.
Weevils	Garlic	Scatter cloves in problem food area.
White Cabbage Butterfly	Sage, rosemary, hyssop, thyme, mint, wormwood	Interplant to protect members of cabbage family (broccoli), cauliflower, Brussels sprouts).

minuta) is highly effective and very similar to pyrethrum. In parts of Africa it is used to repel flies, fleas, and lice by hanging dried leaves in the problem areas. I located a seed source and am growing, experimenting, and tabulating the results with this herb. Don't confuse this with Mexican marigold mint *(Tagetes lucidia),* a lovely perennial. The latter has yellow button-like flowers and foliage with a licorice fragrance.

I have mentioned several herbal sprays and organic powders to help control destructive insects. I say *control,* for total elimination is unnecessary. One reason we don't need total elimination is that natural pruning is beneficial for many of the vegetables. We've been brainwashed to think that if there's a blemish on a fruit, it's no good, or that a head of lettuce is unfit to eat if there's a hole or two in a leaf. It just isn't so.

In addition to sprays, several of the herbs are great companion plants for certain vegetables. Some herbs hinder the growth of some vegetables. Combinations of certain varieties of herbs are beneficial; other groupings are not. Alphabetically listed below are some helpful plantings and some to avoid.

Anise—does well with coriander
Basil—don't plant near rue
Chives—helps the growth of carrots
Coriander—retards growth of beans and tomatoes
Caraway—does not do well near fennel
Dill—aids cabbage, but suppresses carrots
Fennel—bad influence on beans and tomatoes
Garlic, Chives, Leeks and Shallots—inhibit beans and peas
Hyssop—increases grape crop, decreases carrot crop
Mint, Rosemary and Sage—aid cabbage family
Parsley—helps tomatoes
Rosemary and Sage—help each other
Southernwood—plant near cabbage
Wormwood—plant off in a corner
Yarrow—increases fragrance of most herbs

Several of the herbs act as trap crops, i.e., the harmful insects are attracted to them instead of nearby vegetables. Mustard and nasturtium attract several of the destructive garden insects. They are particularly useful planted near cabbage, cauliflower, Brussels sprouts, broccoli, and radish. African marigold and white geranium attract and kill the Japanese beetle, and lemon grass repels the African tsetse fly.

Some, but not enough, experimenting with herbs as natural insecticides is being done. Hopefully, this research will expand and more ways to use herbs and other plants as natural repellents will be discovered.

Herb Oils

Commercial herb oils are extracted by distillation. If you don't own or have access to a still, here's a method that will enable you to extract the oil of many herbs. Use a gallon-size ceramic crock, filling it with clean leaves and blossoms of the herb of your choice. Use rain or distilled water, pouring enough in the crock to cover the material. The crock should be set outdoors in the full sun. Should it rain, either cover your crock or bring it indoors. In five to eight days a scum, the herb oil, will form on the surface of the water. You can soak up the oil with a cotton ball and carefully squeeze the liquid into a small container. Inspect your crock on a daily basis, removing the oil as it forms with the cotton and transferring it to the smaller container. Over an extended period you may have to add more rainwater to the crock. When the oil appears to be extracted from the crock, usually after several days, place gauze or cheesecloth over the mouth of the small container of herb oil. This will allow the water that is mixed with the oil to evaporate. In about a week you should have pure herbal oil that can be transferred to a small, clean opaque bottle with a tight-fitting lid. It is now ready for use or storage.

Herbs that lend themselves to extraction of oil include: mints, thyme, basil, marjoram, sage, lemon verbena, lemon balm, and many more. Oils from fragrant woods can be extracted in the above manner, too. The wood needs to be reduced to shavings prior to filling up the crock.

Herbal Baths, Rinses, & Body Lotions

Camomile, lemon verbena, and rosemary make excellent rinses for the hair. Blondes can use rinse of camomile flowers to bring out the highlights.

Place a gauze bag filled with dried leaves of your favorite herbs and hang it over the spout of your tub. You'll smell nice all over.

Rinses are easy to make with herb leaves and tender tips. Use either rain, distilled or softened water (there are too many harsh chemicals in most tap water). Simmer 2 cups of the leaves in a quart of water for 30 to 60 minutes. When your mixture is cool, strain off the liquid and store in a clean container. It's available when you are. I've mentioned a few herbs, but there are many more that make fragrant hair rinses.

Body lotions (pomades) are not difficult to prepare. Leaves of the mints, marjoram, lemon balm, lemon verbena, lavender, pineapple sage, scented geraniums—the list is endless—all make lovely fragrant body lotions. Blend two cups of your favorite herb or herbs with a small amount of alcohol. Plain alcohol can be purchased at any drug store. Add enough alcohol to your mix to fill up an inch or so of a quart bottle. Cap this bottle tightly and shake it vigorously every few days over a couple of weeks. At the end of two weeks, strain off the liquid into appropriate bottles.

Does an herb bath appeal to you? You can boil a gauze bag filled with 2 to 3 cups of a fragrant herb for 20 minutes, pouring the liquid in the full tub of water. Another method is to take the same gauze bag with herbs and hang it over the spout, allowing the warm water to pour through it. Not only will you smell nice, but an herb bath is most refreshing. You can use some of the same herbs that are used for body lotions.

Teas

There are two methods in making tea: *infusion*, where boiling water is poured over the leaves until

Herbal R_x

Historically, the most important uses of herbs were medicinal. They have been prescribed to treat human infirmities for at least 5,000 years. The sixteenth century was the great age of herbals, and it's these texts that hold, in my opinion, the most interesting and unusual potions to aid or cure ailments ranging from ingrown toenails to noises in the ears.

Among many uses of sweet marjoram, Culpepper tells us:

It is warming and comforting in cold diseases of the head, stomach, sinews, and other parts taken inwardly or outwardly applied. The decoction thereof being drunk, helps diseases of the chest, obstructions of the liver and spleen, old griefs of the womb, and the windiness thereof, and the loss of speech, by resolution of the tongue. Made into powder, and mixed with honey, it takes away the marks of blows and bruises. It is good for the inflammation and watering of the eyes, if mixed with fine flour and laid into them. The powder snuffed up into the nose provokes sneezing, and thereby purges the brain.

I like what Culpeper says about southernwood:

The ashes mixed with old salad oil (not new or fresh, but old), helps those that are bald, causing the hair to grow again on the head and beard.

Did you see my picture? Didn't work on my head. I guess it only half works.

Here's what he has to say about tobacco:

The smoke of tobacco injected in the manner of a clyster, is of efficacy in stoppage of the bowels, for destroying small worms and for the recovery of persons apparently drowned.

A priceless prescription, author unknown, for constipation:

Take an equal amount, preparing as a tea, of each of the following—wormwood, wood betony, bugle, mountain mint, germander, hyssop, ground ivy, yarrow, periwinkle, marjoram, rosemary, sanicle, sage, thyme, vervain, catsfoot flowers, and coltsfoot flowers.

To be honest, I'm afraid to try this.

There are some unusual potions for treating premature wrinkles, wounds, warts, to purify the blood, expel worms, to restore normal functions of the body, and on and on. In an herbal text written in the early 1600s, an index is compiled of diseases and herbs that can cure them. I've listed several that, in my opinion, are fascinating.

Disease	Herb(s) That Cure	Comments
Baldness	Beets, yarrow	Doesn't work
Belchings	Betony, burnet	Burnet is great in salads
Blastings by lightning	Purslane	No comment
Bad breath	Mint, rosemary	They both work
Forgetfulness	Agrimony	I forgot if it works
Baldness	White mustard	No way
Lust	Hemlock	It's a poison; it'll stop you forever
Sun-burnings	Betony, cucumber	This could be the answer

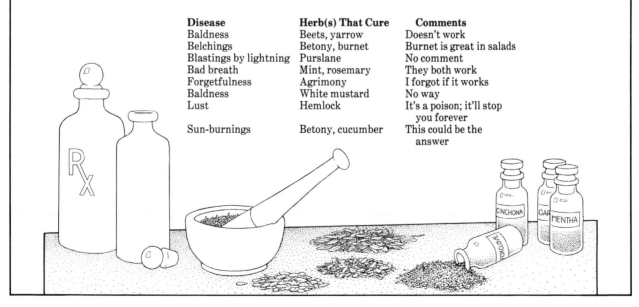

it is strong enough, and *decoction*, where the water and herb are boiled to bring out the oils. The best container for preparing tea is either porcelain or glass; never metal. Fresh or dried leaves and flowers can be used. Mix your own special brand of herb tea. Keep a record of the different combinations you try and eventually you'll find your favorites. Half a dozen herbs will make a large number of combinations, all different in taste.

Teas used for relief of colds include catnip, yarrow, lemon balm, and sage. Lemon balm, peppermint, rosemary, lemon verbena, and marjoram are teas that have a calming effect. For years, wintergreen tea has been used for relief of rheumatism. My favorite herbal tea is lemon grass; the leaves can be dried in a week or so in the open shade in hot summer. Spread the leaves out on a newspaper and move it inside if it looks like rain.

Herbal Dyes

Many of the herbs produce such fine colors that they are used for coloring and dyeing. A fixative, or mordant, is necessary in the process, for not only will it fix the color but in many instances it will bring out a brighter and sharper color. I suggest that if you are interested in pursuing this further, get a book on dyeing. Listed below are some herbs, flowers, vegetables, and trees that are used for dyes, stains, and inks.

Plant	Part Used	Color
Agrimony	Entire herb	Yellow
Daphne	Seed	Yellow
Date palm	Roots	Brown
Elecampane	Roots	Blue
Eucalyptus cineria	Leaves	Red, yellow, gold
Hops	Stalks	Brownish-red
Hyssop	Leaves plus copperas	Green
Indigo	Plant	Blue
Juniper sp.	Berries	Yellow or brown
Lily of valley	Leaves	Green
Marigold	Flowers	Yellow
Parsley	Leaves	Green
Rhododenron	Leaves	Grey
Safflower	Flowers	Yellow
Saffron	Flowers	Yellow
Tansy	Stalks plus alum	Green-grey
Yarrow	Flowers plus alum	Yellow
Yarrow	Leaves	Green
Yellow flag	Roots plus sulphate of iron	Black
Zinnia	Flowers	Yellow

Reputed Herbal Medicinal Properties

"Reputed" is a common word used in describing medicinal properties of many of the herbs. There are some really vague expressions regarding herbal curative properties. But many of the herbs *do* have excellent medicinal properties, and I'll list some at the end of this discussion. Here are some other phrases commonly used.

This herb is *known medicinally*, or this is an *ancient known stimulating tonic plant*. Back in Roman days, *Pliny told us elecampane would relieve indigestion*. (I'm skeptical of today's attorneys; why should I listen to one 1900 years ago?) Another herb is *said to relieve indigestion*. Who said so?

The juice of this particular herb *is said to be a good medicine for diarrhea*, and the juice of another *is listed as an aid for diarrhea*. A certain nut is mentioned, and if they are eaten in quantity, *laxative effects may be noted*.

The mints are *seemingly all good for aiding digestion*. Seemingly? What does that mean? And yet another: *Everyone knows it stimulates the appetite*. An herb is mentioned as an aid to rheumatism, but a footnote tells us one reference says it's not too reputable. Here's one for our part of the country: In the South where the magnolia grows, *reports are that the mild astringent qualities of the leaves are an alleviant for rheumatism*. The juice of another herb is *thought to be good for rheumatism*.

The best one is out of an herbal remedy book in my library. At the end of the book is a bibliography with works from Moses up to modern authors. Some of the references include the Scriptures, Culpeper, and Gerard. The author *dares the reader to challenge the validity of the authorities cited*. A couple of his works have "author unknown." I can't challenge them.

In my opinion, there are too many medicinal qualities attributed to the herbs, and, unfortunately, these appear to many people as factual. But many herbs *do* have medicinal value, and a large number are being researched. I've mentioned that aloe vera is good for burns. Garlic juice was used as an antiseptic during World War I. The oil of certain species of the eucalyptus is used as an astringent. Jewel weed (impatiens) is good to treat poison ivy. The juice from the stems dries up this painful skin irritation. If you have been in the woods and think you were exposed to poison ivy, oak, or sumac, it's a good idea to use the juice on exposed portions of your body.

I suggest that you check the reported medicinal qualities of many herbs before relying on them to benefit your particular ailment. Enjoy growing them, smelling them, tasting the culinary ones; be careful when you use any medicine, herbal or otherwise.

Recipes from Texas and Other Areas

Arno's was a fine Italian restaurant in Houston, Texas. The chef used many herbs from my garden for flavoring. My wife and I ate there many, many times and what they did with herbs for flavor was a gourmet delight. Pancho Garrison, a good friend and chief chef, was kind enough to give me the recipes I've listed below. They are written exactly as he gave them to me.

Potate al Forno

Wash potatoes well. Cut into chunks. Place in baking dish large enough so that they are not atop one another. Mix with olive oil, salt and pepper (fresh-ground) and a liberal amount of rosemary leaves. Bake in 400° oven for about 20 minutes or until tender inside and crispy outside. Stir them occasionally.

Pollo al Forno

Delicious and simple chicken dish prepared in the precise manner above.

Flounder with Sage

Lightly flour a filet of flounder and drop in pan with some butter. Add several fresh sage leaves. Keep flame at about medium force. Turn fish over after a few minutes. Salt. Remove when fish is cooked—it should be slightly crisp on the outside. Squeeze juice from half a lemon in pan and deglaze pan with a few drops of water or white wine, stirring everything stuck to the bottom of the pan into a delicious sauce. Pour over the filet of flounder.

Filetto Rosmarino

Cook a fine cut of choice tenderloin in some butter with some rosemary, 2 sage leaves and 1 bay leaf. Salt and pepper. Cook to taste, then toss in some brandy or cognac, let it flame, then stir up the drippings with a few drops of water, and serve.

Modified Mousseline Sauce

Melt ½ pound butter with the juice of two or three lemons and a large tablespoon or two of tomato paste. Separate four egg yolks from the whites. Beat the yolks and remove melted butter from fire, adding yolks. Stir vigorously with wooden spoon (if it starts to curdle, add a few drops of hot water). It should become thick. It may need some stirring by placing the pot inside another pot with hot water. Remove from heat, then stir in one cup of whipped cream. Salt if necessary. Chop up about ½ cup of chives and/or dill stems and leaves. This is a great sauce for all fish.

Penne Alla Salvia

Any short pasta (penne, rigatorri, ziti, conchiglie) will do. Boil in abundant salt water. Meanwhile, melt butter in a skillet and add a small handful of sage leaves. Let the butter absorb the flavor, then add a bit of heavy cream. Strain the pasta; it is ready when, upon biting into it, you get a faint taste of the raw pasta still in the center (*al dente* which is Italian for firm yet tender). Drop the pasta into the skillet and add more cream if it appears too dry. Salt and pepper, and add a healthy handful of Parmesan cheese (only imported Italian Parmesan will give pasta dishes their true character). Stir and serve.

Saltimbocca Alla Romana

You'll need thin milk-fed veal scalloppini for this dish. (Available at Jamail's in Houston.) On each scalloppini, put two or three large fresh sage leaves; cover with a very thin slice of prosciutto, which is a salted Italian ham; fasten this onto the veal with a couple of toothpicks. Sauté in skillet with butter. Salt lightly (proscuitto is quite salty) and coarse-grind some pepper. It cooks very fast, and should be done over high heat to get some brown on the pan. Remove and deglaze with some water to make a delicious sauce for a delicious dish which translates as "jump in the mouth."

Pesto Sauce

Blend together:

4 tbsp. chopped fresh basil	3 garlic cloves
	6 tbsp. olive oil
1 tbsp. chopped pine nuts	1 tbsp. chopped parsley
	1 tbsp. Pecorino cheese
3 tbsp. Parmesan	(a goat cheese)

Cook pasta—preferably homemade fettuccini. Mix with sauce, butter, plus some of the boiling water you cooked the pasta in. Serves three or four.

Herb Vinegars

Try flavoring vinegars with your favorite herbs. This is a great way to add something new and different to your salads, sauces, and marinades. Use either cider or wine vinegars for best results. Place about one pint of dried leaves in a jar (tarragon, carraway, bay, rosemary, and thyme are all good; try what you prefer), then pour 1½ pints of vinegar over the leaves. Cover and keep airtight for a week or two. Strain off the vinegar and bottle.

To make a garlic vinegar, pound six or eight garlic cloves and place in a jar. Bring one pint of vinegar to a boil, and pour into the jar. Let the mixture steep two or three weeks, strain, and bottle.

Herb Butters

You can make a zesty spread of your favorite herbs. Simply boil some dry leaves in a little water, drain, and blend briskly with butter. Use enough butter to suit your taste; three ounces of butter to two ounces of herbs makes a pleasing, yet not overseasoned, spread. This recipe is also excellent if you substitute cream cheese for butter.

To make a herbal fondue, follow the same procedure with the herbs, and add to your favorite cheese melted in a double boiler. Add wine, beer, or milk to give the fondue the consistency and taste you like.

Herbal Dip

2 cartons (6 oz.) cottage cheese	¼ cup parsley
1 cup diced cucumber	1 tbsp. salad burnet
¼ cup chives	1 tbsp. borage
	¼ cup chopped radishes

Chop the herbs finely, and blend all the ingredients thoroughly. Chill, and garnish with parsley, nasturtium buds, or whatever you like. You can add lemon juice, milk, or wine to liquify further. Play around with this recipe: add whatever suits you. Chopped nuts, watercress, shallots, garlic—the list of alternatives or additional ingredients is limitless.

————————

Mint Julep

1 ounce whiskey (bourbon, a blend, or scotch)
6 mint leaves (spearmint is best; others are suitable)
1 teaspoon sugar

Make a syrup of half the liquor, mint leaves, sugar and a small amount of water. Add the syrup to a glass half filled with crushed ice. After stirring, add the balance of the whiskey and more crushed ice. Stir final mix, or use a shaker, and it's ready for consumption. You may want to increase or decrease the number of mint leaves to suit your taste.

————————

From my dear friend, Janie Couvillon, of Baton Rouge, Louisiana

Fromage de Porc Glace

3 lbs. pork rump and 1 lb. beef chuck	6 ribs celery
1 qt. water and 1½ cups water	1 cup parsley
2 large dry onions	6 bay leaves
2 bunches of green onions	¼ tsp. red pepper
3 tsp. minced garlic	¼ tsp. thyme
2 large bell peppers	1 tsp. basil
	1 tbsp. vinegar
	¼ cup Lea & Perrins
	3 packages gelatin
	Salt and pepper to taste

Cut meat in 1-inch squares; cut off excess fat. Put the meat in a deep pot and cover with one quart of water. Dice vegetables and add meat, along with the bay leaves, thyme, basil, Lea & Perrins, red and black pepper, salt, and vinegar. Cook until the meat falls apart. Transfer to a pan, discard the bay leaves, and mince with your hands. Then dissolve the gelatin in 1½ cups of water and add to the meat mixture; stir well. Taste to be sure seasoning suits your taste. If not, add more salt, red and black pepper. Pour this in a pan about 14 by 8 inches. Chill at least four hours before serving.

Beer Soup

1 can warm beer	¼ tsp. each: sweet basil, oregano, dill seed and bay leaf
2 cubes beef bouillon	
1 cup water	
¾ cup apple juice	1 tsp. powdered onion
2 tbsp. Worcestershire sauce	1 tsp. parsley
	salt and pepper to taste

Combine and simmer for ½ hour.

Chicken Liver-Sausage Jambalya

1 lb. chicken livers (frozen)	1 cup green onions
2 lbs. hot sausage	¼ tsp. Worcestershire sauce

½ cup bacon drippings
1 large bell pepper
1 large onion
6 cloves garlic
3 ribs celery
¼ cup parsley
1 tsp. sweet basil
1 cup dry sherry
1 cup water
6 bay leaves
3 cups rice
Salt and pepper to taste

Cut sausage in 1-inch pieces and fry in bacon drippings. Add chopped onions, bell pepper, garlic, celery and seasonings and chopped liver (frozen liver is easier to chop). Add this to sausage and cook for 15 minutes. Add water, wine, Worcestershire, green onions, parsley, bay leaves and sweet basil. Cook for ½ hour, then add cooked rice. Mix well and serve.

Chicken Liver Paté

1 lb. chicken livers
½ lb. sliced bacon
1 large onion (dry)
4 pods garlic
4 bay leaves
2 tbsp. Worcestershire sauce
¼ tsp. red pepper
½ tsp. nutmeg
1 tsp. dry mustard
⅛ tsp. ground cloves
1 tsp. salt

Wash liver, put in covered pan with cut-up bacon. Add bay leaves, onion, garlic, salt, pepper, and Worcestershire sauce. Bring to a boil and cook for 20 minutes in just enough water to cover. When done, discard bay leaves and add rest of ingredients. Put in blender, then pour into molds. This will keep in refrigerator for a week. It will also freeze well.

Bayou Border Buttermilk

1 can (8 oz.) concentrated orange juice
6 jiggers (total 9 oz.) rum, vodka or bourbon
3 tsp. honey
2 tsp. vanilla
2 raw eggs laid by *small* hen

Blend above mixture thoroughly before adding crushed ice, a handful at a time, and then blend again vigorously. A little nutmeg may be sprinkled on top before serving in champagne or sherbet glasses. Serves 10-12. This drink is great. To classify this as an herb recipe, I'm calling two raw eggs laid by a small hen a new exotic south Louisiana herb.

Deep Squash (From Camille Waters)

Steam six medium-sized whole zucchini. With a spoon, scoop and hollow zukes so they resemble boats. Put scooped zucchini innards in skillet with:

6 green onions, chopped
4 stalks celery, minced
1½ lbs. boiled shrimp
4 tbsp. butter
½ cup toasted bread crumbs

Sauté. Add 1 tsp. dill (½ tsp. dried) or ½ tsp. basil or ¼ tsp. white pepper. Add 1 cup grated monterrey jack cheese. Mix. Put stuffing into boats and bake 20 minutes at 350°. Serve with gazpacho or cold plum soup.

Some Creole Cookery

These recipes are from the *Cajun Country Cookbook* by Tony Chachere. Tony was kind enough to give me permission to incorporate these here. Some grocery stores carry *Tony's Creole Seasoning;* this is the same Tony.

Dove Casserole

6 doves
6 small onions
6 tbsp. chopped parsley
½ cup butter
1 garlic clove, minced
2½ cups canned
  tomatoes or
  2 cups tomato sauce
6 oz. canned mushrooms
1 large onion, chopped
½ tsp. thyme
¼ tsp. dried basil
1 tsp. salt
Fresh-ground black
  pepper

Stuff each dove with one onion, one teaspoon parsley and one teaspoon butter. Sauté garlic in remaining six tablespoons butter for 5 minutes. Add doves and sauté 10 minutes. Put doves and garlic butter in deep casserole, add other ingredients. Cover and bake 375° about two hours. Serves six.

Tony's Creole Seasoning

(Use as you would salt; store in airtight jar.)

26-oz. box Morton salt
1½-oz. box ground
  black pepper
2-oz. bottle ground
  red pepper
1-oz. bottle pure
  garlic powder
1-oz. bottle chili powder
1-oz. carton Accent

To season seafood, use 3 tsp. of above and add: 1 tsp. powdered thyme; 1 tsp. bay leaf; 1 tsp. sweet basil.

Fried Shrimp

1 lb. fresh shrimp
2 tbsp. vinegar

1 small can evaporated
milk
2 eggs
1 tbsp. Calumet
baking powder

1 cup flour
*Tony's Creole Seasoning
to taste*
Season to taste

Make a mixture of eggs, evaporated milk, baking powder, and vinegar. Marinate shrimp for at least one hour. Remove and season lightly with *Tony's Creole Seasoning*. Dip in flour and fry at 380° for not more than 10 minutes.

Cold Plum Soup (From Camille Waters)

Pit eight large elephant-heart plums. (Try to resist smearing them over your body.) Simmer with ¾ cup honey and three cups water for 30 minutes. Cool. Blend. Add ½ tsp. nutmeg. Serve cold with a dollop of whipped cream.

———————

The following recipes are from *Concord Cuisine* published by the Junior Charity League of Concord, North Carolina.

Black-eyed Peas and Pork

1 lb. (2¼ cups)
black-eyed peas
1½ lbs. smoked ham
or ham hocks
1 large onion
1 clove garlic

Few sprigs parsley
1 bay leaf
⅛ tsp. thyme
Pinch crushed red pepper
2 tsp. salt
⅛ tsp. pepper

Cover peas with water and soak overnight. Next day, drain and rinse thoroughly. Cook ham or ham hocks in two cups water for 30 minutes, then add peas, chopped onion, crushed garlic, chopped parsley, herbs, and seasonings. Add enough water to cover peas, bring to boil, reduce heat, and cover. Cook slowly for about two hours or until peas are tender. Don't cook to the mushy stage. Cut meat into chunks before serving. Serves four to six.

Baked Stuffed Zucchini Squash

6 large zucchini squash
¾ tsp. salt

¾ lb. ground beef or
round steak

1 can (lb. 13 oz.)
Italian tomatoes
3 oz. tomato paste
1 egg, slightly beaten
½ cup bread crumbs
⅓ cup onion, chopped
Dash of pepper
1 tbsp. vegetable oil

½ tsp. oregano
½ tsp. basil
1 clove of garlic, mashed
½ cup pitted olives,
sliced
½ cup onion, sliced
⅓ cup Parmesan cheese,
grated

Wash squash, remove and discard ends. Cut thin slice lengthwise from top of squash. Scoop out seeds, leaving shell ⅛ to ¼ inch thick. Cook squash in boiling salted water five minutes. Drain well, upside down. Combine tomatoes and tomato paste in bowl; break up tomatoes. Mix three tablespoons of tomato mixture, egg and bread crumbs. Sauté onion and pepper in oil in skillet for three minutes. Add ground beef; cook until brown. Add salt, pepper and bread crumb mixture. Fill squash with mixture. Place in greased 2-quart casserole. Heat oven to 350°. Combine remaining tomato mixture, oregano, basil, garlic, olives and sliced onion. Pour around zucchini. Sprinkle with Parmesan cheese. Cover and bake for 30 minutes; uncover and bake for ten more minutes. Serves six to eight.

French Herb Loaf

1 stick butter or
margarine
1 tsp. garlic juice
½ tsp. salt
¼ tsp. pepper
¼ tsp. sage, crushed

¼ tsp. rosemary
¼ tsp. thyme
¼ tsp. dry mustard
¼ tsp. tarragon
3 tbsp. parsley

Mix all ingredients. Spread on slices of French bread; reassemble loaf. Wrap in foil. Serve hot. Fine for outdoor suppers.

Gary's Scallops Kasmir

1 bunch celery
1 large onion
1 tbsp. cumino seed
Big pinch of tarragon

1 pint buttermilk
½ stick butter
1 cup white wine
2 lbs. scallops

Sauté the fresh scallops in butter with celery, onion and white wine for 20 minutes. Add cumino seed, tarragon, and buttermilk. Simmer 20 minutes and serve over saffron rice. Superb!

The Herbs

The herbs described in this section are presented in alphabetical sequence. Though some of the herbs are of the same genus, they're quite different in culture, appearance, and use. Thus, they are listed individually; i.e, pennyroyal, a member of the mint family, is listed separately. An "A" following an herb's common and latin name designates it an annual; a "B" means biennial and a "P" perennial. Full sun means sun all day; partial shade refers to more sun than shade. Only a few herbs will survive in complete shade. With the exception of a few, I have grown every herb discussed in the pages that follow.

ALOE *(Aloe vera)* P

Propagation: By vegetative offshoots from the mother plant

Width & Height: 1' x 2'

Soil: Average to slightly sandy

Exposure: Full sun or partial shade

Water: Average

Aloe vera leaves, a few inches wide and up to 2 feet long, form a gray-green rosette. The center stem reaches a height of about 4 feet. Flowers form in a spectacular yellow-orange cluster almost a foot in length. Along the Gulf Coast (zones 9 & 10), aloes can reach 4 feet in height and get almost as wide. Don't confuse the agaves (century plants) with the aloes. Aloes have soft, pulpy leaves, while the agaves have stringy, tough leaves.

Culture. Aloes need a well-drained, moderately rich soil and do best with partial shade. They dislike wet feet and an excess of nitrogen.

Uses. I have seen ads extolling the aloe's virtues as an ingredient in cosmetics, but its prime use is medicinal. The juice from the leaves is used to treat burns, abrasions, and minor skin diseases. It is also very effective for sunburn. You can save the

The leaves of the aloe vera contain a mucilaginous substance soothing to minor skin irritations, abrasions, and burns.

leaf you've used by covering it with cellophane and storing in your freezer till you need it again. Your plant will heal itself, sealing off the break in the leaf.

Remarks. The aloe is native to South Africa but is quite common to the arid regions of the United States, Mexico, and the Mediterranean (there are more than 200 varieties). They do quite well on a sunny windowsill indoors, and weekly watering with minimum fertilizing will make an attractive plant. Would you believe they belong to the lily family? They do, and so do the onion, tulip, and asparagus, but don't use these on the burns. Enjoy the beauty of the tulips, and eat the asparagus and onions.

ANGELICA
(Angelica archangelica) P

Propagation: Seed

Width & Height: 2' x 5'

Soil: Average

Exposure: Full sun or
partial shade

Water: Frequent

This large, handsome plant can get to be 6 feet high and almost 3 feet wide. The leaf stems are unusual in appearance in that they start as a sort of sheath, developing into a compound five-segment leaf. Leaves can reach 5 inches or more in length and almost as wide. Green flowers are in rounded clusters and rise several feet above the main foliage of the plant.

Culture. Angelica likes average moist soil and cooler climates. It does best in the eastern portions of zones 7 and 8.

Uses. An oil is extracted from the leaves and roots for use in the manufacture of perfumes. This oil is also used to flavor liqueurs. Leaves and stalks can be eaten as a salad.

Remarks. Because the herb gets so tall, make sure it's in the background of your garden. Culpeper tells us this herb is good for "deafness, toothaches, and bites of mad dogs." Well, . . . maybe.

ANISE *(Pimpinella anisum)* A

Propagation: Seed

Width & Height: 1' x 2'

Soil: Average

Exposure: Full sun

Water: Average

The leaves of anise are lobed and finely cut, with small white flowers developing in flat clusters. Plants can reach 2 feet in height and should be thinned 8 to 12 inches apart.

Culture. A well-drained, moderately rich soil in a sunny location.

Uses. The fresh leaves are used in salads, and the seeds in bread, cake, soup, and as a medicinal tea. Commercial uses include: soap, perfume, tea, dental preparations, and flavoring for cough drops and liqueurs.

Remarks. Anise does well as a companion plant with coriander. Anise has a long taproot, and so it resents transplanting, but it's no problem if you've grown your plants in containers and then transfer them to the garden.

(Sweet) BASIL
(Ocimum basilicum) A

Propagation: Seed

Width & Height: 2' x 2'

Soil: Average

Exposure: Full sun

Water: Average

The most common of the basils, sweet basil, is a medium-size bushy plant reaching 2 feet in width and height. The leaves are 2 inches long and 1 inch wide, with a clove-pepperish taste and odor. There are many varieties of basil: the large-leaf plant reaches 3 feet tall; lettuce leaf, a Japanese basil, is a large plant with sawtooth leaves 4 inches long that resemble a leaf of lettuce; compact bush basil,

Basil is an easy herb to grow; it does well with minimal watering. Our warm southern climate forces basil to seed prolifically after flowering, so look for volunteer seedlings each fall.

(Sweet) BAY *(Laurus nobilis)* P

Propagation: Seed or cuttings

Width & Height: 5' x 10'

Soil: Average

Exposure: Full sun or partial shade

Water: Average

Bay is an evergreen shrub or tree that can reach up to 60 feet. The bark is olive-green with a reddish hue. The dark green leaves are 3 to 4 inches long. Bay is compact and multi-branched; the mature tree has a pyramidal appearance. Small yellow flowers turn to black berries twice the size of a pea.

Culture. Average well-drained soil, in either full or filtered sun. This is a slow plant to propagate, as are most trees. It takes four to six months to root cuttings, and seed viability (ability to germinate) is low, averaging about 25 percent.

Uses. Bay is used to flavor poultry, fish, pasta, and sweet dishes. Try a leaf in a pot of beans. Leaves can be used fresh or dry.

Remarks. Bay is hardy to 10° and can be grown outdoors in zones 8, 9, and 10. It makes a fine potted plant or hedge and can be pruned to any size.

This is a seedling of bay, a classic for all savory dishes. This plant will become a tree up to 60' high.

less than a foot tall, has leaves no larger than a fingernail; opal basil, both the compact as well as the large-leaf variety, is very striking in color; sacred basil has an unusual fragrance and reaches 18 inches in height; and lemon basil, an unusual variety, is my favorite. I don't believe I've seen seeds of this latter variety for sale. Every garden should have this herb. If you can't find any seeds, drop me a note and I'll send you a gift of some of mine.

Culture. Basil is grown from seed in the spring and germinates in seven to ten days. Seedlings are easily transplanted. A light, well-drained medium rich soil in full sun is a good environment for this herb. Fertilize lightly after a moderate pruning. You can extend the life of your plant if you don't allow it to flower.

Uses. This versatile flavoring herb enhances soups, stews, salads, cottage cheese, and many other foods. My wife uses the leaves in conjunction with other herbs to flavor roasting chicken, and, I might add, her chicken is a gourmet's delight. Basil's prime commercial use is in perfumes.

Remarks. Basil is a very easy herb to grow, and it manages very well with minimum water. The bush and opal varieties make lovely border plants requiring little or no care. In most of Texas, with over six months of warm weather, a flowering basil plant drops many seeds, resulting in many volunteer plants.

BEE BALM *(Monarda didyma)* P

Propagation: Seed, cuttings, or division

Width & Height: 2' x 3'

Soil: Average

Exposure: Full sun

Water: Average

Bee balm is a bushy plant to 3 feet in height. Leaves are up to 6 inches long. Flowers are in dense clusters in red, pink, purple or white, depending on variety.

Culture. Sun to partial shade in moist, slightly acid soil.

Uses. Used for tea, to flavor jellies, in fruit salads, and in potpourri.

Remarks. Commonly known as Oswego tea or bergamot, bee balm is native to the northeastern U.S., though some subspecies are natives of Texas. It is hardy to −20° and does quite well in all zones. The middle of the plant has a tendency to rot, so use outer shoots and roots when you propagate by division.

BORAGE *(Borago officinalis)* A

Propagation: Seed

Width & Height: 1' x 2'

Soil: Average

Exposure: Full sun or partial shade

Water: Minimum

This plant can reach 3 feet tall. The gray-green leaves are covered with bristly hairs and get up to 6 inches long. Borage has lovely blue star-shaped flowers that tend to droop downward.

Culture. Soil can be somewhat poor and on the dry side. Too much moisture will kill this plant. Borage does well in sun or partial shade.

Uses. The leaves have a cucumber-like flavor and are used in salads or cooked as greens. The flowers can be candied or used in iced drinks.

Remarks. Borage is an excellent bee plant. Culpeper tells us that it's a useful antidote for the venom of serpents. Nitrate of potash is one of the chemicals in this plant, and when burned it spews sparks with a slight explosive sound.

BURNET *(Sanguisorba minor)* P

Propagation: Seed or root division

Width & Height: 2' x 2'

Soil: Average

Exposure: Full sun

Water: Average

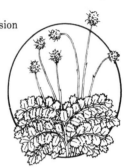

A bushy, full plant with lacy leaves, burnet reaches a height of up to 2 feet. The leaves are serrated in opposite pairs along the stalks. It is hardy to −25° and is evergreen in all zones.

Culture. Does well in average soil in full sun. In the North it takes a few years for a well-established plant; here in Texas, one growing season produces a vigorous, healthy plant.

Uses. Burnet has a fresh cucumber flavor and the leaves can be used in salads, iced drinks, cream cheese, and as a garnish.

Remarks. Makes a nice low hedge requiring minimum care. It is native to England and Europe and was brought to this country by the early settlers.

CAMOMILE *(Anthemis nobilis)* P

Propagation: Seed, root division, or layering

Width & Height: ½' x 1'

Soil: Sandy

Exposure: Full sun or partial shade

Water: Average

There are two varieties, English *(Anthemis nobilis)* and German *(Matricaria camomilla)* with both herbs having similar characteristics. The leaves are lacy with small flowers very similar to a daisy. The English variety grows in a soft mat, with flowers reaching a foot high. German camomile does not have a mat appearance but has delicate foliage surrounding the daisy-like flowers.

Culture. Camomile likes full or partial sun and a moist sandy soil.

Uses. The blossoms are used as a hair rinse for blondes. The dried blossoms make a mild tea. The oil is used in perfumes.

Remarks. The German variety flowers in a shorter period than does the English, and it self-sows throughout the year in zones 9 and 10. In mild winters I have German camomile blooming all year.

CARAWAY *(Carum carvi)* B

Propagation: Seed

Width & Height: 1' x 3'

Soil: Average

Exposure: Full sun

Water: Average

Caraway is a hardy biennial that sets seed the second year. This 2-foot plant has lacy foliage similar to carrots and does very well in southern gardens. The umbels, or seed heads, are creamy-white in color and reach 5 or 6 inches in diameter.

Culture. Sow in light soil, spacing so mature plants are a foot apart. Caraway has a long taproot and so is difficult to transplant. It's no problem grown in its own container and then set out in the garden, though.

Uses. The leaf is used in salads and soups. Caraway seeds, a favorite in German cooking, are used to flavor rye bread, cake, saurkraut, baked apples, goulash, and soup. It's used commercially for perfume, liqueurs, and soap.

Remarks. In Texas, seeds can be planted in early fall and the plants will set seed heads the following summer. Broadcast seeds throughout the garden rather than restrict them to a bed. To have an appreciable amount of seeds, you need 40 to 50 plants. Seeds need to be harvested just before they are ripe or the wind will get most of them. Viability for seeds is several years; the fragrance improves with age.

Dioscorides advised pale-faced girls to partake of the oil. It was thought the seed would keep lovers from being fickle and would prevent fowl and pigeons from straying.

CATNIP *(Nepeta cataria)* P

Propagation: Seed, cuttings, or division

Width & Height: 3' x 2'

Soil: Average

Exposure: Full sun or partial shade

Water: Average

Catnip reaches 3 feet in height and can grow more than 4 feet wide. The gray heart-shaped leaves are up to 3 inches long. White flowers (with a lilt of purple) in dense clusters on spikes, make this a fine accent plant.

Culture. This herb does well in most any soil but will grow best in sandy soil. It self-sows, and plants are easily transplanted to other areas of the garden. Catnip does well in full or partial sun. It tends to get scraggly and needs to be pruned several times during the growing season.

Uses. Leaves make a hot tea that some drink to ease the discomfort of a cold. Large doses of warm tea induce vomiting. Catnip acts as a mild narcotic for most cats. Some cats enjoy fresh leaves; others prefer them dried. Leaves can be dried and sewn in a small sachet for your cat to play with.

Remarks. Protect your catnip until it's a foot tall—a cage of chicken wire is good. Your cat or your neighbor's can destroy a plant very quickly. My daughter's cat is not interested in catnip but prefers lemon grass, but what can you expect from a cat that drinks water from the faucet.

Catnip is avoided by rats. Either the odor is very disagreeable to them, they smell the recent presence of a feline, or experience has given them bad associations with the plant. Culpeper advises that catnip juice added to wine is good for bruises, whereas the tea applied to the head will heal sores.

CAYENNE *(Capsicum minimum)* P

Propagation: Seed

Width & Height: 1' x 2'

Soil: Average

Exposure: Full sun or
partial shade

Water: Average

There are many varieties of hot peppers (cayenne is just one), with pods ranging from 1 to 6 inches in length. It is perennial in its native tropical climates, but grows as an annual outside its native habitat. The leaves are half an inch wide and up to 2 inches long. The fruit, a seed pod, can be red, blue, yellow, or green. The plant grows up to 18 inches tall and wide.

Culture. Cayenne does well in most soils and in full or partial sun and doesn't require much care.

Use. An absolute must for flavoring Mexican food.

Remarks. Cayenne, with its many colorful pods, is an excellent border or accent plant. Peppers in your garden can be potted and brought indoors before the first freeze. There are many unusual varieties of hot peppers from Mexico. Regardless of what they look like, they all have the same hot flavor. Wash your hands thoroughly after handling this pungent herb.

CHERVIL *(Anthriscus cerefolium)* A

Propagation: Seed

Width & Height: 1' x 2'

Soil: Sandy

Exposure: Partial shade

Water: Average

This annual reaches a height of up to 2 feet, with very lacy light green leaves. The flowers are delicate white in flat heads. Chervil resembles flat-leaf parsley, although it is a more dainty plant. It turns red in the late fall.

Culture. Chervil does best in well drained soil with some shade. Plant close to taller herbs or vegetables to provide the necessary shade. Chervil self-sows, and in areas of Texas we can have several crops in a year.

Uses. There is a curled variety that has an anise flavor. The leaves are used in salads, soups, and as a garnish in much the same manner as parsley.

Remarks. A lovely, easy-care plant. The ancient Roman author Pliny advises that the seed taken in vinegar gets rid of hiccups.

CHIVES *(Allium schoenoprasum)* P

Propagation: Seed or division

Width & Height: ½' x 1'

Soil: Average

Exposure: Full sun or
partial shade

Water: Average

Chives are probably one of the most familiar and widely used herbs. This hardy perennial has small bulblets growing very close together in dense clusters. Its slender hollow leaves are cylindrical and grow to about 12 inches tall. The pale-purple flower heads are densely packed in a conical umbel. The small seeds are black and similar to onion seeds. As the plant gets larger the leaves have a tendency to droop. This is normal for chives.

Garlic chives (*A. schoenoprasum* var. *sibricum*) have a mild garlic flavor. At maturity, garlic chives (Chinese chives, oriental chives) are the same size as a tubular chives plant. The flowers of the garlic variety are white and grow in attractive star-like clusters. This herb usually flowers in late July or early August.

Culture. Both varieties do well in any garden soil. Clumps should be divided into smaller clumps with eight or ten bulblets. You can cut your clump of chives several times a year. Fertilize after each cutting. Chives will not flower with continual pruning. If you use them as border plants, don't prune till the flowers have set seed.

Uses. Chives are great in salads, soups, and many other dishes. I take a handful of either variety and, with a scissors, snip them into very small pieces. Mixing chives with scrambled eggs makes a very tasty breakfast dish.

Remarks. As members of the onion family, chives deter many harmful insects in the vegetable garden. I randomly plant both varieties in my garden.

COMFREY
(Symphytum officinale) P

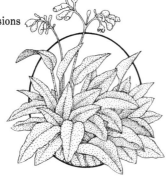

Propagation: From root divisions

Width & Height: 2' x 3'

Soil: Average

Exposure: Full sun

Water: Average

The main stem of comfrey is covered with bristly hairs and can reach 3 feet tall. Leaves on the lower part of the plant are largest (up to 10 inches long), decreasing in size as they grow up the stem. Like the stalk, the leaves are quite hairy and promote itching when handled. The drooping flowers, usually purple, bloom through the greater part of the summer. There are several varieties of comfrey, but *S. officinale* is the most common.

Cultivation. Comfrey does well in full or partial sun and in average soil. Plants should be spaced 3 feet apart. Several cuttings a year can be made from this perennial (it's hardy to −30°). It's a heavy nitrogen feeder and should be fertilized after each cutting.

Uses. This herb, rich in calcium, phosphorous, potassium, and high in protein, makes an excellent supplement for livestock and poultry. The young leaves can be used in salads, cooked as greens, in soups, or as a tea.

Remarks. A small bit of root means another plant, so plant this herb where it will be happy for years

Comfrey produces drooping purple flowers that bloom throughout the summer.

to come. I'm sure a plant or two will be very happy off in a corner of your garden. I've been trying to reduce my 30 or so plants down to 10. It's very difficult, but I'm making some progress. Comfrey leaves are excellent for your compost pile. Allantoin, which promotes healing of cuts and lacerations, is a valuable component of comfrey. Culpeper tells us that comfrey is good for gout, ulcers, bruises, wounds, ruptures, and helps mend broken bones.

CORIANDER
(Coriandrum sativum) A

Propagation: Seed

Width & Height: 1' x 2'

Soil: Average

Exposure: Full sun

Water: Average

The Egyptians and Israelites used coriander over 2,500 years ago. Note the volunteer plants that have sprouted at the bottom of this large specimen.

COSTMARY
(*Tanacetum balsamita*) P

Propagation: Root division

Width & Height: 1' x 2'

Soil: Average

Exposure: Full sun or partial shade

Water: Average

This hardy perennial can reach 3 feet tall. The plants in my garden are usually 1½ feet tall. The leaves are large, up to 8 inches long and 4 inches wide, with a sharp minty fragrance and flavor. The flowers are small, pale yellow and button-like in appearance. The roots spread very easily and costmary can cover a large area in one growing season.

Culture. This herb prefers full sun but will thrive in partial shade. It likes almost any soil as long as it's fairly dry and well drained.

Uses. In England, costmary was used to flavor ale: "Alecost" is another of its common names. It is used in salads and potpourri.

Remarks. In colonial days, churchgoers used costmary as markers for their Bibles, hence another common name, "Bible leaf."

The stem of coriander gets up to 3 feet tall and quite slender and branched. Leaves are almost round and slightly lobed. The flowers are off-white and compliment the plant's bright green appearance. Seeds should be picked just before they are ripe or the wind will random plant them for you.

Culture. Coriander does well in any well drained soil in full sun. It has a long taproot and is difficult to transplant. It's no problem if it's grown in its own container and then planted outdoors.

Uses. Flavors liqueurs, an ingredient of curry powder, good in breads or as a condiment.

Remarks. The foliage and seeds of coriander have an unpleasant musty odor. They lose this odor when dry, and the seeds become more fragrant the drier they get. This herb is one of several used by the Egyptians and Israelites over 2,500 years ago.

DILL (*Anethum graveolens*) A

Propagation: Seed

Width & Height: 1' x 3'

Soil: Average

Exposure: Full sun

Water: Average

This hardy annual, similar in appearance to fennel, grows from 2½ to 3 feet tall. It usually has one stalk with sparse feathery leaves. The umbels, or flat seed heads, are 4 or 5 inches across. The flowers are a pretty yellow and add quite a bit of

Be sure to clip the seedhead of dill just after it turns brown. Otherwise, the wind will scatter the seeds everywhere.

color when randomly planted in the garden. The entire plant is very aromatic.

Culture. Dill grows well in most any well drained soil.

Uses. The seeds and leaves are used to flavor soups, sauces, fish, and in pickling cucumbers. The French flavor their cakes and pastries with dill seed.

Remarks. This native of the Mediterranean region was used as a drug in the 10th century. Magicians used it to combat witchcraft. Culpeper tells us that it strengthens the brain, controls hiccups, and helps to expel "wind." Dill seeds should be collected when they first turn brown. If you neglect to collect them, it's only a matter of a few days before the wind random plants them for you.

DITTANY OF CRETE
(*Amaracus dictamnus*) P

Propagation: Seed, cuttings, or
plant division

Width & Height: 1' x 2'

Soil: Sandy

Exposure: Full sun

Water: Minimum

Dittany of Crete is a very ornamental plant with soft hairy grey leaves ½ inch long and wide. The slender stems grow about a foot long. The flowers are purple and quite small.

Culture. This herb does well with full sun, minimum watering, and sandy soil.

Uses. Dittany is a culinary herb for Greek and Italian cooking. The flowers are used for tea.

Remarks. This herb makes an excellent ground cover. It is fine for rock gardens and makes a spectacular hanging basket plant with its long leafy trailing stems.

ELECAMPANE
(*Inula helenium*) P

Propagation: Seed or
root division

Width & Height: 2' x 4'

Soil: Sandy

Exposure: Partial shade

Water: Frequent

Elecampane is one of the largest of the herbs. The stem grows to 5 feet, with leaves up to 18 inches long and 4 inches wide. The undersides of the scalloped leaves are velvety. Elecampane usually blooms through the summer with large, bright yellow flowers 4 inches in diameter. If you grow it from seed, however, it won't flower until the second year. When the flowers are spent and have fallen, the seed head has a very unusual geometric pattern.

Culture. It does best in moist, well drained soil in partial shade.

Uses. Roots are candied for a cough medicine. In Europe the roots are used with wormwood foliage in the preparation of absinthe. It is given to horses to improve their coats.

Remarks. The 16th century authors tell us this herb is good for fevers, the plague, and destroys worms in the stomach.

FENNEL *(Foeniculum vulgare)* P

Propagation: Seed

Width & Height: 2′ x 4′

Soil: Average

Exposure: Full sun

Water: Average

Fennel is a large herb, 4 or 5 feet tall, with a bright green, almost polished appearance. The leaves are feathery or lacy, very similar to the dill leaf. Bright golden-yellow flowers adorn this plant. Florence fennel *(F. vulgare* var. *dulce),* also called finocchio, is an annual and a much smaller plant. It has a swollen base with white stalks. This annual reaches a height of 15 to 18 inches, with flowers similar to vulgare. It usually blooms earlier than the perennial variety.

Culture. Fennel is easily grown from seed, likes full sun, and does well in any well drained soil. Florence fennel requires more watering and a richer soil.

Uses. The leaves are used for garnishes, in salads and puddings, and to flavor Italian sausage. The tender stems are soaked in water and eaten raw like celery. Seeds are used to flavor cordials and liqueurs. Fennel also makes a good tea.

Fennel is an excellent all-purpose kitchen herb. Use for garnishes, in salads and meats; the slender, white stalks can be eaten raw like celery.

Remarks. This native of temperate Europe and the Mediterranean has followed civilization, usually where Italians have traveled. In medieval times this plant was hung over the doors to keep away evil spirits. The ancient Greeks tell us that partaking of the herb increases the life span and gives strength and courage.

FOXGLOVE *(Digitalis purpurea)* B

Propagation: Seed; low germination percent

Width & Height: 1′ x 4′

Soil: Average

Exposure: Full sun

Water: Frequent

Foxglove is classed as a biennial, but sometimes it can flower for several years. This handsome plant produces a flower stalk up to 4 feet tall. Large leaves, almost a foot long, grow at the base of the plant. The long bell-shaped flowers are 2 inches long and purple or white with speckled throats. The flowers are borne on stalks a few feet above the foliage.

Culture. Does best in rich, friable, moist soil in full sun.

Uses. Foxglove is a source of digitalis, a heart stimulant.

Remarks. The true medicinal plant has deep pink or magenta flowers; the pale-flowered variety does not produce the drug. This is a beautiful plant and should be grown for show.

GARLIC *(Allium sativum)* P

Propagation: By cloves from the bulb

Width & Height: 1′ x 3′

Soil: Average

Exposure: Full sun

Water: Average

This 2-foot tall herb, in my opinion, belongs in every garden. The bulb consists of several cloves enclosed together in a thin white skin. The stem is smooth, surrounded at the bottom by tubular leaf sheaths from which the long, flat linear leaves grow. The flower umbel is at the top of the main stalk. The white flowers comprising the umbel are usually sterile.

Culture. Garlic does best in rich, sandy, moderately moist soil in full sun. Cloves should be planted, pointy end up, about 2 inches deep and 6 to 8 inches apart. Keep your garlic bed hoed and free of weeds. Mulching will help to conserve moisture and reduce weed growth. When the leaves dry and turn brown (after four to six months), the bulbs are ready to harvest, dry and store.

Uses. Garlic is a widely used seasoning for many Italian dishes. It's a fine additive to spice up almost any food. It was used as an antiseptic during World War II. Research is currently in progress testing garlic for possible use in treating various cardiovascular diseases. A friend had a year-old dog in very poor health. She fed him a daily ration of garlic and it helped restore him to health in about 4 months.

SCENTED GERANIUM
(Pelargonium spp.) P

Propagation: Seed or cuttings

Width & Height: ½' x 1'

Soil: Sandy

Exposure: Full sun or
          partial shade

Water: Minimum

Scented geraniums *(Pelargonium spp.)* comprise a very extensive genus. I'll give a general description of some of those I grow. Coconut-scented geranium has a round medium green leaf, about an inch or so across, with lovely tiny pink flowers. It's a trailing variety and has to be in a hanging basket, for it'll trail 2 feet down the sides. There's an apple-scented geranium that has small white flowers and also does well in a hanging basket; its leaves get as large as 2½ inches wide and long. Nutmeg-scented geranium, with inch-long gray-green leaves and

Among the various scented geraniums are an amazing array of fragrances; coconut, rose, apple, mint, cinnamon, lemon, lime, orange, and more. This nutmeg-scented geranium has delicate white flowers and makes a fine container specimen.

small white flowers makes a fine container plant. Cinnamon-scented has leaves an inch wide and long, also produces small white flowers, and is another nice pot plant. There is lemon-rose, which has very large, rounded leaves; rose-scented has large leaves that are more wrinkled than lemon. Attar of rose and crowsfoot are very similar in appearance, but the leaves on crowsfoot are more sharply cut back. Leaves of both species are so sharply divided that they appear fernlike; the flowers of both are a medium purple. Lemon-scented has small ¾-inch leaves, whereas lime-scented has very tiny crinkled leaves.

My favorite geranium is the peppermint-scented variety. The leaves are quite large (3 inches wide and long) and hairy. To me it has one of the most pungent fragrances of all the scented geraniums. All the rose species need at least a gallon-size container or larger, for they can reach 2 feet in height.

Culture. Sandy, well drained soil, and at least 6 to 8 hours of sun a day. Geraniums like it a bit dry. If the lower leaves get yellow, you're overwatering. Purple leaves mean a lack of phosphorous. One-half a teaspoon of bonemeal sprinkled on the surface and watered in will remedy the deficiency.

Uses. Commercially, the fragrant oils are used in perfumes. The leaves flavor jellies, jams, custards, and puddings. Scented geraniums are also fine additions to potpourri.

Remarks. These herbs are very easy to grow and care for, and their exotic fragrances are a must for every home and garden. They do very well in containers or in the ground. Get some, you'll love them.

A Word of Warning

The yew *(Taxus baccata)* is included here as a warning—it is deadly poisonous. This applies to all parts of the tree, even those which appear in ancient herbals as cures for one thing or another. Its delicate pink seeds and dark green leaves have tempted many children with tragic consequences.

I point out yew, but many of the old herbal texts list all sorts of potions for several plants that are poisonous. Many folks enjoy collecting wild herbs these days, but a number of plants in the field and forest can be fatal. All parts of the buttercup, if ingested, can severely damage the digestive system. Jimson weed—the entire plant—has proven to be fatal in many instances. From time to time I read in the newspapers that someone has become very ill or has died from collecting and eating wild mushrooms. *Be very careful* of old herbal

remedies, and *absolutely* identify any wild plant that you intend to either eat or use in a tonic or potion.

An herb that can cause skin problems is *Dictamnus Albus*, whose names include fraxinella, burning bush, and dittany. It is a showy herbaceous perennial with fragrant ash-like leaves and many large flowers. The flowers of the *rubra* variety are pink; those of *alba* are white. This plant can cause painful burns and leave residual skin discoloration for months. Three prerequisites for skin disorders caused by this herb are: moist skin from water or sweat, contact with the plant, and exposure to the sun. I suggest that if you grow this herb, wear gloves, a long sleeve shirt, and don't perspire when pruning or even getting near it.

GERMANDER
(Teucrium lucidum) P

Propagation: Seed, cuttings, or root division

Width & Height: 1½' x 1'

Soil: Average

Exposure: Full sun

Water: Minimum

This hardy perennial, 1 to 1½ feet tall and 2 feet wide, needs frequent clipping and makes a good hedge. The small stiff leaves are a dark glossy green with serrated margins similar to those of an oak leaf. The rose-colored flowers are in whorls on 4- to 6-inch spikes.

Culture. Germander does well in any well drained soil in full sun with minimum care.

Uses. Years ago this herb, in conjunction with other herbs, was used as a cure for gout.

Remarks. The herbalists of the 15th and 16th centuries tell us that mixed in wine it's very effective against the poison of serpents and diseases of the brain. So, not only will it make a lovely hedge, but with a bottle of wine, you're protected from poisonous serpents in your back yard. Quite a number of the herbs, according to the ancient herbalists, are great as medicines to combat venomous serpents.

GINGER *(Zingiber officinale)* P

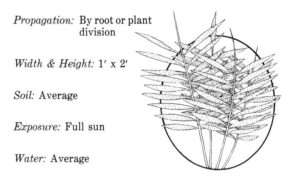

Propagation: By root or plant division

Width & Height: 1' x 2'

Soil: Average

Exposure: Full sun

Water: Average

Ginger, a perennial root, grows and increases underground in tuberous joints. The stalk is ap-

Aloe Vera, p. 37

Angelica, p. 38

Arugula, p. 77

Sweet Basil, p. 38

Purple Ruffles Basil, p. 74

Cinnamon Basil, p. 77

Bay, p. 39

Borage, p. 40

Burnet, p. 40

Camomile, p. 40

Chives, p. 42

Comfrey, p. 43

Comfrey, p. 43, and Costmary, p. 44

Dill, p. 44

Fennel, p. 46

Elephant Garlic, p. 74

Society Garlic, p. 46

Rose Geranium, p. 47

Lamb's Ear, p. 58

English Lavender, p. 59

Lemon Grass, p. 60

Lemon Verbena, p. 61

Lion's Ear, p. 75

Luffa, p. 75

Makrut, p. 77

Apple Mint, p. 62

Licorice Mint, p. 63

Mexican Marigold Mint, p. 61

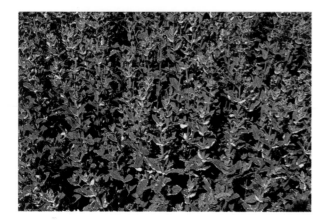

Pineapple Mint, p. 62

Ohja Santa, p. 77

Thai Pepper (Plik), p. 77

Rose Campion, p. 76

Rosemary, p. 65

Golden Sage, p. 67

Jerusalem Sage, p. 75

Mexican Sage, p. 75

Pineapple Sage, p. 67

Santolina, p. 68

Southernwood, p. 69

Winter Savory, p. 68

French Shallots, p. 69

French Sorrel, p. 76

French Tarragon, p. 71

Thyme, p. 71

Violet, p. 76

Wormwood, p. 73

Golden Yarrow, p. 73

White Yarrow, p. 73

proximately 2 feet high with several spikes of white or yellow blossoms. The leaves, 2 inches long and half as wide, have a very fragrant odor of—that's right—ginger.

Culture. My ginger grows in average garden soil in full sun. I've had to cut back the bed several times in past years.

Uses. Ginger is used as a condiment; medicinally, it is an aid in treatment of gastritis. A hot tea for relief of colds is also made from the roots.

Remarks. Jamaica and the West Indies cultivate and export most of the ginger used in the U.S. There is a wild ginger, *Asarum canadense*, native to North America and found in Eastern portions of zone 7. This stemless perennial is a low, spreading, little plant that may reach 12 inches tall. The leaves are heart-shaped, with brown-purple drooping flowers. The entire plant has a strong ginger fragrance and was used by the North American Indians to cover up the smell of spoiled meat.

GINSENG *(Panax quinquefolium)* P

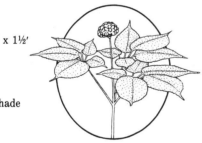

Propagation: Seed

Width & Height: 1' x 1½'

Soil: Average

Exposure: Partial shade

Water: Average

Ginseng is a wild herb with a large, fleshy, very slow-growing root approximately 3 inches long and an inch thick. The root divides into a fork with side shoots resembling a human form. The plant grows to 18 inches tall. The leaves are cinquefoliate (in sets of five), and in its third year the plant produces greenish-yellow flowers followed by clusters of red berries. It takes up to eight years for a ginseng root to mature.

Culture. Ginseng grows best in light, well drained, rich soil in the woods on protected north slopes.

Uses. This herb is prized by the Chinese, who consider it a remedy for most diseases.

Remarks. I have seen many ads telling how much money you can make growing and selling ginseng. Balderdash! As I said above, it takes several years and absolutely perfect growing conditions for roots large enough to sell. Incidentally, these people will sell you seed (rather expensive) and a book (also expensive). If you want to experiment, that's fine, but don't plan to realize many dollars from your ginseng farm.

HOREHOUND
(Marrubium vulgare) P

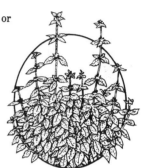

Propagation: Seed, cuttings, or root division

Width & Height: 6' x 1½'

Soil: Average

Exposure: Full sun

Water: Minimum

Horehound usually is no more than 2 feet tall, but it can reach 6 feet in width. The leaves are very wrinkled and are covered with white hairs. The stem becomes woody in a year-old plant. The flowers, off-white in color, are small and inconspicuous.

Horehound has distinctly furrowed leaves. It is used to brew ale and to flavor candies.

Culture. Does well in poor soil in full sun.

Uses. Its prime use is for horehound candy used for coughs and colds. In England this herb is the ingredient for horehound ale, reputed to be a very healthful beverage.

Remarks. Here's another herb that ancient herbalists say was good for the bite of serpents—and mad dogs too! Black horehound *(M. nigrum)* is distinguished by its foul odor. It is a very unattractive plant.

HORSERADISH
(Armoracia rusticana) P

Propagation: Root division

Width & Height: 1' x 2'

Soil: Average

Exposure: Full sun

Water: Average

The root of horseradish (the portion used for flavoring) reaches deeply into the soil, branching in all directions. Roots are long and cylindrical, with a cream-colored skin and white flesh. The leaves are very large, up to 14 inches long and 5 to 6 inches wide. The plant usually attains a height of 18 to 24 inches. The flowers are white with a green cast, on a stalk not much taller than the plant.

Culture. This herb grows best in a rich, well drained soil, but it will develop a fair root system in dry soil. Plant it off in a corner. When you dig your roots late in the fall, you must get every bit of root, for any bit of root left in the ground means another plant next spring.

Uses. The roots are grated and used as condiment for seafood and meat. Horseradish is one of the bitter herbs the Jews eat at the Passover. It is a powerful stimulant and an excellent aid in digestion. My mother made horseradish, and one taste would make you gasp and bring tears to your eyes. Horseradish is also a rich source of vitamin C.

HYSSOP *(Hyssopus officinalis)* P

Propagation: Seed, cuttings, or
plant division

Width & Height: 1' x 1'

Soil: Sandy

Exposure: Full sun

Water: Minimum

This evergreen shrub reaches 1 to 2 feet high and is a very attractive border plant. It has dark foliage and flowering spikes of pink, white, or blue, depending on the variety. The small leaves, a dark green, have a sharp taste and a fragrance reminiscent of sage. The flowers have a spicy balsam odor.

Culture. Hyssop does best in dry, sandy soil in full sun.

Uses. The oil is used in perfumes, and a tea is made from the leaves and stems to treat rheumatism. It also is used as an ingredient in liqueurs.

Remarks. This herb is mentioned frequently in the Old Testament: David mentions it in a prayer, and Moses tells the Israelites to dip hyssop in the blood of a lamb.

LAMB'S EAR *(Stachys lantana)* P

Propagation: Seed or plant division

Width & Height: 1' x 1'

Soil: Sandy

Exposure: Full sun

Water: Minimum

This hardy perennial is a foot tall with soft, downy long linear grey leaves up to 3 inches long and half as wide. When stroked gently, the leaves feel like a lamb's ear. The entire plant has an almost silvery appearance. Most of the leaves grow from the root, and the purple flowers grow on a long stalk, rising a foot or so above the plant.

Culture. Lamb's ear likes full sun and a sandy soil. As this plant increases in size and the leaves touch and cover the ground it becomes a breeding place for pill bugs. Periodically, gently lift the lower leaves around the entire plant and brush the bugs out. They can destroy a well-established plant.

Uses. The dried leaves make a tea to relieve headaches and calm the nerves.

Remarks. I've read that the juice can be used to heal cuts and old sores. I'm old, so I presume it will heal any sores I have.

LAVENDER *(Lavandula spp.)* P

Propagation: Seed or cuttings

Width & Height: 1' x 2'

Soil: Sandy

Exposure: Full sun

Water: Minimum

There are many varieties of lavender, with the most common and largest being *L. spica,* or English lavender. Depending on the variety, this herb ranges from 1 to 4 feet tall and up to 3 feet across. It is a woody plant and has very fragrant flowers, usually lavender or deep purple in color. The narrow grey leaves are 2 inches long and make lovely contrasting plants with the predominant greens of other herbs. In addition to a number of dwarf varieties of lavender, there are Spanish *(L. Stoechas),* French *(L. dentata),* and spike lavender *(L. Lafifolia),* all approximately the same size as English lavender.

Culture. All lavenders need full sun, a sandy well drained soil, and I suggest a raised bed to improve drainage. Most varieties need winter protection in zones 7 and 8.

Uses. Fragrant oils of lavender are used in toilet water, soap, perfume, and the blossoms for potpourri.

Flowering French lavender.

Remarks. It takes 60 pounds of flowers to produce 16 ounces of oil. This is another herb used as an antidote for the bites of mad dogs and serpents.

LEMON BALM *(Melissa officinalis)* P

Propagation: Seed, cuttings, or plant division

Width & Height: 1' x 3'

Soil: Average

Exposure: Full sun or partial shade

Water: Minimum

The stem of lemon balm is upright and hairy with ovate, opposite leaves. The light- to dark-green leaves are 2-3 inches long with scalloped edges. The leaves at the base of the stem are largest, diminishing in size toward the top of the plant. The flowers are usually sparse, white, and quite small. The leaves, when bruised, have a strong lemon odor.

Culture. Lemon balm does well in most well drained soils, in full sun or partial shade. It tends to wilt during extended dry spells (which do occur here in the South, in spite of all our rain). Pruning is necessary to keep this plant in bounds; it can be cut back any time of the year.

Uses. This herb makes an excellent tea and a garnish for fish. The oil is used as a base for perfume and for furniture polish. Dry leaves are used in potpourri.

Remarks. The name *Melissa* is from the Greek word for bee. Dioscorides, a Greek physician in the first century, said that lemon balm can be used as a remedy against the bite of a mad dog by steeping the leaves in wine, drinking it, and also applying the leaves externally. Lemon balm tea, according to one 15th century herbalist, is good for female complaints. If your wife complains, about anything, fix her a cup of tea and advise me of the results.

LEMON GRASS
(Cynbopogon citratus) P

Propagation: Plant division

Width & Height: 1' x 2'

Soil: Average

Exposure: Full sun

Water: Average

This lovely herb has leaves 2 feet long and an inch wide. It looks very similar to a clump of Johnson grass. The strongly lemon-scented leaves rise from the root. If you don't divide the plant periodically, it can reach more than 2 feet in width.

Culture. Lemon grass does well in full or partial sun and with average watering. It is hardy in zone 10 but needs winter protection in zone 9. It can manage 20° weather with 8 to 10 inches of mulch. When you divide the plant for propagation, cut off all but a few inches of leaves, making sure that each small clump has some root system.

Uses. Its prime use is in the manufacture of perfume. In my opinion, it makes one of the tastiest herb teas. It is also used to flavor Oriental dishes.

Lemon grass, a very tropical-looking herb, makes a delicious tea.

Remarks. This native of the tropical climes is grown commercially in India and Ceylon. This is one of the many scented grasses that include: *C. nardus* grown in Ceylon, Java, and Burma, and *C. martine* grown in India.

LEMON TREE
(Eucalyptus citriodora) P

Propagation: Seed or cuttings

Width & Height: 3' x 10'

Soil: Average

Exposure: Full sun

Water: Average

This Australian native will reach a height of 30 feet there. It can get that tall in zone 10, and perhaps 10 feet in zone 9. It is hardy to 20°. I have one about 5 feet tall that I keep pruned to bush size. New leaves have a lovely almost irridescent color. As the tree grows the leaves become a medium green. The spear-shaped leaves have a lovely lemon scent and are 4 to 5 inches long and an inch wide.

Culture. I'm growing my tree in full sun in compost-enriched soil. It looks quite pretty pruned to a bush.

Uses. The oil distilled from the leaves is used to make perfume. This citron-scented gum tree contains up to 98% of citronellol, a prime ingredient for perfumery.

Remarks. The genus Eucalyptus contains over 300 species native to Australia and Tasmania. They grow very quickly, and one of the tallest known trees is *E. Amygdalin*, which attains a height of almost 500 feet.

LEMON VERBENA
(Lippia citriodora) P

Propagation: Seed or cuttings

Width & Height: 2' x 4'

Soil: Average

Exposure: Full sun

Water: Average

Lemon verbena, in my opinion, is "Queen of the Herbs." This leafy shrub can reach a height of 10 to 12 feet in zone 10. It is an excellent pot plant, and in a 10-gallon container it can grow to 6 feet tall. The leaves, up to 5 inches long and less than an inch wide, are a shiny light green. They are slightly rough to the touch, with a delightful lemon fragrance. The flowers are very small, purple and white, and grow in slim terminal spikes.

Culture. Lemon verbena likes full sun and average well drained garden soil.

Lemon verbena can grow to 6' tall. Its redolent lemon fragrance is one of the most delightful of all.

Uses. The leaves are used for tea, perfume, and to flavor jellies. A few leaves in water make a fragrant finger bowl for the dinner table.

Remarks. The leaves dry very quickly, usually in a week, spread out on a newspaper in the open shade. This herb needs winter protection in zones 8 and 9.

MARJORAM
(Marjorana hortensis) P

Propagation: Seed or cuttings

Width & Height: 3' x 1'

Soil: Average

Exposure: Full sun

Water: Average

This fragrant herb can reach 18 inches in height and 3 to 4 feet across. The stems tend to get woody, and the small oval leaves are light green in color on top, with the underside having a grey-green cast. The flowers, white in color, grow in small tight clusters.

Culture. Sweet marjoram does well in most soils in full sun.

Uses. We are all familiar with marjoram as a culinary seasoning. The oil is used in soap and perfume.

Remarks. It takes in excess of 200 pounds of leaves to produce 16 ounces of oil. It was the custom of Greeks and Romans to make a crown of sweet marjoram for newlyweds. American colonists used the oil on furniture.

MEXICAN MARIGOLD MINT
(Tagetes lucidia) P

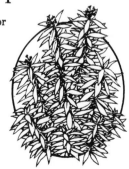

Propagation: Seed, cuttings, or plant division

Width & Height: 1' x 2'

Soil: Average

Exposure: Full sun

Water: Average

Mexican marigold mint has a strong licorice fragrance. Try in potpourri.

This delightful bush reaches a height of near 2 feet and a width of 1½ feet. The leaves, a light green color, have a strong licorice fragrance. They are 1½ inches long and about ⅓-inch wide. Flowers, ½ inch buttons and yellow in color, are produced in late summer. The seeds are identical to French marigold seeds and look like small black and white spears about ½ inch long.

Culture. Full sun means a very tight bushy plant; they tend to get scraggly in partial shade. I have this herb growing in several types of soil: sandy compost—enriched, and heavy. They all do well with average watering.

Uses. The leaves make an unusual tea and are a great substitute for French tarragon.

Remarks. Mexican marigold mint makes a lovely low hedge, a planting against the house, or out in your herb garden. Hardy in zone 9; winter protect in zone 8.

MINT *(Mentha spp.)* P

Propagation: Seed, cuttings, or plant division

Width & Height: 3' x 1'

Soil: Average

Exposure: Full sun or partial shade

Water: Average to frequent

There are three important species of mint: peppermint, spearmint, and pennyroyal. The latter is discussed separately. Spearmint, probably the most common, has a bright green wrinkled leaf with serrated edges. The leaves are an inch to 1½ inches long and are half as wide. The erect stems reach 2 feet in height, and in mid-summer the entire plant is covered with tiny pink flowers in a circular pattern around the upper leaves. Wrigley's spearmint, with a fragrance of its own, is very similar to spearmint except that this variety has leaves that are more rounded. Once you've seen and smelled both mints, there's no mistake as to the proper identification.

In the peppermint group, blackstem peppermint is probably the most common. The dark green leaves are an inch long and half an inch wide and are shaped like an arrowhead with a blunted point. Violet flowers are in cylindrical clusters near the upper leaves. The stems reach approximately a foot in height. Mild peppermint is quite different in appearance, fragrance and size. The leaves of this plant are up to 2 inches long and only ½ inch wide. Stalks can reach over 2 feet tall.

Pineapple mint, with its varigated leaves, is a very striking plant. Apple mint with its large, almost round, very hairy leaf is another fragrant member of the Mentha family. Another varigated mint is golden mint. This is the last mint to produce foliage in the spring. It's less than a foot tall, with beautifully varigated yellowish-gold and green leaves. Orange mint or bergamot, has purple-tinged leaves and a citrus fragrance. Probably the largest mint leaves in my garden belong to red-stem apple mint. The leaves are up to 3 inches long and 1½ inches wide. The erect reddish-tinged stems reach a height of 2 feet.

Leaves of spearmint.

Corsican mint rarely gets over an inch tall and grows in a dense mat. Its tiny leaves and purple flowers are lovely in a rock garden. I have a water mint, a native of Oregon, that a friend brought me several years ago. It has a smooth rounded leaf and the stem is 18 inches tall.

Another variety is licorice mint. It has a strong licorice fragrance. It makes an excellent tea.

Culture. Mints like moisture and do quite well in full and partial sun. They'll grow in most any soil, but will do best in rich, friable soil. Roots need to be dug up to restrict the bed or mint can take over your entire garden. It likes a balanced fertilizer on a periodic basis.

Uses. Mints' prime use is culinary, but the oils are used in many other items such as shampoo, fragrant sprays, toothpaste, and in some medicines that have an otherwise unpleasant taste.

Remarks. The Greeks and Romans used mint to add fragrance to their baths. The mint was a highly esteemed herb: this herb was a tithe to the rulers of Egypt.

MUGWORT *(Artemisia vulgaris)* P

Propagation: Seed or cuttings

Width & Height: 3' x 2'

Soil: Average

Exposure: Full sun

Water: Average

Mugwort can get as tall as 3 feet, sprawling to 4 feet in width. The smooth, dark green leaves are slightly lobed, and have a feathery delicate look. The flowers are in small oval-shaped patterns and are red or yellow. It's an unusual looking plant, and when pruned properly, it's very graceful.

Culture. My mugwort does quite well in full sun in average well drained garden soil.

Uses. In the early 1900's, when tea was expensive. in England, many people brewed tea from the leaves. It is used as a culinary herb in Europe. It is

Properly trimmed, mugwort makes an interesting, graceful low hedge.

taken as a warm infusion with pennyroyal and southernwood leaves at the first sign of a cold.

Remarks. The ancient herbalists used this herb for hysterics, to kill worms, and to treat ailments of the liver.

NASTURTIUM *(Tropaeolum spp.)* P

Propagation: Seed

Width & Height: 1' x 2'

Soil: Sandy

Exposure: Full sun

Water: Average

This perennial, grown as an annual, is known primarily for two varieties. *T. majus* is a climber, and with support can reach over 6 feet. *T. minus* is much smaller averaging 12 to 18 inches tall. Both species have shield-like leaves approximately 2½ inches wide, dark green on top and a lighter green on the underside. The flowers, shaped like elongated bells, ranging in colors from dark red, orange, or yellow to an off-white.

Culture. Several hours of sun a day in sandy soil is a good environment for this herb. Too rich a soil will produce lush foliage but not many flowers.

Uses. It has been used as a dye plant, in perfumes, and the leaves and flowers in salads.

Remarks. Nasturtium should be planted around the roots of your squash plants to repel the squash bug.

OREGANO *(Origanum vulgare)* P

Propagation: Seed, cuttings, or plant division

Width & Height: 1' x 2'

Soil: Average

Exposure: Full sun or partial shade

Water: Average

This 2-foot tall native of Europe spreads by invasive underground runners. The stems are very leafy, with flat clusters of small pink blossoms at the end of the stem. The leaves are an inch long, hairy, and medium-green in color. Greek oregano (*O. prismaticm*) is very similar to vulgare, having a slightly different flavor and brown flowers. It spreads more rapidly, covering a large area in one growing season. I have another variety called

Oregano in a planter box; a classic for cookery.

Origanum majorana. It has a perfume-like fragrance and is evergreen in South Texas. Like the *vulgare*, it can spread quite a bit in a growing season. The leaves are smaller, and the more you cut, the larger the plant will grow.

Culture. Oregano likes full sun; my plants have done well in average well-drained garden soil.

Uses. A culinary herb for many Italian dishes.

Remarks. The *majorana* is, in my opinion, mistakenly called sweet marjoram. The two herbs have similar fragrances, but marjoram is a tender herb, and *majorana*, much larger, is hardy in South Texas.

PARSLEY *(Petroselinum hortense [crispum])* B

Propagation: Seed

Width & Height: 2' x 1'

Soil: Average

Exposure: Full sun or partial shade

Water: Average

Curled, or moss curled parsley, is the most popular of several species. The leaves are quite large, measuring 6 inches in length and width. They are generally a lustrous green with some softer shades. The stalks are hollow, and the flowering stem does not appear until the second year. When parsley blooms, it will die; it is a true biennial. The seeds, grey-green and very small, are borne in flat umbels. With proper pruning, this herb can be as tall as 18 inches and 3 feet across. Other species include plain-leaf parsley, a much rangier plant with flat leaves and a different taste, and a Hamburg parsley, which is grown for a root that is cooked to flavor soup.

Culture. Parsley likes a moist, well-drained soil; my plants do best when some shade is provided. I plant them close to taller plants.

Uses. Parsley leaves garnish almost all meat dishes, can be used on and in salads, and give a nice flavor to soup. A medicinal tea is prepared from the dried leaves.

Remarks. Curled parsley makes a fine border plant along the walk or driveway. In most of the South several plantings of parsley can be made during the year. Store in freezer.

PENNYROYAL
(Mentha pulegium) P

Propagation: Seed, cuttings, or plant division

Width & Height: 2' x .1'

Soil: Average

Exposure: Partial shade

Water: Average

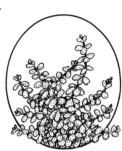

Pennyroyal is one of the smallest of the mints. It is prostrate in habit, with stems up to a foot long that root at the nodes. The leaves are roundish, hairy, grey-green, and are 1 inch long and ½ inch wide. The flowers are a reddish-purple to light blue and are borne in clusters just above the nodes. This herb makes a nice ground cover and covers a considerable area in a growing season.

Culture. My pennyroyal does well in partial shade in sandy soil, with a little extra water every now and then.

Uses. It is used in infusions to promote perspiration. A handful of the leaves rubbed into the coat of your dog or cat will repel fleas.

Remarks. This herb needs winter protection in zone 9. I pile a leaf and grass mulch around my beds, and, when a frost is predicted, completely cover my pennyroyal. I uncover it the next day, saving my mulch for the next frost.

PYRETHRUM *(Chrysanthemum cinerariaefolium)* P

Propagation: Seed or root division

Width & Height: 1' x 2'

Soil: Sandy

Exposure: Full sun

Water: Average

This herb reaches 2 feet tall, with beautiful white, crimson or pink daisy-like flowers. (Daisy is a member of this genus.) The plant can be cut back to bloom again. The leaves are dark green and finely cut.

Culture. Pyrethrum needs full sun and sandy, friable, moderately rich soil. Its seed is difficult to germinate; use sterile soil and propagate indoors. It's easier to grow from root division in early spring.

Uses. An organic insecticide powder is derived from the flowers of this herb. It is effective against many harmful vegetable insects and is harmless to warm-blooded mammals (you and me). An insect repellent is also prepared that can be used on exposed skin to keep away insects.

Remarks. This is a difficult herb to get started, but one well worth it. Plant 30% more plants than you'd like to have. For no apparent reason, hale and hardy plants expire.

ROSEMARY
(Rosemarinus officinalis) P

Propagation: Seed or cuttings

Width & Height: 2' x 3'

Soil: Average

Exposure: Full sun or partial shade

Water: Average

The evergreen leaves of this shrub-like herb are an inch long, dark green on top and a lighter green on the underside. The light blue flowers are very small and bloom through most of the summer. This species is about 4 feet tall and 2 to 3 feet wide. I prefer *R. prostratus*, which is a low-growing species and makes an excellent low hedge. Prostrate rosemary is almost bonsai in appearance, with its woody twisted branches. This variety is a foot tall and 2 to 3 feet wide. The leaves are very similar to *R. officinalis* (upright rosemary), but not quite as long or wide. Leaves of both species, have a piney odor. This is a very fragrant herb. There are a least a dozen varieties of this herb.

Flowering rosemary.

RUE *(Ruta graveolnes)* P

Propagation: Seed, cuttings, or
root division

Width & Height: 1' x 2'

Soil: Sandy

Exposure: Full sun

Water: Minimum

This hardy, shrubby, evergreen, a native of southern Europe, reaches a height of 2 feet and perhaps a foot wide. The leaves are blue-green, and can reach 5 inches in length and half as wide. The flowers are a bright yellow, button-like, and ½ inch wide. The entire plant has a strong and, in my opinion, disagreeable odor. The taste is best described in one word—ugh!

Culture. Rue does best in poor, dry sandy soil in full sun. I read that rue and basil should not be planted together, so, as an experiment, I planted them side by side. The sweet herb, basil, overpowered the malodorous one, and the rue expired in about four weeks. Basil must release a chemical or exude a gas that kills rue.

Uses. Italians and Greeks use rue in salads. It is also used in some perfumes.

Remarks. Go easy on fertilizing rue. It is excellent as a low hedge or border plant along a walk or driveway.

Culture. Does well in any well drained soil and can manage on minimum water. It does best in full sun but can tolerate some shade during the day.

Uses. Rosemary is an excellent culinary herb for flavoring many meat dishes. Oil of rosemary has been used for relief of headaches. It is an ingredient in hair lotions and has been used as a rinse for the prevention of dandruff. It is a common ingredient in colognes.

Remarks. A lovely herb for the garden or a container. Rosemary won't get as large grown indoors, but it will do very well.

Spanish legend has it that the Virgin Mary, while journeying to Egypt, draped her cloak over a bush of white-blooming rosemary. When she removed her cloak from the bush, the blooms had taken on the blue color of her garment.

Rosemary is also known as the herb of remembrance. Centuries ago this herb was used for happy occassions such as weddings, festivals and banquets. Sorcerers and witches say it is useful in casting spells. *R. officinalis* (upright) is more cold-hardy than prostrate rosemary.

Showy yellow flowers of rue make it an attractive border or hedge. Don't plant near basil.

SAGE *(Salvia officinalis)* P

Propagation: Seed and cuttings

Width & Height: 2' x 3'

Soil: Sandy

Exposure: Full sun

Water: Minimum

This herb can reach 3 feet in height and width. The leaves, depending on the species, can range from 3 to 6 inches in length and half as wide. The leaves are finely wrinkled and gray-green in color. The purple flowers are in whorls. The stem becomes quite woody before the plant reaches full maturity. There are many varieties of sage, i.e., red, golden, narrow-leaf, varigated, and several others. In addition to the common, I grow varigated and golden, two very striking plants.

Golden sage.

Variegated sage.

Culture. All species like sandy, well drained soil in full sun. I suggest a 6 to 8 inch hill to plant your sage, and no matter what the average rainfall is in your particular zone, don't water after your plant reaches maturity. You can fertilize lightly after pruning. Sage is hardy in all zones.

Uses. Sage is used to flavor many foods. It is also used to flavor wines, and a tea is made from the leaves. A gargle can be made from the leaves, and dried leaves can be smoked like tobacco.

Remarks. Like many of the herbs, the ancient herbalists ascribed magical properties to sage. According to them, sage, too, is great for the venomous bites of serpents.

(Pineapple) SAGE *(Salvia rutalins)* P

Propagation: Cuttings

Width & Height: 3' x 4'

Soil: Average

Exposure: Full sun or partial shade

Water: Average

The semi-woody stems of pineapple sage can grow over 4 feet tall, and the entire plant can get as wide as 6 feet. The leaves, a medium to light green, are 2 to 3 inches long and up to 2 inches wide. The rough, pointed leaves, with a delicious pineapple fragrance, decrease in size and increase in number as they approach the terminus of the stem. The flowers, up to 2 inches long, are deep red and appear in early summer.

Culture. This plant does well in any garden soil and has a tendency to wilt when it needs water. If you notice wilting, a good watering will take care of it.

Uses. The fragrant leaves are excellent for potpourri and are used to flavor cold drinks.

Remarks. In our long growing season, pineapple sage can get to be quite large. Allow for adequate space; I suggest planting it in the background of your garden.

SANTOLINA
(Santolina chamaecyparissus) P

Propagation: Cuttings

Width & Height: 3' x 1'

Soil: Sandy

Exposure: Full sun

Water: Minimum

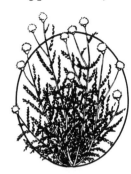

This grey, woody shrub is 2 feet tall and wide. The grey leaves are very small and form a dense coral-like mound. The flowers are clustered yellow buttons that appear late in summer. Both leaves and flowers have a pungent odor. Lavender, cotton or grey santolina are other common names. Another species, *S. vireus,* is about the same size, but the foliage is green and not as dense as the grey. The flowers of green santolina are a green-yellowish color. Both santolinas have an almost menthol fragrance.

Culture. Santolinas thrive in full hot sun, in sandy, well drained soil with minimum watering.

Uses. The oils have been used to treat ringworm, and the leaves and twigs are a moth deterrent amongst your woolens. The oils are also used in the manufacture of some perfumes.

Remarks. A beautiful edge plant as a low hedge; I insist that you secure a few of each species for your yard.

SASSAFRAS *(Sassafras albidum)* P

Propagation: Seed and cuttings

Width & Height: 8' x 30'

Soil: Average

Exposure: Full sun or
         partial shade

Water: Average

This North American tree can reach 100 feet in height, though I've never seen one that tall. Most get to 20 or 30 feet. The leaves are downy on the underside and vary in shape from ovate to elliptic, entire or three-lobed. The lobed leaf looks like a mitten. The flowers are small, yellow, and inconspicuous.

Culture. Sassafras does best in sandy, acid soil with a fair amount of sun. Try and find trees that are native to your area. If you live in zone 9, don't send off to a nursery in zone 3; you may have problems adapting that particular tree to your backyard.

Uses. The oil distilled from the rootbark is used in the manufacture of perfumes and soap. The wood and bark furnish a yellow dye. Tea is made from the roots, and young shoots and leaves are used to thicken gumbo.

Remarks. Everyone should have a sassafras tree. The fall color of the leaves is absolutely lovely.

SAVORY *(Satureja hortensis)* A

Propagation: Seed

Width & Height: ½' x 2'

Soil: Average

Exposure: Full sun

Water: Average

Summer savory is a hardy annual with slender stems that reach up to 16 inches tall. The flowers are very small, like the medium green leaves, and are a light lilac color. The stems become quite woody, and the entire plant has an almost wind-blown appearance. Winter savory, *S. montana,* is a perennial and is quite different in appearance. It's usually 2 to 3 feet across and a foot tall. The small leaves are dark green, shiny, and arranged in opposite pairs on the stem. The white flowers are less than a ¼ inch across with several on a cluster. Both herbs have a very pleasant spicy scent.

Culture. Both summer and winter savory like sandy well drained soil but will do well in any soil. They can manage with minimum water. Summer seedlings transplant very well.

Uses. Summer savory is the preferred condiment, and the leaves being used to flavor salads, meats, beans and other foods. It's a good plant for bees.

Remarks. This is one of my wife's favorite herbs, and because she's my favorite, it's one of mine. Winter savory makes a nice low hedge, requiring minimum care.

SHALLOTS
(Allium cepa ascalonicum) P

Propagation: By individual cloves or bulbs

Width & Height: 1' x 3'

Soil: Average

Exposure: Full sun

Water: Average

I grow the Louisiana shallot (Delta Giant), which does well in all zones. The mature plant will reach 3 to 4 feet tall, and a clump can reach 18 inches in width. The hollow, cylindrical leaves are very similar to chives but are much larger. Shallots flower in mid-summer in ball-shaped clusters of white seed heads 3 inches wide.

Dried shallots, ready for storage.

Culture. Shallots like rich, well drained soil and do best in full sun.

Uses. A highly prized culinary for meat, soups, stews and many other foods. Young shallots can be eaten like green onions. Shallots are a bit stronger than chives but have a more delicate flavor than onions.

Remarks. I have grown shallots from bulbs I purchased in the northeast. They were a brown-skin variety and didn't do too well in my garden. I prefer the Louisiana shallot.

It takes approximately 6 months for shallots to bulb up. To tell when they are ready, just brush the soil away from the top of the clump. You can pull the shallots up after a few months growth, prune off the tops, separate into bulbs (or cloves), and replant. They need to bulb-up before they can be stored. When they're bulbed-up, pull the entire plant up, wash off the soil, and hang in open shade with good air circulation. A clean, hot attic or garage is a good place. In 3 to 4 weeks, the tops should dry and fall off and the bulbs can be stored in a cool place.

SOUTHERNWOOD
(Artemisia abrotanum) P

Propagation: Seed, cuttings, or plant division

Width & Height: 2' x 3'

Soil: Average

Exposure: Full sun or
             partial shade

Water: Minimum

This feathery gray-green plant, or small shrub, is 18 inches tall and 3 to 4 feet across. It is an interesting specimen, with a bonsai appearance. The leaves are finely divided and give the plant a delicate, graceful look. My plants haven't flowered, but I've seen southernwood outside the South with yellowish-white flowers.

Culture. This plant does well in poor soil in full or partial sun.

Uses. Southernwood is used as a culinary herb in Italy. It is also used, in conjunction with other dried herbs, as a moth repellent for stored woolens.

The lacy foliage of southernwood.

Remarks. According to Culpeper, Dioscorides said it was good for worms in children. Years ago in Europe, a sprig of southernwood was included in a bouquet the young men gave to their girls.

SWEET FLAG *(Acorus calamus)* P

Propagation: Root division

Width & Height: 5' x 10'

Soil: Average

Exposure: Full sun or
partial shade

Water: Average

This native plant has long slender, lily-like leaves that get as tall as 6 feet. The yellow-green leaves, approximately ¾ inch wide, rise from a sheath. A flower stalk projects at a slight angle to the leaves, and the 3-inch cone-shaped spadix is covered with minute yellowish-green flowers. The leaves and root have a strong lemon scent. As the root gets drier, its scent becomes stronger.

Culture. This hardy perennial thrives in full sun in moist soil, but it will do well under fairly dry conditions.

Uses. Pieces of root are used as protection from household insects that attack books and furs. The candied roots are used for coughs and colds in Europe. The leaves are used as flavoring for custards and puddings. The English use oil extracted from the root bark to flavor beer.

Remarks. In fields and along the marshes this plant reaches 6 feet. In your garden it may reach 3 feet. Sweet flag is an interesting and unusual plant.

TANSY *(Tanacetum vulgare)* P

Propagation: Seed or plant division

Width & Height: 2' x 3'

Soil: Average

Exposure: Full sun or
partial shade

Water: Average

This herb can reach 3 feet in height and almost as wide. The fern-like leaves, dark green and sharply cut, are 6 inches long and about 4 inches wide. The yellow flowers grow in round, dull button-like clusters. The stems die down every year and reappear in the spring. There are several varieties of tansy.

The dark green, fernlike leaves of tansy are a fly-repellant.

Culture. Tansy thrives in most well drained soils in full or partial sun.

Uses. Tansy oil is used in some perfumes. This herb has been used to treat some skin diseases. If taken internally in large doses, it can be harmful.

Remarks. The origin of the name is thought to be derived from the Greek *Athanaton* (immortal) because the flowers last for a long time. Tansy leaves also deter flies. It is said that if the leaves are rubbed on spoiled meat, it'll keep the flies off.

TARRAGON
(*Artemisia dracunculus*) P

Propagation: By root division in early spring

Width & Height: 1' x 2'

Soil: Sandy

Exposure: Partial shade

Water: Average

French tarragon: a naturally drooping plant and a culinary staple.

This perennial grows to a height of 2 feet and 1½ feet wide, with 3-inch long, narrow dark green leaves. Tarragon rarely blossoms; when it does, it is late in summer, with small round yellow flowers dashed with black. Tarragon is a rather floppy looking plant and looks almost as though it has permanent wilt. There are two varieties of tarragon: French (A. *dracunculus*) and Russian (A. *redowski*). Russian is propagated by seed, root division, and cuttings, and is very similar in appearance to French, though Russian tarragon's leaves are a lighter green. Russian tarragon has absolutely no flavor. It tastes like Bermuda grass.

Culture. Both varieties like full sun, sandy soil and minimum fertilizing. French tarragon is very difficult to grow in the hot summer of most zones. It will do best in the northeast portion of zone 7.

Uses. Tarragon is used as a culinary herb for flavoring many types of salads; it's also excellent in vinegar.

Remarks. The name tarragon is a corruption of the French *Esdragon*, derived from the Latin *dracunculus* (little dragon), by which it is sometimes called.

THYME (*Thymus vulgare*) P

Propagation: By seed or cuttings

Width & Height: 2' x 1'

Soil: Sandy

Exposure: Full sun

Water: Minimum

This hardy perennial, English thyme, reaches a height of 1 foot and a width of 2 feet. The gray-green leaves are ¼ inch long, slightly wider at the base, and slightly hairy. The stems and roots become quite woody in a brief growing period. The light pink flowers are in conical spikes at the ends of the branches; they'll bloom twice if the plant is pruned after its initial flowering.

Culture. *T. vulgare* is hardy in all zones; the other varieties are hardy in zone 9 but need winter protection in zone 8. Thyme does best in full sun in most any soil with minimum water. If thyme is grown with only a few hours of sun, the leaves will be light green and the stalks tend to droop.

Uses. Thyme's principal use is for flavoring. Oil is extracted and used in colognes and soaps.

Remarks. There are many varieties of thyme. French thyme has a narrower, lighter green leaf

Creeping golden thyme, a beautiful ground or rock cover, has numerous culinary uses; bees love it, too.

but botonically is still considered *T. vulgare.* Mother of thyme *(T. sergyllum)* is an excellent rock garden herb. This ground cover plant makes a lovely carpet in one growing season. If you want to cover a large area, plants should be set out on 12 inch diagonals. There is golden lemon thyme *(T. citrodorus aures)* with golden leaves. *T. nutmeg,* another mat-forming thyme, has purple flowers. There are also a pine-scented thyme, marjoram wooly thyme, and several others.

This is an excellent herb for bees. Honey flavored with thyme commands a higher retail price than other honey. Mother of thyme *(T. serpyllum)* grows wild in Europe, and bee hives are set out to take advantage of the herb's nectar.

WINTERGREEN
(Gaultheria procumbens) P

Propagation: Seed or plant division

Width & Height: 1' x 1'

Soil: Sandy

Exposure: Partial shade

Water: Minimum

Wintergreen is a native of North America and occurs as far south as Dallas. It is a low-growing shrub, usually less than a foot tall. The woody stems are covered with oval dark green leaves 1½ inches long and ½ inch wide. Young leaves are green with a slight yellow-red cast. The leaves have a peppermint fragrance. The berries, usually produced in late summer and early fall, have a pleasant taste.

Culture. Wintergreen likes partial shade and sandy, fairly rich soil.

Uses. Wintergreen oil was used to treat muscle aches and pains.

Remarks. Wintergreen can be grown in your yard, and it does best in the eastern portion of zones 7 and 8.

(Sweet) WOODRUFF
(Asperula odorata) P

Propagation: Plant division

Width & Height: 1' x 2'

Soil: Average

Exposure: Partial shade

Water: Average

This attractive plant is a lovely low-growing ground cover that spreads rapidly. The smooth stems reach 6 to 8 inches tall, and are covered with whorls of tiny white flowers. The yellow-green leaves are quite small and have a vanilla fragrance when crushed.

Culture. Sweet woodruff needs quite a bit of shade and will do best under trees or when shaded by tall plants. It requires more than average moisture and rich, friable, sandy soil.

Uses. The flowers are used in May wine or in hot tea.

Remarks. I have found sweet woodruff difficult to grow here in Houston. It's too hot along the coast, but it should do well in the eastern portions of zones 7 and 8.

WORMWOOD
(Artemisia absinthium) P

Propagation: Seed or cuttings

Width & Height: 2' x 2'

Soil: Average

Exposure: Full sun

Water: Minimum

Wormwood is probably the most familiar of the Artemisias. This herb reaches 4 feet in height and width. The leaves are a blue-gray and shaped somewhat like those of a chrysanthemum. The yellow flowers are very small and button-like. This is a very handsome plant, but it tends to get rank. Pruning your plant is necessary in late spring or early summer.

Culture. I found that wormwood does well in full sun and heavy soil.

Uses. It was used as an ingredient in conjunction with other herbs to treat gout. In France it was used to make absinthe, and it is now used in the manufacture of Vermouth. Wormwood is one of the most bitter herbs.

Wormwood, used in making absinthe and Vermouth, has a very fresh, clean fragrance, but a rather bitter taste.

Remarks. Sagebrush *(A. tridenta)*, a native of the American West, was a very useful herb for the Indians. It furnished dye for their cloth and is edible. I have seen sagebrush 12 feet tall.

YARROW
(Achillea milleofolium) P

Propagation: Root division

Width & Height: 2' x 1'

Soil: Average

Exposure: Full sun

Water: Minimum

This perennial, hardy in all zones, grows in dense clumps, covering a large area in a growing season. Yarrow reaches 2 feet tall with very finely divided fern-like leaves. The flowers are white and grow in flat umbels 3 inches across. Other varieties include: *A. m. rosea*, 8 to 10 inches tall with pink flowers; and *A. filipendulina*, a 4-foot tall plant with bright yellow flowers.

Culture. Yarrow likes full sun, minimum moisture, and does well even in poor soil.

Uses. If you have any sick sheep, it is reputed to make a tea which restores their health. Yarrow is used as a tea for colds, as a tonic, and as an ingredient in salads.

Remarks. A very easy herb to grow; the fern-like leaves are excellent with flower arrangements. When the leaf dries it retains the original leaf pattern.

Umbels of yarrow flowers.

Other Herbs for Your Garden

Agrimony *(Agrimonia eupatoria):* This native of Britain is commonly used to flavor tea and wine, having a flavor reminiscent of the apricot. Unlike most herbs, agrimony is harvested when in flower (usually in late May or June). The flowers are produced in elongated yellow spires, and when grown amidst other herbs, agrimony will give your garden a pleasant, wild look.

It is tolerant of a wide range of soils and situations, but always provide good drainage, a reasonable amount of sun, and some organic matter to enrich the soil.

Basil *(Basilicum):* I mention several varieties of this herb in an early section of the book. However, there are many more wonderful varieties that need to be described. Purple ruffles is probably the most striking with large crinkly purple leaves tinged with green. The lower leaves are almost a golden color. These leaves grow up to 3 inches long and half as wide. The herb can be used just like regular green basil. A close relative to this plant is green ruffles basil. The plant is a bit larger, but the leaves are the same size as purple ruffles.

Another variety is spicy globe basil that grows as a perfect round clump about 18 inches across and half as tall. It looks like it was pruned to its perfect shape, but nature did that for you. The leaves are rounded and are the size of my 11-month old granddaughter's finger nail.

Licorice basil leaves have a very unique fragrance. You guessed right, they smell like licorice. The plant is a bit over 16 inches tall and half as wide, with leaves a couple inches long and an inch wide. You can use a few leaves at a time in a salad or add some to the pesto you're making.

All these basils can be used as a garnish, and the plants should be available at your favorite nursery.

Chicory *(Cichorium intybus):* The roots of this herb are roasted and crushed for commercial use as an additive to coffee. Chicory produces lovely star-shaped blue flowers, which are strewn along the stem and only last a few hours, after which they are quickly replaced by new ones. The plant varies in height from one to three and one-half feet, and likes a light, slightly alkaline soil (the wild plant is commonly found growing in soils rich in calcium carbonate, an alkaline compound).

Camphor *(Cinnamomum camphora):* This evergreen tree grows to 40 feet high and can spread to 20 or 30 feet across. The leaves, when crushed, yield a characteristic aroma of camphor. Bunches of crushed leaves placed in plastic bags, liberally punctured, can be hung among clothing to protect from moths. By extracting the essential oil from the leaves (try the method suggested on page 30) and combining with Vaseline, baby oil, or soft wax, you can make a very effective balm for relief of minor skin irritations, abrasions, and chapping.

This tree makes a beautiful shade tree, but may be considered messy because of the large quantities of fruit it produces; it also has a rather shallow root system.

Elephant garlic *(Allium ampeloprasum):* When you see the size of the bulb and cloves, you understand why it's called elephant. Some of the bulbs can exceed a pound. The flavor is sweeter and not as strong as regular garlic. I would suggest planting this herb in the autumn. It does better through our fall and mild winters. Usually it matures in 120–150 days. Garlic contains a lot of vitamins, and is not only a healthful herb, but it adds zest and wonderful flavor to all the dishes it flavors.

Fennugreek *(Trigonella faenum-graecum):* This is one of the most ancient plants in cultivation. The Egyptians used it as a constituent of embalming oil; today it is the principle source of an extract used in imitation maple syrup, as well as an ingredient in many spice blends, such as curry powder. It tolerates a wide variety of conditions, but prefers a fairly dry soil. The plant can be grown from seed (which germinates quickly after sowing) or from cuttings. Fennugreek is thought to aid in the production of diosgenin, a compound used to produce steroidal hormones such as progesterone, and so may have future use in contraceptive treatments.

Gentian *(Gentiana lutea):* According to the Greek, Dioscorides, this medicinal plant was first put to use by Gentius, King of Illyria, from 180-167 B.C., who extracted the bitter juice from the root. Gentian is a rather slow-growing, long-lived plant (up to 50 years), and its huge spongy root extends as deep as 3 feet into the soil. It likes a slightly alkaline, preferably calcareous, rich clay soil. Fall is the best time to harvest the roots, for that is when they are richest in gentianin, the bitter medicinal substance.

Gentian can be grown from seed germinated indoors and transplanted, or you can purchase starter plants. Remember—once you situate the plant, you'll have to leave it there because of its deep root.

Jasmine *(Jasminum officinale):* This is a gracious addition to any garden. This native of the Near and Middle East is highly valued for perfumery. Jasmine grows as a woody, flowering vine and makes an excellent ground cover or border planting. Average fertilizer and moisture are suitable, and it can take either full sun or partial shade. Propagate by layering or from cuttings; prune in the fall, after flowering.

Jerusalem sage *(Phlomis fruticosa):* This beautiful plant has gray foliage and bright yellow flowers that attract hummingbirds. The flower is edible, but the leaves are not. It is a perennial and attains a height of 4 feet.

Juniper *(Juniperus silicicola):* The Gulf Coast juniper, an evergreen tree, gets to 30 feet high and spreads to 15 or 20 feet across, but you can keep it as a shrub with judicious pruning. Another variety, *J. communis 'Compressa,'* is an excellent specimen in rock gardens, with its gray foliage and white lilt.

The oil juniper berries is used medicinally as an aid to digestion; it is also added to wine to stimulate the appetite. Juniper berries are also used in the distillation of better brands of gin. The Gulf Coast juniper is tolerant of highly humidity and is widely adapted to growing conditions here in the South.

Lion's ear *(Leonotis leonurus):* This wonderful herb can reach 6 feet tall and half as wide. It has beautiful deep orange flowers. It is hardy along the Gulf, is drought resistant with minimum water requirements. The hummingbirds love the color, and if they are in your area they will find the flower. Lion's ear can be used as a border or hedge row. It is used medicinally in Africa.

Luffa *(Lufa aegyptica):* This is not an herb in the true sense, but it's such a wonderful plant it needs to be included. This annual plant does best along a chain link or similar open fence. The plant, like cucumbers, sends out little vines that attach themselves to the fence as the vine grows. If you grow along a wooden fence, these little vines need to be attached to the fence. Another alternative would be to loosely attach several strings a foot apart along the wood fence. The plants can easily grow 15 or 20 feet in a growing season.

The bright yellow flowers become a small edible fruit, and if allowed to grow, reach up to 2 feet long and 3-4 inches thick. Most fruit will be about 16 inches long. These large gourds make an excellent body sponge for shower or tub as well as a scrubber for pots and pans. Dirty ones, that is.

If planted in late March, some of the fruit will be large enough to pick in late July. The plant will produce fruit until the first freeze. Pick the fruit when the skin is slightly yellow. Squeeze hard with both hands to break the skin. Do this many times to make it easier to peel off the skin. Rinse several times, a hose is easiest, to wash out the juice. Squeeze out the excess water and set in the open shade to dry. When dry, shake out the seeds and save them for next year. Save only the black ones. There are many seeds in each fruit, and enough to supply all your neighbors.

Another method of removing the skin is to boil the luffas. You'll need a large pot of course. After about 30 minutes of boiling, allow to cool and then peel off the skin. This method results in a very light colored (cream) sponge. The seeds must be discarded.

I have left fruit on the vine till it turns brown, and then peeled off the skin. The seeds are fine to save, and you don't need to rinse the gourd. The sponge will be darker, a light brown.

If you have trouble finding seeds, send me a self-addressed envelope and I'll send you some.

Mexican bush sage *(Salvia leucantha):* This herb has lovely purple flowers, and as you suspect, the hummingbirds love to come to visit it. It is a perennial and grows to 4 feet. It makes a lovely hedge or group planting, but the leaves cannot be used for flavoring.

Mullein *(Verbascum thapsus):* This is good plant for background plantings or as a centerpiece in a more formal garden. A group planted together have a stately, almost ethereal appearance. Mullein makes a very colorful display in the summer, when spires of yellow flowers are produced. Try mixing in some of the cultivars, which have pink, rose, or salmon-colored flowers.

The thick, white velvety foliage is rather sparse, and the juice extracted from the leaves has been used for centuries as a decongestant for coughs and colds. Plant in any well drained soil, in sun or partial shade! Propagate from cuttings or by layering.

Rose *(Rosa gallica officinalis):* Though we usually plant roses for the decorative value of their flowers, the plants are also grown for the distillation of their essential oil and for the medicinal value of rose hips. The distillate is used to make rose water, a refreshing drink or fragrant finger bowl. The essence, of course, is also used in perfumes.

Rose hip tea, rich in vitamin C, is fairly simple to make. Gather the hips after the first frost, when they will be slightly soft to the touch. Crush them with a pestle or rolling pin (avoid using a metal utensil, for this will discolor the rose hips and oxidize the vitamin C), and soak 4 tablespoons of crushed hips in five pints of water for 24 hours. Afterwards, simmer gently for one-half hour, but don't boil. Strain and store in tinted bottles or earthenware jars. Sweeten with honey when ready to use.

Roses require excellent drainage (raised beds), in a sunny location, for optimum growth. They like good, rich soil, slightly acidic (pH 6.5), and regular fertilization (about four times a year) with a balance such as 12-24-12. Give them plenty of water, and mulch year-round to protect in winter and to hold water and moisture in summer. For more details on rose culture, see *A Garden Book for Houston and the Gulf Coast*, Pacesetter Press, Houston.

Rose Campion (*Lychnis coronaria*): This plant is often found growing as a weed in the wild, though its rose-colored flowers make it a popular item in the garden. Wild species are commonly found throughout the U.S. and Europe.

Rose campion, like other members of the *Lychnis* family, has historically been valued as an ornamental rather than as a medicinal plant; the ancient Greek Dioscorides called it Lychnis (from the Greek "Lychnos," or lamp), a clear bright and light-giving flower.

It grows well in light soils, so add some sand or vermiculite to heavier soils to provide the necessary drainage and porosity. Flowers appear in May and last through June.

Sorrel (*Rumex acetosa*): If you like a green with a bite and a slightly acidic taste, you'll love sorrel. Most sorrel is the common variety, although it is referred to as French sorrel. The plant is a foot tall and almost as wide and resembles a clump of leaf lettuce. The leaves are an inch or two wide, and the more you cut, the more it will produce. It is a perennial and can manage an average winter up to 100 miles or so north of the coast.

The flowers are reddish and should be pruned when they appear. This will extend the availability of good, tasty leaves. This plant is found in Europe, Asia, North America, and even in Greenland. The tangy flavor of the leaves apparently is appreciated more by the French. I have grown this herb in past years. It has lost its popularity here, but perhaps it will come back again.

Violet (*Viola odorata*): This is another plant steeped in antiquity. The Greeks and Romans used it for numerous purposes (cosmetic, medicinal, and symbolic). Syrup of violet has a chemical property that renders the substance red on contact with acids and green on contact with alkalis. Violet is a North American native, and it grows by means of long stolons that root at the ends, giving the plant a prostrate habit. It can tolerate dry soil and is winter hardy in zones 7, 8, and 9. Violet does best in rich soil, in a sunny location. Propagate from seed, division, or cuttings. The easiest way is to plant runners (divisions) in spring or fall, in friable, humus-enriched soil. Remove dead leaves before planting, and keep the plants moist for the first few weeks. This is a lovely border or accent plant.

You can press the flowers and spray them with a solution of gum arabic, sugar and water to make candied violets. After spraying, dry in the oven at 100°. Be sure you store them in an airtight container to retard deterioration or invasion by roaches and other ugly bugs.

Watercress (*Nasturtium officinale*): Watercress was introduced in the U.S. by early European settlers and can be found growing wild along the banks of rivers and estuaries. Since it is a hydrophyte (growing with roots submerged in water or very moist soil), you'll have to grow it in gravel beds or in beds of very sandy soil, with a constant source of slow running water.

Watercress is usually propagated by inserting a cutting of a plant in the growing medium on an angle complementary with the direction of the current. They will root quickly, and you can harvest as soon as healthy, lush growth has begun.

High in vitamin C and iron, this herb is a classic in green salads. Its nutritive value is dimished by cooking, so always prepare it fresh. Watercress is also a good substitute for spinach, and it is delicious when chopped and minced with butter or your favorite sandwich spread.

Herbs from Around the World

Arugula, Rugula, Roquette Riquette, Garden Rocket (*Eruca vesicara*): Seeds can be sown all year long in south Texas. Arugula is hardy to about the mid-20s. The dark green leaves can almost be mistaken for oak leaf lettuce. During the cooler months the plant reaches 2 feet in height and width. In the hot months, it is perhaps half as large. Never let arugula go to seed. Prune off the seed heads to prolong the life of the plant.

For the summer growing season, plant seeds every few weeks for a constant supply. Italy and France are probably the origin of this plant, and friends who have visited there tell me it's all over the countryside.

Arugula's nutty flavor goes great with a dollop of goat cheese and sliced tomatoes. It's a love/hate affair; either you love arugula or you hate it. Some restaurants mix it with other greens such as lettuce or radicchio.

Seeds are available as Garden Rocket from Nichols. (See Sources).

Cinnamon Basil: According to my Thai friends—and I have several—this herb is Thai in origin. The plant is about 1½ feet by 1½ feet, and leaves are 1½ inches long and half as wide. As the name implies, they have a strong fragrance. The seed heads are a lovely light purple in color, and they are very attractive plants for your herb garden. I'm not much of a cook. Wait a minute! I'm not a cook, but people I know mix some of these leaves with sweet basil for Pesto.

Epazote (*Chenopodium ambrosioides*): A native of Mexico, this plant reaches up to 3 feet tall and 4 feet wide. The long narrow serrated leaves are about 3 inches long and an inch wide. They have an almost camphor smell, which is far removed from a fragrance.

In hot weather, the plant goes to seed, but the foliage can be extended by pruning. Once you've planted epazote, it will drop seeds and it can take over a growing area. I know it does well ± 100 miles north of the Houston area and grows well in and around Austin.

It is said (by whom I don't know) that cooking black beans and adding epazote will eliminate the aftereffects—not true. Seeds are available from Shepards (See Sources).

Makrut, Makrood (*Citrus Hystrix*): I found out recently, after growing this Thai citrus for several years, that it is also called Kaffir lime. In a very large pot, 20-gallon size or so, the plant can reach 10 feet tall. The green, very shiny leaves grow as doubles, one an extension of the other. The thorns are over an inch long, and care must be taken around this plant. The leaves have a wonderful citrus fragrance, and sliced thin, are used in many Thai dishes. Don't pick individual leaves to use, but rather a cutting with a few leaves. The latter method induces more growth.

This is a very tender citrus and must be protected in cold weather.

Ohja Santa (*Piper auritum*): This semi-woody plant dies back in the winter and, like magic, reappears in the spring. It manages quite well along the coast and north to Austin. I sent some plants out to Portland, Oregon and they didn't make it. But then it gets below zero there. It is a multiplier and in a few growing seasons can cover a large area. Leaves reach up to 16 inches long and half as wide. The more you cut, the more it reproduces.

My wife uses it to wrap and bake fish, fowl, and pork chops. Chefs I know chop it up and use these sarsaparilla-flavored leaves with other greens in salads.

This Mexican herb came to me from my dear friend Lucinda Hutson, author of *The Herb Gardening Cook Book* (available from Gulf Publishing Company). She has some wonderful recipes for Mexican and Thai herbs.

Plik (*Thai Pepper*): Here is a small, thin 1 to 2-inch hot pepper, and I DO MEAN HOT. The plant can reach 4 feet in height and width. The peppers are green, turn almost black, then red, and regardless of color, are hot. It is used to flavor several of the spicy Thai dishes. Panang, like a curry, is my favorite.

Thai Basil (*Kah Prow*): I don't know if this is a true basil. I have tried to get my Thai friends to find the Latin name—no such luck.

In full sun the upper two-thirds of this 2 feet by 2 feet plant are reddish-purple, the lower third green. Leaves are small, about an inch long and half as wide and add a slight bite to food they are used to flavor. Many Thai dishes are flavored with this herb, and seeds are available at Nichols Nursery (See Sources) or contact your local nursery.

The Herbs at a Glance

Herb	Plant Habit A=annual B=biennial P=perennial	Light		Water			Soil		Dimensions	Evergreen Zone(s)	Propagation S=seeds C=cuttings D=plant or root division	Plantings			Teas	Remarks
		Full Sun	Partial Shade	Min.	Avg.	Freq.	Avg.	Sandy	Width & Height (feet)			Hang. Basket	Does Well Indoors	Ground Cover		
Aloe	P	X	X		X		X	X	1 x 2	9, 10	†		X			Good for skin irritations
Angelica	P		X			X	X		2 x 5	9, 10	S					Plant in background
Anise	A	X			X		X		1 x 2	—	S					Plant with coriander
Basil	A	X			X		X	X	2 x 2	—	S, C	X	X			Very easy to grow
Bay	P	X	X		X		X		5 x 10	9, 10	S, C					Pot plant in zones 7 and 8
Bee Balm	P	X			X		X		2 x 3	8, 10	S, C				X	Pretty flowers
Borage	A	X	X	X			X		1 x 2	—	S					Beautiful flowers
Camomile (English)	P	X	X		X	X		X	2 x 2½	9, 10	S, C, D			X	X	Lovely, fragrant mat
Camomile (German)	A	X .	X		X	X		X	½ x 1	—	S		X			Pretty daisy-like flowers
Caraway	B	X			X		X		1 x 3	8, 9, 10	S					Unusual seed head
Catnip	P	X	X		X		X		3 x 2	9, 10	S, C, D				X	Gets scraggly — prune
Cayenne	P	X	X		X		X		1 x 2	10	S					Hot! Grown as annual
Chervil	A		X		X			X	1 x 2	—	S		X			Lacy light green leaves used like parsley
Chives	P	X	X		X		X		½ x 1	All	S, D	X	X			Great culinary herb
Comfrey	P	X			X		X		2 x 3	9, 10	D				X	Plant off in the corner
Coriander	A	X			X		X		1 x 2	—	S					Plant with anise
Costmary	P	X	X		X		X		1 x 2	All	D				X	Unusual mint fragrance
Dill	A	X			X		X		1 x 3	—	S					For pickling
Dittany of Crete	P	X		X				X	1 x 2	9, 10	S, C	X	X	X		Great for hanging basket
Elecampane	P		X			X		X	2 x 4	9, 10	S, D					Large daisy-like flower
Fennel (Florence)	A	X			X		X		1 x 2	—	S					Eat stalks like celery
Fennel	P	X			X		X		2 x 4	9, 10	S				X	Big herb; seeds used for flavoring Italian sausage, cordials, liqueurs
Foxglove	B	X				X	X		1 x 4	9, 10	S					Beautiful flowers, showy; yields digitalis, a heart stimulant.
Garlic	P	X			X		X		1 x 3	—	D					Random plant
Garlic Chives	P	X	X		X		X		½ x 1	9, 10	D	X	X			A must for salads
Germander	P	X		X			X		1½ x 1	All	C					Beautiful flowering hedge
Ginger	P	X			X		X		1 x 2	10	D			X		Lovely fragrance
Ginseng	P		X		X		X		1 x 1½	—	S					Tough to grow
Horehound	P	X					X		6 x 1½	9, 10	S, C				X	Gets scraggly —
Horseradish	P	X			X		X		1 x 2	—	D					Dig up every bit of root
Hyssop	P	X		X				X	1 x 1	All	S, C, D					Lovely low hedge plant
Lambs Ear	P	X		X				X	1 x 1	9, 10	S, D					Soft, furry leaves
Lavender	P	X		X				X	1 x 2	8, 9, 10	S, C					Plant in raised beds; flowers have exquisite fragrance
Lemon Balm	P	X	X	X			X		1 x 3	8, 9, 10	S, C, D	X	X		X	Gets scraggly
Lemon Grass	P	X			X		X		1 x 2	9, 10	D				X	Excellent tea
Lemon Tree	P	X			X		X		3 x 10	9, 10	S, C					Lovely Eucalyptus
Lemon Verbena	P	X			X		X		2 x 4	9, 10	S, C	X	X		X	Pungent lemon fragrance
Marjoram	P	X			X		X		3 x 1	9, 10	S, C	X	X			Very pretty plant; culinary herb
Mexican Marigold Mint	P	X			X		X		1 x 2	9, 10	S, C, D	X	X		X	Licorice fragrance
Mint Spp.	P	X	X		X	X	X		3 x 1	9, 10	S, C, D	X	X		X	Great for teas
Mint, Corsican	P		X		X	X	X		3 x .1	9, 10	S, C, D	X				Only an inch tall
Mugwort	P	X			X		X		3 x 2	8, 9, 10	S, C				X	British used it for tea
Nasturtium	P	X			X			X	1 x 2	10	S		X			Grown as an annual

*I've estimated on some of the northern limits of evergreen zones and have included zones in which I am confident they will be evergreen. It may well be that in some cases they are evergreen another zone north. The criteria for evergreen zone(s) is average mean temperature, and an unusually cold winter can change some of the classifications.

†Aloe — Propagation by vegative offshoots from the mother plant.

**Scented Geraniums; coconut, apple, and nutmeg for hanging baskets.

The Herbs at a Glance

Herb	Plant Habit A=annual B=biennial P=perennial	Light		Water			Soil		Dimensions	Evergreen Zone(s)	Propagation S=seeds C=cuttings D=plant or root division	Plantings			Teas	Remarks
		Full Sun	Partial Shade	Min.	Avg.	Freq.	Avg.	Sandy	Width & Height (feet)			Hang. Basket	Does Well Indoors	Ground Cover		
Oregano	P	X	X		X		X		1 x 2	8, 9, 10	S, C, D	X	X			Great for Italian foods
Oregano (Majorana)	P	X	X		X		X		4 x 1	10	S, C	X				Great for many foods
Oregano (Greek)	P	X	X		X		X		2 x 1	9, 10	S, C, D	X	X			Makes an interesting Bonsai
Parsley, moss	B	X	X		X		X		2 x 1	8, 9, 10	S	X	X			Good border plant
Parsley, flat leaf	B	X	X		X		X		2 x 2	8, 9, 10	S		X			Best parsley
Pennyroyal	P		X		X		X		2 x .1	9, 10	S, C, D	X		X	X	1 inch tall
Pineapple Sage	P	X	X		X		X		3 x 4	9, 10	C	X			X	Delicious fragrance; good background plant
Pyrethrum	P	X			X			X	1 x 2	9, 10	S			X		Organic insecticide powder
Rosemary (Upright)	P	X	X		X		X		2 x 3	8, 9, 10	S		X		X	Excellent culinary or decorative herb
Rosemary (Prostrate)	P	X	X		X		X		1 x 2	8, 9, 10	S	X	X		X	Excellent culinary or decorative herb
Rue	P	X		X				X	1 x 2	8, 9, 10	S, C, D					Don't plant near basil
Sage	P	X		X				X	2 x 3	All	S, C	X	X		X	Needs good drainage; plant on mounds or in raised beds
Salad Burnet	P	X			X		X		2 x 2	All	S, D		X		X	Cucumber flavored leaf
Santolina	P	X		X				X	3 x 1	All	C		X			For low hedge
Sassafras	P	X	X		X		X		8 x 30	–	S, C				X	A lovely tree
Savory, Summer	A	X			X		X		½ x 1	–	S		X			A fine culinary herb
Savory, Winter	P	X			X		X		3 x 1	8, 9, 10	S, C		X			Low hedge
Scent. Geraniums	P	X	X	X				X	½ x 1	10	S, C	**	X			Delicious fragrances
Shallots	P	X			X		X		1 x 3	–	D					Random plant
Southern wood	P	X	X	X				X	2 x 3	All	S, C, D					Does well in any soil
Sweet Flag	P	X			X	X	X		1 x 6	8, 9, 10	D					Fine lemon fragrance
Sweet Woodruff	P		X		X		X		1 x 2	9, 10	D			X		Beautiful ground cover
Tansy	P	X	X		X		X		2 x 3	9, 10	S, D					Pretty herb; inedible; deters flies
Tarragon (French)	P		X					X	1 x 2	9, 10	D	X	X			Naturally wilted appearance; minimal fertilizer
Tarragon (Russian)	P	X	X						1 x 2	9, 10	S, C	X	X			Easy to grow along the coast
Thyme	P	X		X				X	2 x 1	All	S, C	X	X			Very hardy plant; plant near bee hives for flavored honey
Wintergreen	P		X	X				X	1 x 1	All	S, D				X	A nice bush; pleasant mint taste
Wormwood	P	X		X			X		2 x 2	8, 9, 10	S, C					A graceful plant; once used to make absinthe
Yarrow	P	X		X			X		2 x 1	9, 10	D				X	Dried leaves hold shape, good in floral arrangements

*I've estimated on some of the northern limits of evergreen zones and have included zones in which I am confident they will be evergreen. It may well be that in some cases they are evergreen another zone north. The criteria for evergreen zone(s) is average mean temperature, and an unusually cold winter can change some of the classifications.

†Aloe — Propagation by vegative offshoots from the mother plant.

*Scented Geraniums; coconut, apple, and nutmeg for hanging baskets.

In the Vernacular...

English	Botanical Name	French	German	Spanish	Italian
agrimony	*Agrimonia eupatoria*	agrimoine soubeirette	kleiner Odermennig	agrimonia	agrimonia
angelica	*Angelica archangelica*	angélique	Angelika Engelwurz	angélica	angelica
basil	*Ocimum basilicum*	basilic	Basilienkraut	albahaca alabega	basilico
bay	*Laurus nobilis*	baie	Lorbeer	laurel	lauro
bee balm	*Monarda didyma*	bergamote	Bergamotten-baum	bergamota bergamoto	bergamotta
borage	*Borago officinalis*	bourrache	Borretsch	borraja	borragina borrana
burnet	*Sanguisorba* spp.	pimprenelle	Pimpernell	pimpinella	pimpinella
caraway	*Carum carvi*	carvi	Kümmel	alcaravea carvi	carvi
catnip	*Nepeta cataria*	herbe aux chats cataire	Katzenminze	menta de gato	nepeta erba dei gatti
camomile	*Anthemis nobilis*	camomille romaine	Kamille	manzanilla camomila	camomila
chervil	*Anthriscus cerefolium*	cerfeuil	Kerbel	perifollo	cerfoglio
chicory	*Cichorium intybus*	chicorée	Zichorie	achicoris	cicoria
chives	*Allium schoenoprasum*	ciboulette	Schnittlauch	cebollino cebolleta	cipollina
comfrey	*Symphytum officinale*	consoude	Schwarzurz	consuelda	consolida
coriander	*Coriandrum sativum*	coriandre	Koriander	cilantro	coriandolo
costmary	*Tanecetum balsamita* (syn. *Chrysanthemum balsamita)*	herbe Sainte-Marie tanaisie balsamite	Alecost		tanaceto balsamatico
dill	*Anethum graveolens*	aneth fenouil bâtard fenouil puant	Dill	eneldo	anito
elecampane	*Inula helenium*	aunée	Alant Alantwurzel	énula	enula campana
fennel	*Foeniculum officinale*	fenouil	Fenchel Schwarzkümmel	hinojo	finocchio
fenugreek	*Trigonella foenum-graecum*	fénugrec	Bockshornklee	alhoula	fieno greco
foxglove	*Digitalis purpurea*	digitale	Fingerhut	digitalis dedalera	digitale

In the Vernacular...

English	Botanical Name	French	German	Spanish	Italian
garlic	*Allium sativum*	ails	Knoblauch	ajo	aglio
gentian	*Gentiana lutea*	gentiane	Enzian	genciana	genziana
geranium	*Geranium* spp.	géranium	Storchschnabel	geranio	geranio
horehound, black	*Ballota nigra*	marrube noir	schwarze Bulte		marrubio nero
horehound, white	*marrubium vulgare*	marrube blanc	weisse Andorn	marrubio	marrubio comune
horseradish	*Cochlearia rusticana*	raifort	Meerettich	rábano picante o rústico	rafano
hyssop	*Hyssopus officinalis*	hysope	Ysop	hisopo	issopo
jasmine	*Jasminum officinale*	jasmine	Jasmin	jazmin	gelsomino
lavender	*Lavendula officinalis*	lavande spic	Lavendel	lavándula espliego	lavanda spiganardo
lemon balm	*Melissa officinalis*	mélisse	Melisse	balsamita	balsamo
lemon verbena	*Lippia citriodora*	citronnelle	Eisenkraut	verbena	berbena
marigold	*Calendula officinalis*	souci	Dotterblume Ringelblume	cálendula flamenquilla	calendula fiorrancia
marjoram (sweet)	*Marjorana hortensis*	marjolaine	Marjoran	megorana	maggiorana
mint	*Mentha* spp.	menthe	Minze	menta	menta
mullein	*Verbascum thapsus*	molène bouillon blanc	Wollkraut	verbasco gordolobo	verbasco
nasturtium	*Tropaeolum majus*	capucine	Kapuzinerkresse	capuchina nasturcia	nasturzio
onion	*Allium* spp.	oignon	Zwiebel	cebolla	cipolla
oregano	*Origanum* spp.	origam	Majoram	oregano	oregano
parsley	*Petroselinum crispum*	persil	Petersilie	perejil	prezzemolo
pelargonium	*Pelargonium* spp.	pelargonium	Pelargonie	pelargonio	pelargonio
pyrethrum	*Pyrethrum coccineum*	pyrèthre	Pyrethrum	piretro	piretro
rhubarb	*Rheum officinale*	rhubarbe	Rhabarber		rubarbaro
rose	*Rosa* spp.	rose églantier odorant	Rose wilde Rose	rosa escarmujo olorosso agavanzo	rosa rosa selvatica
rosemary	*Rosmarinus officinalis*	romarin	Rosmarin	Rosmarino Romero	Rosmarino

In the Vernacular...

English	Botanical Name	French	German	Spanish	Italian
rue	*Ruta graveolens*	rue	Raute	ruda trago amargo	ruta
saffron	*Crocus sativus*	safran	Safrangewürz	azafrando	zafferano
sage	*Salvia officinalis*	sauge	Salbei	salvia	salvia
santolina	*Santolina chamaecyparissus*	santoline	Buschzypress	santolina	santolina
savory	*Satureja* spp.	sarriette	Bohnenkraut	ajedrea	savore
tansy	*Tanacetum vulgare*	tanaisie herbe aux vers	Rainfarn Gänserich	tanaceto balsamita minor	tanaceto
tarragon	*Artemisia dracunculus*	estragon	Estragon	tarragon estragón	tarragone dragoncello
thyme	*Thumus* spp.	thym serpolet	Thymian	serpoleto tomillo	serpillo timo
violet	*Viola odorata*	violette	Veilchen	violeta	violetta mammola
wall germander	*Teucrium chamaedrys*	chéneau	Batenikel Berggamander	pinillo maro	germandria
watercress	*Nasturtium officinale*	cresson de fontaine	Brunnenkresse	berro	crescione di fonte
wintergreen	*Gaultheria procumbens*	gauthérie couchée	Wintergrün		tè di montagne
woodruff, sweet	*Asperula odorata*	aspérule odorante	Waldmeier		raspello odoroso
wormwood	*Artemisia* spp.	absinthe armoise	Absinth	alcachofa arcacil	carciofo
yarrow	*Achillea millefolium*	millefeuilles herbe aux charpentiers	Schafgarbe	milenrama	millefoglie

Sources

When you order herb plants, have them sent by air rather than surface mail. They'll arrive in a few days and in good condition.

Taylor's Herb Garden Inc. ($3.00 for catalog)
1535 Lone Oak Road
Vista, CA 92084

A great selection of seeds and live herb plants. The largest mail order company for live herb plants in the country.

Richter's Herb Seed Catalog ($1.00)
Goodwood, Ontario LOC IAO

One of the largest listings of herb seeds.

J. L. Hudson, Seedsman ($1.00 for catalog)
P.O. Box 1058
Redwood City, CA 94064

Their catalog is a fascinating little book listing many varieties of herb seeds. It also lists seeds of rare and unusual plants, shrubs, and trees.

Nichols Garden Nursery (Free catalog)
1190 North Pacific Highway
Albany, Oregon 97321

An excellent selection of herb plants and seeds. They carry seeds of unusual vegetables from around the world, including some from the Peoples Republic of China, Japan, Italy, France, and other countries.

Park Seed (Free catalog)
Greenwood, South Carolina 29647-0001

Seed for some of the scented geraniums and many different herbs.

Burpee Seed (Free catalog)
Clinton, Iowa 52732

Many varieties of herb seeds and plants.

Shepards Garden Seed
6116 Highway 9
Felton, CA 95018

A good seed selection that includes epazote and Thai peppers.

Graingers

Check telephone directory for store nearest your home. Solenoid valves and time clocks are available from their catalog.

Index

Boldface numbers denote color photographs.

About the Author

Sol Meltzer grows and sells herbs from his garden. He wrote a monthly garden column for **The Houston Gardener** and **Houston City Magazine,** has done many radio and television shows on herbs and organic gardening, taught courses on herbs and organic gardening, and is a guest lecturer to garden clubs throughout Texas. By profession, he is a petroleum geologist (retired), formerly with Cities Service Oil Co.

Mr. Meltzer grows almost every herb he has written about. He supplies several chefs with the fresh culinary herbs they use in their entrees. He also supplies health food stores, nurseries, plant shops, and other retail outlets with potted herb plants. He and Thelma, his wife, live in Houston, Texas.

MORE GARDENING BOOK GREATS

A Garden Book for Houston and the Texas Gulf Coast
Fourth Edition
Edited by the
River Oaks Garden Club of Houston

Now in its seventeenth printing, here's everything a Gulf Coast gardener needs to know: from design to pests.

396 pages, color photos throughout, index, appendixes, 6 x 9 hardcover.
ISBN 0-88415-350-9 . . . . #5350 . . . . $27.50

Great Gift! Order a Second Copy!

Herb Gardening in Texas
Second Edition
Sol Meltzer

With more than 25,000 copies sold, this revised and expanded edition now has more herb descriptions and beautiful color photos. Learn how to propagate, grow, and use more 90 different herbs.

1992. 88 pages, color photos, index, 8 x 11 paperback.
ISBN 0-88415-043-7 . . . . #5043 . . . . $11.95

Growing Fruits, Berries & Nuts
Southwest-Southeast, Second Edition
George Ray McEachern

Here's the acclaimed guide that shows you how to grow and harvest more than 20 species and 130 varieties of tasty fruits, berries, and nuts.

100 pages, figures, photos, index, 8 x 11 paperback.
ISBN 0-88415-040-2 . . . . #5040 . . . . $12.95

Bestseller!

Native Texas Plants
Landscaping
Region by Region
Sally Wasowski with Andy Wasowski

"**You can't go wrong with this paperback version of the Wasowskis' book,** which drew praise as one of the best references on state flora when first published in 1988. It contains not only regional landscape plans but also lengthy plant profiles, accompanied by color photographs. Buy two copies—one for a gardening friend and one for yourself.**"
—*Houston Chronicle*

1991. 406 pages, 300 color photos, region and speciality plans, figures, bibliography, index, 8 x 11 paperback.
ISBN 0-87719-201-4 . . . . #9201 . . . . $27.95

The Herb Garden Cookbook
Lucinda Hutson

Transform the simplest meal with herb garnishes, eye-pleasing presentations, herbs in place of rich sauces, and add vitamins all at the same time with the help of this beautiful book. An updated source list adds to the usefulness of this unique cookbook.

1992. 230 pages, 30 color photos, bibliography, index, 7 x 10 paperback.
ISBN 0-87719-215-4 . . . . #9215 . . . . $21.95

❖ *Visit Your Favorite Bookstore* ❖

The Ultimate
Flower Gardener's
TOP TEN LISTS

Happy gardening!

The Ultimate
Flower Gardener's
TOP TEN LISTS

70 Garden-Transforming Lists,
Money Saving Shortcuts,
Design Tips & Smart Plant
Picks for Zones 3 through 7

Kerry Ann Mendez

LONE OAK PRESS

The Ultimate Flower Gardener's Top Ten Lists:
70 Garden-Transforming Lists, Money Saving Shortcuts,
Design Tips & Smart Plant Picks for Zones 3 through 7

ISBN: 978-1-935534-907 (Second Edition)

Plant Characters: Created by artist, book writer, and teacher, Daniele Ippoliti.
                  owner of Character of Nature. www.characterofnature.net.

Photo Credits: Robin Wolfe, Wolfe Enterprises;
                  Bluestone Perennials (www.bluestoneperennials.com);
                  Gardener's Supply Company (www.gardeners.com);
                  Perennial Resource (www.PerennialResource.com);
                  Perennially Yours (www.pyours.com);
                  Plant Delights Nursery (www.Plantdelights.com);
                  Pride Corner Farms (www.pridescorner.com);
                  and Proven Winners (www.provenwinners.com).

Book Design: Melissa Mykal Batalin

Printed by: The Troy Book Makers
                  Troy, New York
                  www.thetroybookmakers.com

Publisher: Lone Oak Press
                  Ballston Spa, New York

Editing: Margaret Morrone, Rita Fassett, Sergio Mendez and Evan Mendez

Book orders: Perennially Yours,
                  P.O. Box 144, Ballston Spa, NY 12020
                  Phone: (518) 885-3471
                  Email: pyours@nycap.rr.com

To order additional copies of this title, contact your favorite local bookstore
or visit www.tbmbooks.com

In loving memory of my dear mother
who had a contagious joy for life,
a heart for serving others,
and was special in every way.

Acknowledgements

My heartfelt appreciation to all who have supported and encouraged me in my gardening walk. There are far too many individuals to list by name but I could not have done this without all of you. My dearest husband and son have been my fan club from the start, making many sacrifices to make this book a reality. And my salute to the loyal patrons of Perennially Yours. You have assisted with every aspect of this book, from creating the title to the topics included. My deepest thanks to Melba Higgins and Margo Richards, my first gardening mentors, who took me under their masterful wings and fueled my passion for gardening. I am also very thankful to all those who have provided photographs for this book: Robin Wolfe; Bluestone Perennials; Gardener's Supply Company; Perennial Resource; Plant Delights Nursery; Pride Corner Farms and Proven Winners. And I am extremely appreciative to PerennialResource.com for their invaluable plant library and images collection. I cherish the delightful plant characters provided by my gifted artist friend and business owner, Daniele Ippoliti. Her Coneflower Dancer and I are 'soulmates'. And where would I have been without the expert editing by my friends Margaret Morrone and Rita Fassett? Thank you. Thank you all.

And above everything, praise to the Lord for so remarkably orchestrating events to lead me down this garden path and for His blessings on the journey.

Contents

Introduction

Lists. Usually I hate them. They mean work. I am the queen of making lists. Grocery shopping, household chores, bill payments, my teenager's lost privileges for 'poor decision making'. My goal is to make lists disappear. I get a twisted pleasure out of pressing down hard when scratching an item off the list. Even better, when the list is all crossed off (I remember that happening once in 2004), crunching up the paper into a tight wad and triumphantly 'stuffing it'.

The lists in this book are designed to cause rejoicing. After twenty-five years as a tough-love garden teacher, designer and coach, my sweat-earned knowledge from successes and failures are yours. I sorted through pages and pages of my 'tear-stained' notes and grouped them into practical lists for creating ever-blooming, low-maintenance gardens.

The plants featured in this book have hardiness zones ranging between 3 and 7. Gardeners in colder zones (3, 4 and 5) have challenges unknown to gardeners in warmer climates. We stare at our bloomless mophead Hydrangeas in disgust; curse our short growing season; sigh as huge piles of snow crash upon unsuspecting foundation plantings; groan at ice storms that disfigure trees and evergreens; and shake our heads at 'confused' spring blooming bulbs and perennials that break dormancy during midwinter thaws. That said, the warmer zones (6 and 7) have their own crosses to bear; wicked heat that beats down plants and humidity that encourages fungal diseases. Regardless of which group you fall into, this book provides 'I wish I had known', tried and true gardening solutions for gorgeous perennial gardens including how to jump-start gardens in spring and extend fall color.

My bottom-line lists include what plants thrive in specific locations; time-saving tools and maintenance shortcuts; the best defensive strategies for offensive lines of rabbits, deer, voles, chipmunks and slugs; rewarding design tips and plant combinations; and money-saving angles. Plant lists also include design tips and cultural advice. Chapter Six features colorful photographs of some outstanding plants as well as garden vignettes. I've also answered the most frequently asked questions culled from thousands of gardeners in lectures and classes. And because we all could laugh more, included are some hilarious gardening stories collected from strolls down the garden path.

This book cuts through a lot of mumbo jumbo. I have walked in your muck boots. I know what it feels like to be overwhelmed and frustrated by excessive information not necessary for creating my little backyard paradise. I feel like a deer in the headlights when someone rambles off long Latin names and

photo courtesy of Daniele Ippoliti

talks about espaliering their fruit tree. I promise I will not do that to you. I will say it straight, without any frou-frou language. As your 'garden coach', my job is to cut through all that complicated jargon and distill it to what is really necessary for your dream garden. And I will share this information in a way that empowers and inspires, not overwhelms and intimidates. I will only discuss plants that are in the tough, work-with-me-I-have-a-life, catagory. I am a realist and so are you. That's why you are reading this book. What you have been doing in the garden is not working, or it could be better. There are a million things in our lives that we cannot control; our gardens should not be one of these nail-bitters. Predictable, refreshing, and uplifting gardens are what we need and they must be the least of our time and money drains. The good news is that we can have them, and I'll show you how.

Let's begin, shall we?

CHAPTER 1

On Your Mark, Get Set...STOP!

Right Plant, Right Spot, Right Results

Before you dig into the lists, let's first make sure we are on the same page as far as sunlight definitions and hardiness zones. I can give you proven plants for specific sites but if you plant them in the wrong light, we all look bad. And wrong zones are a killer.

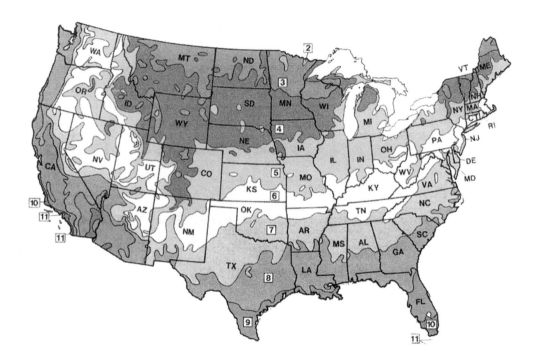

Blinded by the Light (or Lack Thereof)

Allow me to shed light on one of the most common reasons for lackluster gardens. Many people are in la-la land when it comes to understanding their garden's light conditions. The lighting is determined more by what plants grabbed their attention and pocketbooks at the garden centers versus the actual hours of sunlight the garden receives. Backwards thinking, or, as Dr. Spock would say on Star Trek, illogical. If we want healthy, bloom-splendiferous gardens, we need to be good matchmakers. Pairing plants to their required light condition is a must.

It is a common myth that full sun beds are more beautiful and easier to grow than their shadier cousins on the other side of the railroad ties. How did this fairy tale get started? I think it is because most people are more familiar with sun-loving plants and therefore conclude shade gardening offers few choices; translating to boring. But just because you haven't been introduced to the magical and exquisite world of shade plants, doesn't mean they don't exist. In reality, there are many super shade perennials that are unparalleled in their beauty. And I am not referring to just green hosta and pink bleeding hearts. I'm talking Foamflowers, Bishop's Hat, Siberian Bugloss, Bugbane, Toad Lily, Masterwort and many other exotic beauties.

I much prefer shade gardening. Shade beds have an allure of their own. They are much more intriguing and provocative than sun gardens plus they need far less maintenance. There are four reasons why shade gardens allow more time in the lounge chair. Typically they demand less water, have fewer weeds and require less deadheading, a task I detest. Many shade perennials will not rebloom with deadheading. Once the flowers are spent, you can whack them off or leave them on for dried flower interest. Some folks complain that shade perennials don't bloom as long as their sunnier counterparts. I have a solution for that. Spray paint (not a typo). It works especially great on astilbes. Once the plumes have dried, grab a can of your favorite color and spray away. I've had some real head turning results with fluorescent orange. Glittery silver and gold make a more refined statement. But don't stop at astilbes. Spray paint can also dress up dried Hydrangea, Goat's Beard, Masterwort, and Allium blooms. The fourth factor contributing to less work in shade beds has to do with sunlight. Because there is less light, plants tend to grow more slowly which means less frequent dividing. Yes, dividing is good in that you get more plants and it stimulates new roots and better flowering, but it also takes our time and energy - not good.

Refer to the light definitions provided and then track how much sunlight your garden really receives. This may surprise you. I find that most people err in overestimating the amount of sunlight. This only leads to problems down the garden path. What happens when you place sun-loving plants in too little light? The plants usually grow taller than they normally would, become scraggly, lean towards the light, and bloom little or not at all. And how do most of us respond when our plants aren't blooming like we want them to? Yup. We grab the Miracle-Gro and blast them with blue water. The result? Taller, scragglier, tilting plants with no flowers. Unless you do something to let in more light (such as limb up a tree), this frustrating cycle will only continue as the plants stretch towards the light source and amass leaves in an attempt to capture the limited sunrays. It would be so much easier to buy plants that thrive in lower light, remain compact, bloom magnificently and don't resemble the leaning Tower of Pisa.

ASSESSING SUNLIGHT

Full Sun: six or more hours of direct sun between 10:00 a.m. and 6:00 p.m.

Part Sun: four to five hours of direct sun between 10:00 a.m. and 6:00 p.m.

Part or Filtered Shade: filtered light throughout the day or two or less hours of intense sun, especially between 10:00 a.m. and 4:00 p.m.

Shade: early morning sun (before 10:00 a.m.) or late day sun (after 5:00 p.m.)

And a few cautionary words to those of you still prone to manipulating data so your garden falls into the full sun category. When assessing light, especially for sun-loving plants, you cannot count early morning sun. You need to track the sun throughout the entire day, especially between 10:00 a.m. and 6:00 p.m., to see if you hit the full or part sun lottery. And it is no fair running out to assess light before trees leaf out in spring. I'm up to your games. I have done them all myself and suffered the consequences. If after doing your homework you are still waffling between light conditions, fight your desire to pick the sunnier category. Trust me. If you are wrong in your analysis and your garden actually gets more sun than you thought, the lower light plants will do just fine. It backfires big time when you put sun-lovers in lower light. We're back to scraggly, unattractive, non-flowering plants.

I'm commonly asked what time of year is best to assess a garden's light. Earth Science 101: the sun is lower in the sky in fall than it is in the spring, increasing the amount of shade cast by an object. This means sections of our garden may be shaded in September but be in full sun in June. This seasonal fluctuation is unchangeable. We should follow suit and stop changing our minds about our garden's light category. When we waffle in our assessment, we resemble a squirrel darting back and forth across the road. Pick one light category and stay the course. I recommend folks track sunlight between May and July. Most plants do the majority of their growth in the spring and early summer so it is vital to meet the plant's required light during this time of tremendous change. Not unlike children during major growth spurts. They need proper nutrients and rest during such energy-demanding periods. Also be aware that a garden may have several light conditions in the same bed, especially larger ones. Track the light carefully. Some people have found it helpful to take photographs of their gardens every two hours as references.

The other party killer is when we purchase perennials, bulbs, shrubs and trees that are outside our hardiness zones. If you are not sure of your zone, please refer to the USDA Hardiness Zone Map. If a plant is not rated for your area, why invest a lot of time and money on it just so it can kick the bucket come winter? This book is all about making smart choices for beautiful gardens that are not time and money hogs. Sure, there is room in our low maintenance gardens for some annuals and tropicals but these are placed with realistic expectations. We need to be very choosy about which prima donnas are escorted into our beds. Tough, hardy perennials and flowering shrubs that can survive winters without any blankies (winter mulch) are a must. Heartless as it sounds, I refuse to give any of my perennials winter protection. They must meet me on the other side of Old Man Winter's best blows, if not, I'll find a plant that will.

Hardiness zones represent a range of average annual minimum temperatures in a region. There are eleven zones in the USDA Plant Hardiness Zone Map. Zone 1 is the coldest; zone 11 is the warmest. Zones are divided into ten degree sections. If you really want to get technical, these sections are further divided into two subsections, A and B (A being the colder half). Personally, I don't get bogged down with the A's and B's (except when it comes to my son's report card). Most plant descriptions don't go into this detail anyway. If a plant is rated to a certain hardiness zone, let's say zone 5, it should survive winters in that zone as well as warmer zones (zone 6 and above). Notice I said should. If you can't stand the thought of seeing a few dead plants each spring then go with plastic or silk flowers. There are simply no guarantees in life, other than my son not making his bed in the morning.

I find that many folks like to push the envelope when it comes to deciding their hardiness zone. Let's be honest. It's all about shopping. The warmer the zone, the more plants there are to choose from. I'm here to help you fight the temporary insanity that overtakes us as we drool over knockout plants requiring more temperate climates. Somehow we northern gardeners become color-blind when looking at the hardiness zone map. Agreed, there may be microclimates in your yard, areas that are one, perhaps two zones warmer, but for simplicity sake let's stick with plants that work within your hardiness zone. Those few irresistible gems that hail from warmer neighborhoods

can be tucked away in those sweet, milder spots. A few locations where you may be able to push a zone warmer are along the southeast foundation of your home or next to stonewalls and boulders, especially on the downwind side. If after staring at the zone map you are still confused, contact your regional cooperative extension, local garden club, garden center, or neighborhood Master Gardener for advice.

Cold temperatures are not the only potential plant terminators. Snow cover, mid-winter thaws, wind and elevation also play roles in how successfully your plants make it through the winter obstacle course. Regardless of how you personally feel about snowy winters, they are good for our gardens. Snow is a super insulator, a natural blankie for gardens. During periods of little snow cover, I'll grab my shovel and transfer snow from the lawn to the base of my roses, Butterfly Bush and Blue Mist Shrub. My neighbors find it a little odd when I show up with my wheelbarrow and ask if I can shovel their lawns (they use salt on their driveways) but no matter. Plant survival overrides com-

mon sense. But sometimes common sense should triumph. Even I shake my head at the reactions of some desperate gardeners during extended winter warm spells. I've seen folks do crazy things in an attempt to prevent, or slow down, perennials from breaking dormancy. Anything goes, from shelter-ing warming areas with strips of insulation, um-brellas, tarp, insulated grocery bags, pine boughs and straw. The reality is most of these emerging plants will survive just fine, despite their mid-win-ter confusion. Wind and higher elevations can also stress plants with the insult of generating even colder temperatures and desiccating evergreens. If either of these last two factors are a reality for you, buy plants that are one zone colder to reduce heartache in the spring.

Now on to the lists

In the fifteen years since I started my gardening business, Perennially Yours, I've helped thousands of gardeners in their quest for growing gorgeous, low-maintenance flower gardens and landscapes in zones 3, 4 and 5. The following perennial lists provide workhorse plants for a range of conditions. Lists include the plant's common name, botanical name (the hard to pronounce word), the range of plant heights in that family; the hardiness zone (the number provided indicates the coldest zone of one or more varieties in that family) and other comments I thought you would find helpful. **Also noted is if a plant is drought tolerant (🌿) or deer resistant (⚐).** I also included some uncommon plants instead of the 'same old, same old'. I recognize that new cultivars are constantly being introduced. It wouldn't be fun if they weren't. But the plant families on these lists are gold medalists and will endure the passing of time with accolades.

CHAPTER 2

Top Ten Perennial Lists

Top Ten Spring Blooming Perennials for Full to Part Sun

🍂✥**Carnation, Pinks** (Dianthus) 4" - 20" Many recent introductions are superior to older varieties. The plants bloom longer and the foliage stays neater and well mounded after flowering. Some of my favorites are in the Star Series. 'Eastern Star' (red), 'Neon Star' (bright pink), and 'Spangled Star' (red and white) are great. The Dessert Series is sweet. 'Cranberry Ice', 'Raspberry Swirl' and 'Strawberry Sorbet' are shades of pink, burgundy and white. Both series have nice blue-grey foliage. ' Bath's Pink' has been around for a long time; a solid performer with soft pink blooms and blue foliage. All dianthus prefer sharply draining soil (another way of saying sandy). If you have clay you can cheat by working gravel or chicken grit into the soil and mounding the planting area slightly to increase drainage. Zone 4

✥**Woods Phlox** (Phlox divaricata) 6" - 14" Woods Phlox boasts masses of flowers for a good five weeks. Blooms can be white, pink or lavender. All are extremely fragrant! Woods phlox are equally happy in sun or dappled shade. After flowering, shear them back to within two inches of the ground for a pleasing green mat. Woods Phlox is my pick over the more common creeping phlox (sometimes called moss phlox). Woods phlox is fragrant, weed-smothering, longer blooming, and deer resistant; not so creeping phlox. Zone 3

🍂✥**Peony** (Paeonia) 15" - 3' + I'm going to assume you are already well acquainted with the common herbaceous (lactiflora) peony. Me too. Nice plant. But why not branch on to some more exotic types? Like Tree Peony (P. suffruiticosa). These hardy 4' - 5' shrubs have massive flowers in colors unavailable in common peonies: dreamy apricot, purple, near black and wisteria blue. Of course red,

photo courtesy of Robin Wolfe

whites and pinks abound too. Tree Peonies never require pruning and can handle full sun or dappled light. These long-lived plants are quite drought tolerant once established. But be patient with them; they are slow growing but worth the journey. Zone 3

✥**Blue Star Flower** (Amsonia) 12" - 3' What's not to love about this perennial? Soft blue, starry flowers decorate smooth, willow-like leaves born by stiff stems that don't flop. The foliage of A. tabernaemontana and A. hubrichtii turn a glowing orangey-yellow in fall. Simply breathtaking next to fuller bodied fall blooming sedums and wispy Japanese anemones. Zone 4 (some catalogs say zone 5 but I have found Blue Star Flower very hardy)

❀☩False Indigo (Baptisia) 10" - 4' False Indigo is a tough, tap-rooted plant that wants to stay where it's planted. Think long and hard before plopping the pot down in the garden. Most folks are familiar with the rich blue flowering indigo (australis), but there are also white, yellow, purple, and multicolor varieties. Two of my favorites are 'Twilite PrairieBlues' (purple and yellow) and 'Carolina Moonlight' (soft yellow). All Baptisias have attractive seedpods. Baptisias take a few years to get established before sending forth flowers. This is one plant I would 'splurge' for a gallon sized pot versus a four inch container. Zone 3

❀☩Cushion Spurge (Euphorbia) 6" - 24" This family has a lot of funky members with foliage that is a lot showier than their spring flowers. Either way, they make a statement. The most commonly sold variety is polychroma. It has bright yellow flowers in spring and green leaves. But why not step it up a notch and plant 'First Blush' (pink, white and green leaves), 'Bonfire' (burgundy-red leaves) or 'Chameleon' (bronzy-purple leaves)? All have bright yellow flowers and benefit from a hard shear after blooming to create a neat, tight mound. Don't be timid when pruning these back. I shear them by 1/3 to ½ their height. If you have sensitive skin, wear gloves when pruning spurges as the sap may cause a rash. Polychroma, Zone 3. All others are Zone 5.

❀☩Lady's Mantle (Alchemilla) 6" - 18" Lady's mantle is a must for cottage gardens. Its frothy greenish-yellow flowers foam forth from crisp, scalloped leaves. I like placing Lady's Mantle along a garden's edge so it can billow onto hard surfaces and soften transition lines. To keep it looking pretty all season, prune older leaves with browning edges to reveal fresh new leaves below. For a petite look, use A. erythropoda that only get 6" - 8" tall. A. alpina is the same size as erythropoda but each of its leaves has a silvery edge giving it a very elegant look. Zone 3

❀Carolina Lupine (Thermopsis) 2' - 5' I love lupine but I hate how short-lived it can be, its propensity to get white aphids and ratty looking after blooming. Carolina Lupine (sometimes nicknamed False Lupine) is Lupine's twin but it's long lived and remains attractive all season. Carolina Lupine has buttery yellow flowers in spring, blooming at the same time as Catmint and Geraniums. After blooming, I shear it back by 1/3 for fresh new growth. Zone 4 (some references say 3, others 5)

☩Goat's Beard (Aruncus) 10" - 5' This family has members that barely reach 10" and others that soar to 5' or more. They all have delicate, astilbe-like white flowers that sway above mounded foliage. The 'baby' in the group, aethusifolius, has tiny, ferny green leaves and puffy white flowers. On the other end of the scale, dioicus, at 5', holds court when in full bloom. My favorite is 'Misty Lace'. This is not too big, too small, but just right. It grows between 2' and 3' and has darker, contrasting stems. I like to leave Goat's Beard's spent flowers for interest. You can even spray paint them fun colors to add a whimsical feel to the garden. Zone 3

🌿✝ **Rock Soapwort** (Saponaria) 8" - 10" The striking pink flowers on this cascading plant are enchanting. Use its trailing habit to tumble over stone paths or rock walls. Soapwort can also be tucked between stepping stones or crevices in rock walls. Shear it to within a few inches of the ground after flowering to promote a thick mat. And if you run out of soap, use its leaves and roots to make your own sudsy substitute. Zone 3

Okay, before I move on to the next list, I know some of you are wondering why I did not include German Bearded Iris or Siberian Iris for spring bloomers. There are surely other beauties that are also noticeably absent. Why? My goal for writing this book was to create an All Star team of ten plants, per category. It was an extremely difficult exercise for assembling these lists. I must have one hundred spring blooming perennials in my yard, no small feat given my property is only a quarter acre. German Bearded Iris and Siberian Iris are some of these. In many ways, the challenge of selecting plants for these lists was comparable to the challenge you probably face walking into garden centers. One can become delusional confronted by hundreds of beautiful, blooming plants seeming to scream "Pick me! Pick me!" I feel your angst. Hopefully my 'wrestled down' lists will make it easier for you the next time you go shopping. Oh, and if you want to know why German Bearded Iris didn't make the cut, it has a tendency to get ratty leaves after its relatively short bloom period. The gross Iris borers it gets didn't help its case either. Siberian Iris got dinged because of its short bloom and fast growth rate requiring frequent divisions. Plus it's a bear to divide, even when wielding a machete, ax or chainsaw.

Top Ten Summer Blooming Perennials for Full to Part Sun

Tall Garden Phlox (Phlox paniculata) 15" - 48" I cannot imagine a sunny garden without Phlox. These fragrant beauties have been a backbone of cottage gardens for centuries. The only nasty habit phlox has is a tendency to get powdery mildew. Thanks to research and hybridizing, there are now many cultivars that keep this fungus at bay. Plant tags state if the plant is mildew-resistant. The king of no mildew is 'David', a bold white phlox. Other standouts are 'Robert Poore' (rich pink), 'Laura' (purple with white center), 'Bright Eyes' (soft pink with bright pink center) and 'Franz Schubert' (soft lilac with lighter edges). There are also several dwarf phlox series with plant heights ranging between 15" and 22". Flame, Junior and Pixie are three popular series proving to be mildew resistant. And if you also want striking foliage to compliment colorful flowers, check out 'Goldmine' (green and bright gold foliage); 'Becky Towe' (green with creamy-yellow margins) and 'Nora Leigh' (green with white margins). Zone 3

Geranium 'Rozanne' 18" - 20" This hardy geranium won the Perennial Plant of the Year in 2008. And it wins mine for one of the easiest, longest blooming perennials I've ever grown. The blue-violet flowers open in mid-June and continue right through October with no deadheading. 'Rozanne' has long trailing stems blanketed with flowers. One plant can easily cover a 2' to 3' square area. Because of its cascading habit, it also works well in containers and window boxes. If the plant gets a little too enthusiastic, simply prune back the stems to the desired length. This geranium is different than many others as it doesn't set seed and it is slow to increase in clump size. It can be divided in spring every third or fourth year. Be aware that it pouts when divided but it will come back. Don't lose sleep over it. Other high performing geraniums include 'Jolly Bee' (looks like 'Rozanne' but grows taller) and 'Heidy' (pinkish-lavender flowers with dark veining). Zone 5 (although I know 'Rozanne' thrives in many Zone 4 gardens)

Coreopsis 'Moonbeam' 15" - 18" This is one of the threadleaf Coreopsis. It has soft yellow flowers that bloom for six weeks or more without deadheading. I find 'Moonbeam's color much easier to pair with other flowers versus the egg-yolk yellow of other varieties. 'Moonbeam' does best in full sun, the hotter the better. I have been disappointed with some of the newer cultivars that have had a hard time wintering in my borderline zone 4/5 garden. Some big time failures include 'Creme Brulee', 'Autumn Blush' and 'Heaven's Gate'. Coreopsis rosea also struggled. It has limey green foliage and weak pink flowers, a combination that made me happy it died. Zone 3

Masterwort (Astrantia) 15" - 3' Masterwort is one of those delicate 'see through' plants. It has pincushion-like flowers on long wiry stems that shoot forth from neat foliage mounds. You can plant it at the edge of a garden and easily see through its long stems to flowers behind it. Flowers are white, pink or burgundy. With a tad bit of deadheading, it will bloom June through August. 'Sunningdale Variegated' has striking yellow and green variegated leaves in spring that slowly turn green in summer. Masterwort is happy in sun or shade. Zone 4

❦Daylily (Hemerocallis) 8" - 5' Daylilies are so forgiving. They can truck along and look terrific with no handholding. Their only downfall is they're deer candy. Check the Top Ten list to keep deer from noshing plants. There are early, mid and late bloomers as well as repeat bloomers. A repeat bloomer (also called twice bloomers or rebloomers) will send up additional bud-loaded stems after the first round has finished. 'Stella D'Oro' was the first of these to hit the market but there are now far superior choices. Check the Top Ten Daylilies list. 'Golden Zebra' (not a repeat bloomer), at only 15" tall, has bold green and white variegated leaves. Very striking. And please don't plant the orange species daylily from the roadside (sometimes called a ditch daylily) or accept it from a well-intentioned friend. It will run you out of house and home – literally. Zone 3

❦⚕Yarrow (Achillea) 3" - 40" The only reason yarrow made it to my top ten is for the yellow varieties and the outstanding Seduction series. I find most others can become scraggly, thuggish and rather milk toast in color. My favorite yellows are 'Moonshine' (I love its gray, feathery foliage), 'Coronation Gold' (this is the tallest at 40") and 'Anthea' (very soft yellow flowers). The Seduction series was the clincher for me. These plants have stiff stems, rich green foliage and bold flowers all summer. 'Strawberry Seduction' was the first to entice its way into my garden bed and I'm glad it did. Fiery red flowers with gold centers add months of sizzle. Other Seductors are 'Yellow Seduction' (buttery-yellow flowers) and 'Saucy Seduction' (rosey-pink). Zone 3

False Sunflower (Heliopsis) 30" - 48" There are only two cultivars in this family that made it on this list but they are exceptional. 'Prairie Sunset' has burgundy-red stems, dark green leaves and golden daisy-like flowers with wine-red markings. 'Loraine Sunshine' has cheerful yellow flowers but it's the foliage that makes it a winner. Leaves are silvery-white with contrasting green veins. All Heliopsis can get a little tall for their britches and look leggy, especially in rich soil. I pinch stems back by 1/3 in early June. This triggers side branching and results in a compact, heavily flowered plant. Bingo! Zone 3

❦⚕Fleece Flower (Persicaria) 15" – 4' I discovered this plant in 2007 and it's a gold mine. 'Firetail' has striking red, spiky flowers that open in July and persevere into November. And that is without deadheading. It's also a butterfly and honeybee magnet. 'Orangefield' (orangey-pink flowers), 'Blackfield" (deep red flowers) 'Pink Elephant' (pink flowers) are introductions that I haven't trialed yet but I'd be surprised if I wasn't as thrilled with them. Zone 4

Helen's Flower (Helenium) 25" - 6' Many gardens start to look tired as summer draws on. Helenium adds pop at just the right time, late July into September. These stiff-stemmed wonders covers themselves with masses of daisy-like flowers. Color choices include yellow, orange, bronzey-red, dusky-red, pink and bicolor. Most Helen's Flowers get around 4' tall but 'Red Army' stays low and bushy at 25". 'Sahn's Early Flowerer' has been hybridized to bloom earlier then the rest of the gang. It powers up in early July. And 'Red Jewel' breaks to color barrier with reddish flowers with a blue undertone. Zone 3

✥**Shasta Daisy** (Leucanthemum) 8" - 40" Shastas just seem to shout 'Smile'. And I always do except when they don't make it through our cold, wet winters. Thankfully there are some tough nuts and those are the ones I plant. 'Snowcap' and 'Snow Lady' are both reliable. They top out around 10" and make a great show at the front of the garden. Moving back in rows, 'Silver Princess' at 15" is lovely and 'Becky' is unstoppable at 3'+. 'Becky' is the only shasta that restrains herself until July to bloom and then struts her stuff into September. 'Broadway Lights' has also been an outstanding performer in my beds, with powdery yellow flowers in tight clumps that reach 18". Zone 3

photo courtesy of Jacob Davis

Top Ten Fall Blooming Perennials for Sun to Part Sun

🌿**Stonecrop** (Sedum) 3" - 36" How could 'the broccoli plant', as my son calls it, not make the top ten for fall? Sedums come in so many flower and foliage colors plus they can be upright or creeping. They add architectural interest all three seasons. 'Autumn Joy' with its green foliage and brick red flowers is most commonly known. Frankly, I think there are far better choices. For instance, 'Matrona' has pinkish-burgundy stems and soft dusty-pink flowers; 'Purple Emperor' has intriguing purple leaves with pink flowers; seiboldii 'Mediovariegatum' has coil-like stems with frosty blue, creamy yellow and pink foliage and 'Angelina' acts as a groundcover, sporting needle-like, yellow foliage that gets coppery tips in fall. Upright sedums won't flop open in fall if you pinch them by half their height in early July. Why not consider creating a stunning 'quilted blanket' groundcover by planting 'patches' of colorful creeping sedums? Creeping sedums come in many foliage colors including red, bronze, yellow, shades of green and blue as well as bicolors and tricolors. Zone 3

✛**Windflower** (Japanese Anemone) 24" - 4' Japanese Anemones are dancers. Their delicate blooms atop long dark stems twirl in fall breezes. What a nice change of pace from heavier framed fall bloomers like sedum. Great contrast. Flower colors are white or shades of pink. There are single and double-petaled flowers. 'Whirlwind', a double white anemone, has been a hit in my gardens for years. I find the double-petaled anemones have more 'umph' than singles, especially when viewed from a distance. The one anemone I would caution you on is ' Robustissima'. Its pale pink flowers are lovely but it can be quite thuggish. Zone 3

Aster (Aster) 8" - 4' Asters provide masses of daisy-like flowers in white, pink, lavender, blue and purple. Some have a nasty habit of getting mildew on their 'lower legs'. These benefit from placing shorter, full-foliaged plants like daylilies, in front of them to hide their unsightly legs. The Wood Series are remarkably mildew resistant and stay compact at 12" - 16". 'Purple Dome' is grand with deep, totally purple flowers (no yellow centers). I also like Aster e. 'First Snow'. It looks quite different with ferny leaves, arching stems and sprays of tiny white flowers. Taller asters like 'Alma Poetschke' can be pinched by 1/3 their height in early July for shorter, compact flowering plants. This also reduces the need for staking. Zone 3

🌿✛**Bolton's Aster** (Boltonia) 18" - 6' Bolton's Aster has clouds of daisy-like flowers on slender stems with narrow leaves. 'Snowbank', at 4', has bluish foliage, stiff stems and masses of white, starry flowers. 'Pink Beauty' is another tall lady at 4' - 5' but its weaker legs benefits from some support. 'Jim Crocket' has impressed me with its lavender flowers, blue-green leaves and compact 18" growth. It also starts blooming in August,

16   **Kerry Ann Mendez**   🌿drought tolerant   ✛deer resistant

earlier than others in this family. 'Nana' is another short cultivar only reaching 2' with lilac-pink flowers. Zone 3

Burnet (Sanguisorba) 18" - 4' This provocative plant has won my heart. It's a workhorse needing little attention. Most Burnets start blooming in mid-July and continue to look fabulous into fall. Arching, bottlebrush flowers can be white or burgundy-red. The leaves have a nice 'pinked' edge. My favorite variety is Great Burnet (officinalis) with its stately 5' height and large maroon flowers. 'Lemon Splash' only gets 24" and its variegated gold and green leaves provide interest right from the get go. Most Burnets are hardy to Zone 4 but 'Dali Marble' (4' tall, maroon flowers) pushes it one zone colder. Zone 3

⋓⁺Goldenrod (Solidago) 8" - 4' No, Goldenrod this does not cause hay fever! This poor native gets pegged for ragweed's mischief, as the two flowers look similar. The clump forming Goldenrods on the market are splendid for fall color plus they are butterfly magnets. 'Peter Pan', at 22", throws forth lemony-yellow flowers starting in September until late October. 'Fireworks' is spectacular with long golden sprays that fizzle like sparklers at 4'. 'Little Lemon', in contrast, is the most compact of the group at 8" - 12" with soft yellow flowers. Zone 3

⁺Hardy Ageratum (Eupatorium coelestium) 3' This lovely lady looks just like annual Ageratum but it is a perennial. I love combining its misty purpley-blue flowers with Sedum 'Matrona' and white Japanese Anemones. Hardy ageratum can spread pretty quickly by its roots where happy. Sometimes I sink it into a pot to control its enthusiasm; other times I just yank it where it has pressed my patience. Hardy Ageratum is a great cut flower and butterfly magnet. Zone 5 (although I would not think twice about planting it in Zone 4)

⋓⁺Allium 'Ozawa' 8" - 10" This member of the onion family is left alone by all wildlife, except butterflies that love it. It has rosey-purple umbrel-shaped flowers than nod from 8" - 10" stems into November. The foliage is said to turn orange in late fall but mine stubbornly refuses. In midsummer 'Ozawa' sends up funky, spear-shaped buds above grassy foliage. It's a sweet, unusual addition to the garden. Zone 4

⋓⁺ Montauk Daisy (Nipponanthemum) 3' This showy sub-shrub covers itself with large 2" to 3" white daisies in September and October. It can easily get 3' wide and 3' tall and does best in full sun. Like many fall bloomers, butterflies love it. To keep it looking tidy, cut it back hard to within a few inches of the ground, in early June. You will be pleased with the results when you see it perform in September. Montauk Daisies are difficult to divide due to their crown's woody nature. Stem cuttings tend to be the norm for propagation or simply buy another container. Zone 5

⋓⁺Ornamental Grasses 6" - 7' Warm season grasses come into their glory in the fall with brilliant 'flowers' that are especially dramatic when backlit by the sun. Check the Top Ten list for grasses hardy in zones 3, 4 and 5.

Top Ten Spring Blooming
Perennials for Part Shade to Shade

🌿⚕️**Lenten Rose** (Helleborus) 12" - 24". This 2005 Perennial Plant of the Year has nodding flowers that come in white, yellow, pink, red, burgundy as well as multicolor. Deep green leathery leaves are semi-evergreen in zones 5 and colder, a questionable benefit when they are buried under a foot of snow. Plants are ignored by deer, rabbits and other munchers thanks to their poisonous nature. 'Ivory Prince' is one of a number that break the traditional nodding flower posture. It has upward facing blooms. This allows you to better appreciate the delicate stamens without lying on your back. Lenton Rose is drought tolerant once established. Zone 5 and colder.

⚕️**Siberian Bugloss** (Brunnera) 10" - 15" Bright blue, forget-me-not like flowers billow over Siberian Bugloss's mounded, heart shaped leaves. Leaves can be solid green or have silver, creamy yellow or white markings. I prefer the variegated cultivars for their ability to reflect light in darker spots. Plus the solid green leaved plant, macrophylla, can seed about where happy. 'Jack Frost' has silvery leaves with green veins; 'Looking Glass' has solid silver leaves; and 'Variegata' and 'Hadspen Cream' have green leaves with bold white margins. I 'deadleaf' all of these periodically in summer to remove leaves with brown edges. This also stimulates new leaves to unfurl. Zone 3

🌿⚕️**Barrenwort, Bishop's Hat, Fairy Wings** (Epimedium) 4" - 20" This is my favorite groundcover for dry shade. It sneers at thirsty maple tree roots. Although it is frequently labeled a groundcover, I find it much less vigorous than others like Ajuga, Vinca and Pachysandra. Flowers can be white, pink, sulfur yellow, orange and bicolor. All flowers dangle from wirey stems that sweep up from the elongated, heart-shaped foliage. Barrenwort's leaves have a pleasing burgundy cast in spring and sometimes again in fall. These make great underplantings for spring and summer flowering shrubs. Zone 4

Bleeding Heart (Dicentra spectabilis) 2' - 3' I can't imagine a garden without old fashioned Bleeding Heart. Gracefully arched stems with dangling white or pink flowers are a spring hallmark. 'Gold Heart' displays all of the same graceful characteristics of its siblings but it sports screaming yellow foliage that glows in shade. Some might call it gaudy with its bright pink flowers and yellow leaves; I say encore! After our

photo courtesy of Jane Carlson

Kerry Ann Mendez   🌿drought tolerant   ⚕️deer resistant

long cold winters 'Gold Heart' is a refreshing sight. Most spectabilis varieties start to die back and go dormant in mid-summer. The more sun they get, the faster the 'adios'. Surprisingly, 'Gold Heart' is slow to fade and usually remains unfazed by warmer weather. I give it a quick trim after blooming and it becomes a pretty backdrop to summer bloomers. The best time to divide spectabilis varieties is as they start to go dormant. Speed up their retreat by whacking back the foliage to within 6" of the ground, dig out the clump and cut it into sections with a sharp knife. Reset the divisions, water in well and smile. Zone 3

ꙮ⚜Foamflower (Tiarella) 8" - 13" Foamflowers are a must for shade beds. They have delicate white or pink flowers on wiry stems carried above colorful foliage. There are many different leaf shapes, most displaying rich black markings. Some of my favorite cultivars are 'Black Snowflake' (white flowers), 'Pink Bouquet' (pink flowers), 'Mint Chocolate' (creamy white) and 'Heronswood Mist' with 'fuzzy' creamy-green leaves and white flowers. Most Foamflowers are clump formers but 'Cascade Creeper' and 'Running Tapestry' will root along their stems to create a pretty, drought-tolerant groundcovers. Zone 3

ꙮ⚜Lungwort (Pulmonaria) 10" - 15" These shade stalwarts always bring a smile. Most varieties have flowers that start out pink and then turn blue as the flower matures. 'Sissinghurst White' is a white flowering cultivar and 'Bertram Anderson' is a lovely gentian blue. Leaves can be solid green, spotted, silvery or green with white margins. 'Redstart' is the earliest to bloom in spring. Lungwort does have a bad habit of getting yucky looking leaves after flowering from powdery mildew. Fix the problem by cutting back all foliage to within 2" of the ground. The emerging new foliage will look great. Of course you are wondering how Pulmonaria got the catchy common name of Lungwort? When the Bubonic Plague ('Black Death') swept across Europe in the 1300's, Pulmonaria was used along with another herb, wormwood, as a possible cure. Pulmonaria was also sometimes referred to as "Herb of Mary" and used to supposedly prove if a person was a witch or not. It was a hot seller at Halloween. Zone 3

ꙮ⚜Dwarf Crested Iris (Iris cristata) 4" - 6". This charming little spring perennial never fails to entertain visitors. Small, sword shaped leaves spring from petite rhizomes. Flowers are blue, violet or white. Like its larger cousin, German Bearded Iris, Dwarf Crested Iris does not like to have its rhizomes buried under soil or mulch. Leave the top half enjoying fresh air. Because of its small size, place it at the entrance of a path or near a sitting area so it can be best appreciated. I like planting it around trees, especially near tough to plant spots next to a trunk's flare line. Dwarf Crested Iris needs very little soil to sink its roots into and is quite drought tolerant. One word of caution. If you have children or pets that are 'ground feeders', think twice about Crested Iris. Its rhizomes are poisonous. Zone 3

Shooting Star (Dodecatheon) 8" - 20" Shooting Star's dart-shaped flowers dangling from long green stems are a joy to behold. Flowers are white or pink. The leaves are a crinkly, medium green and lay close to the ground. By midsummer, Shooting Stars go dormant. They are in the ephemeral plant category. After blooming in spring and as the temperatures rise, they 'sink'. But don't despair. They'll cheerfully return next spring. Shooting Stars look especially nice next to fuller bodied plants like Hosta. Zone 4

⁜**Paeonia japonica** (Woodland Peony) 15" - 24" Hold the phone! Here is an enchanting Peony for shade. It has papery white petals and bright yellow stamens. It is probably the most asked about plant in my May gardens. And the show doesn't stop after it finishes blooming. The seed pods open in August to reveal bright pink shells and blue seeds. The leaves of Woodland Peonies look quite different from traditional peonies. They are grayish-green and held in clusters of three. These exotic beauties may be slow to get going, but once happy and settled in, they will grow into a nice clump. A word of caution on dividing these. I assumed they would be easy like other peonies so I hacked mine in late summer. Sadly, only one of five potted divisions survived, along with my 'mother plant' in the garden. Woodland Peonies can be hard to find at garden centers. You can find these at Plant Delights Nursery (www.plantdelights.com) and Seneca Hill Perennials (www.senecahillperennials.com), both great mail-order sources. Zone 4

⚘⁜**Dead Nettle** (Lamium) 4" - 8" These are workhorses for dry shade. There are many varieties, although most gardeners are only familiar with silver leaved ones. 'Beedham's White' has chartreuse leaves with a white strip down the center; 'Anne Greenaway' is green, gold, and white; 'Aureum' has solid gold leaves and 'Friday' has green and yellow leaves. All march across the soil and set roots from their stems, creating more self-sufficient plants. Almost all varieties of Lamium are terrific plants but there are a few I steer clear of. 'Beacon Silver' tends to get a rust on its leaves and 'White Nancy' sometimes wimps out over time. Zone 3

Top Ten Summer Blooming
Perennials for Part Shade to Shade

✣ **Astilbe** (Astilbe) 8" - 4' Astilbes can handle sun or part shade. They really don't bloom well in full shade. I prefer the chinensis cultivars which are more drought tolerant than others. How can you tell if an Astilbe is a 'camel-like' chinensis one? You will either see that word chinensis or c. before the single quote marks. For example, Astilbe c. 'Visions'. To enjoy these colorful white, pink, red, lavender, or purple blooms throughout the summer, make sure to buy Early (mid-June through early July), Mid (July) and Late blooming (mid-July through mid-August) varieties. Astilbes are heavy feeders. To encourage impressive plumes, work in some slow-release fertilizer such as Plant-Tone (organic) or Osmocote (14-14-14) into the soil once a year in early May. Zone 3

photo courtesy of PerennialResource.com

✣ **Ligularia** (Ligularia) 20" - 4' What a funky group of plants. They all have intriguing leaves, both in their shape and coloration. The flowers are 'crunchy' too. The most common, 'The Rocket', has tall yellow spikes in July. 'Little Rocket' takes it down a notch at 3' tall. 'Othello' and 'Desdemona' have chocolate-green, scalloped leaves. 'Britt-Marie Crawford' goes the extra mile with dark chocolate-purple foliage and purple undersides. 'Othello', 'Desdemona' and 'Britt-Marie Crawford' all have orangey-yellow, flowers topping tall stalks in August. Ligularias want a moisture-rich site. Along the water's edge is super. If you don't have a wet area, create a mini-bog by digging a hole, lining it with some pond liner or heavy plastic, backfill with soil amended with organic matter (compost or aged manure along with some peat moss) and plant. Zone 4

✣ **Cardinal Flower** (Lobelia) 24" - 5' Cardinal Flowers hit their peak in late July and August. Cardinalis is most commonly available with its electric red flower stalks that can reach 4'. It can be finicky and short-lived for some. I find 'Monet Moment' with rosey-pink flowers and 'Fan Scarlet' to be much more reliable. L. siphilitica has stunning blue flowers in August and September. Although it can seed around, given that blue is such a rare color in late blooming perennials, I'll take it. 'Queen Victoria', with its captivating burgundy foliage and red flowers, has never wintered in my gardens, despite the claim it is hardy to Zone 5. Zone 3

Hosta 4" - 4' Call me snobby, but I primarily buy Hosta for their foliage. I usually whack off the flowers. There are a few exceptions. I love the white flowering Hosta that reflect light in shady spots. Hosta with white flowers include sieboldiana 'Elegans' (blue leaves), 'Frances Williams' (blue and chartreuse leaves), 'Love Pat' (blue leaves) and 'Spilt Milk' (white streaks on blue leaves). Fragrant flowers are always a plus. Perfumey Hosta include 'Fragrant Bouquet' (apple green and creamy yellow leaves), 'Royal Standard' (green leaves), 'Fragrant Blue' (blue leaves), 'Guacamole' (apple green and chartreuse leaves) and 'So Sweet' (green and creamy-yellow leaves). The thicker the leaves (substance), the more resistant the Hosta is to deer, slug and snail damage. Most Hosta with blue leaves have a heavy substance. Zone 3

Corydalis (Corydalis) 9" - 16" These are 'Ever-Ready Bunnies' in shade or Part sun. They bloom May through September with no deadheading. They can be short lived and seed if happy, but a perennial that bangs away flowers that long can have a spot in my bed. C. lutea has cheerful yellow flowers with ferny-green leaves. Less common but as impressive is the white corydalis, ochroleuca. Be wary of C. sempervirens, a pink and yellow flowering lady that gets very leggy and is a biennial, not a perennial. The blue flowering Corydalis ('Blue Panda' and 'China Blue') also get low ratings from me. They go dormant in warmer temperatures and can be short lived. 'Berry Exciting' is a newcomer with screaming yellow foliage and purple flowers. Zone 4

⌖Fringed Leaved, Fern-Leaved Bleeding Heart (Dicentra eximia) 8" - 15" These pick up the baton where the earlier blooming, larger Bleeding Hearts fall off. Ferny, blue green foliage complements pink, white or reddish-pink flowers. They dislike dry shade and may go dormant in these conditions. The Heart series is exceptional with frosty blue leaves and heavy flowering habit. Look for 'King of Hearts' (deep pink); 'Ivory Hearts' (white), 'Candy Hearts' (medium pink) and 'Burning Hearts' (rosy-red with white edges). Fringed Bleeding Hearts can be challenging to divide. They don't always respond well (read between the lines). If you are going to divide them, attack in spring. Zone 3

⚘Coral Bell (Heuchera) 6" - 20" Many coral bells thrive in the shade, especially those with yellow, peach or purple leaves. Mounds can be only 4" in height to as large as 12". Most flowers are a non-descript creamy white or pale pink but 'Hollywood', 'Hercules', 'Veil of Passion' and 'Cherries Jubilee' are bright red; 'Rave On' and 'Dolce Mocha Mint' are rich pink. One of my favorites is 'Caramel' with large, showy marmalade leaves. It is one of the few I've found that handles full sun or shade with equal flare. Zone 3

⌖Pink Turtlehead (Chelone) 2' - 4' Pink or white flowers decorate dark green, glossy leaves starting in August. Turtlehead can handle sun or shade as well as drier conditions, despite its fame as being a moistire lover. I had a mass under a silver maple tree and they thrived until the maple was struck by lightning and everything came a'tumblin' down. 'Hot Lips' has deep pink flowers and stays more compact at 2' to 3' than C. lyonii. I am unimpressed with the white Turtlehead. It looks ho-hum. All Turtle-heads have stiff stems that can be pinched in early June for compact, heavier blooming plants. Zone 3

⊹**Athyrium niponicum** (Japanese Painted Fern) 8" - 22" Ferns are a natural for shade gardens. 'Pictum' is the most widely available Japanese Painted Fern with silvery, red and dark green fronds. Nice, but if you want to turn up the color meter more, plant 'Silver Falls', 'Ursula's Red', 'Regal Red' or 'Burgundy Lace'. 'Ghost' is almost all silver and very upright and vase-like in appearance. Japanese Painted Ferns contrast nicely with Hosta and plumy Astilbes, especially the darker red Astilbes that color echo the Fern's burgundy veins. Zone 3

Bellflower (Campanula) 4" - 3' Campanulas do fine in part or dappled shade, especially the gold-leaved ones that tend to fry in full sun. I love using 'Dickson's Gold' along shady paths. It has gold foliage and lavender-blue flowers. The glowing mounds act like runway lights spring through fall. By positioning these at various intervals on each side of a path, the viewer's eye is gently directed forward. Peach-Leaf Bellfowers (persicifolia) also do well in part shade. Flowers can be white, blue or purple. I prefer 'Alba' (white) in shade because it is easier to see. Deadheading always helps extend the bloom period of Bellflowers but all those little flowers drive me bananas. So I wait until most are spent and then I shear them all off, knowing that some fresh buds were sacrificed in the process. So be it. Zone 3

Top Ten Fall Blooming Perennials for Part Shade to Shade

Yellow Waxbells (Kirengeshoma palmata) 3' Yellow Waxbells have delicate, buttery-yellow flowers dangle from 3' arching stems. The foliage looks similar to a maple tree's leaves. Yellow Waxbells form a neat 3' X 3' clump. It rarely needs dividing. I have never divided mine and it is ten years old. It makes a handsome pairing with Astilbes, Toad Lilies and Hosta. Zone 5

Toad Lily (Tricyrtis) 18" - 36" These unique looking flowers are in the orchid family. Blooms can be solid white, or white with pink or purple markings. Leaves are solid green, green and white, or green and creamy-yellow. All Toad Lilies have arching stems with flowers formed along their length. The flowers are petite in size so it's best to plant a number of Toad Lilies together to make a nice show. Also plant them near the front of the bed where these beauties can be appreciated. Zone 4

Gentian (Gentiana) 8" - 30" These uncommon plants make a fetching display in the garden. Most need at least part sun but a few can handle part shade. 'True Blue' has bright blue, upward facing, bell-shaped flowers opening mid-summer and continuing into early fall. It gets 24" - 30" tall. Closed Gentian (andrewsii) has deeper blue, 'closed' tubular flowers and stays shorter at 12" - 18". There is also a pure white variety. Crested Gentian (Gentian septemfida) has brilliant blue, open-faced flowers with white throats. It stays low at 8" and is best planted in multiples. Zone 4

⫟Bugbane, Snakeroot (Cimicifuga) 4' - 6' There are green and chocolate leaved varieties of Bugbane. Chocolate foliaged cultivars have incredibly fragrant flowers. I find the aroma of green leaved ones quite unpleasant. Most Bugbanes send up long, bottlebrush flowers in August and continue into fall. My favorite chocolates include 'Brunette' and 'Hillside Black Beauty'. I have tried 'Black Negligee' several times with no success, in the garden or bedroom. 'Pink Spire' is promoted as having pink flowers, but the blooms were so pale, I needed imagination to 'see' pink. Two of the green leaved varieties that I love for masses of floating 'candlesticks' are Simplex, blooming in September, and racemosa that blooms July and August. Zone 3

photo courtesy of Daniele Ippoliti

Kerry Ann Mendez ⩔drought tolerant ⫟deer resistant

✢**Leadwort, Plumbago** (Ceratostigma plumbaginoides) 8" - 12" Leadwort is a lovely blue flowering perennial opens in August and continues through September. It can handle full sun to part shade. The more sun it gets, the more burgundy the leaves turn in cooler weather. Where happy, it can be a slow spreading groundcover that effectively smothers weeds. Some catalogs list it as a Zone 5, others Zone 6. It will do best in a sheltered area, on the east side of the house or near stonework. I have lost it to Old Man Winter a number of times but it is so gorgeous, I keep buying it. Call me foolish, I'm lovesick. Zone 5/6

✿✢**Fall Blooming Joe Pye Weed** (Eupatorium Chocolate) 3' - 5' 'Chocolate' grows in dry shade and features billowy white flowers September through October. It also does well in full sun. Despite its height, I have never had to stake it. It also does well as a cut flower. Zone 3

✢**Monkshood** (Aconitum) 12" - 5' These resemble Delphinium but are longer lived and handle shade. Plus nothing eats them, they are poisonous. Some Monkshood like nappellis (blue, 4' - 5'), 'Bi-color' (white with blue edges, 4' - 5') and 'Blue Lagoon' (blue, 12") bloom in July and August. Others postpone the show until fall. 'Arendsii' (violet, 4'), 'Barker's Variety' (violet-blue, 5') and carmichaelii or fischeri (wedgewood blue, 4') start in September and bloom for weeks. Many Monkshood have deep green, shiny leaves. Zone 3

Top Ten Short-Lived Perennials

Whenever I get frustrated if a perennial dies, usually due to Old Man Winter's knockout punch, my husband reminds me that plants are living things. They will eventually die. The cause may be winterkill, disease, overwatering, underwatering, the neighbor's dog using it as a fire hydrant, or my son stepping on it with his size 13 foot to get a wayward soccer ball. If I can't stand the heat, get out of the compost pile, or work with plastic plants.

The problem is I love quite a few perennials with short life expectancies, so I purchase these in 4" pots or start them by seed. Fall sales are a great time to pick up reserves. If any in the garden kick the bucket over winter, I simply replace them with back-ups I purchased on sale for under $2 a piece. To winter over sale plants, repot them in gallon pots with fresh soil and move them inside to an unheated garage in late November. Or, if you have an area when you can dig them in for the winter (perhaps a vegetable garden), do so. You can also winter over pots outside above ground by covering them with chicken wire and tarp.

Many short-lived plants crave gravelly, well-drained soil on the lean side. You can 'love them to death' with rich soil and fertilizer. Finally, if a plant's description suggests allowing some to reseed for enjoying more the next season, this is a nice way of saying the plant is short-lived. Heads up.

🌿✛ **Flax** (Linum) 8" - 24" Sun . Summer bloomer. Blue or white flowers. Reseeds easily. Sharp drainage is a must. Zone 5

🌿✛ **Mullein** (Verbascum) 18" - 4' Sun to Part Sun. Summer bloomer. Plum, yellow, rosy-peach, soft pink and salmon flowers. To extend the life expectancy, prune off flowers right after they finish blooming. Zone 5

🌿 **Mallow s. 'Zebrina'** (Malva) 3' Sun to Part Sun. Summer bloomer. Soft pink flowers with purplish stripes. 'Zebrina' is a popular seller, not only because it is pretty but because it is so reliably short-lived. I've never been able to get it to live more than a year. Zone 3

✛ **Larkspur** (Delphinium) 10" - 6' Sun to Part Sun. Early summer bloomer with a second flush in late summer. White, pink, blues, purple and lavender flowers. There are dwarf delphiniums in the grandiflorum group that have very delicate foliage and top out at 15". The New Millennium series are taller varieties hybridized for fuller flower stalks that are not as prone to snapping. 'Connecticut Yankees' and the Magic Fountain Series stay compact at 24" - 36", also reducing the need for staking. Delphiniums can have white or dark 'bees'. Bees are the center of each flower. I think the white bees are more attractive. The dark ones make the flowers look too somber. After Delphiniums flower in early to mid-summer, cut back the stems. Many times, shorter stalks will burst forth in late summer. Zone 3

🌿drought tolerant   ✛deer resistant

Blackberry Lily (Belamacanda) 18" - 3' Sun. Summer bloomer. Yellow, orange with darker speckles and reddish-orange with speckled flowers. Foliage looks a bit like irises. Flowers form shiny black berries in late summer. Reseeds pretty easily. Zone 4

Golden Marguerite (Anthemis) 12" - 3' Sun. Summer bloomer. Creamy white, gold and soft yellow flowers. Small daisy-like flowers cover gray-green foliage. Reseeds freely except for 'Charme' (gold flowers) that has sterile seeds. Zone 3

Lupine (Lupinus) 18" - 4' Sun. Late spring, early summer bloomer. White, yellow, blue, pink, red and purple flowers. There are three popular series. The Popsicle series grows between 18" - 24", the Gallery series between 15" - 18", and the ever-popular Russells run 2' - 4'. Zone 3

Rose Campion (Lychnis coronaria) 20" - 30" Sun to Part Sun. Summer bloomers. Rosy red or white flowers with soft pink centers. All have silvery, fuzzy foliage. Reseeds easily. I find Rose Campions behave like biennials. First year plants have short rosettes of leaves and the next year these shoot forth flower stalks. I transplant first year seedlings around my gardens where I want to see the bright flowers the following year. They have even bloomed in dappled shade, although not as robustly. Zone 3

Blanket Flower (Gaillardia) 10" - 30" Sun. Summer bloomer. Burgundy, yellow, peachy-orange, red and yellow, and orange and yellow flowers. Blanket Flowers require consistent deadheading to look their best. They demand soil with sharp drainage. They have bluish-green leaves with a hairy texture. Most varieties are hardy to Zone 3 but others like the Commotion series are Zone 6 or warmer. Some cultivars have petals with fluted tips making them look like little horns. Zone 3

Broadleaf Tickseed (Coreopsis grandiflora) 6" - 24" Sun. Summer bloomer. Yellow flowers. Flowers can be single or double petaled. Tickseed in this group have 'fatter' leaves than threadleaf family members. Blooms sit atop long wiry stems. Deadheading is a must to keep these blooming well. What a waste of gardener's energy given the plant doesn't live that long. Humbug. Reseeds easily. Zone 4

Top Ten Perennial Reseeders

When I first started gardening I'd get a huge grin on my face when I learned a certain perennial reseeded easily. More was better right? Now I am jumping up and down screaming "Save me" from an invasion of Johnny Jump Ups. Don't get me wrong. I love the flowers you will see on the list below and I have 'many' of them. But now I take steps to control their fertility so I don't feel like the Old Lady in the Shoe.

On a side note, I have not included any biennials on this list. It's a biennial's job to reseed for its preservation. That's what you accept as a gardener when planting biennials. Biennials only live for two years. First year leaves; second year flowers; third year dead. It's just a biennial thing. If you don't want to hassle with making sure reseeding occurs and you don't pull up seedlings that are next year's show, then don't plant biennials. Life will go on. For more on biennials, see my Top Ten list.

Here are some ways to prevent a population explosion of unwanted plants from reseeding perennials:

- Pinch away. Busy hands can be put to work to deadhead flowers before they go to seed. I found a nice match with my son's need to earn money for his XBox games.
- Mulch gardens thickly with 2" to 3" of compost, aged manure, shredded mulch or other organic materials
- Use a pre-emergent weed killer around reseeders. Corn gluten is an organic pre-emergent that is a byproduct of milled corn. It is so safe you can eat it, but it tastes awful. A chemical option (yuck) is Preen. Pre-emergents only kill seeds and not plants that are already leafed out. But be aware that most pre-emergents are non-discriminatory regarding which seeds they terminate. It can be a crabgrass seed or one from your gorgeous white foxglove.
- Pluck seedlings where you don't want them. This is probably the most difficult control method for many gardeners. They cannot 'kill' a plant. Think of it like pulling a tooth. Just close your eyes and pull. Remember, plants are not children. They're easier.

Mallow (Malva a. 'Fastigiata') 3' - 4' Sun. Summer bloomer. Pink or white flowers. Mallows can get very bushy with almost a woody base. They can be sheared in late May to create shorter, compact plants. Mallows have very long taproots and hate being moved once established. If you do have to relocate a plant, prune it back to within a few inches of the ground and then up and at'em. Make sure to keep it watered well for the first few weeks as the plant gets adjusted. Zone 3

Mountain Bluet, Batchelor Button, Cornflower (Centaurea montana) 18" - 24" Sun. Early summer bloomer. Blue, violet, white, and blue and white flowers. Actually, only the blue cultivar, montana, is a zealous seeder in this family. The white flowering 'Alba' and 'Amethyst in Snow (violet centers with white petals) are well behaved. So is 'Gold Bullion' with its brilliant yellow foliage and blue flowers. All Batchelor Buttons get ratty looking after their first flush of flowers. Shear them back to within three inches of the ground after they bloom. They will usually re-bloom later in the summer and their foliage will look much prettier. Zone 3

Corydalis (Corydalis) 9" - 16" Sun to Shade. Late spring through fall. Yellow, white, purple, blue and pink flowers. C. lutea has cheerful yellow flowers with ferny-green leaves and is probably the most enthusiastic reseeder. The white corydalis, ochroleuca, is not far behind. Blue, purple and pink Corydalis are not issues in my borderline Zone 4/5 gardens. They all tend to be very short lived. Zone 4

Cranesbill (Hardy Geranium) 12" Sun to Part Sun. Late spring, early summer bloomer. Magenta flowers. There are dozens of perennial Geraniums. The one I am referring to is, dare I say, common magenta sanguineum. This can become almost a groundcover in gardens. It was in my Grandmother's garden. And that is good. One or two of them that is. Newer Geranium cultivars look similar but are more restrained. Zone 3

Pink or Purple Coneflower (Echinacea) 2' - 3' Sun. Summer bloomer. Pink or purple coneflowers (depending on how your eyes see the color) can happily take over a garden. The white, yellow, orange, red, mango and other color breakthroughs, stay put. Part of the reason they are so prolific is due to our good intentions to leave the seed heads for winter interests and bird feed. Choices, choices. Zone 3

Snowdrop Anemone (Anemone sylvestris) 12" - 15" Sun to Part Shade. Spring, late summer bloomer. White flowers. Delicate, cup-shaped flowers emerge on long stems above mounded foliage. The flowers dance in spring breezes. They will rebloom again in August. Snowdrop Anemones spread by seed as well as rhizomes (roots). Keep them in check or consider using them as a groundcover in a woodland area where the effect can be magical. Zone 3

Chives (Allium schoenoprasum) 12" - 14" Sun to Part Sun. Early summer bloomer. Rosy-lavender flower balls. This group of Chives are superb for cooking but unless you are feeding an army, apply efforts to restrain. Zone 3

Large Flowering Catmint (Nepeta subsessilis) 24" - 46" Sun to Part Sun. Summer bloomer. Lavender, light pink or blue flowers. These Catmints can be rampant reseeders. They have larger flowers and usually get taller than other cultivars. 'Candy Cat', 'Cool Cat' and 'Sweet Dreams' are a few popular sellers. I keep one in my garden for my neighbor's cats that love to nibble the foliage. I feel it's a fair trade for keeping my vole population down. Zone 3

⊹**Northern Sea Oats** (Chasmanthium) 3' Sun to Part Shade. Northern Sea Oats is an ornamental grass with late summer flowers. It is a neat, clump forming grass that slowly expands from the base. It's the seeds that are the issue as the flowers mature. Either hedge trim the flowers off as they start to go by or roll up your sleeves and deal with the 'multification factor'. Zone 3

⊹**Feverfew** (Tanacetum) 18" - 24" Sun. Summer bloomer. White flowers. These ferny-leafed herbs have cute, button-like white flowers that are pleasing cut flowers. Both the green and the yellow foliaged Feverfews seed profusely. Feverfew got its common from the belief that using the dried leaves for a tea took fevers down. Zone 4

photo courtesy of Jane Carlson

⊹**Labrador Violet** (Viola labradorica) 3" - 4" Sun to Shade. Early summer bloomer. Lavender-purple flowers. I was attracted to this perennial because of its chocolate-purple leaves and its ability to bloom in shade. I didn't expect it to act like a groundcover. I also discovered its rich spring leaf color transitions to a greenish-bronze in summer. I still love the little charmers but I'm ruthless about pulling them where I don't want them. Zone 3

Top Ten Perennial Thugs

If we really want lower maintenance gardens, we wouldn't knowingly plant perennials that are out to take over the world with their unrelenting roots. But usually we are caught unaware. Our friends came bearing gifts from their gardens, or we saw a plant marked for $1 at a garage sale, or we mistakenly believed the descriptive word 'vigorous' referred to the plants ability to perform well. Mistake, mistake, mistake.

Unless you do the following to set down the garden rules:

- ❋ Plant the thug in a garden pot in the ground. Recycle your plastic pots (2 gallon or larger) by cutting the bottom off, leaving a good 6" of side attached. Dig a hole in the garden, insert pot (leave about 1" above ground), place the thug in the pot, back fill with soil and tell it to 'Stay!' It will. You can also use large plastic tubs or old plastic swimming pools. Or imprison the thug with heavy duty landscape edging. One of my clients created a huge heart with landscape edging and filled it with red Bee balm. Aaaahhhhh.
- ❋ Don't give it a second thought when you need to ruthlessly plunge a spade into the thug to remove a section where it overstepped its bounds. Share the piece with a 'friend'.
- ❋ Plant it where you want it to be a flowering groundcover.
- ❋ Understand that when a plant's description states it is a groundcover, it is. Use it as a groundcover and you will not get frustrated.

I did not include *&$@#^*mint#%@& that most of us already know.

✛**Bellflowers** (Campanula punctata) 10" - 28" Sun to Part Sun. Summer bloomer. Cherry pink or purple flowers. Don't turn your back on this one. Nodding, bell-shaped flowers dangle from stiff, upright stems making the plant look innocent. Agreed, they are cute, but not in the thousands. Please note, I am only referring to those in the punctata group; there are many other bellflowers that are very well behaved. Zone 3

Loosestrife (Lysimachia) 24" - 3' Sun to Part Sun. Summer bloomer. White and yellow flowers. White Gooseneck (Lysimachia clethroides) has white arching flowers that resemble a goose's neck. It is a tough bird, handling all types of soil conditions with ease. That's the problem. Circle Flower (Lysimachia punctata) has yellow flowers circling each stem at intervals. 'Firecracker' has small, light yellow flowers and chocolate foliage in spring that slowly turns greenish-bronze in summer. Variegated Loosestrifes run at a slower pace. Because variegated leaves contain less chlorophyll, they cannot produce as much food and therefore plants are less vigorous. 'Golden Alexander' has light green leaves with creamy-yellow margins. 'Alexander' has pink, light green and creamy white foliage that becomes mostly green and white in summer. Zone 4

✛**Chameleon Plant** (Houttuynia) 6" - 9" Sun to Shade. Summer bloomer. White flowers (very insignificant). This plant is all about its heart-shaped red, gold, pink and green leaves that race, very quickly, across the ground. It gets its best coloration in moisture-retentive soil and full sun. It wakes up late in the spring so don't get excited too quickly if you think you've finally gotten rid of it in unwanted areas. Take a second look. Don't get me wrong. This is an outstanding groundcover in areas where you want it to be a groundcover. Be decisive before planting. Zone 3

✛**Chinese Lanterns** (Physalis) 12" - 24" Sun to Part Sun. Fall bloomer. Orange flowers that look like Chinese lanterns. Folks love to dry these fun flowers for fall decorations. Fine, but save your sanity by sinking them in heavy duty containers in the ground. Or, you could always buy a plant for your neighbor and ask for some of theirs. Zone 3

✿✛**Evening Primrose, Sundrops** (Oenothera) 4" - 18" Sun to Part Shade. Early summer bloomer. Yellow or pink flowers. The ever popular Evening Primrose (fruiticosa) starts out as purple-tinged, flat rosettes of leaves in early spring. Then stems pop up and are covered with yellow flowers. 'Fireworks' has the same habit but with reddish stems. 'Siskiyou' is low growing (4") with green leaves that have maroon markings. The flowers are large and soft pink. Supposedly 'Siskiyou' has fragrant flowers but my nose has yet to pick up a scent. Of course I would have to be down on my knees to appreciate it. Fat chance. Zone 4

✿✛**Ribbon Grass** (Phalaris) 24" Sun to Shade. Summer bloomer. Airy little white flowers. I know this grass has a purpose. Please tell me. Actually it can make a tough groundcover in hard-to-plant hellstrips. It has a bad habit of getting rust and brown patches mid-summer. Help it out by mowing or weed whacking it down to within 2" to 3". It will regrow and look nice for the remainder of the season and you'll feel better. Trust me. Zone 3

✛**Bee Balm** (Monarda) 9" - 5' Sun to Part Sun. Summer bloomer. Red, white, pink, wine, purple and lavender flowers. I have at least six different varieties of bee balm but I keep them under heavy surveillance. The least aggressive are 'Petite Delight' (lavender-pink, 12" - 15") and 'Petite Wonder' (pink, 9" - 12"). All Bee Balms are great hummingbird and butterfly mag-

photo courtesy of Jane Carlson

Kerry Ann Mendez   ✿drought tolerant   ✛deer resistant

nets, especially the reds. They do tend to get powdery mildew (white stuff) on their leaves. You can prevent this by being proactive and preventing the problem from the get-go. Start spraying the upper and lower surfaces of the leaves in May with one of the following two recipes: one teaspoon of baking soda to one quart water or one part milk (1%, 2%, skim or whole) to three parts water. To either solution add 3 to 4 drops of liquid dish detergent, vegetable oil or Murphy's Oil Soap as an adhesive. Spray every two weeks until mid-July. Simpler yet, buy one of the many mildew resistant cultivars available. Zone 3

Obedient Plant (Physostegia) 2' - 4' Sun to Part Sun. Summer bloomer. White or rosy-pink flowers. The common name tricks you. It actually refers to how you can swivel each of the individual flowers on a flower stem and they will stay in the position you place them. A nice feature for flower arranging I guess. Unfortunately, the plant's roots were never told about the obedient part. Obedient Plant do create exquisite color in late summer when other perennials have started fading. 'Miss Manners' is a 2' tall, white flowering lady that supposedly behaves herself. 'Variegata' has variegated white and green leaves with pink flowers and is a slower marcher given its variegation. Zone 3

Lamb's Ear (Stachys byzantina) 6" - 10" Sun to Part Sun. Summer bloomer. Rosy-pink flowers. I feel badly putting this one on the list. It has such velvety silver leaves that feel like little lamb's ears. But I would be irresponsible if I didn't let you know it is not always as sweet as Mary's Little Lamb. It does make a great edger when kept in check. I prefer to cut the flower stalks off but that is a personal preference. I'm in it for the leaves. If you prefer a non-flowering Lamb's Ear, buy 'Helene von Stein' that has much larger leaves and no flowers. Lamb's Ear hates humidity which causes some leaves to rot. I comb my fingers through plants once a month to pull out unsightly ones. This creates more air flow for the other leaves. Zone 4

Silver King and **Silver Queen Wormwood** (Artemisia) 3' Sun. Foliage plant. Both 'royality' Wormwoods are used for dried flower arrangements and wreaths. They are both aggressive spreaders, especially the male. Never leave these two alone without a 'chaperone', sink them in separate containers. Zone 4

Top Ten 'Needy' Perennials

Before you read on, I have a confession to make. I am a tough love; no nonsense; if you can't perform, I'll find a plant that can; gardener. Does this sound severe? I guess so. But I remind myself that these are plants we are talking about, not children. And yes, I have my soft spots. Truth be told, I have almost every one of the following 'needy' perennials in my gardens, but in limited numbers.

I define 'needy' as plants that:

- require a lot of deadheading to continue blooming
- are prone to insect problems
- are prone to fungal problems
- need staking to prevent flower stems from snapping
- are short-lived and need replacements
- have messy, ugly foliage after blooming
- and anything else that presses my buttons the wrong way

✢**Broadleafed Tickseed** (Coreopsis grandiflora) 6" - 3' Sun. Summer bloomer. Yellow flowers. Popular varieties are 'Sunray', 'Early Sunrise' and 'Rising Sun'. These need consistent deadheading and can be short-lived. Zone 3

✢**Peach-Leaved and Clip Bellflowers** (Campanula carpatica and persicifolia) 6" - 3' Sun to Part Sun. Summer bloomer. White, blue, purple and violet flowers. All of the plants in these two groups (carpatica and persicifolia) are charming but they require a lot of deadheading to look good. Zone 3

✢**Balloon Flower** (Platycodon) 6" - 24" Sun to Part Sun. Summer bloomer. White, pink and blue flowers. Deadheading is a must for best bloom. Zone 3

✢**Lupine** (Lupinus) 18" - 4' Sun. Late spring, early summer bloomer. White, yellow, blue, pink, red and purple flowers. Lupines have a way of captivating people. Yes, they are sensational looking when in bloom but after flowering they can get ratty foliage, white aphids and be short-lived. Strike three you're out. I get my lupine fix by looking at magazines. Zone 3

photo courtesy of PerennialResource.com

Oriental Poppies (Papaver orientalis) 16" - 36" Sun. Late spring, early summer bloomer. White, pink, salmon, red and orange flowers. Few perennials can match the reaction that Oriental Poppies draw when in full bloom from admirers. The problem is they only bloom for about 10 days, if you are lucky not to have rain or wind. After that Oriental Poppies 'go south' for the season and leave their messy foliage as calling cards. Clean up the mess by whacking foliage down to within a few inches of the ground. Plan for their brief stage appearance by planting Baby's Breath or other expanding perennials nearby to fill the void. You can also fill the space with annuals. Zone 3

Blanket Flower (Gaillardia) 10" - 30" Sun. Summer bloomers. Burgundy, yellow, peachy-orange, red and yellow, and orange and yellow flowers. You've got to salute Blanket Flowers for their bright floral display but they need a lot of deadheading and can be short-lived. Zone 3

False Sunflower (Heliopsis) 24" - 48" Sun to Part Sun. Summer bloomer. Yellow and orange-gold flowers. False Sunflowers are cheerful, daisy-like flowers that are charming. My peeve? The can be heavy reseeders (except 'Loraine Sunshine') and are magnets for red aphids. They also tend to get powdery mildew. Zone 3

'Stella De Oro' Daylily (Hemerocallis 'Stella De Oro') 15" Sun to Part Sun. Summer bloomer. Gold flowers. I feel a little like a traitor putting Stella on this list. She was the first repeat blooming Daylily to hit the market in a big way. But frankly, Stella blooms profusely for about three weeks in early summer and then takes a long break. While on 'siesta' we get to look a swollen seed pods. She comes back on stage with the onset of cooler weather. Thanks to hybridizing, there are now many repeat blooming Daylilies with longer blooming periods and larger, showier flowers. Check out the Top Ten Daylilies list. Zone 3

Pincushion Flower (Scabiosa) 6" - 3' Sun. Summer bloomer. Blue, pink, yellow white and lavender flowers. Mounded leaves send up wiry stalks topped with 'pincushion' looking flowers. Less common are 'Moondance' with lemon-yellow flowers and ochroleuca with very pale yellow flowers. The caucasica group can be short-lived. Zone 4

Pacific Giant Delphineum (Delphinium elatum) 3' - 6' Sun to Part Sun. Early summer bloomer with a second flush in late summer. White, pink, blues, purple and lavender flowers. These, and other 'skyscraper' Delphiniums, are the 'grand dames' of the summer garden. Magnificent beauties. But they require staking and tying off every foot to prevent 'timber ho', plus they are short-lived. Zone 3

Top Ten Unusual Perennials

We can't help ourselves. Like proud parents, we want people to notice our unique children. We get our jollies when we own an unusual perennial and it's the talk among garden junkies. Plant envy can be good. Who knows. Maybe you'll have the Paparazzi peeking over your garden fence for photos.

Giant Kale (Crambe) 5' Sun. Summer bloomer. White flowers. This looks like white Baby's Breath on steroids. Giant Kale has a cloud of white airy flowers in July. Like the flower mass, its leaves are also oversized but stay low. Even though Giant Kale is rated to zone 5, I originally saw this eye-popper at Trapp Family Lodge in the mountains of Stowe, VT. I have grown it here in my borderline zone 4/5 garden for years with no babying on my part. It can be a hard specimen to find at garden centers but what joy when you hit gold. Zone 5

Purple Stemmed Angelica (Angelica gigas) 4' - 6' Part Sun to Part Shade. Late summer, early fall bloomer. Purple flowers. Both the funky, dramatic leaves and the large, dome-shaped purple flowers are thrilling. Tropical looking leaves spring from burgundy stems. Angelica, in the herb family, is usually tagged as a biennial or short-lived perennial. I have tried to reseed mine without success so I just buy more pots. Although short-lived, it is worth every penny! Zone 4

⊹**Fernleaf Peony** (Paeonia tenuifolia) 12" - 15" Sun to Part Sun. Spring bloomer. Red or pink flowers. This flower never fails to draw oohhs and aahhs from onlookers. It has extremely feathery leaves that are light to medium green. The flowers can be single or double. Like other peonies, they do not bloom long, but after the flowers gracefully bow out, the foliage remains for an encore. Fernleaf Peonies are very long lived and disease free. In hot summers it may go dormant but don't fret, it will return the following spring in all its glory. These beauties are pricey. They typically sell for $35 - $50. Go for it! Zone 3

⊹**Woodland Peony** and **Japanese Forest Peony** (Paeonia japonica and Paeonea Obovata) 15" - 24" Part Sun to Part Shade. Spring bloomer. White and pink flowers. Hold the phone! Here are enchanting peonies for shade. The Woodland Peony has papery white petals, bright yellow stamens and gray-green foliage. It is probably the most asked about plant in my May gardens. The show doesn't stop after it finishes blooming. The seed pods open in August to reveal bright pink shells and blue seeds. The Japanese Forest Peony (obovata) has pink or white blooms and opens later than the Woodland Peony. They look extremely similar. Seneca Hill Perennials (www.senecahillperennials.com), a great mail-order nursery near Syracuse, NY offers these. Zone 5 (if not Zone 4)

🍂drought tolerant   ⊹deer resistant

Japanese Ligularia (Ligularia Japonica) 36" Sun to Part Shade. Summer bloomer. Orangey-yellow flowers. Okay, no pushing please. And yes, cameras are allowed. This is how I feel when folks cluster about my Japanese Ligularia. It was a gift from a friend years ago. Based on how 'tropical' it looked, I never dreamed it would survive in my tough love gardens. Japanese Ligularia has huge ragged, deep green leaves with orange daisies in August. It is a fascinating plant that needs room to be best appreciated. It can easily get 4' wide. Zone 4

Shredded Umbrella Plant (Syneilesis) 18"- 24" Part Sun to Shade. Summer bloomer. Pinkish-white flowers. This is one fun plant. It emerges looking like fuzzy white, 'closed umbrellas'. It then opens up to deeply divided, flat green leaves. It took my plants three years to finally produce flowers. Small pinkish-white blooms emerged on thin stems above the foliage. And prior to this I thought it couldn't get any stranger looking! The flowers are really not that amazing but the whole ensemble works for generating inquisitive looks. Zone 5 (probably Zone 4)

Dunce's Cap (Orostachys furusei) 4" Full sun. Late summer, early fall bloomer. Orange, creamy yellow flowers. Dunce's Cap is hard to describe…. You know how sometimes your heart just goes out to the ugliest runt of the litter and you feel like you have to give it a home? That's how I felt when I saw Dunce's Cap. I mean, even its name is sad. It has frosty blue-gray, succulent rosettes that hug the ground and then in late summer it sends up 'dunce's caps' of orange, creamy yellow flowers. It absolutely needs sharp draining, gravely soil. Being petite, it does nicely in containers, at the edge of paths or in a trough garden. Some sources list it as a Zone 6. Sunny Border Nursery, a nationally recognized wholesale perennial grower in Connecticut, lists it as Zone 4.

Tricolor Stonecrop (Sedum sieboldii mediovariegatum) 6" - 10" Sun. Late summer bloomer. Greenish-white and pink flowers. This is a strikingly different looking Sedum. It has soft yellow and frosty blue leaves with reddish-pink stems and a corkscrew growing habit. Like what?! A friend gave me a stem cutting of this fas-

photo courtesy of Daniele Ippoliti

cinating succulent and it has grown into a spectacular specimen. By the way, Sedums can be easily propagated by snipping a 3" to 4" stem tip and stripping off the lower leaves (keep two or three on the stem). Allow the cutting to 'cure' in the sun by laying it on the ground for 24 hours and then use a pencil to make a planting hole. Put the stem in (leaves up). No rooting hormone needed. Just be sure to keep it watered as it roots in. Zone 4

Variegated Solomon's Seal (Polygonatum 'Striatum') 18" - 24" Part Shade to Shade. Spring bloomer. White flowers. Many of you know the sold green leaved Solomon's Seal; some of you know the green leaved, white margined Solomon's Seal, but how many of you are acquainted with this one that has sweeping white lines throughout the leaves? It has little white flowers that dangle from stems in spring and then ripen to black berries. The flowers are mildly fragrant. It's a unique, low-maintenance shade lover. Zone 3

Orienpet, OT Lily (Lilium Orienpet) 3' - 6' Sun to Part Sun. Summer bloomer. White, pinks, yellow, raspberry-red, apricot and bicolor flowers. Orienpet lilies are very fragrant, towering liliums that steal the show in July when in full bloom. As the lilies mature, the bulbs get larger and larger producing flower stalks that can be over 1" in diameter. With this girth, they rarely need staking. This exotic beauty is the result of crossing Oriental Lilies and Trumpet Lilies. The resulting merger created huge, fragrant, outward facing blooms. It is fun to watch visitors in my gardens point towards the sky in astonishment as they gape at the flowers. I feel like I'm in a King Kong movie. Zone 4

Top Ten Fragrant Perennials

Picture a stand of heavily flowering lilacs. Take a deep breath. Doesn't the imaginary smell make you smile? Fragrance is the most powerful of all senses for triggering memories. Scents can quickly transport us back to a time in our past.

To get the most bang for your buck when designing with nature's 'AirWicks', consider the following when placing them:

- ✵ Locate them in a sheltered location so the perfume lingers. Usually the warmer the space, the more concentrated the aroma. Many fragrances are often stronger in the evening to attract pollinating night moths. Place plants in the vicinity where you spend time in the evening.
- ✵ Take note of the prevailing direction of breezes. Locate your garden downwind.
- ✵ Remember that low spots in your landscape also capture fragrance.
- ✵ Site fragrant plants near doorways, entertainment areas, patios, open windows, screened porches, gazebos and pathways.

Here are a few tips for selecting sweet-smelling perennials:

- ✵ The older varieties of flowers tend to be more fragrant. Hybridization for bigger and better blooms has not always benefited fragrance.
- ✵ Pick a mix of spring, summer and fall blooming fragrant plants for constant perfume.
- ✵ Remember to include some perennials with fragrant foliage. Their fragrance lasts spring through fall while flowers are only temporary. Some perennials with aromatic leaves (other than culinary herbs) include: Catmint, Lavender, Bee Balm, Geranium macrorrhizum, Gas Plant, Feverfew, Yarrow and Sweet Woodruff.
- ✵ In general, the lighter the flower color, the stronger the scent. White flowers tend to be the most fragrant. Others include off-white, pink, mauve, yellow and lavender.
- ✵ When researching plants, look for those labeled 'strongly or powerfully scented' verses 'lightly scented' to be sure you'll be able to easily smell them.
- ✵ Don't put too many fragrant perennials close together. Stronger scents can overwhelm more delicate ones plus when strong scents mingle the effect can be overpowering instead of pleasant. Think of being in car full of teenage boys 'cologned up with Axe' before a dance?

Oriental, Trumpet and Orienpet Lilies (assorted Liliums) 16" - 6' Sun to Part Sun. Summer bloomer. White, pink, red, yellow, orange, reddish-purple and bicolor flowers. These are all intoxicatingly fragrant. Plant Lilium bulbs as you would spring blooming bulbs, at a depth of three times the height of the bulb. To protect them from bulb-munching critters put chicken grit (crushed oyster shells) in the planting holes. Trumpet

and Orienpets tend to get taller than Orientals. All have yellow pollen that stains clothes or skin so don't get too close to sniff them. You shouldn't need to. As far as blooming, Trumpets are usually first out of the blooming gate, followed by Orienpets, Orientals bring up the rear. By planting all three types you will have fragrance in the garden from late June through August. Zone 4

🌱**Hosta** 16" - 36" Part Sun to Shade. Summer bloomer. White, lavender or purple flowers. Many gardeners admire Hosta for their leaves, not flowers. But there are knockout Hosta with fragrances that will have you sniffing the air. 'So Sweet' (green leaves with white margins, white flowers), 'Fragrant Blue' (blue leaves, lavender flowers), 'Guacamole' (chartreuse centers with blue-green margins, lavender flowers), 'Royal Standard' (green leaves, white flowers), 'Honeybells' (green leaves, violet flowers) and 'Fragrant Bouquet' (green leaves with creamy-yellow margins, white flowers). Hosta can be divided anytime spring until fall. If the plants have grown large, spring is the best time, just as the pips (tips) are breaking through the ground. At that point you are a lot bigger than they are and your confidence should be high. As the Nike ad states "Just do it!" Zone 3

🌱**Daylily** (Hemerocallis) 18" - 30" + Sun to Part Shade. Summer bloomer. All flower colors except blue. The white and yellow daylilies are the most fragrant. And when I refer to fragrant daylilies, I'm not including ones that I have to stick my nose into their throats for a mild whiff. For example, 'Stella D' Oro' is listed as a fragrant daylily. Come on now, really. The following daylilies have some real oomph to them: 'Sunday Gloves' (white, 27" tall), 'Hyperion' (yellow, 40"), 'Buttered Popcorn' (yellow, 32") and 'Amazing Grace' (yellow, 24"). Zone 3

Garden Heliotrope (Valeriana officinalis) 4' - 6' Sun to Part Shade. Summer bloomer. White flowers. Perennial Garden Heliotrope has ferny green leaves that stay within 1' to 2' of the ground. Long stems emerge from the foliage mounds to support fragrant white flowers in June and July that look like Queen Anne's Lace. After blooming, shear off the stems for a neater appearance. Zone 4

✛**Bugbane, Snakeroot** (Cimicifuga) 2' - 6' Part Sun to Part Shade. Late summer, fall bloomer. White and soft pink flowers. If I had to pick one perennial that was the most fragrant, it would be the chocolate-leaved Bugbanes. Their elegant, long 'candle-stick' flowers transmit their sweet aroma all over the property. The dark, ferny foliage is an elegant 'vase'. 'Brunette', 'Hillside Black Beauty' and 'Atropurpurea' all get 4' to 5' tall. 'Chocoholic' is the shortest at 2' to 3'. All have creamy white flowers. 'Pink Spires' has very soft pink blooms. If like me, you are itching for more of these beauties to plant around the property or to give to special friends, the best time to divide them is in spring. Zone 3

German Bearded Iris (Iris germanica) 29" - 38" Sun. Spring bloomer. Many flower colors. Some German Bearded Irises have no scent but others will make you swoon. 'Mariposa Skies; (light and dark blue, re-bloomer), 'Tour de France' (yellow and white), 'Polished Manners' (deep purple), 'Sea Power' (purple-blue), 'Clarence' (pale blue and purple, rebloomer) and 'Feed Back' (blue-violet, rebloomer) are solid choices. Zone 3

Herbaceous Peony (Paeonia lactiflora) 24" - 40" Sun to Part Sun. Spring bloomer. White, pink and red flowers. Peonies are known for their cottage elegance and long-lived nature. Plus many are quite fragrant. 'Eden's Perfume' (white double), 'Monsieur Jules Elie' (rich pink, double), 'Pink Parfait' (pink, double), 'Raspberry Sunday' (white with red markings, double), 'Festiva Maxima' (white with pink markings, double) and 'Sarah Bernhardt' (soft pink, double) will tickle your nose. When cutting flowers to bring inside, make sure to wash off any gypsy ants. The ants do no harm to peonies; they are simply after the sugary syrup the buds emit. Live and let live. Zone 3

Lavender (Lavendula) 12" - 3' Sun. Summer bloomer. Lavender and white flowers. I have a very difficult time growing Lavender in my gardens. They demand hot, sunny locations with sharp drainage. Many Lavenders are only hardy to Zone 6 so check the cultivar before plopping one in your Zone 5 garden (dream on if you are zone 3 or 4). Some more reliable ones are 'Munstead' (lavender, 12' - 16") and 'Hidcote' (lavender, 16"). Some say mulching these prima donnas with white marble chips helps. The stones store heat, reflect light and increase drainage. Personally, I have given up on growing lavender and have use Catmint (Nepeta) instead. Catmint looks similar to lavender and with a little lavender air freshener, smells like it too. Zone 5

Sweet Autumn Clematis (Clematis paniculata) 15'- 20' Sun to Part Sun. Late summer bloomer. White flowers. This heavily flowering Clematis has small white blooms that bury the leaves, resembling a 'blanket of snow'. It can be whacked down to within 8" of the ground each spring and it still scrambles to great heights and blooms in August. It looks divine sweeping over fences, stonewalls, arbors and shrubs. Zone 3

Jupiter's Beard (Centranthus rubre) 24" - 30" Sun. Summer bloomer. Pink and white flowers. I love these old-fashioned flowers with a bluish cast to their leaves. They prefer lean, fast draining soil on the sweet side (a pH of 7.0 –7.5). Jupiter's Beard is one of the few perennials for which I have garden envy. They just don't want to live in my garden. Shucks. Zone 5 (although some sources list them as Zone 4)

Top Ten Butterfly and Hummingbird Perennials

Being the queen of time and money-saving shortcuts that pay big dividends, I decided to provide tips for attracting both of these magical creatures. Many of the same environmental conditions and flowers hit their hot buttons. These winged beauties add color and motion to our gardens, not to mention playing an invaluable role in pollination. Unfortunately I am seeing fewer and fewer butterflies, especially monarchs, in my gardens. It's eerie. Has 'Silent Spring' finally arrived? I pray not.

In addition to planting some of the listed perennials, the following suggestions will make your property a highly favored 'landing strip' for butterflies and hummingbirds:

- Choose a sunny spot sheltered from wind for your garden. If your property is an open area, create a wind barrier with small trees or a fence. A location near a wild meadow is even better, providing a greater diversity of plant material.
- Site the garden near trees and shrubs that provide shelter at night as well as in bad weather.
- Don't use pesticides!
- Don't put bird feeders or birdbaths near the garden. Really now.
- Provide early, mid and late blooming nectar sources.
- Specific to butterflies:
  - Accept the fact that there will be some foliage damage from the butterfly's caterpillar stage. If you can't stand looking at some leaf chomping, switch your focus to the butterfly that just fluttered by your head. Some perennials relished by the caterpillars are Hibiscus, Milkweed (Asclepias) and Parsley.
  - Create 'water puddles'. Butterflies can't drink from open water. They 'sip' from surface moisture on the ground or stones. All you need is a shallow spot where water puddles or make a 'fountain' by sinking a pail or bucket filled with wet sand in the ground.
- Specific to hummingbirds:
  - Hummingbirds migrate from Central America and usually start appearing in zone 5 areas by April. The colder the zone, the later they arrive.
  - Hummingbirds are attracted to flowers based on their color not fragrance. Bright colors are the most effective radars, especially red and orange. Once attracted to the garden, they may dine on less bright colored, tubular flowers.
  - Flower shapes are important. Hummingbirds feed from tubular-shaped flowers.
  - Flowering vines are popular with "hummers". Trumpet Vine, Clematis and Honeysuckle are great drinking fountains.
  - To further entice hummingbirds, hang a hummingbird feeder in the garden. To make your own solution, mix 1 part sugar to 4 parts water, boil for two minutes.

✤ **Bee Balm** (Monarda) 9" - 5' Sun to Part Sun. Summer bloomer. Red, white, pink, wine, purple and lavender flowers. The red flowering cultivars are the most effective for attracting both butterflies and hummingbirds. Mildew-resistant reds are 'Gardenview Scarlet'(3'), 'Jacob Cline'(5') and 'Fireball' (15"). Zone 3

🦋✤ **Butterfly Bush** (Buddleia) 4' - 10' Sun. Late summer, fall bloomer. Purple, pink, white and yellow flowers. Technically this is a shrub not an herbaceous perennial. But it is such a magnet for both creatures, I had to include it. Many resources list Butterfly Bush as a zone 6 plant, some say 5. I have wintered them over with success if I site them in a protected area away from winter winds. As added insurance I hoop chicken wire around them in November and then stuff raked leaves inside the hoop around the stems for added insulation. The time to prune Butterfly Bush is in early spring. Prune them back to within a foot of the ground. New shoots will soar forth and bear luscious blooms later that summer. If no shoots appear by the middle of May, sigh deeply, and decide if you want to roll the dice again. Zone 6 (some say Zone 5)

🦋✤ **Gayfeather** (Liatris) 12" - 4' Sun. Summer bloomer. Rosy-lavender and white flowers. Gayfeathers are bold, spiky perennials that mix-up the flower shapes in gardens. They hate wet soil, so site accordingly. 'Kobold' is the shortest of all the cultivars and earliest to greet butterflies and hummingbirds. L. punctata is an American Plains native and the most drought tolerant of all Gayfeathers. It can even handle hardpan clay. Gayfeathers flower from the top down so they can be easily pruned for weeks of great looking flowers. Zone 3

✤ **Hollyhock** (Alcea) 4' - 7' Sun. Summer bloomer. White, yellow, red, purple, pink, peach, burgundy and almost black flowers. Flowers can be single or double (pom-pom). Most Hollyhocks are biennials but the rugosa group is perennial in nature. Thankfully, all Hollyhocks are easy to start from seed so you can always have these old-fashioned knockouts in the garden. Plant them against buildings, fences or taller retaining walls to help their 'posture'. Rust is a common problem with Hollyhocks. Rust looks like orange or yellow 'bumps' (pustules) on the leaves. It is caused by a fungus in the soil. Pick off infected leaves and dispose of them in the garbage, not compost pile. As of this book's publication, I still do not know of any really effective organic spray for Hollyhock rust. There are harsh chemicals but I refuse to use them. You should too. Zone 3

✤ **Cardinal Flower** (Lobelia cardinalis) 3' - 4' Sun to Part Shade. Summer, early fall bloomer. Red flowers. It is the bright red species Lobelia, cardinalis, native to much of North America, which is best for attracting both hummingbirds and butterflies. It prefers a moisture-retentive soil to do well. If this is not your soil's natural condition, work in organic matter such as compost, manure or leaf mold along with some peat moss to the planting area. Cardinalis will reseed easily when happy. Zone 3

Coral Bell (Heuchera) 8" - 15" Sun to Part Shade. Summer bloomer. Red flowers. Red flowering coral bells are the bell ringer for both hummingbirds and butterflies. 'Firefly', 'Splendens', 'Mt. St. Helens' and 'Ruby Bells' all have brilliant red flowers and green foliage. 'Hercules' and 'Mardi Gras' have variegated green and white leaves with red flower while 'Cherries Jubilee' 'Hollywood', and 'Vesuvius' have darker burgundy-chocolate leaves and, yes, red flowers. Zone 3

Aster (Aster) 12" - 4' Sun to Part Sun. Fall bloomer. White, purple, pink, red and lavender flowers. Asters celebrate the cooler fall weather with blasts of blooms. Hummingbirds and butterflies gladly join the celebration by dining on their nectar-laden flowers before their long migratory trip. The Woods series is very resistant to mildew, a fungus that causes many Asters to get ratty lower stems. Zone 3

Catmint (Nepeta) 8" - 36" Sun to Part Sun. Summer bloomer. Lavender, purple, white, pink and blue flowers. Some of my favorites are 'Blue Wonder' (15"- 20"), 'Snowflake' (12"- 15"), 'Walker's Low' (24"- 36") and 'Six Hills Giant' (2'- 3'). Shear back Catmints in mid-summer for a neater appearance and second round of flowers. Zone 3

Tall Garden Phlox (Phlox paniculata) 15" - 48" Sun to Part Sun. Summer bloomer. Red, white, pinks, lavender, purple, orange and bicolor flowers. The mounded, fragrant flowers of Phlox are one of my favorites. My Mom's garden had masses of these that were cut to fill flower vases in our house. It seems butterflies and hummingbirds are equally enamored with them. Thanks to hybridizing there are many varieties of dwarf phlox that are perfect for smaller gardens and containers. Zone 3

Wand Flower (Gaura) 15" - 3' Sun. Summer bloomer. White and pink flowers. Wand Flower is not reliably hardy in zone 5 or colder but it does reseed where happy. Given that hummingbirds, butterflies and humans are drawn to it for its beauty, length of bloom, nectar and low-maintenance attributes, it is a keeper on this list. Zone 5

Bees, especially honeybees, are important pollinators in our gardens. This is good. But some folks understandably become un-nerved around bees, especially if they're allergic to bee stings. It also makes sense to give busy bees their space. Locate bee-magnet perennials away from entranceways, entertainment areas, swimming pools and other gathering spots. Fragrant perennials are usually favorites for bees. Many of the perennials on this list fall in this category.

Sage 'Purple Rain' (Salvia verticillata) 14"- 20" Sun. Summer bloomer. Violet, smokey-purple and white flowers. Lots of gardeners are familiar with the stiff white, pink or purple spiked perennial Sages but the verticillata gang is different. The flowers are fuller bodied with an arching habit. The leaves are also larger and have a gray tone. Bees love all Sages but especially the verticillatas. In addition to 'Purple Rain' there is also 'Endless Love' (lighter purple) and 'White Rain' (white). If you deadhead these, they will bloom non-stop through September. Zone 4

Stonecrop (Sedum) 3" - 36" Sun to Part Sun. Summer, fall bloomer. Brick red, pink, white, yellow and purple-pink flowers. Sedums are 'chameleons'. They can be ground-hugging summer bloomers or tall, upright 'broccoli' plants that flower in fall. All their flowers lure bees. Pinch back taller cultivars in early July for shorter, stiffer stemmed, blooming plants in fall. Zone 3

Bugbane, Snakeroot (Cimicifuga) 2' - 6' Part Sun to Part Shade. Late summer, fall bloomer. White and soft pink flowers. The chocolate-leaved Bugbanes are elegant, fragrant dining halls for bees. Because they bloom in August and September, they provide a valuable late season pollen source. It also helps that the majority of Bugbanes are tall, requiring they be placed in the back of the border away from human admirers. Zone 3

Thoroughwort (Eupatorium hyssopifolium) 2' - 3' Sun. Late summer, fall bloomer. White flowers. A mass of delicate fuzzy flowers billow above fine foliage starting in September. It is extremely drought and heat tolerant and does best in well drained soil. Zone 4

photo courtesy of Jacob Davis

Hyssop (Agastache) 18" - 3' Sun. Summer bloomer. Shades of purple, blue, pink and apricot flowers. This herb enjoys fast-draining, sandy soil in a hot, sunny location. Be aware that most Hyssops, including many apricot and pink varieties, are rated for Zone 6. I've had great success with 'Blue Fortune' (one of the few Zone 4 Hyssops) as well as 'Golden Jubilee' (bright yellow leaves and lavender-blue flowers). I buy the pink and apricot varieties in 4" pots for under $3 and treat them as low-maintenance annuals. All Hyssops can be pinched in late May for more compact, lush flowering plants. Zone 4

Pincushion Flower (Scabiosa) 6" - 3' Sun. Summer bloomer. Blue, pink, yellow white and lavender flowers. Mounded foliage sends up wiry stalks topped with 'pincushion' looking flowers. Less common are 'Moondance' with lemon-yellow flowers and ochroleuca with very pale yellow flowers. The caucasica group can be short-lived. Zone 4

Joe Pye Weed (Eupatorium fistulosum or maculata) 4'- 8' Late summer, early fall bloomer. Pink flowers. Give these boys room. They can get big, both in girth and height. Even 'Little Joe' that was only supposed to get between 3'- 4' was bumping the 5' mark in my garden. Now there is a 'Baby Joe' that is advertised as only getting 24" -30" tall (maybe that's in its first month). Zone 3

Sea Holly (Eryngium) 6" - 3' Sun. Summer bloomer. Various shades of blue and white flowers. Sea holly has mounded seed heads that sit on 'plates' (bracts) of finely cut leaves in July and August. Some varieties have huge flowers while others look more like thimbles. 'Jade Frost' is the first variegated Sea Holly with showy pink, white and green leaves. 'Blue Hobbit' has steely blue flowers and only gets 8" - 12" tall in full bloom. 'Mrs. Wilmott's Ghost' has bewitching white flowers. It is considered a biennial or short-lived perennial. Zone 4

Thyme (Thymus) 1" - 12" Sun to Part Sun. Late spring, early summer bloomer. Pink, reddish-pink, white and lavender flowers. Most varieties form creeping mats that work well between stepping stones or cascading over walls. 'Peter Davis' is the Jolly Green Giant with dark green leaves and soft pink flowers reaching 12" tall. 'Albus' is a pristine white at the other end of the height scale. It is only 1" tall. Zone 3

Catmint (Nepeta) 8" - 40" Sun. Summer bloomer. Lavender, white and blue-purple flowers. Catmints do best in lean, well drained soil with no fertilizer. They can be sheared back to within 3" to 4" of the ground after the first bloom to create a neat mound and another flush of flowers. Catmints benefit from division every three years for more compact plants. Divide in spring or after the first round of flowers. Zone 3

I am without a doubt a passionate plant collector. I am also broke. But how can a monetary value be placed on the joy one gets when seeing Symphytum 'Axminister Gold' in bloom? Who needs food?

Every year I have a list of plants I'm on the hunt for. We all do, don't we? Here are the newest ones on my list. If you find any of these first, please leave one for me. J

Alpine Clematis (Clematis 'Pamela Jackman') Sun - Part Sun. Spring bloomer. Blue flowers. This clematis blooms earlier than others, bursting into bloom in May. 'Pamela Jackman' has rich dark blue, nodding flowers and grows to 10' - 12'. It blooms on old wood, so a medium to hard shear after blooming is all it needs to keep looking great. 'Pamela' is in the same family line as the ever-popular 'Jackmanii'. Another great thing about 'Pamela Jackman' is it never gets clematis wilt, a fungal disease that attacks many larger flowering clematis. Zone 4

Lady's Slipper Orchid (Cypripedium) Part Shade - Shade. Spring bloomer. Yellow, white, pink and bicolor flowers. Lady Slippers are not a flower for beginners. They can be very temperamental and finicky and at $60 or more per plant, mistakes can be costly. Lady Slippers like organically rich soil with good drainage. An ephemeral, they go dormant after blooming. And needless to say, as a protected wildflower you cannot harvest these from the wild. That is why legally propagated ones grown from seed are so expensive. It can take a minimum of seven years to grow one to flowering size. Plant Delights Nursery (www.plantdelights.com) and Roots & Rhizomes (www.rootsrhizomes.com) both carry these beauties. Zone 3

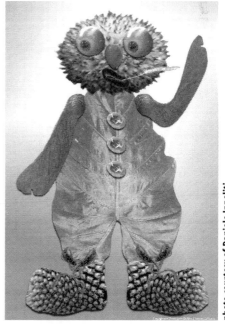

photo courtesy of Daniele Ippoliti

Elephant's Ear 'Lime Zinger' (Xanthosoma) Part Shade. Summer bloomer. White flowers. I have been on the look out for this plant for years. It is a tropical with huge chartreuse leaves that can get 18" long and 12" across. It grows between 3' and 4' depending on how rich the soil. It looks very similar to Elephant Ears (Colocasia) but is actually in a different family. Having said this, if you saw Colocasia 'Elena' you probably couldn't tell the two apart. Either one would work for me! As with other tropicals, 'Lime Zinger' needs to be brought in for the winter. The easiest way to do this is to plant it in a pot, dig the pot into the garden for the summer, and then remove it before the first hard frost to winter over in a cool, dry place inside. I know this doesn't sound like low-maintenance, it is not. I'm lovesick for it so all common sense is tossed to the wind. Pity me.

⊹Comfrey 'Axminster Gold' (Symphytum) Sun - Part Shade. Late spring, early summer bloomer. Lavender-blue flowers. I first saw this spectacular plant in one of my patron's gardens. I was awestruck by it. Its huge, sweeping gray-green and gold leaves are incredible. It produces nodding lavender-blue flowers in spring. 'Axminster Gold' demands sharp drainage and enjoys a nutrient rich soil. It is primarily grown for its leaves. After flowering, whack it back hard to encourage a fresh new foliage display. It can get 2' to 4' tall. Zone 4

⊹Rodger's Flower p. 'Rotaub' (Rodgersia) Sun - Part Shade. Summer bloomer. Creamy white flower. Like all Rodger's Flowers, 'Rotaub's leaves are huge and flashy. Stems of large bronzy-red palmate leaves (five leaves from a central axle) make a fantastic spring display. But the show is not over. In July 'Rotaub' struts sensational, astilbe-like flowers that get up to 5'. It needs a moisture-retentive, nutrient rich soil to thrive. Zone 5 (some sources say Zone 4)

'Ramblin' Red' Climbing Rose Sun - Part Sun. Summer, fall bloomer. Red flowers. 'Ramblin' Red' is from the Knockout line of roses so you know it is a winner. It has medium red flowers on 6' to 8' canes. 'Ramblin Red' boasts the same great flowering habit as its siblings as well as their ability to resist black spot and other fungal diseases. But 'Ramblin Red' is hardier than other family members. It can handle Zone 3 weather just fine whereas most Knockouts only tolerate Zone 4 or 5. Growers also claim the canes are so tough they do not require extra winter protection. We shall see! 'Ramblin Red' may finally be the first, truly ever-blooming, climbing rose. 'Dawn' and 'New Dawn', although marketed as long blooming climbers, have disappointed me.

•Yellow Peony 'Bartzella' Sun - Part Sun. Spring bloomer. Yellow flowers. 'Bartzella' is actually an intersectional peony, a cross between a tree peony and a traditional peony. Although many intersectional crosses are now coming to market, 'Bartzella' is still considered by many to be the best yellow on the market. The flowers are 7" to 8" wide and it grows 36" – 42" tall. I have seen 4" pots of 'Bartzella' selling for around $75 but a plant this size would require a number of years to grow into flower blooming size. I am looking for either a two or three gallon specimen. Call me impatient. Intersectional peonies will die back to the ground like herbaceous ones, unlike tree peonies that maintain a woody structure in winter. Zone 4

Umbrella Leaf (Diphylleia cymosa) Part Shade - Shade. Spring, summer bloomer. White flowers. Here is another plant that I'm eye-balling for its unique architectural attributes. It has large, umbrella-like leaves that can span 18". Dainty white flowers appear in spring and then turn into attractive blue berries on red stems in summer. It grows between 1' and 3' tall. It is a perfect plant for a woodland, low-maintenance garden. Zone 5 (but some sources say Zone 4)

⚜**Woodland Peony** (Paeonia obovata) Part Shade - Shade. Spring bloomer. Pink flowers. This is quite similar to another Woodland Peony I have, Peony japonica but obovata has lush pink flowers and blooms after japonica. Like japonica, it gets 18" tall, has textured gray-green leaves, and the flowers ripens to show seeds later in summer. Zone 4

⚜**Japanese Angelica Tree 'Silver Umbrella'** (Aralia elata) Sun - Part Sun. Summer bloomer. White flowers. I have been trying to find this plant for years. Imagine my surprise when I saw a sweep of these last summer when I was speaking at the Coastal Maine Botanical Gardens in Boothbay, Maine. These striking plants have green and white variegated leaves and white flowered panicles in July and August. The flowers ripen to shiny blue-black berries in fall. It is a multi-stemmed shrub reaching 40". Zone 4.

Top Ten Poisonous Perennials

It makes sense to be aware of this group if you have children or pets that like to put things in their mouths. Poisonous perennials are invaluable where deer, rabbits, groundhogs and other invaders nosh beyond acceptable limits. Before you think I'm a monster, relax. Wildlife are too smart to ingest enough of a poisonous plant to hurt themselves. One nibble and they move on to something more palatable.

photo courtesy of Robin Wolfe, Wolfe Enterprises

✝Monkshood (Aconitum) 12" - 5' Part Sun to Shade. Summer, fall bloomer. Violet, blue, purple, white, soft pink and bicolor flowers. These resemble Delphiniums but are longer-lived and can handle shade. Some Monkshood like nappellus (blue, 4'- 5'), 'Bicolor' (white with blue edges, 4'-5') 'Cloudy' (soft blue, 24") and 'Blue Lagoon' (blue, 12") bloom in July and August. Others postpone the show until fall. 'Arendsii' (violet, 4'), 'Barker's Variety' (violet-blue, 5') and carmichaelii or fischeri (wedgewood blue, 4') start in September and carry the color baton into fall. Many Monkshood have deep green, shiny leaves. Zone 3

✿✝Lily of the Valley (Convallaria) 6" - 8" Sun to Shade. Spring bloomer. White and pink flowers. Lily of the Valley is a well known groundcover for its ability to handle extreme conditions. Its heavenly fragrance is a harbinger of spring and a popular scent for air fresheners, laundry sheets and perfumes. Zone 3

✿✝Lenten Rose (Helleborus) 12"- 24" Part Sun to Shade. Spring bloomer. White, yellow, pink, red, burgundy as well as multicolors. Deep green, leathery leaves are semi-evergreen in zones 5 and colder. Most cultivars have nodding flowers but some newer introductions like 'Ivory Prince' have upward facing flowers. Prune off brown, ratty looking leaves in late winter to trigger fresh new foliage. Lenten Rose is one of the few woodland perennials that prefers a slightly sweet soil (7.0-7.5 pH). Check your soil's pH to see if a correction is needed. I work lime into the soil around my Lenten Roses in the fall to compensate for the towering, shade-producing oak trees (oak leaves are acidic). Zone 5 and colder.

Perennial Foxglove (Digitalis) 2' - 3' Sun to Part Shade. Late spring, early summer bloomer. Pink, yellow, creamy-tan flowers. Zone 3

Ornamental Rhubarb (Rheum) 48" - 60" Sun to Part Sun. Summer bloomer. Pink flowers. This oversized rhubarb looks like it should be in the middle of a tropical rain forest. It has dark green, glossy leaves with purple undersides and rich pink plumes. Given its massive leaves, this is not tolerant of dry sites. It is definitely a plant of fanatical proportions and satisfactory reactions. 'Ace of Hearts' has done fabulously in my garden. Zone 5

Common Tansy (Tanacetum vulgare) 24" - 48" Sun. Summer bloomer. Yellow flowers. This herb has yellow, button-like flowers and green ferny foliage. I made the mistake of planting it in my garden years ago and it became an invasive thug. I liked drying the flowers for arrangements but eventually I decided to 'dry' the entire plant. Zone 3

Rue (Ruta graveolens) 1'- 2' Sun. Summer bloomer. Yellow flowers. This herb has blue, mounded foliage with medium yellow flowers in summer. A milky white sap is released when pruned that can cause skin irritations for those with sensitive skin. Zone 5

Mayapple (Podophyllum peltatum) 6" - 18" Part Shade to Shade. Spring bloomer. White flowers. Mayapple has one or two divided leaves that spring forth from a single stalk. It looks like a big, halved umbrella. The rhizome (root) is the most poisonous part of the plant. Zone 4

Colchicum (Autumn Crocus) 6" Sun to Part Sun. Fall bloomer. White, pink and purple flowers. Many folks think that these are crocus but they are actually in a different family. They are sometimes called 'Naked Ladies' because their foliage comes up earlier in the year, dies back, and the flowers appear on slender stalks, leafless, in fall. Zone 4

Chinese Lanterns (Physalis) 12"- 24" Sun to Part Sun. Fall bloomer. Orange flowers. Folks love to dry these fun, lantern-shaped flowers for fall decoration but be aware the unripe berries and leaves are poisonous. Chinese Lanterns are very, very, very (read as very) invasive. Zone 3

Top Ten 'Blue'-tiful Perennials

Got the blues? I'm not referring to how you may feel as the kids or grandchildren argue over whose turn it is on the X-Box or Playstation. Rather, I am talking about blue flowers in perennial gardens. True blue is such a breathtaking color and an elusive one in the flower world. Thankfully, there are some flowers that come close. Allow me to introduce you to some "blue-tiful" perennials.

✛**Virginia Bluebells** (Mertensia) 12" - 24" Part Sun to Shade. Spring bloomer. Delicate, nodding flowers adorn soft green leaves on arching stems in April and May. After the mesmerizing plant awes bystanders, it goes dormant in early summer. But do not fear, it will come back next spring. Because Virginia Bluebells is an ephemeral, place it where its absence will go unnoticed. I plant it between large Hosta. When the Bluebells disappear, large unfurling Hosta leaves cover their exit. Zone 3

🍂✛**Geranium 'Rozanne'** 18" - 20" Sun to Part Sun. Summer, fall bloomer. 'Rozanne' won the Perennial Plant Association's vote as the Perennial of the Year in 2008. And it wins mine for one of the easiest, longest blooming perennials I've ever grown. The blue-violet flowers open in June and continue through October with no deadheading. Other blue blooming hardy geraniums include 'Brookside' (blue with a white center), 'Jolly Bee' (looks like 'Rozanne' but gets taller, 20" - 24") and 'Johnson's Blue'. Zone 4

✛**Larkspur** (Delphinium) 10" - 6' Sun to Part Sun. Early summer bloomer with a second flush in late summer. The dwarf Delphiniums in the grandiflorum group have some of the most radiant blue flowers. 'Blue Butterfly' (14"), 'Summer Blues' (10"- 12"), and 'Blue Dwarf' (10") have finely cut foliage with masses of flowers. Taller 'sky-reaching' varieties are 'Blue Bird' (5'- 6), 'Blue Jay' (5' - 6'), 'Royal Aspirations' (4' - 6') and 'Sunny Skies' (4' - 6'). All Delphiniums are short-lived perennials. If they make three years, celebrate. If longer, do the Snoopy dance. Zone 3

Gentian (Gentiana) 8"- 30" Sun to Part Shade. Summer, fall bloomer. 'True Blue' has bright blue, upward facing, bell-shaped flowers that open in mid-summer and continue into early fall. It can get 24" - 30" tall. Closed Gentian (andrewsii) has deeper blue, 'closed' tubular flowers and stays shorter at 12" - 18". Crested Gentian (Gentian septemfida) has brilliant blue, open-faced flowers with white throats. It stays 8" and it best planted in multiples. Zone 4

🍂✛**Flax** (Linum) 8" - 24" Sun . Summer bloomer. Flax has gently arching stems and petite leaves. The delicate flowers open in the morning and then drop their petals early afternoon, leaving a delightful confetti blanket around the plant's base. The next day, the party starts again. Sharp drainage is a must. Flax is a short-lived perennial and

🍂drought tolerant   ✛deer resistant

best purchased in 4" pots. They are fast growers and will flower the same season. 'Sapphire', perenne, and 'Nanum Sapphire' are popular varieties. Zone 5

⚜ **Speedwell** (Veronica) 6" - 30" Sun to Part Sun. Summer bloomer. Speedwell is a popular, forgiving perennial. Deadhead it a little and it will be happy. The taller varieties can have a 'relaxed posture'. They benefit from staking or neighboring perennials they can lean against for support. 'Sunny Border Blue' (18" - 24") was the Perennial of the Year in 1993 with its dark blue flowers and spinach-like leaves. Other rich blue bloomers are 'Royal Candles' (15" - 18"), 'Goodness Grows' (12" - 18"), 'High Five' (28") and 'Darwin's Blue' (18"). 'Crater Lake Blue' is the first blue Veronica to bless the gardens in spring. It reaches 12" - 15" and can get floppy, but no one notices because of its so shimmering blue. Shear 'Crater Lake Blue' down to 2" of the ground after flowering for a neat mat the rest of the season. Zone 3

🌿⚜ **Siberian Iris** and **German Bearded Iris** (Iris siberica and germanica) 28" - 38" Sun Spring bloomer. There are a number of rich blue flowering irises in both of these families. Some of my favorite blue Siberian Iris include 'Flight of Butterflies', 'Silver Edge' and 'Harpswell Hallelujah'. German Bearded Iris include 'Blue Suede Shoes' (rebloomer), 'Princess Caroline de Monica' and 'Monet's Blue'. For more about Irises, visit the American Iris Society's web site at www.irises.org. Zone 3

🌿⚜ **Stokes Aster** (Stokesia laevis) 8" - 20" Sun. Summer bloomer. I love the huge, disc-shaped flowers of Stokes Aster. The foliage is smooth, narrow and mounded. 'Blue Danube' (15") is an old favorite. 'Elf' is a dwarf version of 'Blue Danube' topping out at 8". 'Klaus Jellito', 'Peachie's Pick' and 'Blue Star' are other Stokes Asters that do a great job singing the blues. Zone 5

⚜ **Siberian Bugloss** (Brunnera) 10" - 15" Part Shade to Shade. Spring bloomer. Siberian Bugloss is also commonly known as False-Forget-Me-Not because of its dazzling blue flowers that look just like Forget-Me-Nots on elongated stems. Mounded leaves can be solid green or display silver, creamy yellow or white markings. 'Jack Frost' has silvery leaves with green veins; 'Looking Glass' has solid silver leaves; and B. 'Variegata' and 'Hadspen Cream' have green leaves with bold white margins. Zone 3

🌿⚜ **Bellflower** (Campanula) 4" - 3' Sun to Part Sun. Summer bloomer. Bellflowers cup-shaped blooms are charming. I just wish they didn't need as much deadheading to finish the summer strong. There are single and double petaled flowers. Some like 'Blue Clips' (in the carpatica group) are short mounded plants. Others like Peach-Leaf Bellflower (in the persicifolia group) have long stems that shoot up from narrow-leaved foliage mounds. There are even some gold leafed cultivars like 'Dickson's Gold' that do better in part shade. Zone 3

Top Ten Daylilies

I am stating a disclaimer right from the get-go. There are so many superstar daylilies on the market that to only pick ten is truly impossible. But because it's the book's theme, I will do my best. Just don't stop with these ten.

Daylilies do best in full to part sun but I have also planted them in part shade and dappled light with success. Just be aware that in lower light, they will stretch their 'necks' (scapes) to find the sun. Take this into account when siting them. For instance, I will plant dwarf cultivars mid-border since they will grow taller in lower light than the tag indicates. They may also need their scapes staked to support their blooms. Or you can let the flowers rest their 'chins' on Hosta leaves.

Reblooming (repeat blooming, twice blooming) Daylilies double your pleasure by sending up new flower scapes once the first round has finished. Many of the older Daylilies only bloom for three to four weeks before the curtain falls. Rebloomers return for a curtain call.

Daylilies do not need fertilizer to perform well. A nutrient-rich mulch such as aged compost, manure or finely shredded wood does just fine. But if your maternal or paternal instincts nag you, then fertilize in May with a time-released, organic fertilizer like Plant-Tone. Divisions can be done anytime before or after flowering. Be careful not to plant Daylilies too deep or their flowering may be effected. Lastly, as their name suggests, each Daylily blooms last for one day. Once spent, you can let them drop off naturally or deadhead for a neater appearance. Pinch off the spent bloom right at its base. Don't deadhead like my son. I caught him shaking the entire stalk to whip off old blooms. Unfortunately new buds were also spinning from the throttling.

☙'Siloam Amazing Grace' 24" Soft lemony-yellow flowers with very ruffled edges. The petal's have a faint white stripe down the center. The flowers are 5.5" wide and very fragrant.

☙'Sunday Gloves' 27" Satiny white flowers with a soft yellow throat (the funnel where the petals come together). The flowers are 5.25" wide and very fragrant. Repeat bloomer. 'Joan Senior' is another great white Daylily.

☙'Custard Candy' 24" Creamy white flowers sport a dark raspberry-red eye (the ring around the throat). The flowers are 4.25" wide.

☙drought tolerant   ✝deer resistant

🌿 **'Catherine Neal'** 30" This is the richest purple Daylily I've ever seen. It also has a striking chartreuse-green throat. The flowers are 6" wide. Repeat bloomer.

🌿 **'South Seas'** 30" Sizzling tangerine-coral blooms with ruffled edges. The flowers are 5" wide and mildly fragrant. Repeat bloomer.

🌿 **'Baja'** 30" Rich red blooms with a yellow throat. The flowers are 6" wide. Some catalogs list this as a repeat bloomer. All I can say is it's one of the longest blooming Daylilies in my gardens.

🌿 **'Chicago Apache'** 30" Vibrant red with some ruffling on the edges. The flowers are 5" wide. This Daylily doesn't start to open until late July and blooms into September.

🌿 **'Cherry Cheeks'** 28" Cherry rosy-pink flowers. The flowers are 6" wide. Very showy and long blooming.

🌿 **'Pandora's Box'** 24" Creamy white flowers with a cranberry-purple eye. The flowers are 4" wide. Repeat bloomer. Mildly fragrant.

🌿 **'Moonlight Masquarde'** 26" Creamy white flowers with a very wide, deep purple eye. The flowers are 6" wide. Repeat bloomer.

Top Ten Coral Bells

You've hit 'The Easy Button' with Coral Bells. They're no-brainers, my kind of perennial. Drought tolerant, low or nil on the critter buffet, tolerant of most light conditions and can go years without dividing. Their only bad habit is occasionally popping up out of the ground in spring as a result of soil temperature fluctuations. Correct the 'uprising' by pressing Coral Bells back down into the soil or have fun stepping gently on them as I do. I also 'deadleaf' Coral Bells in spring and mid-summer by pruning off the outer, lower rim of leaves for a fresher look.

Coral Bells should be divided when they get large and 'woody' looking. Dig then entire clump out of the ground and use a sharp knife to cut into sections. Make sure each piece has a root and some stems. If the Coral Bell has flowers on it, shear these off. The real trick to getting divisions to take off is replanting them 1" to 2" deeper then they originialy were. Water them in well after resetting and tamping the soil down. All the Coral Bells on this list are hardy to at least Zone 4.

'Caramel' 12" Large caramel leaves that glow in sun or shade make this one of my top 'connector' plants between beds. The flowers are creamy white. I prefer to shear them off and let the foliage take center stage. 'Caramel' is much more robust than 'Peach Melba' and 'Marmalade', although I like these almost as much. 'Georgia Peach' is a belle with more of a peachy-silver coloring. 'Amber Waves' has gotten low ratings in my trials; it tends to wimp out over time. 'Ginger Ale' fizzled out right from the start.

'Snow Angel' 10" - 15" 'Snow Angel's bright green and white flecked leaves and perky pink flowers always draw attention. 'Hercules' has the same foliage but red flowers.

'Firefly' 18" Green mounds are covered by bright red flowers that flag in hummingbirds. Other high point scoring look-alikes with red flowers include 'Splendens' and 'Ruby Bells'.

'Green Spice' 9" - 12" I use this coral bell strictly for its leaves. The creamy white flowers are ho-hum. Foliage is green, silver and red that become more brilliant in fall.

'Citronelle' 12" Bright, non-glossy yellow leaves with silvery undersides make eye-popping mounds in shade. In heavier shade the leaves turn green-yellow. This is another Coral Bell where I sacrifice ho-hum creamy flowers for the leaves. Other fetching yellow Coral Bells include 'Key Lime Pie' and 'Lime Rickey'.

'Midnight Rose' 10" This has dark, purple-black leaves with hot pink spots. Rumba! Flowers are creamy-white and should be forfeited.

drought tolerant   deer resistant

'Plum Pudding' 8" 'Palace Purple' was the first non-green leaved coral bell to wow the plant industry. Now there are many cultivars that display richer purple coloring and that this color better in summer. 'Plum Pudding' is one of them. Its rich purple leaves and undersides are royal winners. Other good purple leaved choices include 'Stormy Seas' and 'Guardian Angel'. All have creamy-white flowers.

'Venus' 8" Silver leaves with purple veining make 'Venus' a winner. Its soft pink flowers are also jewels. Others with a silvery sheen include 'Mystic Angel' (white flowers) and 'Silver Scrolls' (pink flowers).

photo courtesy of PerennialResource.com

'Hollywood' 8" Purple leaves contrast well with blazing ruby-red flowers. Other great purple leaved coral bells with red flowers include 'Vesuvius', 'Veil of Passion' and 'Cherries Jubilee'.

'Dolce Mocha Mint' This has to be one of the longest blooming Coral Bells I've grown. Fuchsia pink flowers dance above silver and purple leaves all summer and well into fall.

Top Ten Coneflowers

There have been so many coneflowers entering the market that I felt compelled to point out some of the great ones as well as others that probably should have been field tested longer.

First let me sing the praises of this plant family. Coneflowers are sensational wildflowers native to the Eastern United States. They thrive on neglect, lean soil, sun and heat. Their only peeve is poorly draining soil or rich, loamy soil. I learned the second dislike the hard way. I kept losing 'fashionably new' cultivars until a gentleman in one of my classes explained it was probably because I had great soil. Coneflowers are prairie plants enjoying sandy, low fertility soil. He told me how to fix the problem. Create crummy soil conditions in the spots where I wanted Coneflowers by removing my rich loam and replacing it with poor soil (I snuck some from my neighbor's garden). I even tossed in handfuls of gravel to insure great drainage. Worked like a charm!

Other 'Conefactors' to be aware of include:
- ❀ Funky cultivars like 'Doubledecker' (two-tiered flowers) and 'Razzmatazz' (big pom-pom flowers) usually don't develop their unusual look until the second year.
- ❀ Many Coneflowers are promoted as fragrant, some are even said to smell like roses. Someone's nose is stretching . Even 'Fragrant Angel', a large white coneflower billed as being heavenly scented, registers zippo with me.
- ❀ Dwarf Coneflowers have a tendency to want to be like their big brothers, tall. An industry joke is that 'Kim's Knee High' should be renamed 'Kim's Thigh High'. That was the case in my garden.
- ❀ Coneflowers are usually quite low on a deer's browse list. Reread the word usually.
- ❀ Finally, be aware that there is serious concern among some horticulturists that new cultivars are being released for sale too quickly. More field testing might be in order. This sadly was the case with a different plant, Coreopsis 'Limerock Ruby'. It was released as a Zone 5 perennial and then 'recalled' and released as a tender perennial (Zone 6 at best).

'All that Jazz' 30" - 36" Lavender-pink flowers. I've been so impressed with this coneflower. It blooms July through October with little or no deadheading. It has a very unique appearance with skinny petals which are spaced farther apart than most Coneflowers. Zone 4

'Magnus' 24" - 36" Rosy-pink flowers. This is one of the 'good old boys', winning the Perennial Plant Association's vote as the Perennial Plant of the Year in 1998. The flowers start out deep pink and fade as they age. The cones are flatter, not as dome-shaped, as other cultivars at that time. Zone 3

'Ruby Star' 24" - 36" Rosy-pink flowers. This is the new, improved 'Magnus' (although it too will be trumped by newer cultivar). 'Ruby Star's petals are richer pink and held more horizontally than 'Magnus'. Zone 3

'Ruby Giant' 36" - 48"" Ruby-pink flowers. Move over 'Ruby Star'. 'Ruby Giant' super-sizes the bloom size. Flowers can be 7" across. Okay, who's next? Zone 3

'Sunrise' 30" - 36" Soft yellow flowers. This was one of the first of the newer Coneflowers I bought. I lost the first few until I started 'crumminizing' my soil. The buttery yellow flowers are sensational. Zone 4

'Razzmatazz' 24" - 36" Rich lavender-pink flowers. I usually steer clear of flowers that look so funky that they border on ugly but 'Razzmatazz' won my heart. It has big pom-pom flowers with a little skirt of petals at their base. Zone 4

Tennesseensis 'Rocky Top' 18" - 30" Pink flowers. This Coneflower is different than others in that it stays shorter and displays narrower petals and leaves. The petals are spaced widely apart and held horizontally or even arch slightly skyward. Fast drainage is a must. Zone 3

'White Swan' 30" - 36" White flowers. 'White Swan' has been around for years. It's a tried-and-true white Coneflower with a golden-orange cone. As with other white Coneflowers, it does not set seed and sow about like many pinks. 'Fragrant Angel', 'Virgin' and 'Kim's Mophead' are also white. Zone 3

'Hope' 30" Soft pink flowers. I have yet to trial this recent introduction but I feel compelled to include it on this list. $.25 of each plant sold goes to breast cancer research. Having lost my mother to this awful disease, I will be purchasing a number of 'Hope's next spring with hopeful expectations on many levels. Zone 3

Big Sky series 30" - 40" Orange, dark magenta, orangey-yellow, melon and reddish-orange flowers. All of the Big Sky flowers are extremely striking in their coloration. The blooms are most intense when they first open and then fade. You can prune off fading flowers to keep pushing newer blooms. Zone 5

Top Ten Hosta

How can you not love Hosta? They ask for little but return great dividends. Their handsome leaves add texture and interest while shading the ground from pesky weeds. They're drought tolerant and do well in a range of soil types.

Hosta can have white, lavender or purples flowers. Depending on your perspective, these can either add to your garden's beauty or be pruned to draw more attention to the leaves. Personally, unless the flowers are white, rich purple or fragrant, they visit the compost pile.

Slugs and snails can be ruthless renegades in the shade bed. These slimers will munch holes and shred leaves. Check out my Top Ten list for dealing with their nonsense.

If deer are an issue (they usually are), the thicker and more puckered the leaves, the less likely they will be nibbled. Many blue-leaved Hosta are also snubbed.

Frosty blue leaved Hosta are one of my favorites. I love the solid colored blues: 'Fragrant Blue', sieboldiana 'Elegans', 'Halycon', 'Blue Mouse Ears', 'Blue Angel' 'Bressingham Blue', Blue Cadet', 'Blue Angel' and 'Love Pat'. Those with blue variegated leaves are also handsome: 'June' (blue and chartreuse), 'Frances Williams' (blue and chartreuse), 'Aristocrat' (blue and creamy white), 'El Nino' (blue and white), 'Regal Splendor' (blue and creamy yellow) and 'First Frost'(blue and white). Whichever blue Hosta you choose, site them in a shady spot. The blue coloration is actually from a waxy coating on the leaves which will 'melt off' in sun, revealing green leaves below. This meltdown will surely give you the blues.

Finally, realize that immature Hosta may not show the same rich coloration and markings of more mature Hosta. It takes them a few years to grow into their good looks. Hosta can also have quite the price range. Many of the more common (but good) ones sell for $5 to $10. Then there is 'My Child Insook' that holds the record for the highest price ever paid. Someone shelled out $4,100 for it at the 1998 American Hosta Society's Convention auction. Choices, choices.

(Note: the height given is for the foliage mound, not flower scapes)

'Frances Williams' 22" - 28' White flowers. Huge, thick blue and chartreuse leaves with heavy puckering make this a popular pick for many gardens.

sieboldiana 'Elegans' 22" - 24" White flowers. Solid blue, thick puckered leaves. The leaves can get one foot across.

'June' 15" Pale lavender flowers. This has to be one of the most asked about Hosta in my gardens. It was the Hosta of the Year in 2001. Blue margins wrap around chartreuse centers.

montana 'Aureomarginata' 27" Soft lavender flowers. Bright yellow leaves edged by narrow dark green rims. This Hosta has an upright, vase shape that distinguishes it from many others. The leaves are very long and ribbed.

'Sagae' 28" Lavender flowers. Huge, undulating leaves with blue, gray-green centers and creamy yellow margins. A favorite of many. Hosta of the Year in 2000.

'Blue Mouse Ears' 6" Lavender flowers. Cute, cute, cute. This petite Hosta has blue, cup-shaped, round leaves. It was the Hosta of the Year in 2008.

'Guacamole' 22" White flowers. Large, ribbed chartreuse leaves with irregular dark green margins make it very showy. The flowers are one of the most fragrant of all Hosta.

'Praying Hands' 14" - 18" Lavender flowers. Very narrow dark green leaves with a skinny gold margin are held stiffly upright. A unique and cherished Hosta in my garden.

'Great Expectations' 20" White flowers. Awesome thick, heart-shaped puckered leaves showcase frosty blue-green, irregular margins surrounding creamy yellow centers. This Hosta is a slow grower and is best for patient gardeners. But the wait is well worth it. After three or four years your great expectations will be satisfied.

'Patriot' 22" Lavender flowers. 'Patriot' has been around for years and is still one of the best green Hosta with crisp white margins for the price. It is also very sun tolerant.

CHAPTER 3

Perennials for Challenging Sites or Specific Uses

Top Ten Perennials for Dry Shade

Dry shade can be a toughy but with the below tips and plant list, you just might find your-self shopping for shade trees.

Helpful tips:

❋ Don't rototill under trees when preparing shade gardens. Tree roots are a drag to tear through plus the process can be stressful to trees. Rather, prepare the bed by shoveling 1" to 2" of loamy soil over the existing grass, weeds or sad-looking soil and rake smooth with a landscape rake. Caution: do not put down a thicker soil layer. This can stress underlying tree roots. Also be careful not to build up soil against the trunk. Now place 6 to 8 pages of newspaper over the thin layer of soil, wet the paper and shovel 2" of mulch of top. Mulch can be compost, aged manure or finely shredded wood. Allow this to sit for four to six weeks for easier planting through the paper. If you are antsy to get going, you can dig plants through the mulch and slice holes in the paper.

❋ To make installing plants easier, purchase smaller sized containers (4" or 6" pots) instead of one or two gallon containers. The less mature roots don't need as large a planting hole.

❋ When digging in plants, add some slow-release fertilizer to the holes. Plant-Tone is a great organic choice, Osmocote 14-14-14 is a synthetic option.

❋ Remember that even drought tolerant perennials need extra watering initially to overcome transplanting adjustments and to develop great roots. Water every three or four days (taking into account natural rainfall) for two, preferably three weeks and then ease off.

❋ In those instances when you can't help yourself and you want to plant thirstier plants in drier spots, create a man-made bog to retain water or use water reten-tive crystals around their roots.

❋ If planting closer than 18" from a tree trunk, use shallow rooted perennials to minimize stress to both tree and perennial.

❋ Many gardeners pay little heed to spacing recommendations on plant tags. We as-sume the suggested spacing applies to others, not ourselves. We need lush look-ing gardens right from the get go. Let me urge you to 'follow the rules', especially when planting in shade created by trees. These shade plants already have tougher conditions than their sun-loving cousins. They're competing against the 'big guys' for light, water and nutrients. Planting them closer together just makes it tougher.

❋ Apply a nutrient-rich mulch such as compost, aged manure or finely shredded wood to shade gardens once a year. This provides nutrients as the material breaks down, reduces evaporation and reduces weeds (another competitor for light, water and nutrients).

- ✤ Dry shade can be caused by overhangs. Consider putting in a stone drip line or make sure you have a watering system to reach thirsty roots under overhangs. Soaker hoses under mulch are a good solution.
- ✤ Dry shade can be in areas where watering systems can't reach or simply don't water effectively. For example, the back of my deeper gardens remain relatively dry after watering due to the limited reach of sprinkler heads.

I did not include Hosta on this list. They have their own Top Ten list.

✤Bugleweed (Ajuga) 2" - 6"

Many gardeners curse Bugleweed for its 'gift' as a ground-cover but it does have its place if used properly. It is extremely shallow rooted and can cling to areas with little soil coverage. I like 'quilting' different Bugleweeds together to create a colorful and functional tapestry. 'Black Scallop' has shiny black leaves, 'Party Colors' has creamy white, pink and dark green leaves (it's an improved sport of 'Burgundy Glow'), 'Toffee Chip' is the most petite variety only getting 2" tall with creamy yellow and grey-green leaves, 'Chocolate Chip' gets a tad taller at 3" with green and purplish leaves and 'Caitlin's Giant' has large bronzy-green leaves. Most Bugleweeds have blue flower spikes in spring but 'Purple Torch' has pink spikes and 'Alba' has white ones. Zone 3

✤Barrenwort, Bishop's Hat, Fairy Wings (Epimedium) 4" - 20"

The roots of this plant were thought to cause barrenness in women, hence its name. Although Barrenwort is frequently labeled a groundcover, I find it much less vigorous than Ajuga, Vinca and Pachysandra. Flowers can be white, pink, sulfur yellow, orange and bicolor. Barrenwort's leaves have a pleasing burgundy cast in spring and sometimes again in fall. These make great underplantings for spring and summer flowering shrubs. A few favorites are rubrum (pink flowers), 'Niveum' (white), 'Sulfureum' (light yellow), 'Bandit' (white) and 'Orange Queen' (orangey-yellow). Zone 4

Solomon's Seal (Polygonatum) 4" - 6'

All varieties of Solomon's Seal have graceful, arching branches. Heights vary greatly. Sweet little 4" tall humile makes a delightful groundcover while Giant Solomon's Seal (biflorum var. commutatum) towers 5' to 6' in the air. Dangling, white tubular flowers appear in spring and then morph to shiny black berries. Most Solomon's Seals have green leaves but 'Variegatum' has white margins and 'Striatum' has white streaking throughout the leaf. Another cool aspect of Solomon's Seal is how it emerges out of the ground in the spring, it's very alien looking. Zone 3

✤Lenten Rose (Helleborus orientalis) 12" - 24".

Lenten Rose's nodding flowers can be white, yellow, pink, red, burgundy or multicolor. Deep green leathery leaves are semi-evergreen in zones 5 and colder. Plants are ignored by deer, rabbits and other munchers. Newer cultivars like 'Ivory Prince', have upward facing flowers so you can better appreciate the delicate stamens. There are also enchanting double-petaled plants like 'Phoebe' (soft pink) and 'Mrs. Betty Ranicar' (double white). Heronswood Nursery (www.heronswood.com) offers a large inventory of unique choices. 'Foetidus', also known as Stinking Hellebore, is an odd duck. It has an upright growth habit with long narrow leaves and greenish bell-shaped flowers. At first I thought it would make a good conversation piece in the garden but then the awful smelling leaves (not flowers) got to me. Bye-bye. Helleborus niger (Christmas Rose) can be more challenging to grow. I recently got one to winter over and I was dancing like a kid at Christmas when I saw it in bloom. It blooms weeks earlier than Lenten Rose. All Hellebores are quite drought tolerant once established. Zone 5 and colder

✢**Siberian Bugloss** (Brunnera) 10" - 15" Bright blue, Forget-Me-Not like flowers billow over heart shaped leaves. Siberian Bugloss makes a great, low-maintenance alternative to Forget-Me-Nots in shade. Siberian Bugloss's leaves can be green or display silver, creamy yellow or white markings. 'Jack Frost' has silvery leaves with green veins; 'Looking Glass' has solid silver leaves; and B. 'Variegata' and 'Hadspen Cream' have leaves with green leaves with bold white margins. 'Langtrees' has silvery markings on each leaf along the outer margin. 'King's Ransom' has creamy yellow margins while 'Spring Yellow' has totally yellow leaves that slowly change to soft green in summer. My vote is still out on 'Spring Yellow'. I think the plant looks on the sickly side. Zone 3

✢**Chinese Astilbe** (Astilbe Chinensis) 6" - 4' All of the chinensis Astilbes are more tolerant of dry soil. Would they prefer more moisture-retentive, organically rich soil? Sure. Chinese Astilbes can be ground-huggers like 'Pumila' with its 6" lavender-pink spikes in August or 'Purple Candles' with rosy-lavender plumes in July that reach 4'. Other great chinensis groupies include 'Visions' (raspberry-red, 15", July), 'Finale' (light pink, 18", August), 'Superba' (lilac, 4', July), 'Diamonds and Pearls' (white, 24", July), 'Veronica Klose' (reddish-purple, 16", July) and 'Maggie Daley' (rosy-purple, 28", July). All Astilbes will generously reward you if you work some organic Plant-Tone or Osmocote fertilizer around their bases in early May. After they finish blooming, you can spray paint the plumes bright colors for late season color. Is nothing sacred? The best time to divide astilbe in colder zones is in spring, not fall. Their roots can get woody and require a handsaw to split. A 'fall saw' can be a little too much stress for them to handle before Old Man Winter barrels in. Zone 3

✢**Big Root Geranium** (Geranium macrorrhizum) 8" - 15" Big Root Geranium makes a spectacular groundcover or individual specimen for dry shade. Spring blooming flowers are either white or pink. It is the only perennial Geranium with fragrant leaves, plus the foliage turns a burgundy-red tint in fall. I've grown 'Bevan's Variety' (deep pink, 10") and 'Ingwerson's Variety' (soft pink, 10") for over 15 years with great satisfaction. A client of mine used Big Root Geraniums as the sole groundcover under limbed up pine trees in the woods behind his house. Pine needle paths weaved through the drifts of geraniums. It was magical and no work. Big Roots are best divided after they bloom. When transplanting, lay the scrappy looking roots almost horizontally, just 3" beneath the soil surface. Zone 3

Foamy Bells (Heucherella) 6" - 12" Foamy Bells are a cross between Coral Bells (Heuchera) and Foamflowers (Tiarella). The resulting offspring retain some of the best characteristics of both parents: showy leaves, drought tolerant, and airy sprays of soft pink or white blooms on long stems. Frankly, I think the leaves steal the show. 'Stoplight', an improved 'Sunspot', has bright yellow leaves with red blotches in the center. 'Alabama Sunrise' looks similar to 'Stoplight' but the leaves are finer cut. 'Burnished Bronze' dazzles with shimmering bronze leaves and pink flowers while 'Silver Streak's has silver and purple leaves with white flowers. 'Quicksilver' was one of the first to come to market with its soft pink flowers and burgundy-purple leaves splashed with a silvery overlay. Zone 4

⁘Wood Fern or Christmas Fern (Dryopteris or Polystichum) 12" - 4' There are many sensual ferns for shade beds but some are more tolerant of dry soil than others. Wood Fern and Christmas Fern are two forgiving choices. The Wood Fern group encompasses many fine specimens including the Crested Male Fern and the Log Fern. The Christmas Fern has dark green, leathery fronds that remain evergreen. All ferns make great companions to Hosta, Astilbe and Lamium. Zone 3

⁘Pig Squeak (Bergenia) 8" - 18" I just had to include this one for its common name, Pig Squeak. Most varieties handle full sun or shade. Pig Squeaks have architecturally interesting leathery, cabbage-like leaves that turn bronzy-red in fall. The more sun they get, the richer the coloring. Stalks of pink or white flowers pop up from succulent leaves in spring. This is a plant you will either love or hate because of its unique look. I choose love. Why is it called Pig Squeak? If you take a wet leaf between your fingers and rub it, you get a noise that sounds like a squealing pig (imagination required). Zone 3

Top Ten Perennials for Baking Hot, Dry Sunny Spots

Let's give these perennials a lot of credit. They handle 'Arizona-like' weather in regions where winter temperatures can get 40 degrees below zero. That's character. Before I give you my top ten, salute of respect list, below are some helpful tidbits.

In general, drought tolerant perennials have one or more of the following characteristics:

- ❋ Succulent leaves and stems to store water. Examples are Sedums, Cushion Spurge and Prickly Pear Cactus (Opuntia, zone 5)
- ❋ Thick roots that store water or long tap roots that dive deep into cooler soil. Plants with canteen-like roots include Peonies and Daylilies. Those with tap roots include Oriental Poppies, Baby's Breath, Malva, and Baptisia
- ❋ Silver or gray leaves as well as foliage with a 'hairy' surface. These colors help reflect intense sunlight while the 'hairs' shade the leaf's surface. Examples are Lamb's Ear, Salvia argentia, Snow-in-Summer, and Silvermound
- ❋ Small leaves. There is less surface area for evaporation. Examples are Flax, Rockcress and threadleaf Coreopsis.

Mulch can be a lifesaver in baking, desert-like conditions. Mulch helps reduce water loss through evaporation and it keeps soil temperatures more consistent. The soil heats up during hot afternoons and then drops with cooler nights. It's like having non-stop hot flashes (my personal interpretation). Applying several inches of compost, aged manure, or finely shredded wood will provide a soothing, insulating blankie. Maybe I will try that.

Winecup, Purple Poppy Mallow (Callirhoe) 8" - 12" Winecup has open-faced, five-petal, magenta flowers that adorn 3' long stems. The leaves are finely cut with a bluish hint. Because of Winecup's trailing nature, I like it cascading over walls or used in containers. You can also position it as a garland on perennials or shrubs. It has a deep taproot so moving an established plant is a bear for you and also stressful to the Winecup. Zone 4

⊹Sea Holly (Eryngium) 6" - 3' Sea holly has mounded seed heads that sit on 'plates' (bracts) of finely cut leaves in July and August. Flower colors can be dark blue, steely blue or white. Some varieties have huge flowers while others look like thimbles. 'Jade Frost' is the first variegated Sea Holly with showy pink, white and green leaves. As my teenage son would say, "sick". 'Mrs. Wilmott's Ghost' has bewitching white flowers. It is considered a bi-

ennial or short-lived perennial. It is crucial to allow 'Mrs. Wilmott's Ghost' to reseed to have more in future years. Folklore has it that Mrs. Willmott, a British gardener, kept these seeds in her pocket and tossed them in gardens, so they would pop up a year later like ghosts. Now don't start getting any crazy thoughts..... Zone 4

✣ **Butterfly Weed** (Asclepias tuberosa) 2' Unfortunately the word 'weed' in its common name puts a damper on its popularity. But in my book, it's hot! A. tuberosa has eye-popping orange flowers in summer that are popular landing pads for butterflies and bees. Then the flowers age to milkweed-shaped seed heads. 'Hello Yellow' is the twin of tuberosa but bright yellow. 'Gay Butterflies' mixes it up with yellow, orange and red flower clusters. All of these are late sleepers in spring so mark their location or you may think they succumbed to Old Man Winter. Zone 3

✣ **Paeonia** (Herbaceous Peony) 24" - 40" Even though these heirloom plants do not bloom that long (especially if you have rainy or windy weather), the show they provide while on stage is breathtaking. And thankfully the foliage is a nice backdrop for summer and fall blooming perennials. There are many flower forms to pick from: double (what most people are familiar with), semi-double, Japanese (two overlapping petals), single, and the bomb (massive center with a ballerina skirt of petals around the base). Flower colors include white, pink and red. There is a yellow peony, 'Bartzella', but technically it's an intersectional peony, a cross between a traditional herbaceous Peony and a Tree Peony. Although 'Bartzella' and others in its unique circle are striking, it's the price that is even more striking; usually around $100 (that's one plant, not a dozen). Recently I have been using more of the single or Japanese peonies. They need less staking and hold up better in poor weather. I don't find their faces in the mud the next day. Zone 3

Daylily (Hemerocallis) 8" - 5' You'll see daylilies on several of my Top Ten lists because they are so versatile and low-maintenance. The only list they will not be on is Deer Resistant. Please refer to my Top Ten Daylilies list for some of the longest blooming, most fragrant, and showiest. Zone 3

✣ **Yarrow** (Achillea) 3" - 40" Yarrows are sensational, summer blooming, heat busters. I've found the Seduction series to be unparalleled as far as their length of bloom and color. 'Strawberry Seduction' (red with gold centers), 'Yellow Seduction' (canary yellow) and 'Saucy Seduction' (rosey-pink) are winners. As far as other yarrows, 'King Edward' has silvery foliage, cheery yellow flowers and only gets 3" tall. It looks terrific planted around other perennials. 'Moonshine' has a soft, gray feathery foliage and dense gold flowers. It is a good mid-border pick at 18" - 24". 'Coronation Gold' is taller at 40" with greener foliage. Yarrow is one of those plants that truly needs full sun not to flop. Zone 3

⚜Russian Sage (Perovskia) 25" - 4' These lavender-flowered beauties reach their peak in August as temperatures also peaks. Russian Sage doesn't even notice the heat waves. Both their stems and leaves are silver. I have a hard time telling some cultivars apart: atriplicifolia, 'Filagran' and 'Longin' all get around 3' - 4' tall with lavender flowers. 'Little Spire', the imp on the block, only gets 25" tall making it perfect for smaller gardens or the front of a garden. All Russian Sages have fragrant flowers and leaves. They demand sharp drainage, the sandier and crummier the soil, the better. Hold the fertilizer as well. Full sun is another must; part sun doesn't cut it. This plant can be difficult to divide, especially as it gets woodier with maturity. I find it best to give an old woody plant a 'proper burial' and replace it with a new one. Am I cold hearted? Zone 4

⚜Perennial Salvia (Salvia) 8" - 30" Most gardeners only grow purple Salvias, and yes these are nice, but why not try some white, blue and pink ones for a change? All Salvias are all tough love plants that start blooming in early summer. Heights range from 8" ('Marcus', deep purple) to 30" ('Cardonna', violet-blue flowers with dark purple stems). I love planting 'Blue Hill', a blue flowering Salvia next to lemon yellow Coreopsis 'Moonbeam'. 'Snow Hill's crisp white flowers add elegance to any setting. 'Eveline' was a pleasant surprise with large, two-toned flowers (pink and light purple). Salvias can be sheared back after the first flush of flowers to generate another round later in summer. Zone 3

⚜Baby's Breath (Gypsophila) 15" - 3' These airy flowers create floral arrangements with any plants lucky enough to be next to them. 'Perfecta' and 'Bristol Fairy' have double white flowers, making them very full bodied and visible. They billow to 36". 'Pink Fairy' has double pink flowers. 'Viette's Dwarf" stays lower at 15" with pinkish flowers that age to white. All have long tap roots that resent transplanting. Baby's Breath makes a great partner with Oriental Poppies and spring blooming bulbs. When these start to go dormant, Baby's Breath flows into their vacated spaces. Zone 3

⚜Wormwood (Artemisia) 8" - 10" 'Silver Mound' is so cute. It forms soft, ferny silver 8" tall mounds. Its only bad habit is after flowering in July. It flops open and looks unkempt. Deal with this messiness by whacking it back within a few inches of the crown (where the stems meet the roots). This stimulates new foliage that will form neat mounds once again. Most other varieties of Wormwoods can be thuggish. 'Silver King' and 'Silver Queen' know no boundaries. Sink these in pots if you want to control their aggressive roots. 'Silver Brocade' is more well mannered. And 'Limelight' should be banned to the back Forty. This green and yellow variegated Wormwood looked like just the plant to dress up my gardens. I have rued the day I every planted this monster. Every time I think I have ripped out the last dastardly piece another pops up, kind of like my teenage son's dirty laundry. All Wormwoods need sharp drainage. Wet soil is the death of them. Zone 3

Most perennials really resent (okay, die) if they are left sitting in wet, soggy soil for an extended period. But the ones on this list are pigs in mud. They love it.

If you don't have a naturally wet area in your garden, you can always try planting these water-lovers:

- ❋ at the base of a rain downspout or where water funnels off the roof
- ❋ at the base of an incline where water flows
- ❋ in your own man-made bog. Dig an area, line it with pondliner or heavier plastic and backfill with moisture retentive soil (topsoil mixed with compost and a little peat moss). Old plastic children's swimming pools also work well.
- ❋ in the vicinity of your (or your neighbor's) sump pump.

⚜Pink Turtlehead (Chelone) 2' - 42" Sun to Part Shade. Late summer, early fall. Pink or white flowers. Chelone glabra, a pale pink 4' native, is commonly known as Swamp Turtlehead. 'Hot Lips' gets 2' to 3' and has deeper pink flowers with shiny, dark green leaves. Don't get seduced by 'Hot Lip's' side kick, 'Pink Temptation'. She is only hardy to Zone 6. 'Alba' has white flowers and gets the tallest at 42". Unfortunately I have never been impressed with 'Alba'. It looks very ho-hum in bloom. All Turtleheads have stiff stems that can be pinched in early June for compact, heavier blooming plants. Zone 3

⚜Astilbe (Astilbe) 8" - 4' Sun to Part Shade. Summer blooming. White, pink, red, lavender or purple blooms. When purchasing these plumey wonders, make sure to buy Early (mid-June through early July), Mid (July) and Late blooming (mid-July through mid-August) varieties for six to eight weeks of color. Astilbes in the Arendsii, Japonica, Simplicifolia and Thunbergii groups do super in wet soil. To encourage impressive plumes, work some slow-release fertilizer such as organic Plant-Tone or synthetic Osmocote (14-14-14) into the soil once a year in early May. Zone 3

⚜Ligularia (Ligularia) 20" - 4' Part Sun to Part Shade. Summer bloomer. Yellow or orange flowers. Ligularias are an interesting group of plants. They all have intriguing leaves, both in shape and coloration plus funky flowers. 'The Rocket' has tall yellow spikes in July. 'Little Rocket' takes it down a notch at 3' in height. 'Othello' and 'Desdemona' have chocolate-green scalloped leaves. 'Britt-Marie Crawford' has even darker foliage with purple undersides. 'Japonica' has huge, deeply lobed green leaves. All four have orangey-yellow flowers in August. Zone 4

photo courtesy of PerennialResource.com

✣**Cardinal Flower** (Lobelia) 24" - 5' Sun to Part Shade. Summer, early fall bloomer. Red, white, blue, pink and purple flowers. Cardinal Flowers hit their peak in July and August. Cardinalis is the most common with electric red flower stalks that reach 4'. It can be finicky and short-lived for some. 'Monet Moment' with rosy-pink flowers and 'Fan Scarlet' are more reliable. L. siphilitica has stunning blue flowers in August and September. 'Gladys Lindley' has white stalks and 'Vedrariensis' boasts deep purple flowers. Both can reach 4'. 'Grape Knee-High' is a compact purple at 18" - 22" tall. I would bypass 'Queen Victoria' with its captivating maroon foliage and red flowers. It has never survived in my garden, despite repeat attempts. Zone 3

✣**Rodger's Flower** (Rodgersia) 30" - 4' Part Sun to Shade. Early summer bloomer. Creamy white and pink flowers. These are cool, tropical-looking plants. They have large, heavily textured, 'five-fingered' palmate leaves that are green or bronze. The flowers look like giant Astilbe plumes. R. aesculifolia has greenish-bronzy leaves and ivory flowers with a soft pink blush. The leaves of 'Chocolate Wings' start out chocolate and change to bronze. 'Elegans' and 'Die Shone' have pink flowers. Zone 4

✣**Meadowsweet** (Filipendula) 8" - 4' Sun to Part Sun. Summer bloomer. White and pink flowers. 'Venusta', sometimes called 'Queen of the Prairie', has fluffy pink plumes that remind me of cotton candy. It and 'Elegans' (very pale pink flowers) can reach 4' or more in rich soil. Their exuberance is also displayed in how quickly they spread. 'Variegata', on the other hand, at 3' has variegated green and yellowish-white leaves with white blooms and is a behaved clumper. 'Kahome' is also well mannered and the smallest of the Meadowsweets at 15" with medium pink flowers. Zone 4

✣**Japanese Iris** (Iris ensata) 24" - 48" Sun. Summer bloomer. White, purple, blue, lavender, pink and multicolor flowers. Japanese Iris have huge, 'winged' blooms that open in early July. They never fail to generate exclamations from onlookers. The leaves are tall and sword-like, making them nice accents before and after bloom. They have a dense, matted root system and can be challenging, but not impossible to divide. Divisions are best done right after they bloom. Japanese Iris hate sweet (alkaline) soil. The pH should be in the low 6.0's for best results. I just dump some naturally acidic coffee grinds on them occasionally and this does the trick. Zone 4

✣**Primrose** (Primula) 4" - 24" Part Sun to Shade. Spring bloomer. Red, white, purple, yellow and pink flowers. Most primroses are easy to grow as long as they have enough moisture. The earliest to pop open in my garden are the drumstick varieties (denticulata). These are followed by polyantha and vulgaris types with Japanese Primroses (japonica) being the last to swoon the crowds. These will seed where happy, especially japonicas. Primroses are easy to divide after blooming. Just pull apart the foliage rosettes with your hands and replant. Zone 3

⊹Joe Pye Weed (Eupatorium fistulosum or maculata) 4' - 8' Late summer, early fall. Pink flowers. You see these native plants swaying high above other wildflowers in late summer. 'Gateway' is a cultivated variety that stays shorter around 5' with lavender-pink flowers while 'Atropurpurem' can get slightly taller. 'Little Joe' is supposed to stay around 3' - 4' but he crept up to almost 5' in my garden. Tish, tish. All Joe Pye Weeds can be pinched back in June to take some steam out of their race to the sky. Zone 3

Culvers' Root (Veronicastrum) 3' - 5' Sun to Part Sun. Summer bloomer. White, pale pink and lavender-blue flowers. This is a sensational plant. It has long (12" or more), narrow, Veronica-looking spikes that sway in the breeze. Whirled leaves follow the stems up at pleasant intervals. 'Fascination' is rosy-lilac, 'Apollo' is soft pink, 'Album' is white and V. sibiricum is lavender-blue. All are magnets for pollen-seeking honeybees. Zone 3

Top Ten Hellstrip Perennials

Hellstrips. You know. Those bear to plant, I can't get anything to grow, areas. You just want to roll out a strip of artificial turf and be done with it. I have a better idea. There are some tough-love, that'a boy perennials that can tackle sites intolerable to many other plants. Potential hellstrip sites can be the section between your sidewalk and road; underneath trees with mega surface roots, on steep slopes and hard to mow areas. Of course you could always go the easier route and simply mulch these spots or use invincible groundcovers (see my Top Ten list for groundcovers). But if you still want to plant a garden, let's get on with it.

Lady's Mantle (Alchemilla) 6" - 18" Sun to Part Shade. Late spring, early summer bloomer. Chartreuse flowers. Great flowers, great leaves. Lady's Mantle will do justice for most sites with minimal attention on your part. There are petite as well as larger ladies to choose from. Zone 3

Stonecrop (Sedum) 3" - 36" Sun to Part Sun. Summer, fall bloomer. Red, white, yellow and pink flowers. These succulents can handle hot, dry areas with ease. Wet areas, no. Sedums come in many flower and foliage colors plus they can be upright or creeping. They add architectural interest all three seasons. Creeping sedums are a favorite as they also march forward and smother out weeds. Zone 3

Snow-in-Summer (Cerastium) 4" - 8" Sun. Late spring, early summer bloomer. White flowers. This is a super plant for hot dry areas. It has silver foliage with crisp white flowers in June. After it finishes blooming, use a mini-hedge trimmer to shear off flowers. This stimulates the leaves to fill out into a lush silver carpet. Zone 3

Coneflower (Echinacea) 2' - 3' Sun. Summer bloomer. Pink, purple, white, yellow, melon and orange coneflowers. It seems there is a never-ending entourage of Coneflowers introduced every year. Unfortunately, some of these could use a few more years of field testing before they hit the market. Thankfully, there are the hallmark purple (or pink depending on how your eyes sees the color) coneflowers that can tough it through our winters in a range of challenging planting sites. 'Magnus', purpurea, and 'Bright Star' are some of the reliable old boys that have us saluting them each summer. Zone 3

Big Root Geranium (Geranium macrorrhizum) 8" - 15" Sun to Shade. Spring, early summer bloomer. White and pink flowers. Large, fragrant, weed-smothering leaves that turn burgundy red in fall are a pleasant accessory to pretty pink or white spring flowers. 'Bevan's Variety' (deep pink, 10"), 'Ingwerson's Variety' (soft pink, 10"), Czakor' (rosey-magenta, 15") and 'Spessart' (soft pinkish white, 15") are all proven winners. Zone 3

Black-Eyed Susan (Rudbeckia) 24" - 5' Sun to Part Sun. Summer, early fall bloomer. Yellow flowers. Some folks think this plant is too 'common' to use in gardens. I say bah humbug! This is one long-lived, resilient plant that handles a wide range of challenging conditions. 'Goldsturm' (24" - 36") is probably the most popular cultivar but fulgida var. fulgida (24" - 30", more slender leaves and later booming than 'Goldsturm') and 'Henry Eilers' (3' - 5') skinny, lighter yellow petals with flower stalks than emerge from mounded leaves) are strong contenders as well. Zone 3

Bugleweed (Ajuga) 2" - 10" Sun to Shade. Spring bloomer. Purple and blue flowers. Dense, ground-hugging leaves eliminate weed competition with ease. Bugleweed is very drought tolerant and can even handle foot traffic without flinching. There are many colorful foliage patterns to choose from including 'Black Scallop' (shiny black leaves), 'Party Colors' (creamy white, pink and dark green leaves), 'Burgundy Glow' (creamy white, pink and soft green leaves), 'Toffee Chip' (creamy yellow and grey-green leaves), 'Chocolate Chip' (green and purplish leaves) and 'Caitlin's Giant' (large, bronzy green leaves). Zone 3

Daylily (Hemerocallis) 8"- 5' Sun to Part Shade. Summer bloomer. All flower colors except blue. Many of us know the wild orange Daylily (sometimes called Tiger Lily or Ditch Daylily). We shudder to think how quickly it can take over gardens. But their better mannered family members are terrific warriors in tough-to-grow spots. Check out the Top Ten Daylily list for great picks. Zone 3

Yarrow (Achillea) 3" – 40" Sun. Summer bloomer. Red, pink, white, apricot, yellow and paprika flowers. Yarrow's ferny foliage can be green or silvery-gray. Be careful of some of the pinks and white flowering varieties. They can become thin, scrappy looking and can wander. On the other hand, the Seduction series has bold, long-blooming flowers, stiff stems and is a good clump grower. 'Moonshine', 'Coronation Gold' and 'Althea' are yellow-flowering, well-mannered varieties. Zone 3

Top Ten Perennial Groundcovers

Groundcovers are great problem solvers. They are marvelous at:

- ❋ Thriving in tough areas under trees where grass won't grow
- ❋ Creating a weed-suppressing blanket between perennials or shrubs
- ❋ Substituting for high maintenance lawns
- ❋ Controlling erosion on slopes
- ❋ Framing the base of trees and shrubs
- ❋ Filling crevices in walls, between pavers and stepping stones
- ❋ Substituting for grass or mulch in areas that are difficult to mow
- ❋ Covering large expanses with low-maintenance plants

Probably the two most commonly used groundcovers are Pachysandra and Vinca (myrtle). No doubt about it, these are good groundcovers, but let's be more creative, shall we?

To help groundcovers spread faster (which is the whole point) fertilize them each spring with Plant-Tone, a slow-release, organic fertilizer. Either apply this right before it rains or water in immediately afterwards to wash off any fertilizer that landed on leaves. You can also use a nutrient-rich, light-weight mulch (aged compost or horse manure) around the plants. I take a shovel full and shake it above the groundcover so the mulch sifts down between the plants.

Prepping the area to be covered also helps a groundcover's success. This does not have to be a labor-intensive process. Simply loosening the soil to four inches deep will help, especially if the area is compacted. Tossing in some compost, aged manure, leaf mold or other organic amendments will also reap tremendous benefits.

Many groundcovers benefit from a good weed whacking, hedge trimming or mowing. This stimulates growth. If you are feeling so inclined, do this in late spring.

When using groundcovers around trees that have a lot of surface-feeding roots, such as maple trees, pick drought tolerant plants that can compete in this challenging environment.

❦✚Barrenwort, Bishop's Hat, Fairy Wings (Epimedium) 4" - 20" Part Sun to Shade. Spring bloomer. White, pink, yellow, orange and multicolor flowers. This is one tough perennial. Spring flowers top dark, wiry stems. The leaves have a lovely burgundy cast in spring and occasionally in fall. I like planting yellow Trout Lily bulbs (Erythronium) among white or pink Barrenworts for a fetching spring display. Zone 4

❦✤Big Root Geranium (Geranium macrorrhizum) 8" - 15" Sun to Shade. Spring bloomer. Pink and white flowers. Big Root Geranium makes a spectacular groundcover. It has large leaves that are pleasantly fragrant. The more sun the plant gets, the richer burgundy-red the leaves turn in fall. 'Bevan's Variety' (deep pink, 10") 'Czakor' (rosey-magenta, 15"), 'Spessart' (soft pinkish-white, 15") and 'Ingwerson's Variety' (soft pink, 10") are remarkable. Zone 3

❦✤Deadnettle (Lamium) 3" - 8" Part Sun to Shade. Spring, summer bloomer. White, pink and purple flowers. Lamiums move pretty quickly across the soil, thanks to their stoloniferous stems and seeding. Foliage can be silvery; green and white; green, yellow and white; or yellow and white. There are many fine cultivars to choose from. 'Pink Chablis' is promoted as one for the longest, consistently blooming Lamiums. 'Cosmopolitan' is the baby of the group, only getting between 3" - 6" tall. Lamiums do not like wet soil or areas where snow piles in winter and is slow to melt in spring. Zone 3

❦Creeping Sedum 2" - 4" Sun to Part Sun. Summer bloomers. Yellow, pink and white flowers. These distinctive succulents make great groundcover tapestries. You can weave a mix of foliage colors, shapes and flowers for a unique look. Creeping sedums have very shallow roots that can hug tough spots with little soil. Zone 3

❦✤Chinese Astilbe (Astilbe chinensis 'Pumila') 6" - 10" Sun to Shade. Summer bloomer. Lavender-pink flowers. This creeping astilbe has matt-forming, ferny leaves covered with spiky flowers in late July and August. You will get more flowers if you treat it to some time-released fertilizer in spring. Zone 3

✤Sweet Woodruff (Galium odoratum) 6" Part Sun to Shade. Spring bloomer. White flowers. Sweet Woodruff's foliage and flowers are both lightly scented. The delicate looking leaves are a nice shade of soft green. Zone 3

❦Stonecrop (Sedum 'Angelina') 3" - 6" Sun. Summer bloomer. Yellow flowers. 'Angelina' has needle-like gold foliage that turns orangey in fall. Bright yellow, flat-shaped flowers smother the plant in summer. I love this unusual looking sedum. I use it in gardens as well as containers. Zone 3

✤Serbian Bellflower (Campanula poscharskyana) 4" - 8" Full to Part Sun. Spring, early summer bloomer. Lavender-blue, blue-violet and white flowers. 'Blue Waterfall' (blue-violet flowers) and 'E.H. Frost' (white flowers) are slower to spread than the species, poscharskyana. Serbian Bellflowers have small, dark green toothed leaves. They send out long stems covered with flowers that will cascade over walls, along paths and down slopes. Zone 3

Bugleweed (Ajuga) 2" - 6" Sun to Shade. Spring bloomer. Blue, blue-violet, pink and white flowers. Most Bugleweeds have arresting blue or blue-violet flowers that holler for your attention in spring. After flowering, shear off spent blooms so the crisp, ground-hugging leaves become the focus. Foliage can be green; burgundy and green; bronzy-green; black; green, pink and white; and soft gray-green and light yellow. Zone 3

Lamb's Ear (Stachys byzantina) 6" - 10" Sun to Part Sun. Summer bloomer. Rosy-pink flowers. It's the leaves that make this a great plant. Soft, velvety silver leaves beg to be pet. If you don't like the slightly raggedy-looking flowers, buy cultivars that flower little or not at all. 'Helene von Stein' (with larger leaves that others in this family) and 'Silver Carpet' are non-bloomers. Lamb's Ear hates wet soil and humidity. The moisture can cause leaves to rot. I comb my fingers through the plants, or gently rake them, once a month to remove unsightly ones. Zone 4

Many folks overlook vertical gardening yet it is such a dynamic element. Drawing the eye upward provides another landscaping dimension, especially important for smaller properties. The sky becomes a 'borrowed view', making the garden seem bigger than it really is.

Climbers can fulfill a number of other design roles as well by:

- ❀ Contributing colorful flowers and/or foliage
- ❀ Camouflaging ugly walls, fences and other eye-sores
- ❀ Creating an interesting backdrop for gardens
- ❀ Acting as a groundcover when allowed to scramble along the ground
- ❀ Decorating shrubs and trees by twining up and over them
- ❀ Attracting hummingbirds and other desired wildlife
- ❀ Providing privacy
- ❀ Providing shade or 'roofing'

When choosing climbers, it is important to know how they ascend. This will dictate what kind of structure they need to achieve their goal. There are three ways for climbers to get where they want to go – up:

Twiners: The plant winds all, or a part of itself, around trellises, poles, string, chain-link fences and other structures. Some plants (Wisteria) wrap their whole 'body' around the structure. These climbers need heavy-duty supports to carry this responsibility. Other plants use tendrils or leaf stalks (petioles) to twirl around slender supports such as chicken wire, netting, string, fishing wire or trellises. Clematis and Morning Glories are in this group. Most climbers fall in the twiners category.

Clingers: These vines attach themselves to solid surfaces by aerial roots or adhesive discs. Potential supports include large trees, masonry surfaces, wood fences and other rough surfaces. Climbing Hydrangea and Trumpet Vine fall into this group.

Scramblers or Ramblers: These plants don't actually climb on their own, they need help being attached with something like twine or string. Climbing roses fall into this category.

You should also take into consideration the following when selecting vines and their placement:

- ❀ The mature height and weight of the vine.
- ❀ The location's light, soil type and ease to get to for maintenance.
- ❀ Don't put vines with sucker-like discs on wooden surfaces, brick or stone walls that could be damaged by their aggressive grip.
- ❀ If you are using a climber to create privacy, think about an evergreen vine, like

English Ivy, for year-round functionality.

✧ Combine vines that bloom at different times for succession of color such as mixing early and late blooming Clematis or early Clematis and Trumpet Vine.

✧ Dress-up ugly chain-link fences with dense climbers like Hydrangea, Trumpet Vine and Honeysuckle.

✧ Use heavier vines to support secondary, lighter vines. For example, Clematis or annual flowering vines can be trained up Climbing Hydrangea.

✧ If you need to get to a wall behind a trellis for maintenance, consider using a hinged trellis that can be pulled down without damaging the vine.

✧ Remember that when flowering vines are grown on a fence, the heaviest blooming will be on the sunniest side.

✧ Chain-link fences are great supports for many vines. The English have a term "fedges", referring to the illusion of a hedge caused by a heavy-duty vine covering a fence. Boston Ivy and Virginia Creeper are good "fedge" materials.

✧ Chicken wire or black netting work well as supports when wrapped around posts, fences, trees and along walls because they are hard to see.

✧ Tomato cages can be used for smaller growing vines in perennial gardens.

✧ Use climbing ivy, Climbing Hydrangea and Euonymus to scramble over tree stumps, rocks and wellheads.

A few specific comments about Clematis:

✧ There are many varieties, colors, bloom times and heights to choose.

✧ Most Clematis like full to part sun but a few are more shade tolerant like 'Comtesse de Bouchaud'.

✧ Clematis uses leaf stalks (petioles) to twirl around slender supports like chicken wire, string and narrow trellis slats.

✧ Clematis can be allowed to scramble over perennials and ornamental shrubs in the garden for an interesting look.

✧ Clematis likes its roots cool and head in the sun. Plant perennials, annuals or apply 2" to 3" of mulch over soil where the roots are.

✧ Make sure to prepare the planting hole well. Dig a hole 1' X 1' and work in plenty of organic matter such as compost or aged manure.

✧ Pruning varies depending on the type of Clematis. Clematis can be in Group I, II or III depending on their pruning requirements. The easiest Clematis to grow are those in Group III that bloom on new wood. Translation: you can cut the vine to within 6" to 8" of the ground each fall when cleaning up perennial beds. They can also be cut back in late winter or early spring. Group I plants bloom early in spring on old wood, prune these right after they bloom. Group II Clematis bloom on old and new wood. They have a heavy flush in early summer and then a second

✧drought tolerant   ⊹deer resistant

bloom later summer but these flowers are smaller and less abundant. Lightly prune Group II Clematis in late winter or early spring and then lightly again after the first bloom.

❋ Some Group III Clematis
    'Betty Corning' (light blue)
    'Dutchess of Albany' (pink with darker pink bars)
    'Ernest Markham' (red)
    'Etoile Violette' (violete-blue)
    'Ramona' (soft lavender-blue)
    'Comtesse de Bouchaud' (rosy-pink)
    'Hagley Hybrid' (soft pink)
    'Jackmanii' (purple)
    'Niobe' (red)
    'Red Cardinal' (red)
    'Polish Spirit' (purple)
    Sweet Autumn Clematis (white)

❋ Clematis 'Duchess of Albany' and 'Gravetye Beauty' are more drought-tolerant than most Clematis.

❋ To train Clematis to climb through branches of small trees and shrubs, plant roots on the shady side of the trunk and the vine will work its way to the sunnier side. It will need a support, such as a bamboo stake, to reach lower branches.

❋ When setting Clematis in a planting hole, place the crown (where the stem meets the roots) 1" to 2" below the soil surface. Also angle the plant slightly in the direction you want it to go.

❋ Clematis wilt is a nasty fungal disease that causes entire stems to rapidly die back to the soil. The fungus typically attacks the vascular system at the stem's base. Infected stems should be cut off and trashed, but not in the compost pile. The disease does not affect the roots so the vine will grow back. Unfortunately many times new stems will also be affected. You can treat this fungal disease with a sulfur product but I have had mixed results doing this. The best solution I found was to dig out the infected plant and dispose of it. Then I dug the soil out where it was planted (a 1' X 1' X 1' area). I filled the hole with 'clean' soil amended with compost or aged manure and planted a new Clematis. Success!

❋ Patio Clematis are great choices for smaller areas or containers. They only reach 2' to 4'. After flowering you can cut all the stems back to 6" from the ground and this usually stimulates another flush of flowers.

And a few final tidbits on climbing roses:

❋ Climbing roses can be used to climb a trellis or arbor. They can also be allowed to ramble along a wall or fence. Remember, these roses don't actually climb on their own like Clematis. Climbing roses are actually shrub roses that produce long flexible canes. You need to help them get to their destination and tie the canes to a support with twine.

- ❋ Climbers range in heights from 5' to 30'. Some bloom once in the spring, others are repeat bloomers.
- ❋ Roses need full sun (at least 6 hours) and rich, well drained soil. When planting a climber, place the rootball at least 15" from the support and lean the root ball slightly towards the support, aiming the canes in the direction you want them to go. To promote good air circulation, the support should be at least 3" from a wall.
- ❋ As the canes climb on the support, tie them in place. Once they've reached the desired height, start training them at an angle. Or 'arc' them right from the start, tying then in place. If the canes are allowed to grow straight up, they bloom mostly at the tips.

⊹Clematis 2' - 30' Sun to Part Sun. Early summer, fall bloomer depending on the cultivar. Many flower colors! There is such an incredible selection of Clematis available. Flowers can be single or double, nodding or open faced, petite or large. Heights range from Patio Clematis that only gets 2' to 4' to Sweet Autumn Clematis that can reach 30'. Sweet Autumn Clematis is the only fragrant Clematis with white starry flowers that mass stems in August and September. 'Comtesse de Bouchaud' (lavender-pink) can handle more shade than most. 'Polish Spirit' has to be the record holder for the longest, consistent bloom in my gardens. This purple Clematis blooms heavily June through September.

Rose (Rosea) 5' - 30' Sun. Late spring through fall bloomers. Many flower colors. There are mini-climbers that get around 5' - 6' tall and extremely vigorous climbers that can reach 30'. A few of my favorites are 'Climbing Iceberg' (white, Zone 4), 'Fourth of July' (red and white, Zone 5), 'John Cabot' (fuchsia, Zone 3), 'William Baffin' (pink, zone 3); 'John Davis' (soft pink, Zone 4) and 'Ramblin Red' (red, Zone 3). Check with the Rose Society in your region for additional suggestions. Don't be surprised if your climbers don't bloom a whole bunch the first few years. The first year they direct a lot of energy into root development, the next year the focus is on cane growth and the third year....paydirt....flowers!

⊹Honeysuckle (Lonicera) 6' - 16' Sun. Late spring, summer bloomer. Pink , white, yellow, orangey-yellow and red flowers, many of which are fragrant. 'Harlequin' has pink, green and cream variegated leaves with pink and white flowers. 'Goldflame' has blue-green leaves with rosy pink and yellow flowers. Honeysuckles are twiners that wrap their entire stems around a structure. Hummingbirds love these. Zone 4

✤**Climbing Hydrangea** (Hydrangea anomala petiolaris) 20' - 30' Sun to Part Shade. Early summer bloomer. White flowers. This vine climbs by aerial roots. I have mine climbing up a huge oak tree. Climbing Hydrangea is breathtaking when in bloom with its white, lacy flowers running 20' up the trunk. The only care I give it is in spring. I prune out some climbing stems at its base to allow more airflow to the tree's bark. I don't want insect or disease problems caused by too much captured moisture. Climbing Hydrangea's leaves turn a golden yellow in fall before dropping. Then peeling bark carries the show through winter. This is not the plant to buy if you are not a patient person. It can take up to seven years for a plant to bloom. When buying Climbing Hydrangea, buy the biggest, most mature one you can for a quicker return on your investment. Zone 4

✤**False Hydrangea Vine** (Schizophragma) 40' - 50' Part Sun to Part Shade. Early summer bloomer. White or pink flowers. This vine looks similar to Climbing Hydrangea but it blooms sooner, at the younger age of three or four years. 'Roseum' is a pink flowering cultivar and 'Moonlight' has white flowers and bluish leaves. False Hydrangeas climb by aerial roots. Zone 5

✤**Dutchman's Pipe** (Aristolochia) 6' - 30' Sun to Shade. Spring bloomer. Yellowish brown flowers. The large, heart-shaped green leaves grow closely together, making Dutchman's Pipe a super shade and privacy vine. The flowers are insignificant. They hang under the leaves and look like a Dutchman's pipe (huh?), hence its common name. This is usually grown on a trellis, pergola or latticework to provide a natural shade awning. It climbs by twining. Zone 4

✤**Fiveleaf Akebia, Chocolate Vine** (Akebia) 12' – 20'' Sun to Part Sun. Late spring bloomer. Purplish flowers. I fell in love with this interesting vine a few years ago. It has five leaflets positioned in a circular pattern that meet at a central point. The leaves have a waxy appearance. The flowers are fragrant and smell a bit like chocolate. Please note that in some warmer regions (Maryland, Virginia, Kentucky, New Jersey, Pennsylvania and Washington D.C.) this vine is considered invasive. Zone 4

Artic Kiwi, Tricolor Vine (Actinidia) 25' - 30' Sun to Part Shade. Late spring, early summer bloomer. White flowers. Small fragrant flowers appear in late spring but it's the leaves that are the main attraction. They are variegated white, pink and green. The coloration becomes more pronounced after several years of growth as well as in more sun. There are male and female plants. Males are the showiest and have the best variegation. Don't get me started. 'Kolomikta' is hardy to Zone 5. 'Artic Beauty' can handle zone 3 but has smaller leaves. Use minimum fertilizer for best leaf color. Zone 3

Wisteria (Wisteria) 10' - 40' Sun. Spring bloomer. Lavender-purple flowers. These are coveted flowers in cold climate gardens. Unfortunately, most of us only get stems and leaves. Bummer. But there are a few cultivars that seem to give Old Man Winter the cold shoulder. 'Aunt Dee' is said to be the most cold tolerant per Estabrook's Nursery (located near my parent's home) in Yarmouth, Maine. 'Aunt Dee', rated at Zone 4, has light lavender, fragrant flowers. It has done well in Maine winters in protected spots such as the east or southeast side of a house. Stalwarts for Zone 5 'Amethyst Falls' (an American Wisteria) and 'Prolific' (a Japanese Wisteria). What's the difference between American and Japanese or Chinese Wisteria you ask? Japanese and Chinese Wisterias can be very fast growing (dare I use the word thuggish?) and require more years to mature before they finally go into bloom. Their buds also seem to be more frost sensitive. American Wisteria are more controlled growers and start blooming at a younger age. Bottom line, buy American. All Wisteria are twiners and need solid supports to hold them. If your Wisteria is stubbornly not blooming, try giving it some super phosphate in spring. Pruning is also recommended twice a year. Once in late winter while it is still dormant, and once right after it blooms. After it blooms, prune all branches coming from the main stems back to 6 inches. Then in late winter while the plant is still asleep, prune these side branches again leaving 3 to 5 leaf buds per branch.

Trumpet Vine (Campsis radicans) 30' Sun to Part Sun. Summer bloomer. Orange, red and yellow flowers. Trumpet Vines are not shy. They grow quickly and can overstep their allowed space if not checked. A strong support is needed for these hefty babes. Prune them hard in late winter or early spring to control their girth. Trumpet Vines bloom on new wood so don't procrastinate pruning. You want to be sure to have those hummingbird magnets in full bloom by summer. These vines use aerial roots to attach themselves to a structure. Zone 4

Perennial Sweet Pea (Lathyrus) 4' - 12' Sun to Part Sun. Summer bloomer. Pink, red and white flowers. This is a fast growing perennial version of the annual Sweet Pea. They look similar but perennial Sweet Pea is, alas, not fragrant. It looks great scrambling up chain link fences, wood fences and trellises. It can self-sow where happy. It is a twiner like Clematis. Zone 3

ᨋdrought tolerant   ⸬deer resistant

CHAPTER 4

Flowering Shrubs, Bulbs, Annuals and Biennials

Top Ten Spring and Early Summer Flowering Shrubs

Daphne (Daphne) 2' - 3' Sun to Part Sun. Spring bloomer. Pinkish-purple and white flowers. 'Carol Mackie' has been one of the most asked about shrubs in my garden. 'She' has extremely fragrant white flowers and variegated green leaves with creamy margins. Like all Daphnes, she requires good drainage, wet soil is the death of her. 'Briggs Moonlight' stays a bit shorter than 'Carol Mackie' and has creamy-yellow centers with green margins. I have found this one to be more challenging to grow even though they are both rated for the same hardiness zone. Mezereum (February Daphne) is supposedly one of the easiest to grow. It starts blooming earlier in spring with pinkish-purple flowers on bluish-green leaves and gets 3' to 5'. Zone 4 (some resources say Zone 5 for 'Carol Mackie' and 'Briggs Moonlight').

Bottlebrush (Fothergilla) 2' - 5' Sun to Part Sun. Spring bloomer. Creamy-white flowers. This native shrub has bottlebrush flowers that emit a delightful honey-like fragrance. The flowers get a jump-start in April before the leaves appear. But the show is not over after the flowers disappear; an encore happens in fall when the shrub explodes into a brilliant orangey-red-yellow glowing spectacle. Burning Bush, which is overused in my opinion and is now listed as an invasive plant, has found its rival in Fothergilla. Not only does Fothergilla cook up brilliant fall color but it also serves fragrant flowers in spring and requires far less pruning to stay at a desirable size. 'Blue Shadow' (frosty blue leaves, 3' - 4'), gardenii (green leaves, 2' - 4') and 'Mount Airy' (green leaves, 4' - 5') are all highly acclaimed cultivars. Zone 4

Azalea (Azalea) 4' - 8' Sun to Part Shade. Spring bloomer. Yellow, pink, white pinkish-purple and orange. Let's face it, most Azaleas struggle in colder climates. I've tried one after another for years, usually grimmacing at the results. But my search is over. The Northern Lights series was developed to make cold climate gardeners smile! These are hardy to 30 to 40 degrees below zero. 'Lemon Lights (soft yellow, 6'), 'Pink Lights' (medium pink, 8'), 'Rosy Lights' (deeper pink, 8'), 'Maderin Lights' (rich orange, 6' - 8'), 'White Lights' (white, 5') and 'Orchid Lights' (pinkish-purple, 3') are a few in this series. 'Orchid Lights' has received the honors of being the hardiest of all, followed by 'White Lights'. Zone 3

Forsythia (Forsythia) 18" - 8' Sun to Part Sun. Spring bloomer. Yellow flowers. Probably the most flamboyant, spring blooming 'woody' is Forsythia. But in northern climates the likelihood of their flowering can be a crap shoot. If it was a bitter, windy winter, many flower buds will have frozen off. If we are lucky, the buds insulated by snow will still make it. Thankfully, newer cultivars have been released with 'thicker winter parkas'. 'New Hampshire Gold' is flower hardy to minus 35 degrees. There has also been a surge of compact introductions for those of us who tire of constantly whacking these shrubs back. 'Golden Peep' gets 18" - 30" and 'Gold Tide' acts more like a groundcover at 24" - 30" tall and 4' wide. And now there are variegated Forsythia. After the flowers electrify the scene, the foliage carries the baton forward. 'Citrus Swizzle' sports soft green and yellow leaves while 'Kumson' has dark green leaves with silver veining. Zone 4

Lilac (Syringa) 3' - 15' Sun. Spring bloomer. Purple, lavender, white, pink and yellow flowers. Take a deep breath. Can't you just smell lilacs from memory? These are hallmarks of spring. Many of the common lilacs (vulgaris) reaching 15' have been around for decades. Of course, hybridizers are always seeking new and better plants. I'm not sure they are better, but there have been dozens of exciting choices in recent years, many of which are shorter and more compact. 'Prairie Petite' (light pink flowers) only gets 3' - 4' while 'Tinkerbelle' has the same flower color but stretches to 4' - 6'. 'Palibin' (purple flowers) comes in between 3' - 5', 'Miss Kim' (pale purple) gets 6' - 7' and 'Sensation' (purple flowers with white edges) is 8' - 10'. 'Josee' (lavender-pink) blooms all summer, although the first flush is the best. Reliable reports have it that the newer 'The Bloomerang' (purple, 5' - 6') puts 'Josee' to shame. Personally, I am interested in getting my hands on a cut-leaf lilac, 'Laciniata'. It tops out at 6' and has fragrant lavender flowers with delicate leaves that are mildew resistant. Then there is the ever-elusive yellow lilac, 'Zhang Zhiming' that Klehms Song Sparrow Nursery sells. Check it out at (www. songsparrow.com). I recently bought a variegated lilac, 'Aucubaefolia', with green and yellowish-white variegated leaves and lavender flowers. I was told to prune it hard in the spring and not let it flower for the best leaf variegation. Eeny, meeny, miny, moe. Zone 3

Rhododendron (Rhododendron) 3' - 12' Sun to Shade. Spring bloomer. White, pink, red, purple and lavender flowers. There are small leaved and broad leaved varieties of Rhododendrons. In general, the smaller leaved Rhododendrons prefer full to part sun while the broad leaves prefer part sun to shade. Small leaf rhodies include 'PJM' (lavender-pink flowers, 3' - 6'), 'Olga Mezzitt' (pink flowers, 3') and 'Purple Gem' (purple flowers, 1' - 2'). Broad leaved cultivars include 'Roseum Elegans' (pink flowers, 6' - 8'), 'Nova Zembla' (red flowers, 4' - 6') and catawbiense album (white flowers, 6' - 8'). Maximum, also known as Rosebay, is one of the most shade tolerant with white to pale pink flowers, growing to 8' - 12'. Zone 3

Weigela (Weigela) 1' - 6' Sun to Part Sun. Spring, early summer bloomer. Pink and red flowers. Weigelas have been loved by gardeners for years. They have tubular shaped flowers that hummingbirds adore. Newer cultivars offer a spin on the standard green leaved selections. 'Wine & Roses' (4' - 5'), 'Midnight Wine' (12" - 18") and 'Fine Wine' (2') all have burgundy-purple leaves. 'French Lace' (4' - 5', red flowers), 'Eyecatcher' (2', red flowers) and 'Gold Rush' (4' - 5', light pink flowers) all have green and gold variegated leaves. 'Rubidor' (4' - 5', red flowers) has dazzling yellow leaves. 'My Monet' sets a whole new standard with pink, green and white leaves that form tight, 12" - 18" tall mounds. Zone 4.

🍃✛**Spirea** (Spirea) 12" - 8' Sun to Part Sun. Spring, early summer bloomer. White flowers. There are many Spireas but for this list I am only going to note early bloomers. Bridal Wreath ('Vanhouttei') is an old time favorite. It has cascading stems bedecked in white flowers. 'Renaissance' is promoted as an improved 'Vanhouttei'. 'Ogon' has long held a commanding spot in my gardens. It has dazzling willow-like, yellow leaves and white flowers. After flowering, I use my mini-hedge trimmer to shear off spent blooms and shape it to be a fine-textured backdrop for summer blooming perennials. 'Tor' stays rounded and compact at 2' to 3'. It has green leaves that turn yellow, orange and purple in fall. 'Snowstorm' is a top seller. It has bluish-green leaves covered with snowy white flowers in spring with leaves that turn fiery, reddish-orange in fall. The time to prune all spring blooming Spirea is right after they have finish flowering. Use a heavy-hand on them, they grow rapidly. Zone 3

🍃✛**Viburnum** (Viburnum) 3' - 8' Sun to Part Sun. Spring, early summer bloomer. White and pink flowers. Viburnums are known for their fragrant flowers and showy fruits. They are also known for getting attacked by Viburnum leaf beetle. In its larvae stage, Viburnum leaf beetle is a little yellow worm with a big appetite. It can defoliate a shrub very quickly. The shrub will struggle back with new green leaves but after several years of this feasting, it may die. Thankfully there are some Viburnums that are resistant to this pest. Those in the burkwoodii (Burkwood), carlcephalum, carlesii (Korean Spice) juddii and rhytidophyllum (Leatherleaf) groups are safe. All of these groups have members with very fragrant flowers except Leatherleaf. I especially like Korean Spice for their velvety-gray leaves. Zone 4

Eastern Redbud (Cercis canandensis) 6' - 10' Sun to Part Shade. Spring bloomer. Rosy-mauve and white flowers. This exquisite plant is covered with flowers in spring before foliage appears. It can be grown as a multi-stem shrub or a single trunk tree. All Redbuds have pretty, heart-shaped leaves. 'Forest Pansy' (rosy-mauve flowers) has lush purple leaves in spring that green up in summer but change to purply-red in fall. 'Covey', also know as 'Lavender Twist', has a contorted trunk and a weeping nature. It is a crowd-stopper in spring when covered with pink flowers. Some resources list Redbuds as Zone 5 plants, other as Zone 4. Gardeners in northern climates should site these out of the path of winter winds for best results.

Top Ten Summer and Fall Blooming Flowering Shrubs

Hydrangea (Hydrangea) 3' - 15' Sun to Shade. Summer, fall bloomer. White, pink, blue and purple flowers. Of all flowering shrubs, Hydrangeas are probably the most frustrating for folks. Usually questions focus on how to prune or why plants aren't flowering. Allow me to provide a quick course on Hydrangeas. There are four main groups:

🌿**Smooth Leaf Hydrangea** (H. arborescens) Sun to Part Shade. These have pink or white flowers and set their flower buds in spring on new wood. All can be pruned hard in late winter or early spring before new growth begins. 'Annabelle' (3' - 5', white ball-shaped flowers) has been around for years and is a tried-and-true winner. 'White Dome' (4' - 6', white dome-shaped flowers) and 'Invincibelle Spirit' (3' - 5', pink ball-shaped flowers) are newer selections. A portion of all plant sales from 'Invincibelle Spirit' goes to breast cancer research. 'Annabelle' is one of the most shade tolerant of all Hydrangeas.

🌿**Bigleaf Hydrangea** (H. macrophylla) Sun to Part Shade. Blue, purple or pink depending on soil pH. This is the Hydrangea group that drives gardeners crazy. There are mophead and lacecap varieties in this group. The reason that most Bigleaf Hydrangeas bloom little, or not at all, is usually related to when they set their flower buds and to your hardiness zone. Many Bigleaf cultivars bloom on old wood. This means flower buds are formed in late summer and need to make it through our blustery winters to bloom the next year. If the shrubs are located on the east side of the house or other sheltered areas, the odds are pretty good you'll be smiling at summer flowers. If not, well, you know..... Thankfully there are now mophead Hydrangeas on the market that set flower buds on old and new wood. Translation: it doesn't mater how many buds freeze off in winter, there will be a whole new round of reinforcements in spring. Another perk of these newer offerings is many are repeat bloomers. After the first round of flowers, more buds will appear through summer into fall. Some great Bigleaf cultivars that bloom on old and new wood are: 'Endless Summer' (4'- 5'), 'Blushing Bride' (3' - 6'), 'Let's Dance Moonlight' (2' - 3'), 'Let's Dance Starlight' (2' - 3', lacecap) and 'Twist-N-Shout' (3' - 5', lacecap). Bigleafs will be blue in acid soil (pH 6.0 or lower) and pink in alkaline soil (pH 7.0 or higher). Sometimes 'Blurple' is the result of pH's between 6.0 - 7.0. As far as pruning Bigleafs, you only need to prune if the shrub has gotten taller than you want. Don't prune just for the sake of pruning. For Hydrangreas that bloom on new and old wood, prune lightly in the fall or late winter. For those that bloom only on old wood, prune right after they flower in late summer or early fall. Zone 4

🍂**Hardy Hydrangea** (H. paniculata) These are grown as multi-stem shrubs or single trunk trees. Most gardeners find the paniculata group the easiest to grow. These set their flowers on new wood in spring. The time to prune, if needed, is in late winter or early spring. Flowers are white or pink but both age to a pretty burgundy-red. Popular cultivars include 'Pinky Winky' (4' - 6', white and pink flowers), ' Limelight' (4'- 6', lime-green flowers), 'Little Lamb' (4' - 6', white flowers), 'Pink Diamond' (6', pink flowers) and 'Quick Fire' (6' - 8', pink flowers and starts blooming earlier in the summer than many others).

🍂**Oakleaf Hydrangea** (H. quercifolia) Sun to Part Shade. This group of Hydrangea are only hardy to Zone 5. They have large, oak-shaped leaves that turn burgundy-red in fall. No other group of Hydrangeas has this rich fall coloring. Another characteristic that sets Oakleafs apart is its peeling bark that makes a nice winter accent. Heights range from 3' to 8'. Oakleafs do best in a protected spot out of winter winds. They set flower buds in fall so if pruning if needed, do so right after they finish flowering in late summer.

🍂⚜**Smokebush** (Cotinus coggygria) 8' - 15' Sun. Summer bloomer. Pink and creamy white flowers. These are magnificent shrubs prized for their unique flowers and leaves. It is nicknamed Smokebush because of the billowy cloud of flowers that rise above the leaves in summer. My personal favorites are 'Grace' (10' - 15', pink flowers) and 'Royal Purple' (8' - 10', creamy white flowers). These have luscious wine-purple leaves. Other worthies include 'Young Lady' (8' - 10', soft pink flowers), 'Golden Spirit' (8' - 10', golden leaves with yellow flowers) and 'Ancot' (8', golden leaves with yellow flowers). All are hardy to Zone 4 except 'Golden Spirit' and 'Royal Purple' are Zone 5. Smokebushes set their buds on new wood so prune in late winter or early spring. I give mine a severe prune (sometimes called coppicing) every spring to keep the plants at 4'.

⚜**Summersweet** (Clethra) 3' - 8' Sun to Part Shade. Summer bloomer. Pink and white flowers. The name is so accurate. Their flowers perfume the summer air with their sweet fragrance. Summersweet is one of the few shrubs that can handle wet soil as well as average soil. They stress out in dry soil. Flower buds are set on new wood so prune in late winter or early spring. 'Sixteen Candles' (28", white flowers), 'Ruby Spice' (3' - 6', pink flowers), 'Hummingbird' (30", white flowers) and 'Vanilla Spice' (3' - 6', white flowers) are all butterfly magnets with showy golden foliage in fall. Zone 4

Ninebark (Physocarpus) 4' - 10' Sun to Part Sun. Summer bloomer. White and soft pink flowers. Ninebark is given its name for what looks like nine layers of peeling bark. It is striking against snow. This native shrub can handle a range of soil conditions. It sets its flower buds on old wood so if pruning is needed, do so after it finishes flowering in summer. But be aware that by so doing you will not get as many beautiful red berries that are cherished by birds. Another strategy to control its height is to whack it to within a foot of the ground in late winter every three or four years. Invigorating both for you and the Ninebark. Some great cultivars include 'Coppertina' (copper foliage in spring that turns to red in summer, 6' - 8'), 'Summer Wine' (dark crimson-red foliage, 5' - 6'), 'Diabolo' (dark crimson-red foliage, 8' - 10') and 'Dart's Gold' (gold foliage, 4' - 5'). Zone 3

Elderberry (Sambucus) 5' - 12' Sun to Part Sun. Summer bloomer. White or pink flowers. The fruit of Elderberry shrubs are prized by both birds and people. Cultivars that are most popular with gardeners are those with showy foliage. 'Black Beauty' (8' - 12') was the first chocolate leaved introduction to wow us. It was quickly topped by 'Black Lace' that has the same rich leaf coloring but lacier leaves. 'Black Lace' also stays shorter at 6' to 8'. Both have flat pink flowers. I personally found 'Black Beauty' to be too sprawling for my taste. 'Sutherland Gold' has large, lacy yellow leaves and flat white flowers that ripen to darker red berries. 'Sutherland Gold' prefers a spot in partial shade to keep the leaves from scorching. Elderberries need good drainage or they will rot (trust me, I speak from experience). They set their flower buds on old wood so prune after flowering in summer. Zone 4

Bush Clover (Lespedeza thunbergii) 12" - 5' Sun. Late summer, fall bloomer. Violet purple and pink flowers. This late blooming, graceful shrub has a weeping habit and flowers that open along its arching stems. I planted mine next to a retaining wall where it could sweep over the edge. 'Gilbralter' and 'Pink Fountains' both get 4' - 5'. There is a tiny version, 'Yakushima' that only grows about 12" - 18". In our colder climates, Bush Clover dies back to the ground, similar to Butterfly Bush. Prune it back hard in the spring. It sets its flower buds on new growth. You may also want to prune out some of the outer stems as it can grow wide. Zone 4

Seven-Son Flower (Heptacodium) 10' - 20' Sun to Part Sun. Late summer, fall bloomer. Creamy-white flowers. As you can see by how tall this big boy gets, it needs a lot of room. Setting it alone in the landscape, surrounded by spring or summer flowering groundcover is a thought. Seven-Son Flower has fragrant blooms starting in August but the real show comes from the red sepals that form after flowering. A bonus is its peeling bark in winter and gentle arching habit. Prune Seven-Son Flower hard in late winter or early spring. Zone 5 (some say Zone 4)

❦✛Bush Honeysuckle (Diervilla) 3' - 5' Sun to Shade. Summer bloomer. Yellow flowers.

This perky shrub is a relative newcomer to my gardens. It tolerates dry, sandy soil with ease and can handle shade if needed. 'Butterfly' has yellow flowers on bright green foliage. 'Cool Splash' displays bold green and white variegated leaves with yellow flowers. It looks like a showier, compact version of a variegated Dogwood. Bush Honeysuckle sends up suckers from the base like Forsythia so remove these just below the soil level if the plant gets too wide for its britches. Prune hard in late winter or early spring. Zone 3

✛Rose of Sharon (Hibiscus syriacus) 3' - 12' Sun to Part Sun. Summer, fall bloomer.

White, pink, lavender, bluish-purple and two-color flowers. When Rose of Sharon is in full bloom, it is spectacular. Flowers can be single or double. Most Rose of Sharons get quite large (8' - 12') and they also grow wide. 'Lil' Kim' breaks this mold with its 3' - 4' stature and red and white flowers. 'Sugar Tip' (8' - 12') is another revolutionary with variegated white and blue-green foliage. Its flowers are double pink. Don't be shy about pruning Rose of Sharon hard in late winter or early spring to control its height and width. In all honesty, I have mixed feelings putting Rose of Sharon on this list. I know many folks love them. My beef is their tendency to seed around and they can have partial dieback if sited in windier areas. To reduce winter damage, plant them in sheltered spots. Zone 5

Rose (Rosea) 6" - 30' Sun. Late spring, summer, fall bloomer. Many flower colors.

This group has a huge number of varieties to choose from: mini's, singles, doubles, climbers, shrubs, hybrid teas, grandifloras, floribundas, rugosas and the beat goes on. Given that I am all about low-maintenance and cold-hardy plants, my pick are those grown on their own roots (not grafted). I'm particularly fond of the Knockout series (shrub roses hardy to Zone 4 but I've seen them handle Zone 3 where sheltered from winter winds), the Canadian Explorer series (shrub roses, Zones 3 and 4), Buck roses (shrub roses, many Zones 3 and 4), Easy Elegance series (shrub roses, Zone 4), 'Morden Blush' (pink, Zone 2), 'Morden Sunrise'(yellow with a pink blush, Zone 3), 'Carefree Beauty' (pink, Zone 4), 'Carefree Delight' (pink, Zone 4), 'Blanc Double de Coubert' (white fragrant rugosa, Zone 4) and 'Iceberg' White (both a shrub and climber are available, Zone 4). Please note this list is not exhaustive. There are many hardy, disease-resistant roses available. Check with the Rose Society in your region for additional suggestions. The time to prune roses (unless they are once bloomers in late spring or early summer) is in April when Forsythia go into bloom. Prune them back by at least half their height. Also remove any dead or broken stems as well as branches directed into the center of the shrub.

❦drought tolerant   ✛deer resistant

Top Ten Flowering Bulbs

Gardeners always seem to be on the quest for more color. Like chocolate, it never seems like we can get enough. We want sizzling action in our beds (ahem, garden beds) and continuous waves of color that will knock our muck boots off. If we can save money and time in this pursuit, all the better. Spring, summer and fall blooming bulbs are an easy solution for creating sensational color.

As a rule, a bulb's planting depth is three times its height. Plant bulbs with the pointy side up. If you are not sure of the pointy side, don't fret. A neat attribute of most bulbs is the ability for an emerging stem to seek the soil's surface despite its orientation in the ground. You can always plant bulbs sideways for added insurance. I recommend planting in multiples; the more the better. And please, not in straight lines. Create sweeps; 5's, 7's and 9's work nicely. Most bulbs require good drainage so they don't rot. Some are more sensitive to moisture than others.

After spring flowering bulbs are finished blooming, remove the flower stalk so energy is directed back into the bulb instead of seed formation. Wait until the leaves are brown before cutting back the foliage. Ideally, you should be able to simply pull the leaves off. The one exception to this rule is for Daffodils. Their foliage takes a long time to cry 'Uncle'. With these I still cut the flower stalks off after blooming but in early July I also shear the foliage to create a short 6" tall 'grassy' clump. If you're the type that impatiently taps your fingers waiting to clean up spring bulb foliage use dwarf or miniature varieties, those that top out at 10". These do their flowery business and go dormant quickly.

For summer blooming bulbs such as Asiatic, Oriental and Trumpet lilies, wait until the flowers have finished blooming and then remove the spent stalks so energy is once again directed to the bulbs versus seed production. Allow the entire stem to brown before cutting it off at the soil line.

If bulb-chomping critters are a problem you can:
- Plant bulbs an inch or two deeper that standard protocol.
- Drench bulbs in a taste repellent like Invisible Fence or Ro-Pel.
- Use chicken grit (crushed shells). Toss some in the hole with the bulb. The sharp fragments feel nasty on tender noses. You can buy chicken grit at farm and feed stores.
- Plant bulbs in large pots. Sink the pre-planted pots in the ground in fall and remove them after they've finished blooming in spring. You can fill the empty spot with annuals or better yet, replace with them with similar-size containers of tender tropicals, such as Cannas or Elephant Ears, that you've overwintered inside.

✽ Use wire cages to protect bulbs, although I find these too much of a drag to fiddle with. Plus I hit them when digging in new plants or dividing perennials.

✽ Finally, you could simply use poisonous bulbs such as Daffodils, Fritillaria, and Colchicums. Although this sounds cruel, the 'muncher' takes one nibble of the bulb and realizes it's bad for tummies and moves on, unharmed.

Many times mail-order companies are some of the best sources for getting unusual bulbs. Some of my favorite 'candy stores' are Dutch Gardens (www.dutchgardens.com), John Scheepers (www.johnscheepers.com), Brent and Becky's Bulbs (https://store.brentand-beckysbulbs.com) and Old House Gardens Heirloom Flower Bulbs (www.oldhousegar-dens.com).

Okay there's 13 bulbs listed... but who's counting?

⊹Checkered Lily (Fritillaria meleagris) 8" Part Sun to Shade. Spring bloomer. Maroon and white flowers. Charming, just charming. Checkered Lily has slender blue-green foliage topped by nodding flowers. There are also pure white varieties. Checkered Lilies naturalize at a polite pace and can tolerate moist soil, unlike many bulbs. Fritillarias are detested by munching critters, including deer. Zone 3

⊹Trout Lily, Dogtooth Violet (Erythronium Pagoda) 8" - 12" Part Shade. Spring bloomer. Yellow flowers. These cheerful flowers, resemble miniature turk's cap lilies, are born on airy stems above broad green, low growing leaves. Zone 4

⊹Narcissi (Daffodils) 5" - 20" Sun to Shade. Spring bloomer. Yellow, white and bicolor combinations. I used to think there were basically two choices for Daffodils; white or yellow and that they were all around 12" tall. Times are a'changin'. Now you can se-lect daffs that are miniature (5" - 6" tall), double cupped (pom-pom looking centers), double petaled, all different cup lengths from petite to those that look like Pinocchio's lyin' nose), and those with orange, pink and 'red' cups. There is a misconception that all Daffodils can handle shade. Per Brent and Becky's Bulbs (a specialty mail-order bulb company in Virginia) only the Cyclamineus group of Daffodils are up for this challenge. Zone 3

Tulip (Tulip) 6" - 30" Sun to Part Sun. Spring bloomer. Many flower colors. Tulips are hands-down the most popular spring bulbs sold. By using Early, Mid and Late bloom-ing varieties, you can have color April into June. There are many styles to choose from: Peony, Double, Single, Parrot, Darwin, Triumph, and a Partridge in a Pear Tree. In gen-eral, most tulips only bloom well for three or four years and then their batteries wear down. Darwin varieties can go four or five years. Other groups of long-lived tulips are the Species and Kaufmanniana tulips. These last two will actually naturalize (increase in numbers) and do well in less sun than other tulips. Zone 3

Allium (Allium) 8" - 48" Sun to Part Sun. Spring, summer bloomers. White, purple, pink, blue, yellow and multicolor flowers. Alliums are always great accents. The globe-shaped balls or nodding heads ranging in diameter from from 1" to 15". Depending on the cultivar, flowering begins in early June. The 'big daddy' of alliums is 'Giganteum' that gets three to four feet tall with 15" wide purple balls. Balls of this girth are best sited in areas sheltered from wind or be ready to give them some support. 'Globemaster' challenges 'Giganteum' with its 10" purple balls and 36" stems. 'Bulgaricum' is always a fan pleaser. It has clusters of green, pink and white flowers that dangle from 36" stems. 'Schubertii' is the Dr. Zeus of alliums with huge, rosy-purple flowers that resemble exploding fireworks. Although short in stature at 18", it packs a wallup of a presentation. Another amusing allium is 'Hair'. It has an alien look with wispy green tentacles twisting around a central ball. Zone 3

Quamash (Camassia) 24" - 30" Sun to Part Sun. Spring bloomer. White, lavender, blue and violet flowers. Quamash is a tall spring bloomer with an airy look. This does best in moisture retentive soil. I love tucking them among Astilbes and Ligularias for early color. Quamash is a native that is rarely bothered by deer. Zone 4

English and Spanish Bluebells (Hyacinthoides) 12" - 15" Sun to Part Shade. Spring bloomer. Blue-violet, pink and white flowers. These deer-proof bloomers have hanging, bell-shaped flowers. English Bluebells (non-scripta) are very fragrant while Spanish Bluebells (hispanica) are not. Both naturalize well and are long-lived. Zone 4

Asiatic Lily (Lilium Asiatica) 10" - 4' Sun to Part Sun. Early summer bloomer. Many flower colors. Asiatic lilies are very popular and are less expensive than many other summer flowering bulbs. They have upward facing, nonfragrant flowers and multiply well. To divide and reset bulbs, wait until after flowering, dig up clumps and pull apart bulbets. Replant bulbs immediately where you want to enjoy the flowers the following year. LA Hybrids are a cross between Asiatic and  Longifloreum lilies. The resulting merger created larger flowers with a waxy appearance, sweet fragrance and better bloom clustering at the stem tips. Zone 3

Martagon Lily (Martagon) 3' - 6' Sun to Part Shade. Early summer bloomer. White, pinkish-purple and burgundy-red flowers. These are rarely seen in gardens, one reason why you want people oohhing and ahhing at them in yours. Martagons have small, downward facing flowers with reflexed petals. They are slow growers but once they get established, they're breathtaking. Mine are five years old and have at least eight nodding flowers per stem. 'Alba' (white) looks bewitching blooming through the leaves of my soft green, fringed-leaf Japanese maple. Martagons are hard to find at garden centers. It is easier to purchase them online at www.vanscheepers.com or www.oldhousegardens.com. But be forewarned. These beauties come at a price: $10 or more per bulb.

Trumpet Lily (Lilium aurelian) 4' - 5' Sun to Part Sun. Summer bloomer. Yellow, pink, white, orange, and pink and white flowers. Trumpet Lilies blast out fragrance and color in mid-summer. The richer your soil, the taller they get. Mine have gotten 6' tall and require staking to hold up their massive flower heads. The large trumpet-shaped flowers are a nice change of shape among other flowers. Sometimes their 'long, skinny legs' look uncomfortable if left bare so I plant a mass of 'Becky' shasta daisies in front of them. 'Becky' has huge white flowers and a full foliage figure that hides Trumpet's legs. Zone 4 Orienpet, O.T. Lily (Lilium Orientpet) 4' - 6' Sun to Part Sun. Summer bloomer. Many flower colors. O.T. Lilies are a cross between Trumpet and Oriental lilies. The resulting progeny are breathtaking. Huge, nodding flowers that face slightly outward burst on the stage in July with a powerful fragrance. These plants look almost tropical in my beds with their 1" caliber stems supporting dozens of flowers and buds. Because of their heavy-duty stalks, I rarely need to stake them. On the other hand, I almost need an ax to chop the stems back in fall. Zone 4

Oriental Lily (Lilium Oriental) 2' - 5' Sun to Part Sun. Summer bloomer. Many flower colors. This is another hugely popular group of summer flowering bulbs. Probably the most well known are 'Stargazer' (raspberry-red) and 'Casa Blanca' (white). Oriental Lilies start blooming just as Orienpets wrap up. Be careful not to place too many Orientals near each other or the fragrance can get overwhelming; almost nauseating (like my teenage son when he douses himself in Axe cologne). Zone 4

⚘Fall blooming Crocus (Colchicums and Crocus) 4" - 6" Sun to Part Sun. Fall bloomer. Rosy-pink, lavender and white flowers. These small stature plants provide the encore in fall. Colchicums and fall blooming crocus look similar except Colchicums have larger flowers. Both bloom on leafless stems. The leaves appear in the spring and then go dormant. If you have critter problems, go with Colchicums. They are poisonous. Zone 4

Even though I am a 'passionate perennialist', I rely on some workhorse annuals as consistent color beacons May through October. Mind you, I insist that these require little or no deadheading and are not water mongers. It doesn't matter if they are in my garden, window boxes, hanging baskets or patio containers.

I also refuse to fertilize annuals every few weeks as instructed by Miracle-Gro. I don't do this for my perennials and shrubs, so why would I give annuals this special attention? They don't even 'thank me' by returning the following year. Harrumph. The only time I fertilizer annuals is at planting time. I use Plant-Tone, a time-released organic fertilizer or Osmocote 14-14-14. This feeds them for three to four months. The other thing I usually do as I'm planting annuals is pinch them back by 1/3. This helps them grow fuller and produce more flowers.

Here are a few more tips when working with annuals:

* The Top Ten annuals list includes great annuals requiring little or no deadheading but this list is by no means exclusive. There are other great annuals to also check out like Cosmos, Cleome, Impatiens, Vinca, Celosia, Nierembergia and Sweet Potato Vine. Whatever you pick, make sure it doesn't stop blooming or go to seed if not routinely deadheaded.
* To reduce the frequency of watering, pick varieties that are drought-tolerant such as Vinca, Portulaca, Zinnias, Gazania, Cleome, Celosia, blue Salvia, Marigolds and Verbena.
* To reduce how often you have to water containers, work water retentive crystals such as Stockosorb into the potting medium. But be careful, a little goes a long way. Some potting mixes already have these incorporated so check the label first.
* To increase drama, build in annuals with striking foliage such as Coleus, Caladiums, Persian Shield, Canna, Perilla (can self seed aggressively), Angel Wing Begonias, Dusty Miller and showy herbs.
* When planting decorative containers or window boxes, I mix approximately ½ topsoil (amended with compost) and ½ potting soil together. This mix does not need to be watered as much and is less expensive that 'top shelf' bagged mediums. The trade off is that my recipe is heavier. So for all but the smallest containers, I incorporate packing peanuts, chunks of Styrofoam, plastic Easter eggs, pine cones, crunched up annual packs or plastic soda bottles to fill air space. This reduces the amount of potting medium needed and the overall weight of the container.
* When selecting containers, remember that pots made out of plastic, fiberglass and metal hold water longer than clay pots, unless the pot is glazed. Also, the larger the pot, the less often it needs watering.
* To keep thirsty shrub and tree roots from stealing water and nutrients from an-

nuals planted nearby, place the annuals in pots in the ground so their space is protected from foraging roots.

Million Bells (Calibrachoa) 6" - 8" Sun. Many colors. There are mounded and trialing varieties. Although Million Bells are commonly used in containers, I prefer planting them in gardens. They provide season-long, colorful anchors and effectively link gardens together. I especially like the trailing varieties spilling onto pathways, cascading over retaining walls and filling gaps left where spring blooming bulbs have gone dormant. Million Bells' only peeve is soggy soil. This is rarely a problem in freely-draining gardens but containers can be a different story. To minimize this stressful condition, steer clear of glazed containers that hold moisture longer. Go for terra cotta that 'breathes' better.

Browallia (Browallia) 10" - 14" Sun to Shade. Blue-purple and white flowers. Browallia receives the MVP award in my gardens, not only for its exceptional performance but also for its ability to trick folks into believing it's a perennial. This 'Energizer Bunny' blooms in sun or shade from May through the first heavy frost. Browallia is quite drought tolerant, making it a great substitute for thirsty Impatiens in dry shade. 'Endless Flirtation' sports crisp white flowers, 'Endless Sensation' has rich blue-purple flowers and 'Endless Celebration' has soft blue flowers.

Begonia (Begonia) 6" - 3' Sun to Shade. Many flower colors. There are lots of great begonias on the market. I use Wax Begonias often in dry shade, especially white flowering ones. Dragon Wing Begonias can get 2'to 3' and have a sweeping habit with shiny green leaves. Bright colored tuberous Begonias add 'pop' wherever they're planted. Probably my favorite Begonias are those in the Mandalay™ series. I trialed Mandalay 'Mandarin' in my gardens and it was a huge head-turner, receiving the most "What's that?" question. Mandalay™ Mandarin reached 12" and was covered with dangling, bell-shaped, single-petaled, orange flowers spring through fall with no deadheading. There are also pink and white varieties. These are also well suited for hanging baskets and window boxes because of their arching posture.

⊹Zinnia (Zinna 'Profusion') 10" - 24" Sun. White, orange, red and pink flowers. Zinnias are a family tradition; they were in my grandparents' and Mom's gardens. I always loved these but hated their propensity for getting mildew and their constant need for deadheading. Thankfully the 'Profusion' series came along. These have the same cheerful flowers but compact mounds instead of leggy stems and they are very mildew resistant. Most annuals in this series grow 10" - 12" tall but 'Profusion Knee High Red' gets 20" - 24". Flowers can be single or double.

⊹Coleus (Solenostemon) 8" - 3' Sun to Shade. Many foliage colors. Coleus has made a grand comeback. In the 1800's Coleus was in high demand but then fell in popularity during the early 1900's. Striking foliage colors, leaf shapes, forms and textures have propelled it back into the spotlight. Some of my favorites include 'Freckles' (chartreuse and orange, 24" - 30"), 'Pink Chaos' (brilliant pink, white and green, 6" - 12"), 'Sedona' (burnished bronze, 18" - 24"), 'Gay's Delight' (screaming yellow with rich red veins, 24" - 30"), 'Saturn' (chocolate-maroon with splashes of chartreuse, 12" - 18"), 'Strawberry Drop' (red, chartreuse, burgundy and green petite leaves, 8" - 12") and Fishnet Stockings (if I can't wear them, at least my gardens can). Most Coleus prefer part sun to shade but new sun tolerant varieties on the market. Coleus are great mixed with other annuals in containers but can make an eye-catching statement by themselves. They also jazz up shaded perennial beds that can become monopolized by Hosta.

When combining Coleus, be careful not to mix too many different variegations or the effect can be overwhelming. And please, pinch off emerging flowers. This is one of those times when flowers play second fiddle. Being a tight wad, I like to save my favorite Coleus from Old Man Winter's death blow. I simply pinch them back to within 4" - 5", plant them in showy containers, spray their leaves with insecticidal soap and bring them inside to a brightly lit room.

Verbena (Verbena) 6" - 12" Sun. Red, purple, pink, white, apricot, lavender and burgundy flowers. Verbena has a sprawling habit, working well as a spiller in containers or groundcover in gardens. The dome-shaped flowers rest on small, dark green, heavily textured leaves. Verbenas are very easy to grow, doing best with a tough love approach. They usually die from too much lovin' (fertilizing and watering).

Lantana (Lantana) 12" - 36" Sun. Yellow, orange, white, red, lavender and multicolor flowers. The other summer I tried Lantana for the first time. Shazam! Luscious™ Citrus Blend™ knocked me over with its screaming red, orange and yellow flowers plus record-breaking growth rate. I planted it with rich blue Salvia farincea and the effect was mesmerizing. Lantana sneers at drought and heat. Like many of us as we age, Lantana tends to get wider than taller. Many cultivars can quickly scramble to three feet across. There is a 'Weeping' collection with trailing stems that are super for cascading down containers in brutally hot locations.

Wave Petunia, Supertunia (Petunia) 4" - 24" Sun. Many flower colors. Wave and Supertunias are fast growers. Flowers can be single or double. They will scramble along the ground, down the sides of containers and retaining walls, and up chain link fences. I thought Supertunia® Vista Bubblegum was going to follow me into the house! I planted one little plug on each side of my front steps and they grew faster than any other petunia I've ever grown. They morphed into soft pink, blossom covered mounds that were easily two feet wide and 18" tall. Both series have choices that are fragrant, single or double petaled, and mounded or trailing.

Sweet Alyssum (Lobularia) 4" - 6" Sun. White flowers. I don't think I have ever been as impressed with an annual as I have been with 'Snow Princess'. It is a very fast grower, covering itself with masses of white, fragrant flowers that never quit until November when it was slammed by snow. It has a billowing, cascading habit making it ideal for containers as well as along garden edges.

Blue Sage (Salvia farincea) 12" - 24" Sun to Part Sun. Rich blue spikes and gray-green foliage makes this a dazzling blue beacon spring through fall. Annual Blue Sage is very drought and heat tolerant. I pinch my plugs when planting for a fuller figured, flowering plant.

drought tolerant   deer resistant

Biennials are a must for cottage gardens but they are not necessarily for low-maintenance ones. Remember, these are plants that only live for two years plus they are moving targets. The first year they only grow leaves, the second year flowers, and the third year it's zippo. In the second year they cast their seeds all over the garden, wherever the wind will carry them. That's their job to survive. It's your job to move the little gypsies where you want them if they haven't already landed there.

Having said this, there are a few tricks for simplifying befuddling biennials.

- ❋ When purchasing biennials, buy one plant in its first year and one in its second year. This way you will have a cycle already started.

- ❋ Buy first year biennials in 4" pots in fall when they go on sale. There are a usually a lot left since most gardeners like to buy perennials in flower. Plant these 'first years' in your garden exactly where you want to see their stately blooms the following year. Basically, you've 'fixed' the game.

- ❋ Make sure not to deadhead all the flowers. You need some flowers to go to seed. Shake the dried flower stalks to scatter seeds at the base of the plant or wherever your little heart desires. Put a marker (garden stake with orange ribbon) by the area to help remind yourself not to weed the emerging seedlings later that summer. You may think these are weeds since the first set of leaves don't closely resemble their mature leaves. I can just hear you say "AHAH", as I did, once I saw the cycle run its course.

English Button Daisy (Bellis perennis) 4" - 6" Sun to Part Sun. Early summer, summer bloomer. White, pink and ruby daisy-like flowers. These petite sweeties need to be planted in mass instead of solo to make the best impression. Zone 3

Forget-Me-Not (Myosotis) 6" - 10" Sun to Part Shade. Spring bloomer. Blue, white or pink flowers. How can you not have these charming spring flowers in your gardens? I thin them out where they have seeded too thickly so emerging perennials don't rot from lack of light or air. Once Forget-Me-Nots finish blooming and start to flop open, I rip them from the ground, shake the seeds over the gardens, and say "thank you" as I toss them in the compost pile. Very satisfying. Zone 3

⚜Hollyhock (Alcea) 3' - 6' Sun. Summer bloomer. White, yellow, pink, nearly black, peach or red flowers. Most Hollyhocks are biennials although there are some perennials. Flowers can be single or double (pom-poms). Hollyhocks are prone to rust (orange spots on their leaves). This is very hard to combat. You can try using a sulfur product. Also strip infected leaves and get rid of them, but not in your compost pile. Sometimes, if the plant is really infected, the best solution is to get rid of it. Fig Leafed Hollyhocks (ficifolia) are less prone to rust and have old-fashioned single flower forms. Zone 3

Sweet William (Dianthus barbatus) 1' - 3' Sun. Late spring, early summer bloomer. White, pink, maroon and red flowers. Some references list this as a short-lived perennial as it will flower from seed the first year. Sweet Williams have mound flower heads that are mildly fragrant. They 'shout' cottage garden. Zone 3

Wallflower (Cheiranthus) 1'- 18" Sun. Spring bloomer. White, yellow and orange flowers. Although this is technically a short-lived perennial it is usually treated as a biennial in our area. Zone 4

Canterbury Bells (Campanula medium) 1'- 3' Sun. Late spring, summer bloomer. White, pink and blue flowers. This flower is also called the cup and saucer plant because of its shape. It's a standard for any English garden. Zone 4

Moneyplant (Lunaria) 2' Sun to Part Sun. Spring bloomer. Rosy-pink flower. The dried seed heads look like silver dollars, a plus in our economy. Zone 4

Foxglove (Digitalis) 2' - 4' Sun to Part Shade. Early summer bloomer. White, pink, apricot and beige flowers. Most Foxgloves are biennials which are the showiest group. Perennial Foxgloves are usually shorter with smaller flowers. 'Pam's Choice' is a popular biennial Foxglove with white flowers and maroon-red speckles inside the throat. Other showboats include 'Apricot', 'Alba' (white), 'Foxy' (mixed colors) and 'Giant Shirley (mixed colors). 'Candy Mountain' is the first biennial to have upward facing flowers for better appreciating its beguiling throat markings. All Foxgloves are no-no's for consumption. They can make a heart race to its death. Zone 3

Sweet Rocket, Dame's Rocket (Hesperis) 3' - 4'. Sun to Part Sun. Spring bloomer. Pink, white, lavender and purple flowers. This wildflower is commonly seen along the roadside in spring. It looks a tad bit like garden phlox and is very fragrant. Sweet Rocket will reseed quickly so think carefully before putting it in a more 'refined' garden. It does best in wildflower gardens where plants are encouraged to seed with abandon. Zone 3

Iceland Poppies (Papaver nudicale) 12" - 15" Sun. Late spring, early summer bloomer. Yellow, orange, pink, rose and white flowers. Iceland Poppies have papery-thin petals that form saucer-shaped flowers on elongated stems. The bluish-green foliage has a hairy texture. As with other poppies, these are difficult to transplant once established. Either start them from seed or buy these in 4" pots and carefully place the whole potting medium with plant into the hole so it never knew a thing. Zone 3

CHAPTER 5

Foliage Plants

Top Ten Ornamental Grasses

Ornamental grasses are so easy to work with and provide four seasons of interest. The rustling sound made by breezes, along with a gentle swaying motion, can lower anyone's blood pressure. The fact that deer leave them alone also helps.

When buying ornamental grasses, make sure you select 'clumpers', not those that spread rapidly by renegade roots (rhizomes) or above-ground stems (stolons). If the tag description is not clear about how they grow, ask.

Grasses provide wonderful winter interest. Leave them be in the fall. You may want to stake larger grasses so they keep 'good posture' in winter after it snows. Prune the foliage to within 2" to 3" of the ground in late winter or early spring. Use a power hedge trimmer or sharp pruning shears for larger grasses. To save time raking up blades, place twine, bungee cord or duct tape around the plant's 'waist' before whacking. Some grasses have razor-sharp blades so use protective gloves when handling them. Shorter grasses like Blue Fescues can be 'deadleafed' by simply running your fingers through the clump and pulling out brown foliage.

The best time to divide grasses is in late winter or early spring after you've cut them back or 'combed' them. Depending on the grass, you may need a saw, ax, machete or chainsaw to get through the dense root mass. Keep going, don't let it get the best of you.

Most ornamental grasses prefer full sun and are quite drought tolerant. Of course, like my teenage son, there are always some that break the rules. Many grasses cannot tolerate our colder winters but there are a number that do just grand. I've listed some of my favorites below.

‡ Japanese Forest Grass, Hakone Grass (Hakonechloa) 12" - 24" Part to Full Shade. Late summer, fall bloomer. Creamy-tan flowers. This is a lovely, cascading grass. It does a superb job softening edges. 'Aureola', with shimmering gold and green variegated blades, was the Perennial of the Year in 2009. 'All Gold' has a more upright habit with sold gold leaves. 'Albo Striata' is green and white and 'Beni Kaze' starts out green and then reddens in cooler weather. Zone 5

❦drought tolerant   ‡deer resistant

Blue Fescue (Festuca) 6" - 12" Sun. Summer bloomer. Tan flowers. Stiff, porcupine-like blue blades create striking textural interest. 'Elijah Blue', 'Boulder Blue', 'Blue Glow' and 'Blue Fox' are intense blue. These benefit from dividing every three or four years to keep their compact habit and rich coloring. I don't prune Fescues in spring, I 'comb out' them. Zone 3

Japanese Blood Grass (Imperata cylindrica) 1' - 2' Sun to Part Sun. Late summer, fall bloomer. Creamy-white flowers. I know, you are thinking this is not for colder zones. I disagree. I have grown this grass for years with no winter protection in my borderline Zone 4/5 garden. Japanese Blood Grass has slender green blades that become rich burgundy-red in late summer. When backlit by the sun, this grass is mesmerizing. Zone 5

Blue Oat Grass (Helictotrichon sempervirens) 18" - 30" Sun. Late summer, fall bloomer. Tan flowers. This is a super-sized blue Fescue. Blue Oat Grass has thicker blades and grows taller. It also has a stiffer habit. 'Sapphire' has richer, steel blue blades than the species, sempervirens. This is another one I 'comb' in spring. Zone 3

Fountain Grass (Pennisetum) 6" - 4' Sun to Part Sun. Summer bloomer. Tan to rosy-pink flowers. There are many great choices in this family. 'Little Bunny' only gets 6" - 12" in bloom, 'Hameln' hits the 24" - 30" mark, while 'Karley Rose' displays nicely arching 40" blades. These are just a few of the great clumpers available. Zone 5

Little Bluestem (Schizachyrium) 2' - 3' Sun. Summer bloomer. Silvery flowers. This native grass defines elegance. It has extremely narrow, fine blue blades with some maroon coloring later in the summer. Little Bluestem sways subliming in summer and fall breezes. Zone 3

Japanese Silver Grass (Miscanthus) 3' - 9' Sun. Late summer, fall bloomer. Silver, tan, burgundy and reddish-tan flowers. This is another family with many tried and true performers for colder climates. Great picks include 'Zebrinus' (horizontal gold bars on green blades, 7' - 8', Zone 5), 'Silver Feather' also called 'Silberfeder' (narrow green blades, 9', Zone 4), 'Gracillimus' (narrow green arching blades, 7', Zone 5), 'Graziella' (green blades with large silver-white flower, 6', Zone 5), 'Purpurascens' (green blades that turn reddish in cool weather, 6', Zone 4), 'Morning Light' (very narrow green and white arching blades, 5' - 6', Zone 5), 'Dixieland' (wider green and white blades, 4', Zone 5), 'Variegatus' (like 'Dixieland' but taller, 6', Zone 5) and 'Huron Sunrise' (green blades with white centers and burgundy plumes, 5' - 6', Zone 4).

Switch Grass (Panicum) 3' - 8' Sun. Late summer, fall bloomer. White and rosy-pink flowers. Many Panicums are more upright and less sweeping than Miscanthus grasses. Outstanding cultivars in this family include: 'Heavy Metal' (upright, steel blue blades with white flowers, 5' - 6', Zone 3), 'Shenandoah', 'Cheyenne Sky' and 'Prairie Fire' (all have green and burgundy blades, 3', Zone 3), 'Prairie Sky' (powdery blue blades, 6', zone 3) and 'Cloud Nine' (blue blades, 6', Zone 3).

✢**Northern Sea Oats** (Chasmanthium) 2' - 3' Sun to Part Shade. Late summer, fall flowers. Tan flowers. Northern Sea Oats has a bamboo look with arching seed heads. It is a clump former but it can seed quite aggressively where comfortable. I reduce its fertility by sheering off the flowers (seed heads) before they ripen. This plant is very versatile. I have planted it in dappled shade, full sun and at the edge of my pond. Zone 3

🍂✢**Feather Reed Grass** (Calamagrotis) 4' - 5' Summer bloomer. Tan flowers. A stiff, upright grass that works well in narrow spots. 'Karl Foerster' with solid green blades was the Perennial of the Year in 2001. 'Overdam' mixes it up with green and white blades while 'Eldorado' has green and gold blades. All are hardy to Zone 3.

🍂drought tolerant   ✢deer resistant

Top Ten Perennials with Honkin' Big Leaves

Part of what makes a garden captivating is contrasting foliage. Contrast can come from color as well as a leaf's size, shape and texture. Leaves entertain the eye before, during and after bloom. We should take greater advantage in this easy, low-maintenance way to add pop to a garden. The following 'big kahuna' leafed perennials will grab one's attention, especially if they are paired with fine foliaged beauties (there is a separate list for these) to add visual tension.

One thing be aware of is that with larger leaves comes thirstier plants. There is a greater surface area for water loss through transpiration. Site these big boys in naturally moisture retentive soil or create a mini-bog.

Giant Kale (Crambe) 5' Sun. Summer bloomer. White flowers. This looks like a white Baby's Breath on steroids. Giant Kale has a cloud of airy flower in July. Like the flower mass, its leaves are also oversized but stay low to the ground. They resemble monster cabbage leaves. Even though Giant Kale is rated to Zone 5, I originally saw this wonder plant at Trapp Family Lodge in Stowe, VT. Now that is definitely not zone 5. I have grown it here for eight years with no babying on my part. Surprised? Zone 5

Butterbur (Petisites Japonica) 24" - 36" Sun to Part Shade. Spring bloomer. White flowers. You'll be rubbing your eyes when you see these monstrous leaves. They are spectacular. And you will also be running for your life if you don't contain it. It is very invasive. Even though it is listed as a Zone 5, I have seen it grown in Lake Placid, NY (Zone 3) for years. The more moisture this plant gets, the happier it is, the faster it advances. There is also a variegated version of Butterbur that has green and white leaves and is a slower runner. Zone 5

Astilboides (Astilboides) 3' - 6' Part Sun to Part Shade. Early summer bloomer. White flowers. The leaves of Astilboides can reach 3' across and float 2' to 3' above the ground. They resemble huge lily pods. The flowers look a bit like white Astilbe that balance on thick 5' tall stalks. As you may guess, because of the huge leaves, this plant prefers a moist setting and lots of room. It is rated as a Zone 5 perennial but I've seen it do great in Zone 4 if planted in a protected spot like the east side of the house. Zone 5

Rodger's Flower (Rodgersia) 30" - 4' Part Sun to Shade. Early summer bloomer. Creamy white to pink flowers. Rodger's Flowers are cool, tropical looking plants. They have large, heavily textured, '5-fingered' palmate leaves that are green or bronze. The flowers look like giant Astilbe plumes. R. aesculifolia has greenish-bronze leaves with ivory flowers that have a soft pink blush. 'Chocolate Wings's leaves start out chocolate and change to bronze. 'Elegans' and 'Die Shone' have pink flowers. The flowers are pretty but the leaves play the lead role in the show. Zone 4

✤**Ligularia** (Ligularia) 20" - 4' Part Sun to Part Shade. Summer bloomer. Yellow or orange flowers. All Ligularias have dramatic leaves. 'The Rocket' has ragged, heart-shaped leaves; 'Little Rocket' echoes these but is one notch smaller in height. 'Othello' and 'Desdemona' have chocolate-green scalloped leaves; 'Britt-Marie Crawford' has dazzling rich chocolate foliage and purple undersides. 'Japonica' looks like a tender tropical with is deeply lobed, green leaves. Zone 4

Hosta 2' or larger. Part Shade to Shade. Summer bloomer. White, lavender or purple flowers. For this top ten list we are only interested in those with monstrous leaves. Large, magnificent, weed-smothering leaves. 'Sum and Substance' delivers with gold leaves that are almost 2' across and nicely ribbed. 'Big Daddy', 'Bressingham Blue', 'Blue Angel' and sieboldiana 'Elegans' have frosty blue leaves. 'Guacamole' is delicious with green margins and chartreuse centers (plus very fragrant flowers), 'Frances Williams' has blue-green leaves with chartreuse margins and 'Sagae' produces gray-green leaves with creamy-white margins. Zone 3

Ornamental Rhubarb (Rheum palmatum) 6' - 8' Sun to Part Shade. Summer bloomer. Red flowers. These dramatic, deep green to dark red leaves with purple undersides, are meant for oogling, not eating. No pies here. This is not a shy wallflower. Give it room and a stage. Zone 5

✤**Ostrich Fern** (Matteuccia struthiopteris) 3' - 6' Part Shade to Shade. Foliage. Large, rich green, tapering fronds look like they should be fanning an emperor. Ostrich Ferns lend a tropical presence wherever they are planted. When happy, they can spread at a good pace from underground rhizomes. Other large ferns include Cinnamon Fern (Osmunda cinnemonea), Royal Fern (Osmunda regalis), and Interrupted Fern (Osmunda claytoniana). Zone 3

Inula (Inula magnifica) 4' - 6' Sun. Summer bloomer. Yellow flowers. One foot long, ragged-edged green leaves provide the backdrop for yellow daisy-looking flowers with finely shredded petals. Best planted at the back of the border so as it starts to fade it can do so in privacy. Zone 4

Purple Stemmed Angelica (Angelica gigas) 4' - 6' Part Sun to Part Shade. Summer bloomer. Purple flowers. There could be a toss up between which is more interesting; its funky, dramatic leaves or the large, dome-shaped purple flowers. Tropical looking, fringed leaves extend from bright burgundy stems. Angelica is usually tagged as a biennial or short lived perennial. Although shorter-lived, it is worth every penny. Zone 4

Top Ten Fine Foliage Perennials

Light and airy foliage can have several dynamic design applications. First, as mentioned earlier, they make great contrasting, tension-builders when paired with large leaved plants. You can also create a visual illusion by placing airy specimens at the back of a border. One gets the sense the garden, or property, is larger than it really is. Fine foliaged perennials work well as translucent veils. They don't totally block the plants behind them. And lastly, the foliage dances at the slightest breeze, adding sensual movement to the garden.

Thread Leaf Coreopsis (Coreopsis verticillata) 15" - 30" Sun. Summer bloomer. Yellow, white, pink and bicolor flowers. 'Moonbeam', with its soft lemon flowers, is a top seller. It mounds nicely and is not as aggressive or prone to winterkill as others in this family. It is my hands down pick for thread leaf varieties. 'Crème Brulee', 'Moonray', 'Full Moon' and 'Sunbeam' are marketed as being improved versions of 'Moonbeam'. On the other hand, 'Autumn Blush', 'Heaven's Gate' and 'Sweet Dreams' have given me nightmares. C. rosea, with its limey green foliage and pale pink flowers gives me indigestion. Zone 3

Yarrow (Achillea) 3" - 40" Sun. Summer bloomer. Red, pink, white, apricot, yellow and paprika flowers. All Yarrows have fine, feathery foliage. Some have silvery-gray leaves ('Moonshine', 'Althea') while others have dark green, stiffer leaves (the Seduction series). Yarrows do best in a fast draining soil with little fertilizer. Zone 3

Flax (Linum) 8" - 24" Sun . Summer bloomer. Blue or white flowers. Flax has gently arching stems with small leaves. The delicate flowers open in the morning and then drop their petals in the afternoon leaving a delightful confetti blanket at the plant's base. The next day, the party starts again. Sharp drainage is a must. Zone 5

Wand Flower (Gaura) 15" - 3' Sun. Summer bloomer. White or pink flowers. Wand Flower is not reliably hardy in zones 3, 4 or 5 but it does reseed where happy. There are two reasons I have included it on this list. It is a nonstop bloomer from June through October with no deadheading. And the airy, arching foliage complements any plants lucky enough to be next to it. I prefer white flowering Wand Flower to pink. White is easier to see from a distance, especially if the blooms are petite. Wand Flowers also make terrific container plants. Zone 5

Blue Star Flower (Amsonia) 12" - 36" Sun to Part Sun. Late spring, early summer. Icy blue flowers. Blue Star Flowers have willow-like leaves. A. hubrichtii has the most feathery foliage and it turns the brightest orange-gold in fall. The other cultivars do not get as brilliant fall color. I shear back hubrichtii to 1/3 its height after flowering for a denser mound of foliage. Zone 3

⚜Maidenhair Fern (Adiantum pedatum) 12" - 18" Part Shade to Shade. Foliage. There are many great ferns with delicate fronds but my pick for the easiest and most delicate is Maidenhair Fern. It has soft green fronds in a circular pattern and jet-black stems. Maidenhair Fern has a mystical appearance as it emerges in spring. Zone 3

⚜Fernleaf Peony (Paeonia tenuifolia) 12" - 15" Sun to Part Sun. Spring bloomer. Red or pink flowers. This flower never fails to draw oohhs and aahhs from onlookers. It has finely cut, feathery leaves that are light to medium green. The flowers can be single or double. Like other peonies, Fernleaf Peony does not bloom for long but after the flowers gracefully bow out, the foliage remains for an encore. Fernleaf Peonies are very long-lived and disease free. Don't fret if it dies back in very hot summers. It's only going dormant and will return the following spring in all its glory. They typically sell for $35 - $50. It is cheaper to buy them bare-root. Zone 3

photo courtesy of Daniele Ippoliti

⚜Fern-Leaved Bleeding Heart (Dicentra) 8" - 15" Part Sun to Shade. Late spring, summer bloomer. White and pink flowers. All Fern-Leaved Bleeding Hearts have lacy foliage, many with a frosty blue hue. I am a big fan of the Heart series: 'King of Hearts' (rich rosy-pink), 'Ivory Hearts' (white), 'Candy Hearts' (medium pink) and 'Burning Hearts' (deep pink with white edges). These resent being divided but if you are feeling adventurous, do so in spring before they set bloom. Zone 3

⚜Jacob's Ladder (Polemonium) 6" - 24" Sun to Part Shade. Spring bloomer. White, apricot and lavender flowers. Jacob's Ladder can have solid green or variegated leaves. P. reptans only gets 6" - 8" tall and covers itself with violet flowers. The variegated varieties are the rage. 'Stairway to Heaven' has pink, white and green leaves, 'Touch of Class' and 'Snow and Sapphires' have mint-green leaves with crisp white margins. 'Apricot Delight' has apricot flowers and green foliage. Stay clear of 'Brise D'anjou'. It has a weaker constitution than others. Zone 3

Ornamental Grasses of course! See the list of Top Ten grasses for great choices.

🌿drought tolerant ⚜deer resistant

Blue leaves add a cool, calming effect. They take down the heat a notch. They are the perfect partner for hot colored red, yellow, orange or fuchsia flowers. The following are a few of my favorites.

Hosta 6" - 4' Part Shade to Shade. Summer bloomer. White, lavender and purple flowers. Frosty blue Hosta are a must in shade gardens. There are smaller cultivars like 'Blue Mouse Ears' (6") and 'Blue Cadet' (15") and then there are the big boys like 'Big Daddy' (36"), 'Blue Angel' (36"), 'Blue Umbrellas' (32") and sieboldiana 'Elegans' (32"). 'Fragrant Blue' (18") has sweet-smelling lavender flowers. All blue Hosta need as much shade as you can give them. The blue is actually caused by a wax coating on green leaves that 'melts-off' in sun and heat or gets washed off by dripping water. Zone 3

Fringed Leaved, Fern-Leaved Bleeding Heart (Dicentra eximia) 8" - 15" Part Sun to Shade. Late spring, summer, early fall bloomer. White and pink flowers. There are medium green, or gray-green leaved Fringed Bleeding Hearts but it's the icy, frosty blue foliaged knockouts that create excitement: 'King of Hearts' (deep pink); 'Ivory Hearts' (white), 'Candy Hearts' (medium pink), and 'Burning Hearts' (rosy-red with white edges). Zone 3

Carnation, Pinks (Dianthus) 4" - 20" Sun. Spring, summer bloomers. White, pink, red, yellow and multicolored flowers. 'Firestar' (red flowers, 8"), 'Eastern Star' (red flowers, 7"), 'Frosty Fire' (double red, 6"), 'Firewitch' (pink, 7"), 'Little Blue Boy' (white, 10") and 'Bath's Pink' (soft pink, 7") are all proven performers. Shear off flowers after their first round to trigger a secondary bloom and thicker blue foliage mat. Zones 4

Ornamental Grasses (numerous families) 8" - 6' Sun. Summer, fall bloomer. White, tan and soft pink flowers. There are a number of steel blue-bladed grasses that provide stiff competition to floral contenders. Panicum 'Heavy Metal' (white flowers, late summer, 5' - 6'), Festuca 'Elijah Blue' (creamy flowers, summer, 8" - 10"), Helictotrichon 'Sapphire' (tan flowers, summer, 18" - 24") and Schizachyrium 'Prairie Blues' (white, late summer, 3') are all blue-eyed beauties. Zone 4

Stonecrop (Sedum) 2" - 18" Sun. Late summer, fall bloomer. Pink and yellow flowers. Sedums always are 'double your pleasure' plants. You get dynamic flowers and foliage. 'Hab Gray' is one of the taller blues (12" - 18") with soft yellow flowers in late summer. Sieboldii spirals out from a central crown and stays low at 6" - 8". Cauticola has tight rosettes hugging the ground at 2" with soft pink flowers in late summer. 'Lidakense' has blue leaves that reach 4" with dusty pink flowers in fall while 'Blue Spruce' has yellow flowers and leaves that resemble the needles of a blue spruce. Zone 3

❧✛**Donkey Tail Spurge** (Euphorbia myrsinites) 6" - 9" Sun. Spring bloomer. Yellow flowers. Springy, coiled blue stems have canary yellow flowers at their tips. A milky sap, released when stems are pruned, can cause skin irritation to those with sensitive skin. Donkey Tail can be a short-lived perennial but it reseeds where happy. Zone 5.

❧✛**Yucca** 4' Sun. Summer bloomer. White flowers. 'Sapphire Skies' has an architecturally interesting look with sword-like leaves and frosty blue coloring. All Yuccas need a lot of space, they can easily get 3' wide. They also demand sharp drainage. Zone 5

✛**Meadow Rue** (Thalictrum) 4' - 6' Sun to Part Sun. Summer bloomer. Sulfur yellow and lavender flowers. Thalictrum glaucum has blue-green leaves that resemble those of Columbine. Airy sprays of sulfur yellow flowers billow to 5' in late June and July. 'Splendide' follows this show with clouds of lavender blooms that can get 6' in July and August. After the flowers are spent, prune them off for a large mound of attractive leaves. Zone 4

❧**Japanese Bluebells** (Mertensia pterocarpa var. yezoensis) 6" - 12" Part Shade to Shade. Spring, early summer bloomer. Blue flowers. This is a challenging plant to purchase but when you find it, grab it! It has rich blue leaves that do not go dormant in the summer like its cousin, Virginia Bluebells. Zone 4

❧✛ **Chives** (Allium flavum) 6" - 12" Sun to Part Shade. Summer bloomer. Yellow flowers. Rich blue, slender leaves send forth yellow flowers in early summer. The small dangling umbrels are a nice contrast to blue leaves. You need a cluster of three of more yellow alliums to make a nice show. I have these in dappled shade next to Hosta, Japanese Painted Fern and dwarf Astilbes. Zone 4

Top Ten Yellow or Gold Foliage Perennials

Glowing yellow and gold leaved perennials illuminate gardens, especially shady ones. Many of these plants do better in part shade where they don't bleach out or scorch.

Hosta 6" - 4' Part Shade to Shade. Summer bloomer. White, lavender and purple flowers. Dwarf gold Hosta include 'Gold Drops' (6", lavender flowers), 'Maui Buttercups' (6", violet flowers), 'Cheatin Heart' (8", lavender flowers) and 'Gold Edger' (7", white flowers). Medium sized golds are 'August Moon' (16", white flowers) and 'King Tut' (18", white flowers). Large golds are 'Sum and Substance' (36", white flowers), 'Gold Standard' (mostly gold with dark green margin, 24", lavender flowers) and 'Sun Power' (26", lavender flowers). Zone 3

Bleeding Heart (Dicentra) 36" Part Sun to Shade. Spring bloomer. Pink Flowers. 'Gold Heart' makes you want to put on sunglasses. Screamin' yellow leaves and bright pink flowers get your blood pumpin'. 'Gold Heart' stays shorter and grows wider than green leaved, spring blooming Bleeding Hearts. Another difference is its ability to hang on and not go dormant as early (or at all) as other spectabilis cultivars. Zone 3

Spiderwort (Tradescantia) 12" Part Sun to Shade. Summer bloomer. Violet flowers. 'Sweet Kate' is one of the few Spiderworts that is a behaved clumper. Some confuse its brilliant gold blades to be an ornamental grass. Shearing it back in mid-summer results in a tighter clump. The only bad habit I've noticed is an occasional effort to revert to solid green leaves. When you see rebellious green blades emerge, pinch these off at their base or divide them out. Zone 3

Coral Bell (Heuchera) 6" - 14" Sun to Shade. Summer bloomer. White, cream and pink flowers. 'Lime Rickey' (8", white flowers), 'Key Lime Pie' (8" - 10", pink flowers) and 'Citronelle' (12", cream flowers) glow in shady beds. 'Citronelle' has silver undersides, a fuzzy surface and remains a gold beacon even in heavier shade. Zone 4

Meadowsweet (Filipendula ulmaria 'Aurea') 2' - 3' Sun to Part Shade. Early summer bloomer. White flowers. 'Aurea' has ferny yellow foliage with misty white flowers in early summer. I prune the flowers off and put the spotlight on the tropical foliage. It looks especially nice next to blue Hosta, purple Coral Bells and violet-blue flowering Geranium 'Rozanne'. It is easy to divide spring through summer. Zone 4

Deadnettle (Lamium) 8" Part Sun to Shade. Spring, summer bloomer. White flowers. 'Aureum' and 'Beedham's White' have gold leaves with white center markings. They look super placed along paths, retaining walls and at the front of borders. Lamiums also work well in containers and window boxes but remove them in the fall and overwinter them in the ground. Lamiums can be propagated by division or stem cuttings. The running stems (called stolons) form roots at various intervals. Use a sharp knife to cut stem pieces from the 'mother plant' and replant. Zone 3

⚘Stonecrop (Sedum 'Angelina') 3" - 6" Sun. Summer bloomer. Yellow flowers. 'Angelina' has needle-like, gold foliage that turns orangey in fall. Bright yellow, flat-shaped flowers smother the plant in summer. This should be treated as a groundcover that can easily be plucked where you don't want it. Zone 3

⚘Japanese Forest Grass (Hakonechola macra) 12" - 24" Part Sun to Shade. Summer bloomer. 'All Gold' has solid gold, slightly wider blades with a less cascading nature than other Japanese Forest Grasses. 'Aureola' has gold and white variegated leaves but looks mostly gold. These clump-forming grasses are pricey so divisions are the way to go. They can be divided at any point before September. Zone 5 (although they can handle Zone 4 if planted in a sheltered area)

⚘Mountain Bluet, Batchelor Button, Cornflower (Centaurea montana) 24" Sun to Part Sun. Early summer bloomer. Blue-violet flowers. 'Gold Bullion' shimmers in the garden. It responds well to a hedge trimmer haircut in mid-July for a more shapely form in August. Many times a second bloom will follow as well. 'Gold Bullion' hates (read as dies) poorly draining soil. Zone 3

⚘Speedwell (Veronica prostrata) 3" Sun. Summer bloomer. Blue flowers. 'Trehane' is not commonly used but it should be. Its yellow matt-like leaves smother weeds. 'Trehane' works well in rock gardens and in containers. Zone 4

⚘drought tolerant   ⚘deer resistant

Silver adds elegance to any plant combination. It 'plays nicely' with all neighboring colors. Most silver leaved plants are also drought tolerant.

Lamb's Ears (Stachys byzantina) 6" - 10" Sun. Summer bloomer. Rosy-pink flowers. Lamb's Ears are meant to be petted. They have such soft, furry leaves. Many shoot forth pink flower stalks in summer that are prized by hummingbirds. 'Helene von Stein' has larger silver leaves and does not flower. 'Silver Carpet' is most commonly available and can be quite 'fleet of foot' in the garden. 'Nana' is the runt of the family with tiny silver leaves and 3" - 6" rosy flower spikes. Lamb's Ears needs sharp drainage and is sensitive to humidity. Once a month I 'rake' rotted leaves from the clump with my hands. 'Thinning' out leaves allows better airflow and more attractive foliage. Zone 3

photo courtesy of PerennialResource.com

Wormwood (Artemisia) 8" - 10" Sun. Summer bloomer. Creamy, white flowers. 'Silver Mound' is a ferny mound until July when it flowers. Then it flops open and looks messy. Deal with this rebellion by whacking it back to within a few inches of the crown. The pruning stimulates new foliage that flushes out to create soft mounds again. Other nice silver family members include 'Silver Brocade' and 'Valerie Finnis'. Avoid 'Silver Queen' and 'Silver King' that are nasty thugs. All Wormwoods need sharp drainage. Zone 3

Silver Speedwell (Veronica incana) 10" Sun. Early summer bloomer. Blue flowers. Stiff blue flowers jump from matted silver foliage and continue to bloom most of the summer if deadheaded. I don't. My vote is for a tight silver carpet that forms after shearing off the spent flowers. Veronica incanca makes a striking groundcover in hot, sunny spots with good drainage. Zone 4

Lungwort (Pulmonaria) 8" - 12" Part Shade to Shade. Spring bloomer. Pink and blue flowers. 'Majeste' has solid silver-white leaves. 'Samurai' is similar to 'Majeste' but has contrasting narrow green margins. 'Diana Clare' has mostly silver leaves with green blotches. All Lungworts can get powdery mildew after flowering. Don't tolerate this. Whack the leaves back to within a few inches of the ground and they will respond with a nice new set. Zone 3

✿‡Dead Nettle (Lamium maculatum) 4" - 8" Part Sun to Shade. Spring, summer bloomers. Pink and white flowers. Lamiums can have silver; green and white; green, gold and white; and gold and white leaves. In my opinion the silver ones are the best. They do a splendid job reflecting light in shady beds in addition to contributing showy flowers. Top performers include 'Pink Pewter' (pink flowers), 'Purple Dragon' (rosy-purple flowers), 'Chablis' (soft pink flowers) and 'Cosmopolitan' (pink flowers). 'White Nancy' with white flowers has failed my appreciation test. It tends to get leggy and die out in sections. 'Beacon Silver' is another one that gets low marks. It frequently gets fungal problems on its leaves later in summer. Zone 3

✿‡Edelweiss (Leontopodium alpinum) 6" Sun. Summer bloomer. White flowers. Silvery, fuzzy leaves are a nice backdrop for stiff stems topped by creamy white flowers. Edelweiss likes sharp drainage and is best used in masses to create the desired effect. I love pressing these flowers for framing or notecards. They also make pretty dried flowers for arrangements. Zone 3

✿‡Snow-in-the-Summer (Cerastium) 4" - 8" Sun. Late spring, early summer bloomer. White flowers. Snow-in-the-Summer can be sometimes tagged as an 'enthusiastic' spreader but it's easy to rip out where not wanted plus it has charming white flowers. After it finishes flowering in late June, shear back spent blooms to prevent a ratty looking appearance in summer. Buzz cuts look good on this plant and stimulates new silver growth. They do best in sandy soils. Zone 3

✿‡Russian Sage (Perovskia) 25" - 4' Sun. Summer bloomer. Lavender flowers. There are quite a few Russian Sage cultivars. Frankly, I can't tell the difference between most of them. The only one I can identify for sure is 'Little Spire' that only gets 25" tall. Atriplicifolia, 'Filagran' and 'Longin' all grow around 3' to 4' tall and look the same to me. All Russian Sage have fragrant flowers and leaves plus demand sharp drainage. The sandier and crummier the soil, the better. Hold the fertilizer as well. Zone 4

✿‡Wooly Thyme (Thymus praecox) 3" Sun to Part Sun. Spring bloomer. Lavender and pink flowers. Delicate flowers bury silver mats of leaves in spring. 'Minor' (2", pink flowers), 'Hall's Woolly' (3", lavender flowers) and 'Doretta Klaber' (2", dark pink) are popular. Wooly Thyme can be used in rock gardens, between stepping stones and in trough gardens. Sharp drainage is a must. Zone 3

✿Pussytoes (Antennaria neglecta var. gaspensis) 2" Sun to Part Sun. Spring bloomer. Pink flowers. I have had trouble getting this to thrive in my garden. My soil is too rich for it. Pussytoes thrive on neglect. The crummier the soil, the happier it is. The only crummy soil it hates is clay. Pussytoes is commonly used between pavers and stepping stones as well as in crevices on rock walls. It feels heavenly between your toes. Zone 3

✿drought tolerant   ‡deer resistant

Top Ten Chocolate, Burgundy or Purple Foliage Perennials

A little goes a long way with chocolate leaves, unlike chocolate candy. Too many dark foliaged perennials elicit a somber mood. Placing these by hot colored flowers or leaves is the ticket. Also, extremely dark, almost black foliaged perennials can be challenging to see against dark mulches. Frame these with silver or yellow leaved groundcovers to bring out their best. For example, Black Mondo grass or 'Obsidian' Coral Bell standout when surrounded with Creeping Yellow Jenny (Lysimachia nummularia 'Aurea') or dwarf Lamb's Ears ('Nana').

Coral Bell (Heuchera) 5" - 24" Sun to Shade. Late spring, summer bloomer. White, pink, red and creamy flowers. Dark leaved Coral Bells are hot. And many of the names sound as delicious as they look: 'Plum Pudding' (8", rich purple leaves, pink flowers), 'Brownies' (olive-brown leaves, 24", white flowers), 'Cherries Jubilee' (7", chocolate-purple leaves, red flowers) and 'Chocolate Ruffles' (10", chocolate leaves with burgundy undersides and curly edges, creamy white flowers). 'Petite Pearl Fairy' is remarkable for the amount of punch it gives for such a small plant (6", burgundy-chocolate leaves, pink flowers). If black is your thing, then so are 'Obsidian' (10", very shiny leaves), 'Blackout' (12" - 18"), and 'Black Beauty' (10", curly leaves). All have creamy-white flowers. Zone 4

Ligularia (Ligularia) 3' - 4' Part Sun to Part Shade. Summer bloomer. Orange and yellow flowers. The large dark, glossy leaves of Ligularias create great drama. 'Desdemona' and 'Othello' have a purple tone to their leaves in spring that slowly fades to brownish-green in summer. I find it difficult to tell the two apart but 'Desdemona' has a slighter richer substance and darker stems. On the other hand, 'Britt-Marie Crawford' leaves no guesswork. Her huge, scalloped leaves are seductively dark and shiny. All three shoot up orangey-yellow flowers on long stalks in August. Ligularias need a moisture-retentive soil to handle the amount of water lost through their leaves. Zone 4

Stonecrop (Sedum) 2" - 30" Sun to Part Sun. Summer, fall bloomer. Pink, red and brick red flowers. Similar to Coral Bells, there are many sultry beauties to choose from in this family. 'Purple Emperor' (16", purple-black leaves, dusty-pink) is one of my favorites. Other good picks are 'Xenox' (20" - 24", burgundy leaves, pink flowers), 'Postman's Pride' (18" - 24", purple-black leaves, rosy-red flowers), 'Sunset Cloud' (12" - 18", purple leaves, rosy-red flowers), 'Vera Jameson' (10" - 12" burgundy-green leaves, soft pink flowers) and 'Dragon's Blood' (3" - 6", burgundy-green leaves, red flowers). Despite the hoopla over 'Black Jack' (24", almost black leaves, pink flowers), I've found its leaves scorch and seem anemic in growth. It was a loser in my gardens. Taller Sedums placed in part sun benefit from pinching the stems by 1/3 to 1/2 in early July. This keeps them from flopping open in the fall. Zone 3

✿⚘Beard Tongue (Penstemon) 2' - 3' Sun to Part Sun. Summer bloomer. Creamy white and pink flowers. 'Husker's Red' made a big splash when it was the 1996 Perennial Plant of the Year. The newer foliage is a bewitching purple-red color. This tends to green out later in summer. It has creamy-white flowers. 'Dark Towers' leaves 'Husker's Red' in the dust with its dark, wine-red leaves that hold their color as the temperature climbs in summer. 'Dark Towers' also switched gears with its purple-pink flowers. Zone 3

⚘Bugbane, Snakeroot (Cimicifuga) 2' - 6' Part Sun to Part Shade. Late summer, fall bloomer. White to soft pink flowers. Rich chocolate and sublime perfume are a girl's best friends. The dark leaved Bugbanes provide both. 'Brunette', 'Hillside Black Beauty', 'Atropurpurea', 'Black Negligee' 'James Compton' and 'Chocoholic' are all 'womanizers'. They have long, slender bottlebrush flowers that dance in late summer breezes. Zone 3

✿⚘Cranesbill (Hardy Geranium) 4" - 16" Sun to Part Sun. Late spring, early summer bloomer. Magenta, lilac and purple flowers. The chocolate, deeply cut leaves of these hardy Geraniums make a splash spring through fall. Most are well behaved 'clumpers' that don't seed around like some other Geraniums. 'Midnight Reiter' is petite and only reaches 6" with lilac flowers; 'Victor Reiter' kicks it up a notch at 20" with lilac-blue flowers and 'Dark Reiter', at 10", boasts handsome plum-purple leaves with lilac-blue flowers. 'Espresso', at 12" - 16", has more of a reddish-brown leaf and pink flowers. The only darker Geranium that caused me to put my hands on my hips in frustration was 'Orkney Pink'. It seemed so harmless and cute at 4" with pink flowers but it seeded around with abandon. Zone 3

⚘Maltese Cross (Lychnis arkwrightii) 8" - 15" Sun to Part Sun. Summer bloomer. Orange with red undertone flowers. This is one fun perennial! It has fluorescent orange flowers on chocolate-green foliage. 'Vesuvius' has graced my gardens for years. It gets 15" - 18" tall while its little brother, 'Orange Dwarf', only hits 8". 'Orange Gnome' comes in at 12" - 15". After flowering, prune the plant back to within 4" - 5" for a neat, rich-colored mound. Maltese Cross hates wet soil. Zone 3

✿⚘Bugleweed (Ajuga) 3" - 6" Sun to Shade. Spring bloomer. Violet-blue flowers. 'Black Scallop' makes you want to eat it right up. Big, black, shiny, crinkly leaves matt the ground, eliminating any hope for weeds to press through. The spiky rich flowers bloom for three weeks or more in spring. I like using 'Black Scallop' around yellow and marmalade Coral Bells for a striking foliage combo. I have also combined it with Geranium 'Rozanne' for three seasons of divine violet blue flowers coupled with attractive black leaves. Zone 3

✿Foamy Bells (Heucherella) 10" Sun to Shade. Summer bloomer. Pink flowers. I fell in love with 'Burnished Bronze' the moment I laid eyes on it. The leaves are nicely cut, glossy, and good sized. Soft pink flowers finish the look. A tough love, drought tolerant perennial that works well in groups. Zone 4

✿✤Switch Grass (Panicum) 3' - 5' Sun. Fall bloomer. Soft pink flowers. Many ornamental grasses have a hard time, if not impossible, making it through zone 5 or colder winters. But lots of Panicums plough through our winters with fortitude. 'Shenandoah' has done fabulously in my gardens. It has burgundy-red and dark green blades that reach 3'. 'Cheyenne Sky' and 'Praire Fire' look like 'Shenandoah' with more intense coloring. 'Huron Solstice' has the same wine-red hues but bluer blades. Leave these standing in winter so they can thumb their dried flower heads at Old Man Winter. Prune them back to within 1" - 2" of the ground in late winter or early spring. This is also the time to divide grasses if needed. Zone 4 (some growers state Zone 3)

Top Ten Bicolor Foliage Perennials

🌿Foamy Bells (Heucherella) 6" - 12" Sun to Part Shade. Early summer bloomer. White flowers. 'Stoplight' will stop you in your tracks. The leaves have glowing red centers surrounded by bright yellow margins. Forget the flowers. 'Alabama Sunrise' looks similar to 'Stoplight' but is supposed to be more tolerant of heat and humidity. The foliage mounds stay tight and neat. I occasionally prune the outer rim of leaves that can fade a bit with age. These Foamy Bells can be pricey so propagate what you have. They divide easily anytime from spring through late summer. Zone 4

False Sunflower (Heliopsis) 24" - 36" Sun to Part Sun. Summer bloomer. Yellow flowers. 'Loraine Sunshine' has silvery-white leaves with contrasting green veins. The leaves almost look like green and white Caladiums on a diet ('Loraine Sunshine's leaves are much smaller). Even though this plant can tolerate part sun, the leaves have better contrast in full sun. Zone 3

🌿Hosta (Hosta) 4" - 4' Part Sun to Shade. Summer bloomer. White, lavender and purple flowers. Needless to say, there are many bicolored Hosta to pick from. 'June' is a favorite of many and was selected as the Hosta of the Year in 2001. It has a blue-green margin and chartreuse center. Please see the Top Ten Hosta list for other winners. Zone 3

Garden Phlox (Phlox paniculata) 30" - 36" Sun. Summer bloomer. Pink flowers. 'Goldmine' is a blue ribbon winner in my book. It has bold green and gold foliage with fuchsia flowers. 'Becky Towe' (green with creamy-yellow margins, pinkish-red flowers), 'Frosted Elegance' (medium green with creamy-white margins, pale and dark pink flowers) and 'Nora Leigh' (green with white margins, soft pink flowers) are also politely flamboyant'. Zone 3

⊹Jacob's Ladder (Polemonium) 14" - 24" Sun to Part Shade. Spring bloomer. Light blue flowers. 'Touch of Class' and 'Snow and Sapphires' have mint green leaves with crisp white margins. Elegant light blue flowers dangle above the stunning variegated foliage in spring. Once the flowers have finished, prune these off for striking 'fern imitators'. Zone 3

🌿Stonecrop (Sedum) 3" - 24" Sun to Part Sun. Summer, fall bloomer. Pink, white, red and yellow flowers. There are many two color sedums on the garden shelf. 'Sedum kamtschaticum 'Variegatum' has green with creamy-yellow edges and is a 5" groundcover. The slightly taller Sieboldii gets 5" - 6" tall with blue-green leaves edged in pink. Other super picks are 'Frosty Morn' (green with white margins, 12"), 'Autumn Delight' (chartreuse with dark green margins, 18" - 24") and 'Autumn Charm' (green with soft yellow margins, 15"). Zone 3

🌿drought tolerant   ⊹deer resistant

Foamflower (Tiarella) 6" - 8" Part Sun to Shade. Late spring, summer bloomer. White and pink flowers. Foamflowers have green leaves with chocolate-black beauty marks. The leaves vary in size and shape. Some knockouts are 'Black Snowflake' (white flowers), 'Crow Feather' (soft pink flowers), 'Mint Chocolate' (creamy white), 'Sugar & Spice' (pink and white flowers) and 'Neon Lights'. 'Heronswood Mist' has fuzzy creamy-green leaves and white flowers. Most Foamflowers are clump formers but 'Cascade Creeper' and 'Running Tapestry' spread slowly and make magnificent groundcovers. Zone 3

photo courtesy of PerennialResource.com

German Bearded Iris and Japanese Iris (Iris germanica and ensata) 18" - 34" Sun. Spring, summer bloomer. Lavender-blue flowers. I use these perennials more for their foliage than flowers because they're not long bloomers. The sword-like foliage makes great accents in the garden. Iris pallida 'Variegata' has green and yellow stripes (34", spring bloomer, violet-blue flowers), pallida 'Argentea Variegata' has green and white stripes (34", spring bloomer, lavender-blue flowers) and ensata 'Variegata' has green and white stripes (30", summer bloomer, blue-purple flowers). After they have finished blooming, remove the flower stalks. The leaves of variegated Irises stay clean throughout the summer, unlike many other Irises that can get ratty looking as the months go on. Zone 3

Daylily (Hemerocallis) 12" Sun to Part Shade. Summer bloomer. Golden-orange flowers. 'Golden Zebra' is a unique daylily that prances bright gold and green streaked leaves in full sun. In shadier spots the yellow fades to white. I have grown this daylily for years and have been very pleased with its compact habit. Plus it has never reverted to a solid leaf, a bad habit of some variegated plants. Zone 4

Yucca (Yucca filamentosa) 2' - 3' Sun to Part Sun. Summer bloomer. Creamy-white flowers. 'Bright Edge' has narrow green leaves with yellow edges. It is very 'Southwestern' looking. It does not grow as quickly as solid green leaved Yuccas which is a good thing. I have found variegated Yuccas to be inconsistent about sending forth stalks of white dangling bells but I'm okay with this. The sensational blades provide four seasons of interest, especially in winter when they stand proudly in the snow. Zone 4

Top Ten Tricolor Foliage Perennials

✛**Athyrium niponicum** (Japanese Painted Fern) 8" - 22" Part Shade to Shade. Foliage plant. Japanese Painted Ferns are the lush 'painted ladies' of the shade garden. The silver, burgundy-red, and green fronds make all 'bed partners' look good. 'Silver Falls', 'Ursula's Red', 'Regal Red' and 'Burgundy Lace' have richer coloring than commonly used 'Pictum'. These ferns look especially lovely near heavier substance perennials like Hosta, Ligularia and Rodger's Flower. Zone 3

Toad Lily (Tricyrtis) 28" Part Shade to Shade. Late summer, fall bloomer. White and lavender flowers. 'Tricolor' has pink, white and green mottled foliage with white and purple spotted flowers. The description may make you queasy but its appearance is unique. If you can't handle the 'plaids and stripes' look, pinch off the flowers. Zone 5

🌱**Stonecrop** (Sedum) 3" - 30" Sun. Summer, fall bloomer. Pink flowers. Sedum seiboldii 'Mediovariegatum' has coil-like stems with frosty blue, creamy yellow and pink foliage tipped with showy pink flowers. 'Tri-color' is a 3" tall groundcover with pink, white and green leaves and pink flowers in summer. Upright Sedums include 'Diamond Edge' (yellow and green leaves with a pink flush plus burgundy-red stems, 18") and 'Samuel Oliphant' (same leave coloring as 'Diamond Edge' but taller at 24" - 30"). Zone 3

🌱✛**Coral Bell** (Heuchera) 9" - 12" Sun to Shade. Summer bloomer. Creamy white flowers. 'Green Spice' is a showy coral bell that thrives in sun or shade. 'Green Spice' has large green, silver and red leaves. 'Tiramisu' and 'Miracle' are like chameleons. In cooler weather (spring and fall) they have pinkish-red and chartreuse leaves but in summer they change to a chartreuse and silvery wardrobe. Interesting. Zone 4

🌱✛**Cushion Spurge** (Euphorbia) 12" - 18" Sun to Part Sun. Spring bloomer. Yellow flowers. Cushion Spurges are no-fuss, top performing perennials. 'First Blush' (12") has pink, white and green leaves and stays compact and mounded. 'Bonfire' (18") is more flamboyant with purple, red and orangey-tan leaves. Be careful when shopping for Cushion Spurge. There are a number of tempting cultivars that are only hardy to Zone 6. Don't zone out. Zone 4

✛**Sea Holly** (Eryngium) 6" - 8" Sun. Summer bloomer. Violet-blue flowers. 'Jade Frost' is the first variegated Sea Holly with showy pink, white and green leaves. It is a narrow growing plant, shooting its flower stalks straight up. As with all Sea Hollies, it thrives on neglect, poor soil and in hot, sunny spots. Zone 5

🌱**Hosta** 13" - 26" Part Shade to Shade. Summer bloomer. Lavender and white flowers. There are many solid colored and bicolored Hosta but those sporting three colors are rare. 'Deja Blu' (blue-green, green and white leaves, 14"), 'Seducer' (dark green, gold

🌱drought tolerant   ✛deer resistant

and white leaves, 26"), 'Striptease' (green, chartreuse and white leaves, 20") and 'Hanky Panky' (green, chartreuse and white leaves, 13") are striking specimens. If unique stem coloring is counted then 'October' has four colors, green, chartreuse and white leaves with red stems. Zone 3

⁜Painter's Palette (Persicaria virginiana) 24" - 30" Sun to Part Shade. Late summer, fall bloomer. Soft, rosy-red flowers. 'Painter's Palette' was a gift to me from another perennial collector. I cherish it. It has creamy yellow and green leaves with a burgundy-red 'V' in the center. The airy flowers are interesting but less so than the leaves. 'Red Dragon' has even showier leaves but I have not been able to winter it over even though it is rated Zone 5. Zone 4

⁜Chameleon Plant (Houttuynia) 6" - 9" Sun to Part Shade. Summer bloomer. White flowers. Don't turn your back on this one. It is an aggressive groundcover that serves a purpose where you want a colorful red, yellow and green leaved, weed smothering, blanket. It has its best coloring in moist, sunny areas. The flowers are insignificant. It is late to wake up in the spring so don't assume you have lost the darling. Zone 3

⁜Jacob's Ladder (Polemonium 'Stairway to Heaven') 1' - 2' Sun to Part Shade. Spring bloomer. Lavender flowers. 'Stairway to heaven' is the most reliable variegated Jacob's Ladder I've grown. It has green, white and pink flushed leaves and grows to 2' in flower. After blooming, shear off the spent flowers to create an impressive ferny mound. Zone 3

⁜Astilbe (Astilbe) 15" Part Sun to Part Shade. Early summer bloomer. Pink flowers. 'Colorflash' is a terrific perennial, providing months of interest. It has pink flowers starting in late June to mid-July. After flowering the foliage starts to really color-up. Burgundy, purple and green leaves shimmer into early fall and then the leaves turn a brilliant reddish-orange. Cameras please. Zone 4

CHAPTER 6

The Photo Gallery

As stated in the introduction, my goals for writing this book were to introduce great plants; warn you about others; and provide design and garden care tips and shortcuts. The book was not created to be an illustrated encyclopedia or coffee table book. There are many great resources and web sites for those purposes. A few great web sites for photo images and additional cultural information are PerennialResource.com (www.perennialresource. com), Proven Winners (www.proven-winners.com), Estabrook's Nursery in Maine (www.estabrooksonline. com), Cold Climate Gardening (www. coldclimategardening.com), Dave's Garden (www.davesgarden.com) and Perry's Perennial Pages (www.uvm. edu/~pass/perry) hosted by horticulturist Dr. Leonard Perry from the University of Vermont.

The following plants are a few award winners mentioned in this book. Under each photo I noted any list the plant is on, or would have been on if more than ten plants were featured. The season – spring, summer or fall – refers to when the plant blooms. Plus I included some snapshots of my gardens for design ideas.

Gentian 'True Blue'
Full Sun - Part Sun. Summer.
Blue flowers, deer, rabbit,
hummingbird
(photo courtesy of PerennialResource.com)

Fleece Flower 'Firetail'
Full Sun - Part Sun. Summer,
fall. Top ten sun summer,
drought tolerant, deer

Sweet Coneflower 'Henry
Eilers' Full Sun - Part Sun.
Summer, fall. Deer, butterfly,
drought tolerant
(photo courtesy of PerennialResource.com)

Siberian Bugloss 'Jack Frost'
Part Shade - Shade. Spring.
Top ten spring shade, blue
flowers, dry shade, deer,
foliage
(photo courtesy of PerennialResource.com)

Monkshood 'Blue Lagoon'
Full Sun - Part Shade.
Summer. Poisonous,
deer, rabbit
(Photo courtesy of PerennialResource.com)

Shredded Umbrella Plant
Part Shade - Shade. Spring.
Unusual, shade
(photo courtesy of Plant Delights Nursery
—www.PlantDelights.com)

False Indigo 'Twilite Prairie-Blues' Full Sun - Part Sun. Spring. Top ten spring sun, drought tolerant, deer, butterfly

(photo courtesy of PerennialResource.com)

Japanese Ligularia Sun - Part Shade. Summer. Unusual, deer, butterfly, wet

(photo courtesy of Plant Delights Nursery – www.PlantDelights.com)

Bugbane, Snakeroot 'Hillside Black Beauty' Part Sun - Part Shade. Summer, fall. Fragrant, bee, chocolate foliage, top ten fall shade, deer, rabbit.

(photo courtesy of PerennialResource.com)

Helen's Flower 'Red Jewel' Full Sun - Part Sun. Summer. Top ten summer sun, butterfly

(photo courtesy of PerennialResource.com)

Geranium 'Rozanne' Full Sun - Part Sun. Summer, fall. Top ten summer sun, blue flowers, deer, rabbit

(photo courtesy of PerennialResource.com)

Barrenwort 'Bandit' Part Shade - Shade. Spring. Top ten spring shade, dry shade, groundcover, foliage

(photo courtesy of Plant Delights Nursery – www.PlantDelights.com)

Foamy Bells 'Stoplight' Full Sun - Part Shade. Summer. Dry shade, bicolor foliage, drought tolerant

(Photo courtesy of PerennialResource.com)

Woodland Peony Full Sun - Part Shade. Spring. Unusual, deer, rabbit, drought tolerant

Bleeding Heart 'Gold Heart' Part Sun - Shade. Spring. Top ten spring shade, yellow foliage, deer, hummingbird

Fernleaf Peony Full Sun - Part Sun. Spring. Unusual, fine foliage, deer, rabbit

(photo courtesy of Robin Wolfe, Wolfe Enterprises)

Ligularia 'Britt-Marie Crawford' Part Sun - Part Shade. Summer. Wet, chocolate foliage, top ten design tips, deer, butterfly

(photo courtesy of PerennialResource.com)

Cushion Spurge 'First Blush' Full Sun - Part Sun. Spring. Tricolor foliage, top ten spring sun, deer, rabbit, drought tolerant

(photo courtesy of PerennialResource.com)

Elderberry 'Black Lace' Full Sun - Part Sun. Summer. Top ten shrubs summer, fine foliage, deer

(photo courtesy of Proven Winners - www.provenwinners.com)

Blue Star Flower's fall foliage color Full Sun - Part Sun. Spring. Top ten spring sun, fine foliage, deer

(photo courtesy of PerennialResource.com)

Bellflower 'Dickson's Gold'
Part Sun - Part Shade.
Summer. Top ten summer
shade, yellow foliage, deer,
hummingbird
(photo courtesy of PerennialResource.com)

Variegated German Bearded
Iris Full Sun - Part Sun.
Spring. Bicolor foliage, deer,
rabbit, drought tolerant
(photo courtesy of PerennialResource.com)

False Sunflower 'Loraine
Sunshine' Full Sun - Part Sun.
Summer. Top ten summer
sun, top ten design tips,
bicolor foliage, butterfly
(photo courtesy of PerennialResource.com)

Variegated Sedum Full Sun
- Part Sun. Fall. Tricolor foliage, top ten fall sun, rabbit,
butterfly, drought tolerant,
hellstrip
(Photo courtesy of Proven Winners –
www.provenwinners.com)

Hydrangea 'Invincibelle Spirit'
Full Sun – Part Shade. Summer. Top ten shrubs summer
(photo courtesy of Pride Corner Farms)

Phlox 'Laura' next to teak
bench

Daylily 'Sunday Gloves' Full Sun - Part Sun. Summer. Fragrant, top ten daylily, Q&A's, hellstrip, drought tolerant

(photo courtesy of PerennialResource.com)

Meadow Rue 'Splendide' Full Sun - Part Sun. Summer. Blue foliage, deer

(photo courtesy of PerennialResource.com)

Browallia 'Illumination' Full Sun - Shade. Summer, fall. Annual, drought tolerant, blue flowers

(photo courtesy of Proven Winners – www.provenwinners.com)

Climbing Hydrangea framing Harry the tree gnome watching 'Robert Poore' Phlox Full Sun - Part Shade. Summer. Climber

Hosta 'Guacamole' Part Shade - Shade. Summer. Fragrant, top ten summer shade, top ten hosta, honkin leaves, hellstrip, drought tolerant, hummingbird

(photo courtesy of PerennialResource.com)

Geranium 'Bevan's Variety' Full Sun - Shade. Spring. Dry shade, hellstrip, groundcover, deer, rabbit, drought tolerant

(photo courtesy of Bluestone Perennials – www.Bluestoneperennials.com)

Climbing Rose 'Ramblin Red'
Full Sun. Summer, fall.
Kerry's wish list, climber
(photo courtesy of Bailey Nurseries)

Coral Bell 'Caramel' Full Sun
- Shade. Summer. Foliage,
drought tolerant, deer
(photo courtesy of PerennialResource.com)

Yarrow 'Strawberry Seduction'
Full Sun. Summer. Top ten
sun summer, hellstrip, baking
hot sun, deer, rabbit, butterfly, fragrant, drought tolerant
(photo courtesy of PerennialResource.com)

Stokes' Aster 'Blue Danube'
Full Sun. Summer. Rabbit,
deer, butterfly
(photo courtesy of PerennialResource.com)

Dianthus 'Frosty Fire' Full Sun.
Spring, summer. Blue foliage,
drought tolerant, deer,
butterfly
(photo courtesy of PerennialResource.com)

Coneflower 'Hope' Full Sun -
Part Sun. Summer. Coneflowers, butterfly, deer, fragrant,
drought tolerant
(photo courtesy of PerennialResource.com)

Peony 'Bartzella' Full Sun -
Part Sun. Spring. Kerry's wish
list, drought tolerant, deer
(photo courtesy of PlantDelights.com)

Martagon Lily 'Fort Knox' Full
Sun - Part Shade. Late spring,
early summer. Bulb, unusual
(photo courtesy of PlantDelights.com)

Blue Switch Grass 'Heavy
Metal' Full Sun. Fall. Top ten
grasses, blue foliage, deer
(photo courtesy of PerennialResource.com)

Japanese Iris Full Sun.
Wet, deer
(photo courtesy of Plant Delights Nursery.
PlantDelights.com)

Orienpet 'Shocker' in the
gardens Full Sun - Part Sun.
Summer. Bulbs, fragrant

Color echos: lilac phlox,
purple daylily, yellow foliage
of Blue Star Flower

Shade Gardens in Spring   Foliage in a shade garden   Double Knockout Rose and
                                                               Wand Flower

Gardens in July   Forget-Me-Nots and Tulips   Thalictrum glacum and Lych-
                                                               nis Rose Campion

CHAPTER 7

Garden Design

Top Ten Design Tips for Sensational Gardens

∾ Play the Foliage Card. Foliage, unlike flowers, provides interest and drama three, if not four, seasons. Some favorites: Coral Bells ('Caramel', 'Peach Melba', 'Obsidian', 'Plum Pudding', 'Green Spice'); ornamental grasses; Ligularia 'Britt Marie Crawford' and others in this family; Lamiums ('Pink Chablis', 'Beeham's White', 'Anne Greenaway'); Hosta (of course); Heliopsis 'Loraine Sunshine'; variegated Phlox paniculatas ('Becky Towe', 'Norah Leigh'); blue leaved Dianthus ('Frosty Fire', 'Firewitch', 'Blue Boy'); silver leaved plants (Artemisia 'Silver Mound', Lamb's Ear, Snow-in-Summer); Foam Flowers ('Mint Chocolate', 'Black Snowflake') and others. See the Top Ten foliage list.

∾ Bulb It! Use spring, summer and fall blooming bulbs as fillers. I pack spring blooming bulbs (Tulips, Daffodils, Checkered Lilies, Trout Lilies); summer blooming bulbs (Asiatic, Trumpet, Oriental, Orienpets) and fall blooming bulbs (Crocus and Colchicum) among perennials and shrubs for a riot of color. See my Top Ten bulbs list.

∾ 'Annualize'. Even low-maintenance gardeners rely on annuals to carry the 'color baton' May through October, especially in shade. A few well placed annuals can unify gardens and 'keep the light on' when others around them have checked out. See the Top Ten annuals list.

∾ "Do I have to repeat myself?" Yes. Repetition in the garden is a good thing. Repeating the same plant (you can change the colors) at various intervals ties one or more gardens together.

∾ Color me beautiful. Color is a powerful design tool. Hot colors (red, yellow, orange, fuchsia) grab our attention quickly. These bold colors excite and appear closer than they really are. White is also considered a bold color. Cool colors (blue, silver, purple) are calming, appear farther away than they really are, and are difficult to see from a distance. You can use these impressions to your advantage. For instance, you can direct the eye towards a focal point by planting hot colors near it while you can also direct the eye away from an eyesore by placing these same colors at a distance from it. Gardens appear smaller if you use brighter colors in back; deeper if you use cool colors behind. As noted, colors also elicit emotions from the viewer. My twin sister loves her garden jammed with hot colors. Orange flowers, next to red ones, next to fuchsia flowers. After strolling her beds I feel like I've had five cups of coffee. My other sister planted a hot garden in full sun using only brilliant yellows, reds and oranges. Her goal was to have people feel thirsty after seeing it. It worked. I asked for a lemonade. My garden on the other hand is mostly cool colors. It's filled with lavender, purple, soft pink, pale yellow and silver. I use the bolder colors as carefully placed 'exclamation marks'. Having said this, there is no right or wrong when using colors in your garden. Beauty is in the eye of the beholder - yours.

❧ Give the eyes a rest. Well placed urns, benches, containers, bird baths, statuary and other objects allow the eye to take a refreshing break from moving among flowers and foliage. These objects provide a dynamic change, not just from living to inanimate, but great architectural value. Picture large, puckered blue leafed Hosta leaning on a silver gazing globe, or Japanese Painted Ferns cascading over a moss-covered stone stature, or wispy white Baby's Breath billowing around a black iron obelisk. I love using large pottery pieces or antique urns without any flowers planted in them.

❧ Reach for the sky! Creating vertical interest in the garden is another dynamic design element. The eye is drawn upward and the sky becomes a 'borrowed view'. Flower or foliage covered trellises, arbors and pergolas work nicely. So do tall perennials like Thalictrum 'Lavender Mist' (6' - 8'), many fountain and switch grasses, Joe Pye Weed (6'), Culver's Root (5'), climbing vines (Clematis, Climbing Hydrangea) and Plume Poppy (8', can be very invasive). Ornamental trees (flowering and non-flowering) are also good 'eye elevators'.

❧ The more the merrier. Planting in multiples makes for showier gardens. 'Gumdrop' gardens (one of everything) can cause indigestion. Odd number groupings (threes, fives, sevens) create more natural, flowing impressions than using a lot of even numbers. In general, the smaller the plant's size, the more you need to generate the coveted oohhhh reaction.

❧ Edgy? A neat garden edge is like a beautiful frame enclosing a picture. It finishes the look. Edging defines a garden. Edging choices include stone, aluminum, steel and brick. It could be flush with the ground or raised. Or it could be the 'natural look', nothing between grass and garden except a clean sliced edge. If you vote for the natural look, save your back with one of the great lawn and garden edgers available. Sometimes called a sod cutter, the heavy duty machine rolls on four wheels and encloses an adjustable steel blade. It's easy to push along a bed and makes a noticeably different cut than lighter weight edgers. Troy-Bilt and MTD are two manufactures.

❧ Shape up. Mixing a variety of flower shapes is an easy way to increase a garden's beauty and intrigue. Flowers can be spiky (Salvia, Veronica), mounded (Phlox, Sweet William), flat (Yarrow, Butterfly Weed), irregular (Bee Balm, Sea Holly), rounded (Globe Thistle, Allium), open-faced (Geranium, Coreopsis), funnel-like (Daylily, Trumpet Lily) or daisy-shaped (Shasta Daisy, Asters). When placing plants next to each other that bloom at the same time, don't only consider how the colors work together but also how the flower shapes differ.

Top Ten Ways to Get Color Without Flowers

Let's face it. Flowers are beautiful but they are work. Living things are like that. Most flowering perennials need nutrients, water and some loving kindness to thrive. And their neediness doesn't stop after blooming. They still need to be deadheaded, tidied-up and watered. Harumph! Wouldn't it be nice to have color in the garden with minimal involvement on our part? Below are ten ideas to add pizzazz, but let me start by saying mulch is not one of them. I know I risk offending some folks, but I believe mulch should be understated (not orange) and used as a functional backdrop, not the focal point. There, I said it.

✧ Leave it to the leaves. Admit it or not, leaves are the backbone of your perennial gardens. They play an invaluable, and usually thankless, role. Great leaves can complement flowers and bring out their best, just like in a beautiful bouquet. Leaves can also hide eyesores and carry the interest when there are no blooms in sight. When designing gardens, I count on at least one out of three perennials to contribute striking leaves. And leaves are little or no work. Some great perennial families with sassy leaves include Coral Bell (Heuchera), Deadnettle (Lamium), Ligularia, Hosta, Foamflower (Tiarella), ornamental grasses, Lungwort (Pulmonaria), Sedum and Snakeroot (Cimicifuga). Refer to the Top Ten foliage plant list for more ideas.

✧ Colorful containers and urns help breakup 'boring' expanses of flowers. You don't even have to fill them with flowers. Besides, planting them only defeats the purpose of reducing maintenance. Tuck interesting pieces among perennials and shrubs or set them by themselves as focal points. I am a huge fan of glazed blue containers, especially in the shade where blue flowering perennials are a rare find.

✧ Chairs and benches add pop. They can be made from many different materials, providing both an architectural dimension as well as color. Bright pink, purple, blue, yellow and chartreuse are popular furniture colors. Natural finished wood is less flamboyant but can make an equally strong impression. I use many teak chairs, benches and tables in the landscape. These are es-

photo courtesy of Ann Van Wie

pecially striking when surrounded by an apron of cool green leaves of various hues, sizes and textures. Very soothing. To keep the wood looking rich and lustrous, I apply an annual application of Penofin, a protective oil. This also increases their longevity. I also rub some on myself.

❧ Gazing globes, birdhouses, birdbaths and other entertaining pieces are always fun. Let your personality shine. Glowing globes are becoming the rage. They contain a special material that absorbs sunlight, turning them into solar-powered beacons at night. You can also buy glowing gnomes and fairies. I tend to be on the conservative side and stick with gazing globes. I tuck blue gazing globes of varied dimensions (4", 6" and 10" diameter) throughout my gardens. Some are placed on the ground, nestled among cool foliaged plants, while others sit atop stands or in birdbath basins. These ornaments subtly carry the eye from one garden bed to the next with no handholding on my part.

❧ Statuary and fountains are a no-brainer. My favorite. The added bonus of fountains is the soothing sound of running water they provide. My only comment on statuary and fountains is to be careful they are in scale to the surrounding area. If they are too large or tiny for the space, they look silly.

❧ Outdoor lighting can be a unique color source. Agreed, we are talking primarily in the evening but this is when many of us actually have time to enjoy our gardens. When locating the lamps, think creatively. Don't just blast an area with 'stadium lights'. Outdoor lighting is an art form and there are landscape specialists in this area. Uplighting, down lighting and backlighting create a magical atmosphere. Don't just think 'white' light. Use different colored bulbs to make a light show second to none. And by using LED powered 'projectors', you also save money. You can direct lighting to focal points, pathways, walls, water features, graceful branched trees and through special light panels in decking.

❧ Stonework (natural stone or man-made tiles) and stamped colored concrete are solid choices. Concrete acid stains have now evolved from earthy color selections to greens, blues and lavender.

❧ Obelisks, armillaries and sundials add a 'cottagey' dimension. I like planting delicate, wispy flowers or foliage around their base to act as ballerina skirts. Theme 'panels' that are placed on walls or freestanding can also add punch. Usually these are in sections or they come as folding panels with colorful artwork painted on them.

❧ Don't discount how much interest well placed pillows and throws are in a garden setting. Of course they work better on furniture than tossed among plants.

❧ Spray paint can be likened to duct tape. Very functional. I spray spent flower heads of Alliums, Astilbes and Hydrangeas to extend color into fall (and winter if I don't whack the plants back). You can spray just about anything to add excitement. Heck, one of my students even spray-painted the tail of a friendly gray squirrel in his yard bright blue. Is nothing sacred?

Top Ten Tips for Planting Containers

Container gardening has become the rage. You can transform a blah entrance into a magnificent focal point with some well appointed, lushly planted urns. Or how about adding a dash of color and fragrance to a shady retreat? Creating your own masterpiece is a fun way to express the Picasso in you. Just get your hands in the potting soil and let it fly.

When designing containers, I insist they be low-maintenance like my gardens. No prima-donnas that need a lot of handholding. Translation: I don't want to have to do much, if any, deadheading; as little watering as possible; and no weekly fertilizing. I can achieve these no-fuss containers by being savvy about how I choose the container, potting soil, plants and fertilizer.

❧ Containers styles and sizes are only as limited as your imagination. There is an incredible selection available from massive antique urns, to grungy L.L. Bean boots, to old barbeque grills. If it rings your bell, plant it. But as you reach for your container, consider:

- The larger the container, the less frequently you will need to water it.
- Plastic and glazed pots transpire less water than terra cotta.
- Hanging baskets made of coco fiber or moss will dry out faster than those made from plastic.
- Containers made with lightweight materials such as resin are much easier to move around than heavy ceramic pots. But they also blow over easier.
- The darker the container's color, the hotter and faster it will dry out in sun.
- Make sure the container has adequate drainage in the base or plants will rot.

❧ If you are working with a large container, to save money on potting soil and reduce the container's weight, fill ½ to 2/3 of the space with packing peanuts, broken styrofoam, bubble wrap, pinecones, crunched up plastic annual packs or plastic soda bottles. Pack your filler of choice into the planter, cover with a piece of landscape fabric or hardwire cloth, and scoop potting soil on top. I also use this technique for window boxes so they are not as heavy.

❧ Potting soil is key for growing healthy containers. Buy a good potting soil such as Coast of Maine's Bar Harbor Blend or any other premium mix that includes compost so it does not need as much watering. The other option is to mix your own potting medium. My formula calls for ½ unamended potting soil, ¼ loamy topsoil and ¼ compost.

❧ To reduce watering requirements, use water retentive polymers such as Sta-Moist, Soil Moist, Water-Gel Crystals and Watersave. These little crystals can hold water up to

400 times their density in water, slowly releasing it to thirsty roots. You can save money by purchasing these polymers separately instead of buying potting soil with them already added. Hydrating the crystals before adding them to the potting mix works best. One time I learned this the hard way. I made the mistake of using too generous a scoop of dry crystals. I filled the container with the potting soil and crystals, artistically set colorful annuals in place and then watered in my masterpiece. To my horror, the whole thing started to slowly bubble up and ooze over the container's edge as the crystals swelled to their full size. Ugly and messy. You can also use these crystals in your gardens when planting new shrubs or moisture-loving perennials. Just add some hydrated crystals to the planting hole before putting the plant in. These environmentally friendly, non-hazardous crystals will last up to five years in soil.

photo courtesy of Proven Winners – www.provenwinners.com

Reduce the need for frequent fertilizing by using a time-released fertilizer that slowly feeds plants for three to four months. Choices include Plant-Tone (5-3-3), Osmocote (14-14-14) and Multicote (17-17-17). You can buy potting soil that includes time-released fertilizer but it is cheaper to buy the fertilizer separately. You don't need the fertilizer throughout the container, only around the plant's roots. So rather than add this fertilizer to the entire mix, I simply work some around the base of each plant when setting it in place. I'm not only frugal with my time but my money as well.

When selecting the plants, pick those that match the light conditions where the container will be located. Thankfully, if you are wrong, it is simple to correct by moving the container to the right light. Also consider the plant's water needs. If they are drought and heat tolerant, they will do well in terra-cotta or dark colored pots as well as in spots where there is a lot of reflected heat. If the plants need more moisture, glazed pots will hold water longer.

Go for easy going annuals that require little or no deadheading; are drought tolerant; have attractive foliage; and stand up to light frosts with courage. A few sun loving favorites are Periwinkle (Vinca); Wave Petunia or Supertunia; Million Bells; 'Profusion' Zinnia; Verbena; Lantana; Sweet Alyssum 'Snow Princess'; Portulaca and blue Salvia. Shade lovers include Browallia, New Guinea Impatiens, Wax Begonias, Lobelia, Potato Vine, Torenia and Coleus.

Perennials also make superb container choices. One of my favorites is Geranium 'Rozanne' that blooms June through October. Repeat blooming Daylilies, Creeping Yellow Jenny, ornamental grasses, colorful Color Bells, Coreopsis 'Moonbeam', Japanese Painted Ferns, Lamiums, Masterwort, and showy Hosta also work well. At the end of the growing season, simply dig perennials into the ground for the winter and you will have twice the bounty the following year.

When placing 'spiller' plants (those that cascade in containers) plant them so they are slightly tilted towards the edge. I also pinch off any stems that are aimed in the wrong direction, like the center of the container. As the plants grow on, I am also quick to pinch back those that have gotten too big for their britches and are bullying their neighbors. I have the same policy in my gardens.

photo courtesy of Daniele Ippoliti

When designing your container, go wild and pack in lots of plants to make a spectacular statement. This is not the time to be shy. Make sure you have a large 'thriller' plant for vertical interest (usually positioned in the center or back); lots of 'fillers' billowing around the 'thriller', and lush 'spillers' that cascade over the side of the pot. The more the better. Trust your well prepared soil and time-released fertilizer to power up to the assignment. Rarely do pots bursting with bodacious color disappoint; it is the anemic, skimpy looking ones that sadden. There are too few opportunities in life to pull out all stops and go wild; let potting containers be one of them.

Top Ten Perennial Combinations

This is another difficult list to compose. There are so many fabulous combinations. Please do not assume this is an exclusive list. Have fun mixing up your own favorites. As a general rule, when creating combos I try to include one plant with great foliage or form to carry the show for three or more seasons. I grouped three different perennials in these vignettes. Typically, the smaller the plant's size, the greater the number I plant to balance the display. I also used color echoing to unify the grouping and create more drama. Color echoing is when a color is repeated in two or more plants. The color could come from flowers, foliage or stems. Finally, I noted the range of light conditions by each vignette and its zone.

❧ Sun - Part Sun. Zone 4 (possibly 3). Coreopsis 'Moonbeam' (soft yellow flowers, June-August, ferny green leaves), Geranium 'Rozanne' (blue flowers, June-October) and Sedum 'sieboldeii' (pink flowers, August-September, frosty blue succulent leaves)

❧ Sun. Zone 4. Blue Star Flower hubrichtii (soft blue flowers, May-June, brilliant yellow-orange needle-like leaves in fall), Russian Sage (lavender flowers, July-August, silvery leaves and stems) and Fleece Flower (Persicaria) 'Firetail' (reddish-pink flowers, July-October)

❧ Part Shade - Shade. Zone 4 (possibly 3). Astilbe 'Montgomery' (burgundy-red flowers, July); Japanese Painted Fern (foliage plant, silver and green leaves with burgundy veins) and Lamium 'Pink Pewter' (soft pink flowers, May-June-August, silver leaves)

❧ Sun - Part Sun. Zone 4 (possibly 3). Shasta Daisy 'Becky' (white flowers, July-August); Phlox 'Laura' (purple flowers with white eye, July-September) and Coreopsis 'Moonbeam' (soft yellow flowers, June-August, ferny green leaves)

❧ Sun - Part Sun. Zone 5. Sedum 'Angelina' (yellow flowers, July-August, yellow succulent foliage that gets coppery-orange tips in fall); Colchicum (poisonous bulb, rosy-pink flowers, September) and Japanese Blood Grass (foliage, red-tipped grass that stays 2' or less).

❧ Sun - Part Sun. Zone 4 (possibly 3). Masterwort 'Hadspen Blood' (deep red flowers, June-August); Daylily 'Custard Candy' (yellow with a burgundy-red eye zone) and Veronica 'Purple Candles' (deep blue, June-September).

❧ Part Shade - Shade. Zone 5 (possibly 4). Hosta 'June' (foliage, frosty blue and chartreuse); Japanese Forest Grass 'Aurea' (variegated gold and green grass, 18" and cascading) and Fern-leaved Bleeding Heart 'King of Hearts' (pink flowers; June-September, frosty blue delicate leaves).

❧ Sun - Part Sun. Zone 3. Culver's Root sibiricum (lavender flowers, July-September, gray-green leaves); coneflower 'White Swan' (white flowers, July-August) and Daylily 'Cherry Cheeks' (cherry-pink flowers, July-August).

❧ Part Shade - Shade. Zone 4. Coral Bell 'Caramel' (creamy-white flowers, June-July, large caramel leaves); Jacob's Ladder 'Stairway to Heaven' (lavender-blue flowers, May-June, pink, white and green variegated ferny leaves) and Astilbe 'Veronica Klose' (rosy-lavender flowers, June-July).

❧ Part Sun (possibly full sun but Bugbane may scorch in hotter weather). Zone 3. Bugbane 'Brunette' (creamy, white fragrant flowers, August-September, chocolate, lacy leaves); False Sunflower 'Lorraine Sunshine' (yellow flowers, July-August, variegated silver and green leaves) and Spiderwort 'Sweet Kate' (Violet-blue flowers, July-August, bright yellow leaves and non-invasive).

Top Ten Tips for Interesting Winter Landscapes

Most of us stare at bleak winter landscapes for at least five, if not six, months of the year. That's of course if you are not a 'snowbird'. But there is no reason to throw up our arms in despair when the gardens are buried under snow. By making some simple wardrobe adjustments, you can have a dazzling winter wonderland that is both beautiful and less work than summer gardens. Here are some ideas.

❧ Plant flowering shrubs and trees with attractive bark. Deciduous red and yellow twig Dogwoods have striking bark that glows against snow. 'Artic Fire' Dogwood is a particularliy striking cultivar with red stems. To keep the stems a vibrant color, prune off the oldest stems in late winter or early spring. Stems older than three years lose their brilliance. Peeling (exfoliating) bark is interesting. I love birch trees. For those with smaller spaces, there are dwarf weeping birches that stay under 12' like 'Little King'. Paperbark maples are gorgeous and will top out around 20'. Flowering shrubs with peeling bark include Ninebarks (Physocarpus), Oakleaf Hydrangea and Climbing Hydrangea.

❧ Evergreen shrubs and conifers are always a nice addition to the winter landscape. Rhododendrons, Mountain Laurel (Kalmia) and Japanese Andromeda (Pieris) are spring flowering shrubs. Some flowering shrubs stay semi-evergreen in colder climates including Daphne 'Carol Mackie' and Abelia. Red and yellow berried hollies are bold. Remember, you need both male and female hollies to have berries. Boxwood and Inkberry make zippy green structures and are also deer resistant. And the world of conifers is extraordinary. The choices are endless with sizes, needle colors and shapes.

❧ Deciduous trees and shrubs with unique branching can be great focal points. Some of my favorites are Harry Lauder's Walking Stick (sometimes called contorted filbert), Redbuds (Cercis) and dwarf Japanese maples. There are also weeping or twisted varieties.

❧ Perennials left uncut in the fall are pretty, plus many serve as bird feed. Astilbes, Coneflowers, Black-Eyed Susans, Sedums and Globe Thistle are excellent picks. Ornamental grasses are stars of the winter landscape, especially the taller Fountain grasses.

❧ Garden statuary, benches, trellises, birdhouses and other inanimate objects dance on the winter stage. I bring in my pottery containers to protect them from cracking but everything else I leave out for interest. I particularly love an inexpensive bird bath I spray painted cobalt blue. It is striking against snow.

❧ Gazing balls are glamorous in the snow. I tuck large, medium and small balls around the landscape. Of course after a heavy snowstorm, they disappear for a while but soon their shiny surfaces reemerge. An even cheaper version of gazing balls is to buy Christmas ornaments at post holiday sales. The large ones designed to be hung from porches are ideal. Last year I picked up some glittery gold, ball-shaped twine ornaments. These were dazzling hanging from the branches of my miniature crabapple tree. You can easily make your own rustic balls by using grape or bittersweet vine. They look like huge 'dust bunnies' in the winter playroom. Let your imagination run wild!

✿ Fences, arbors and pergolas add winter interest. I'm a big fan of cedar and teak structures in snow.

✿ Dried flowers on spring, summer and fall flowering shrubs and trees are intriguing in winter. Hydrangeas are probably the number one plant used for this. My only advice is to remove spent flowers before winter on younger plants. Allow younger Hydrangea trees to mature a few years so their branches are strong enough to support the weight of snow or ice-covered flowers without tearing or breaking.

✿ Fruiting trees and shrubs add colorful berries to a white world. Holly, Winterberry Holly and Viburnum are popular picks. Witch Hazel (Hamamelis) actually flowers in late winter. Its orange, red or yellow blooms are a sight to behold. Most get 12' - 20' tall but there are some dwarfs like 'Little Susie' that only gets 4'.

✿ Okay, call me silly but I love the gnome smiling face on my oak tree. I look out at it and he always smiles back. I cannot say that for everyone in my house. You can get all different expressions as well as other cutesy figures.

✿ Stone retaining walls of various heights help breakup the flat expense of snow. I also use these as platforms for my little boulder owls. Stone Age Creations has many fun pieces. Check them out at www.stoneagecreations.com

Top Ten Tips for Designing with Foliage

Admit it or not, leaves are the backbone of your perennial garden. They play an invaluable, and usually thankless, role. When interviewed by a national gardening magazine about how I design such beautiful, three season gardens, I gave foliage much of the credit. Great leaves complement flowers and bring out their best. Leaves can also hide eyesores and carry the interest when there are no blooms in sight. When designing gardens, I count on at least one out of three perennials to contribute striking leaves.

A leaf's color, shape, size and texture all play into the game as well as the plant's overall form (upright, prostrate, vase, mounded, arching or spiky).

❧ Be careful when using dark leafed plants such as chocolate or purple-black. Too much can produce a somber feeling. But a dash here and there can create a real statement, like a simple black dress. Chartreuse plants really 'pop' next to these.

❧ You can create an enchanting effect when placing tall delicate flowers or grassy foliage, such as Baby's Breath, Crambe or Miscanthus 'Morning Light' behind darker, thicker leafed plants like Sedums or Hosta.

❧ Arching or weeping branches provide a serene feeling. Working some of these through a bed, along a walk or at the top of a wall, adds a soothing touch to the garden.

❧ Bold, spiky foliage can have a very dramatic effect, provide 'shock value' and work as super 'exclamation marks' or focal points. Just picture a large Yucca in the landscape.

❧ Be careful when combining variegated plants. Too many can cause a 'dizzying effect'. When placing different variegated plants together try to combine plants with 'reverse' variegation next to each other. For example, a gold margined plant with a green center next to a green margined plant with a gold center. Also tuck in some solid leaved plants that repeat one of the variegated colors. You can put plants with the same variegated pattern next to each other but change the size or form of the plants.

❧ Use foliage color to unify a garden and to build continuity in your landscape. For example, use gold foliaged plants periodically down the length of a garden - some at the front, some mid-border, others in the back - to carry the eye along. Repeat some of these plants in other gardens to unify the landscape.

❧ Cover-up or disguise eyesores in your landscape or your neighbor's by siting large perennials, grasses, shrubs, trees or climbing plants appropriately. Plants should be evergreen to achieve their mission year-round.

☙ Foliage can be a peacemaker, a 'soothing respite', between flowers with strong, clashing colors. Silver and darker colored foliage plants do this especially well.

☙ Foliage plants can make a sensational backdrop for flowers. Picture dark, purple leaved Smoke Bush (Cotinus coggygria) or 'Black Lace' Sambucus (Elderberry) with pink and white flowers in front. Or how about glowing yellow weigela 'Rubidor' or golden conifers (Chamaecyparis p.f. 'Mops') framing rich blue or purple flowers?

☙ Add statuary, rocks, water features and other fixtures to add contrast to foliage in the landscape. Visualize feathery leaves against a rock; soft, hairy foliage falling over a glistening glass globe and sharp, blue-needled branches rubbing against a moss-covered, weathered statue. Take pictures of your garden with black and white film. This can be an eye-opening exercise to see how interesting foliage shapes, textures and forms are without the benefit of color.

CHAPTER 8

Garden Care

Top Ten Pruning Tips for Flowering Shrubs

There are two primary seasons for pruning flowering shrubs. One is during a shrub's dormant season in late winter or early spring. At this time the plant is still 'asleep'; it doesn't even see you coming. The second opportunity is in its active growing season.

There is a misconception among some gardeners that all shrubs must be pruned every year, as if this is a golden rule. Not. Just because you plant a shrub doesn't mean the pruners must come.

Reasons for pruning include:

- ❁ To remove dead, damaged or diseased wood.
- ❁ To maintain a shrub's size and proportion. Don't try to manipulate a larger shrub into a smaller space by severe pruning. It's better to buy a shrub that matures to, or close to, the size you ultimately want.
- ❁ To promote a healthy, more vigorous shrub by thinning out older wood and allowing younger wood to replace it. This typically encourages more blooms since the plant's energy is channeled to fresh blooms instead of supporting older wood.
- ❁ To rejuvenate older shrubs and bring them back to a healthy state.
- ❁ To remove branches on shrubs that bloom on old new wood while the plant is still dormant. This way it doesn't waste energy directing food to limbs that will be cut off.

❧ Prune spring flowering shrubs right after blossoms fade. They bloom on old wood, branches that have gone through the winter. Prune summer bloomers in late winter or early spring before new growth starts. Most summer bloomers flower on new wood that comes off older wood. And some flowering shrubs rarely need pruning like Bottlebrush (Fothergilla) and Daphne 'Carol Mackie'.

❧ As a rule of thumb, don't prune flowering shrubs in fall. This can stimulate new growth and if the plant doesn't have time to harden-off this growth, damage can occur.

❧ If a shrub sends out suckers (new sprouts from the base that 'suck' energy from the main plant), remove these just below the soil surface. If the plant has been grafted, the suckers will outgrow the desired variety. Suckering shrubs include Lilac, Forsythia, Flowering Quince and Kerria.

❧ Many shrubs that bloom on prior year's wood benefit from an annual pruning to stimulate new growth for next year's flowers and to maintain size. Think of a common Lilac that has not been pruned for years. Soon the branches soar out of reach, the Lilac produces fewer and fewer flowers on old branches, it gets scraggly, and suckers abound.

❧ Prune non-variegated leaves that show up on variegated shrubs. The non-variegated leaves are more vigorous and will take over the plant if allowed to remain.

❧ Prune flowering hedges so that the bottom is slightly wider than the top to allow sun to reach the bottom. Some flowering shrubs to consider for hedges: Forsythia, Rose Of Sharon, Roses (Knockout series), Lilac, Burning Bush, Bottlebrush (Fothergilla), Viburnum and Hydrangea.

❧ Use hand pruners and loppers to prune flowering shrubs, not hedge shearers or hedge trimmers. Your goal is to carefully and selectively prune stems of flowering shrubs, not to shear off all of the stems at the same length as you would with evergreen boxwoods and yews.

❧ To keep many flowering shrubs in their best shape, do maintenance pruning by:
- ◆ systematically cutting out older wood, allowing new shoots to replace them
- ◆ pruning dead or damaged branches
- ◆ pruning branches that rub against each other
- ◆ thinning some stems in the shrub's interior to allow in more air and light
- ◆ pruning for height or shape
- ◆ pruning shrubs grown for winter stem color, like red and yellow Dogwoods, in late winter for more colorful bark the following winter. After the stems get older than three years, their color fades. By removing the oldest stems each year and allowing younger ones to take their place, you have brilliant color every winter.

Top Ten Perennials to Whack Hard for Secondary Blooms

There are some perennials that enjoy a buzz cut after they've finished flowering. Many times this will stimulate a 'redo', although the second flush of flowers is not as heavy. It is important to prune back flower stems right after the first bloom to allow enough time for the plant to recover and set new buds. In most cases (unless otherwise noted) prune stems and foliage down to within three inches of the ground.

🌿✛**Perennial Salvia** (Salvia) 8" - 30" Sun. Summer bloomer. Violet, purple, white and pink flowers. Zone 3

🌿✛**Catmint** (Nepeta) 8" - 36" Sun to Part Sun. Summer bloomer. Lavender, purple, white, pink or blue flowers. As noted in the Top Ten reseeders list, I recommend you avoid the subsessilis group due to their high fertility. The faassenii Catmints are a better behaved bunch. Some of my favorites are 'Blue Wonder' (15" - 20"), 'Snowflake' (12" -15"), 'Walker's Low' (24" - 36"), and 'Six Hills Giant' (2' - 3'). Zone 3

🌿✛**Thread Leaf Coreopsis** (Coreopsis verticillata) 15" - 30" Sun. Summer bloomer. Yellow, white, pink and bicolor flowers. I have never needed to whack back my coreopsis in mid-summer to encourage a second flush but I know many say it helps to give it a buzz cut in late July. Zone 3

🌿✛**Mullein** (Verbascum) 18" - 4' Sun to Part Sun. Summer bloomer. Plum, yellow, rosy-peach, soft pink and salmon flowers. Cutting back the first round of flowers not only encourages more blooms but can also help extend the plant's life expectancy so energy is not wasted on seed production. Zone 5

✛**Speedwell** (Veronica) 6" - 30" Sun to Part Sun. Summer bloomer. Pink, white, blue, lavender and bicolor flowers. Speedwell has bold, vertical flower spikes that jazz up any garden. 'Giles van Hees' is the baby in the family, topping out at 6". You need to plant a number of these to make a visual impact. 'Sunny Border Blue' was the Perennial Plant of the Year in 1993 with its dark blue flowers and green, spinach-like leaves. Unfortunately it can get a fungal problem on its 'lower legs' and look rather sad. 'Royal Candles' has the same rich coloring but it is more resistant to this fungus. 'Aztec Gold' has shimmering gold foliage and does best when given some afternoon shade. 'Foxy Lady' is the first bicolor blooming Veronica with pink and white mottled flowers. 'Waterbury' is a light blue flowering groundcover that blooms in early summer. Zone 3

Spiderwort (Tradescantia) 12" - 24" Sun to Shade. Summer bloomer. Pink, white, purple and blue flowers. I agree with you. Most Spiderworts are thugs but there are some good ones in the seed tray. 'Sweet Kate' has bright yellow foliage with violet-blue flowers and she stays where you put her. Other obedient Spiderworts include 'Zwanenburg Blue' (rich blue flowers, 18") and 'Satin Doll' (fuchsia flowers, 12"). All Spiderworts, thugs or not, look better if sheared back by half their height after the first bloom. Zone 3

✣Mountain Bluet, Batchelor Button, Cornflower (Centaurea montana) 18" - 24" Sun. Early summer bloomer. Blue, violet, white and blue and white flowers. Yup, you saw this also listed as a rampant reseeder. Shearing it back to within three or four inches of the ground after the initial bloom will put a huge dent in the next generation. When the second flowering occurs, deadhead regularly to reduce the number of seeds that get away. After most of the flowers are spent, whack it back a second time and you'll have neat silver-gray mounds into fall. Plus whacking is a great stress reliever (for you, not the plant). Zone 3

✤✣Carnation, Pinks (Dianthus) 4" - 20" Sun. Spring, summer bloomer. White, pink, red, yellow and multicolor flowers. Pinks can have single or double flowers. I personally have found the double petaled ones (those that look like florist carnations) to be very challenging to winter. Very. Pinks can have green or blue foliage. All are mildly fragrant. Many of the newer cultivars will rebloom if the flowers are sheared after the first bloom. Some foliage may be swiped in the process if you are moving fast with the mini-hedge trimmer. No big deal. Some stars to check out are the Star Series and the Dessert Series. Zones 4

✤✣Reblooming Iris (Iris germanica) 29" - 38" Sun. Spring, fall bloomer. Many flower colors. Reblooming Irises sound great, don't they? Unfortunately dreams don't always come true given our shorter growing season in zones 3, 4 and 5. To give Reblooming Irises the best odds for September flowers, plant them in shelterd areas near foundations or stone structures with a southern or western exposure. The fall blooms are smaller in size and have shorter stalks. After the first round of flowers in spring, cut the flower stalks to their bases. Some touted rebloomers for colder regions include 'Immortality' (white, 29", slightly fragrant), 'Painted Clouds' (pink, 38"), 'Clarence' (pale blue and violet, 35", fragrant) and 'Feed Back' (Violet-blue and yellow, 36", fragrant). Zone 3

✣Delphinium (Dephinium elatums) 3' - 6' Sun to Part Sun. Summer bloomer. White, pink, purple, blue and lavender flowers. Many Delphiniums will send up a secondary bloom in late summer. To encourage rebloom, cut off spent flower stalks to within a few feet of the ground. Delphiniums are heavy feeders and benefit from an application of time-released fertilizer in early May. Plant-Tone is a good organic choice. This will feed the plants for three to four months, helping push a second bloom. Zone 3

Top Ten Ways to Eliminate Weeds

Weeds are probably gardener's number one enemy. They steal nutrients and water from our precious perennials and make gardens look unkempt. Here are some ways to smother their attack.

🪶 A weed in time, saves nine. Pull weeds when they are small and before they bloom. If you do a little weeding each time you stroll through the gardens, you'll be amazed at how this helps. Weeding becomes less and less necessary as gardens mature.

🪶 Mulch is a great weed barrier. Reapply as it breaks down to maintain a 2" to 3" layer. I do this every spring. Make sure to remove weeds before applying mulch.

🪶 Try not to disturb the soil after you've got weeds under control. You'll unearth new weed seeds that will germinate.

🪶 Water beds well before weeding or weed after it rains. Moist soil makes it easier to remove the renegades.

🪶 Hoeing weeds with a stir-up hoe is very efficient. This cool tool looks like a horse stirrup. It's sharp on both sides of the hoe. Simply pull it back and forth along the top inch of soil and it slices or uproots weeds without disturbing much soil.

🪶 To remove weeds in gravel or between stepping stones or sidewalk cracks, spray organic post-emergent products like Burnout II or Nature's Avenger. Simpler yet, use boiling water from your tea kettle. Burnout II or Nature's Avenger can also be applied to weeds in flower beds but be careful, anything it hits, it kills. If you are working in a tight spot you can:
  ◆ paint the solution on with a paintbrush
  ◆ Use cotton gloves to dip your fingers into the solution and then touch the weeds. To be on the safe side, wear plastic or pharmaceutical gloves under the cotton gloves.

🪶 Solarization is a good choice for killing weeds or grass when prepping new gardens located in sun or part sun. Simply loosen the soil with a spade, rototiller or pitchfork, and then water the area well. Cover with thick clear plastic and secure edges with mulch, stone or landscape pins. Wait at least 4 to 6 weeks for the sun to heat up and steam weeds, as well as their seeds to death. After removing the plastic, work in some aged compost or manure into the top 6" of soil to introduce organic matter and microorganisms. Be careful not to disturb the soil deeper than 6" when planting or you'll bring a whole new crop of weed seeds to the surface.

🌿 After cutting back gardens in fall, weed one more time. It makes a huge difference eliminating weeds, especially perennial weeds in fall. I'm the first to admit I don't always know which is an annual weed or which is a perennial weed. Just pull 'em all. You'll be smiling in the spring when you have a lot less weeding to do.

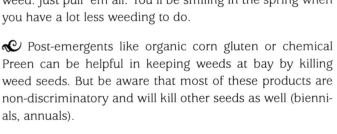

photo courtesy of Gardener's Supply Company

🌿 Post-emergents like organic corn gluten or chemical Preen can be helpful in keeping weeds at bay by killing weed seeds. But be aware that most of these products are non-discriminatory and will kill other seeds as well (biennials, annuals).

🌿 If you are open to unconventional methods, how about a weed dragon? This nifty hand-held machine is a flame-thrower attached to a propane tank. You scorch weeds in the lawn, flower bed, driveway and walkway with 'flare'. This method works best (and makes the fire department happiest) if done after it rains. You actually steam the weeds to death instead of burning them.

Top Ten Gardening Mistakes

Let me start by saying most of these, okay all, I have done myself so I am not pointing fingers. I garden, I learn. When asked about my academic background in horticulture, I like to respond that I graduated Magna Cum Laude from UHK, the University of Hard Knocks. Allow me to share some of my notes on top gardening mistakes.

❧ Placing plants in the wrong light. Most people err in planting perennials, annuals, shrubs and trees in less light than they require. The results:
- plants grow taller and leggier than they should
- few or no blooms
- plants are more prone to disease and insect damage due to a stressed state
- plants are more prone to winterkill due to a stressed state
- plants may lean towards the light

Buy plants that match your light conditions. If you are going to fudge, assume you get less light than you do. This will lead to little or no disappointment instead of the other way around.

❧ A garden's foliage is all, or mostly, just green. Yawn. There is very little variation in foliage color, leaf shape, size, texture and plant form. Yawn. Foliage is the backbone of a garden. It is there before, during and after flowering. Cool colored foliage plants (deciduous and evergreen) are an easy way to ramp up a garden's eye-appeal. Refer to my section on Top Ten foliage plants.

❧ The garden is 'mulchless' or the wrong mulch is being used. A nutrient-rich mulch has many benefits:
- weed control
- conserves moisture
- provides cooler roots, insulating them from daily temperature swings
- prevents erosion
- improves fertility and physical structure of the soil
- is an attractive backdrop for plants

Mulch options include:
- rotted manure (i.e., horse, cow, lama, sheep, rabbit)
- aged compost
- peat moss mixed with another organic material such as compost or manure
- shredded leaves. Some leaves are more acidic (oak, pine) and others more alkaline (hardwoods like maple).
- composted bio-solids (sludge). Do not use on edibles

- mushroom compost
- cocoa bean hulls. These may get moldy during extended warm, damp weather but the mold doesn't hurt plants. Do not use these where dogs may get to them. Chocolate is toxic to dogs.
- grass clippings. Only apply these at a depth of one inch if fresh, two inches if dried. Grass clippings decays rapidly and are a great source of nitrogen. Don't use clippings if the lawn is treated with herbicide.
- newspaper. Use black and white pages, approximately 6 to 10 pages thick. Water down and cover with compost or topsoil to hold in place.

Depth and application of mulch:
- usually 2" to 3" thick
- keep mulch away from plant stems. If mulch builds up on stems it may cause conditions for disease and insect damage.
- apply mulch in the spring after emerging perennials are approximately four or five inches tall and the soil has warmed up.
- never apply mulch to bone dry soil. Make sure the soil has moisture first.
- if your soil is poor, apply a second mulch application in fall after cutting back the gardens. Apply compost, manure or another material of choice approximately 3" thick around perennials, not on top of them, just as if you were mulching in the spring.
- calculating how much mulch to buy:

Bulk: 1 cubic yard will cover approximately 100 square feet 3" thick or multiply the length of the area (in feet), times the width (in feet), times the depth (in inches) for a total. Then divide this total by 324 for the number of cubic yards needed. Round the number up.

Bagged mulch: Divide total square footage of the planting bed by 18 sq. ft. for number of 3 cubic foot bags needed to apply 2 inches of mulch OR divide by 12 sq. ft. if using 2 cubic foot bags

❧ German Bearded Iris rhizomes are covered by soil or mulch. The top half of the rhizomes (they look a bit like Idaho potatoes) should be above ground, baking in the sun. If they are covered they are prone to rot and will not bloom as well. If you need to reset or plant new German Bearded Iris, dig a hole and then make a mound of soil in the center of the hole (like an old fashioned juicer). Place the rhizome on top of the mound, spread the roots over the sides of the mound, and back fill the hole with soil covering the roots and the bottom half of the rhizome. Cut back foliage to within three inches of the rhizome so the weight of the leaves won't tip the rhizome out of the soil. It will take a few weeks for the roots to anchor the plant.

❧ Landscape fabric is used in a perennial bed in an effort to reduce weeds. Sorry, in the long run this only causes headaches. I find weeds actually lodge themselves better into fabric than topsoil or mulch. Plus the fabric reduces the ability for nutrient-rich mulches to be incorporated into the soil. Fabric also doesn't allow for the expansion of perennials as they grow.

❧ Plants are dug in at the wrong depth. Usually they are planted too shallow instead of too deep. The plant should be set at the same depth that they were in the container. The plant's crown (where the stems meet the roots) needs to be at soil level. As I dig in a plant, I hold it at the correct level with one hand, and with the other hand I backfill the hole with soil.

Bare-roots are even more 'misunderstood'. Bare-root plants are grown in fields and then harvested in fall when they go dormant. They're graded according to their root size and sold in a dormant condition. Perennials commonly sold this way include Peonies, Hosta, Daylilies and Bleeding Hearts. Plants may look 'dead' when they arrive but will quickly revive. They should be stored in a cool, dark location and ideally planted within three days of arrival. Make sure to soak them in warm water for at least two hours before planting. If you can't plant for at least 5 days then soak roots and pot them up in potting soil. Keep the pots watered and in filtered light until you can plant outside. The benefit of buying bare-roots are they are usually less expensive than potted plants, shipping is less because of the lightweight and compact material, and plants don't go through the shock and stress that leafed-out plants do when shipped. When planting a bare-root plant, follow the same procedure as with German Bearded Irises. Spread the roots over a central soil mound and hold the crown at soil level while backfilling with soil. This approach is also used with bare-root shrubs and small trees.

❧ Planting thugs in disguise. What was I thinking planting this thug in my garden? Answer: you weren't. Sometimes we are our own worst enemy. Thugs can be plants that can't keep their roots to themselves or that seed all over the place. Before I provide some tips for reining these in, let's remind ourselves how they got in our gardens in the first place. Usually they came from well intentioned friends sharing surplus. Next time a friend bears plant gifts, before accepting kindly ask why they have extras. Then, if the answer is related to the plant's enthusiastic growth rate, you can plant with necessary precautions.

- Some perennials that advance quickly by roots: Bee Balm, Obedient Plant (Physostegia), Lamb's Ear, Yarrow, Evening Primrose (Oenethera speciosa and youngii), Ajuga (Bugle Weed), Lysimachia (Gooseneck) and do I have to even say Mint?
- Eager self-sowers are: Purple Coneflower, Malva, Feverfew, Lobelia siphiliticata (Blue Cardinal Flower) and Centaurea montana (Batchelor Button). To keep seeding under control, be religious about deadheading or use a pre-emergent, organic weed killer like corn gluten.

- Beware of plant descriptions that include the words naturalizes easily, vigorous or groundcover.
- To contain an overly-enthusiastic plant you can sink it in a pot with the bottom cut out leaving 5" of siding surround the area designated for the plant with 4" to 5" deep landscape edging.
- Another approach to controlling aggressive plants is to surround the plants you don't want invaded with landscape edging to protect them from the oncoming invasion.

❧ Gardeners 'manhandle' their garden soil while doing maintenance, cutting flowers, fishing for errant baseball and soccer balls and planting new plants. When you go tromping around in the garden, you compress the soil everywhere you step. One of the attributes of healthy soil is open channels for air and water to move through the soil. You can avoid stepping on soil by incorporating paths or placing flat topped stones to step on when accessing deeper sections of the garden. I have stones tucked all around my gardens. You cannot see them once the gardens are grown in; they are only meant for my eyes and access. I even carry a long plank around with me when doing maintenance so if I can't reach an area by stepping stones, I can 'walk the plank' (distributing my weight) to reach my goal. Think about it. If you have a hard time digging a hole in compacted soil to install a plant, how hard do you think its roots will have to work to break through that soil?

❧ Poor watering is the death of many a plant. For those with automatic watering systems, the damage is usually due to shallow watering or overwatering. Gardeners who rely on manual watering techniques or 'mother nature', can usually 'thank' erratic watering, or lack of water, for sad plants. Correct watering encourages healthier plants that are more disease and insect resistant, produce showier flowers and foliage, and experience less winterkill.

- Deep watering is key to healthy gardens. Most gardens do fine with one inch of water per week. Water once or twice a week depending on natural rainfall. And when you do, water for longer periods of time but less often. Deep watering is better than shallow watering. It encourages healthy, deep roots. Shallow watering encourages roots to stay near the surface, making them more impacted by drought as well as freezing and thawing soil fluctuations in winter. To check how well you've done watering the garden, after you've finished, push back the mulch and place your finger into the soil. If you have sandy loam, it should feel damp to the touch 6" - 8" deep. If clayey loam, then 4" - 5" deep. When I used to water with an overhead sprinkler, I would run it about 45 - 50 minutes on each garden. Now with an inground irrigation system, I set each zone for about 40 minutes depending on the type of heads (mister or large rotary).

- Correct watering is especially important for newly planted gardens. When perennials are just getting established, shallower and more frequent watering is needed because the plants are not yet deeply rooted. Water the garden well every second or third day for the first two weeks, depending on your soil type (sandy, clay), the amount of natural rainfall received, the amount of wind (wind pulls moisture from the soil and leaves) and the temperature (warmer temperatures cause more evaporation than cooler temperatures). After two weeks it is time to back off watering as frequently to toughen up the plants. Once or twice a week should be adequate, or less depending on rainfall.

- The best time of day to water is early to mid-morning. Afternoon sun is usually too hot, causing increased evaporation and possibly burning plants. Don't water at night. This can foster fungal diseases.

- In late summer and early fall start lengthening the intervals between watering to start readying plants for winter.

- Remember to keep watering gardens in fall. They need a good drink of water before going to bed for the winter. This is especially important for spring blooming shrubs. Many people make the mistake of zoning out on their gardens in fall. After I cut back the beds in October, I still water them deeply once a week (if there has been little rain) and I continue to do this until late November.

Not spacing plants correctly when planting. It seems many gardeners feel that the recommended spacing recommendations on plant tags are for their neighbor's benefit, not theirs. We all want full, lush gardens right from the get go. It's as if seeing soil between plants is a no-no. But planting closely will not serve your plants well. Spacing recommendations take into account the roots' need for nutrients and water. By crowding plants you force them to compete. How much better they would grow if each plant had its own 'dining hall', especially in

photo courtesy of David Chinery

their youth. They would fill out faster, be healthier and not requiring dividing as soon as those that are bunched together. Resist the temptation to plant too closely. If you can't stand seeing space between plants in a newly installed garden, then use annuals to a fill in.

Any garden tool that helps get the job done quickly and correctly is a friend of mine. Personally, I have a special fondness for power tools. They are a form of therapy. After a tough day at work; with kids; battling traffic; or seeing the price after filling my car with gas; I simply grab a power tool and have a go at it in my gardens. It's usually a win-win for the gardens and me. I also have an odd sense of entertainment. I get a kick out of watching people's reactions as they watch me work in the gardens. There are mixed reactions, ranging from surprise, delight, amusement, appreciation and horror. I keep smelling salts on hand. Some suggest I designate the property as a hard hat area and surround it with yellow caution tapes.

❧ Bulb auger. 24" steel augers make digging spring, summer and fall blooming bulbs fun. Really. I used to dread this project but now I'm a fan. I'll even drill in my neighbor's bulbs. Simply place the auger into an electric or battery-operated power drill and feel the power. You can also use it for digging in annuals, smaller perennials and for aerating soil as well as compost piles. Heck, I bet it would even work in the kitchen.

photo courtesy of Gardener's Supply Company

❧ Hedge trimmers. I have battery and electric trimmers as well as different bar sizes to fit the job at task. I use the larger bar to whack back gardens in fall like a Samaria warrior. The shorter bar works magic. Like a Ninja, I flit about cutting off spent flowers, shaping Boxwood, pruning flowering shrubs or 'pinching back' taller perennials. I especially like the petite battery-operated trimmer. It's lightweight so my arm doesn't tire as quickly plus I don't risk cutting the cord. I did this once with the electric trimmer and it wasn't pretty. When I feel my upper body needs a workout, I get out the good ole hand-held hedge shears. Black and Decker sells many great trimmers and power tools.

❧ Hand pruners. There are a number of excellent pruning shears on the market. A few brands to look for are Felco, Fiskars and Corona. You can choose between right or left handed pruners plus those that are ergonomically designed. Use bypass pruners instead of anvil pruners because they make a clean cut and don't crush the stems. Don't be cheap when buying hand pruners. The more expensive ones outlast the cheaper versions, stay sharper longer and have parts that can be replaced when they wear out. I cannot count the number of cheap pruners that sent springs popping into the air. Your projects will go much more quickly if you keep the blades sharp. Special hand-held steel sharpeners can be purchased that also sharpen spades, knives used for divisions, and scissors. Istor, a Swiss company, has gotten good reviews. To reduce the chance of losing hand pruners or other smaller tools in the garden, wrap bright orange tape on them.

෴ pH soil test kits and soil probes. Your soil's pH is an important factor in your garden's health. If the pH is askew, roots cannot efficiently utilize nutrients from the soil. Ideally, you should recheck your soil's pH every two or three years. For more about soil pH, see the Top Ten soil pH tips list. You can do this yourself or take samples to a cooperative extension office. Many garden centers also provide this service. There are many kits on the market. Some require the sample to be dry, others moist. Follow the kit's instructions carefully for accurate results. There are also pH soil probes available. You simply put the probe into the soil and read the meter. More expensive probes can also measure moisture and nutrient (N-P-K) levels. I am a big fan of Rapitest products that are sold at many garden centers.

෴ Stirrup hoe. This u-shaped tool is very effective at eliminating shallow weeds as well as aerating the top inch of soil. It is also called a scuffle or hula hoe. Simply pull it back and forth along the top inch of soil and the two-sided sharpened edges slice or uproot weeds without disturbing much soil. The long wooden handle is great for those of us with back problems. There are also short handled stirrup hoes for more intimate weeding around smaller plants.

෴ Knife. A sharp knife is a handy thing in the garden. I use a large knife to divide plants. I simply lay my target on its side, eyeball it to see where to slice between roots and stems, and then commence to 'Just do it' as Nike says. The majority of my plant divisions are done with a knife. A knife can also be used for taking stem cuttings and for cutting through woody branches.

෴ Garden spade and shovel. A spade has a rectangular blade while a shovel has a curved tip and slightly concave face. Garden spades or small-sized shovels are for day-to-day tasks in the garden, digging, dividing, planting and edging. Large shovels are for lifting and moving quantities of material such as topsoil, compost, mulch, gravel or pea stone.

෴ Garden twine. I never leave the garden shed without it. I grab a roll of twisty tie and some bamboo stakes whenever I head out to the gardens. There is always some plant that needs a helping hand for support.

෴ Garden stakes and hoops. Stakes can be made of metal, plastic or bamboo. Stakes should blend in and not draw attention. For taller perennials like Delphinium, stake each stalk separately. Stakes should be about 6" shorter than the mature plant. Place the stake in the ground about 1" from main stem then tie the stem. Don't tie it too tightly to the stake, allow some movement. When tying the stem use a figure 8 loop to secure it to the support. Hoops as well as twigs and branches are options too. Place these into the ground while plants are small so maturing plants can weave their way through the supports.

The Weed Hound. This nifty tool was first introduced to me by an organic lawn care company. Its ease of use and effectiveness blew me away. I immediately bought one for my husband's Father's Day present. It has a steel plunger and tines that grab leaves and roots. It works best on broadleaved weeds, especially those with taproots. Check it out at www.hound-dog.com. They also sell other tools including a snazzy poop hound. American ingenuity.

Top Ten Soil pH Tips

pH isn't phooey. I used to think pH was only something that Master Gardeners, professional landscapers or chemists had to be concerned with. To explain, I will use the KISS approach (Keep It Simple, Silly). pH affects a plant's ability to take up nutrients from the soil. If your soil's pH is not in the optimum range, then your plants can become anemic, weakened, prone to disease and stunted in growth. Allow me to use my son's love of macaroni and cheese as an illustration. I could put a huge bowl of that awful, fluorescent orange, boxed macaroni and cheese (his favorite) in front of him and tie his hands behind his back so he couldn't (theoretically) get it into his mouth. All of that 'good stuff' is right there next to him but he is unable to partake. Same thing with nutrients and your plants' roots. You could put a lot of sweat equity into working organic amendments into your soil and if the pH is off, you are not seeing the results of your hard work. And if like many, you try to make up for the garden's lackluster appearance with fertilizer, you would just be wasting money as the fertilizer also bypasses the roots.

Soil pH is measured on a scale from 1-14. Seven is considered neutral. Anything above 7 is alkaline (also referred to as basic or sweet). Anything lower than 7 is acidic. Most perennials, annuals, bulbs, shrubs and trees prefer to be in the 6.0 – 7.0 range. Of course there are always exceptions to the rule. Acid loving shrubs like Rhododendrons, Azaleas, Mountain Laurels, blue Hydrangeas, Blueberry bushes, and Japanese Andromedas prefer a pH between 5.0 – 5.5. Most woodland perennials like a pH in the upper 5's to 6.5. Swinging to the other side of neutral are Lilacs, pink Hydrangeas, Clematis, Dianthus, Delphinium, Lavender and Lenten Roses. These enjoy 7.0 – 7.5. If you choose to do you own pH test, follow the kit's instructions carefully. Some require the sample to be moist, others dry. There are also pH soil probes available. You simply put the probe in the soil and read the meter.

Some areas in your yard are particularly prone to pH extremes. Refer to the chart for potential trouble spots.

POTENTIAL pH PROBLEM AREAS

Likely to be Alkaline
Where limestone is a predominant rock
Where there is a lot of stonework, retaining walls
Along the foundation of older homes
Near lawns that have been annually limed

Likely to be Acidic
under oak and pine trees
where peat moss has been used
woodlands, especially evergreens
where pine needles are used as mulch

~ When collecting samples, each area should be tested separately. Brush away any surface mulch or debris; dig down about 5" to 6"; slice a ½ cup sample from the sides and bottom of the hole with a stainless steel trowel or large spoon; and place the sample in a baggie. Label each baggie so you know where the sample came from. Also note what is, or what will be, planted there. For example, perennial gardens, Rhododendrons and other evergreens, lawn or vegetable garden. Recommended soil pH will vary based on the plantings. If the area to be tested is large, collect five to eight samples from different spots, mix them together in a clean plastic bucket or mixing bowl and scoop ½ cup into a baggie as the representative sample. When preparing a new garden bed, take the sample after all the soil amendments have been incorporated.

~ Many pH test kits require the sample to be dry. If there is a lot of moisture in the sample, the results can be skewed. I used to dry my samples on the kitchen counter until my son once thought it was his after school snack. Tells you a lot about my cooking. One harried student of mine had a different approach. He was running late from work and had forgotten to collect a soil sample for my class that night. Unfortunately it had rained all day and the soil was soaked. He called on his cell phone as he raced to collect the sample and asked if he could microwave it. I chuckled and said no, this would affect the reading. He was quiet for a moment and then asked if he could blow dry it on low. Creative thinking.

~ If a pH adjustment is required, apply lime to raise pH, sulfur to lower pH. Follow package directions for the amount needed based on the desired change. If your soil was tested by a service, the summary will include what amendment is recommended and its specific amount. Simply work the recommended number of pounds per one hundred square feet into the top few inches of soil with a cultivator or hoe and then water in well.

~ Apply lime or sulfur with a handheld spreader (Scotts makes a snappy one for under $15), a broadcaster if your space allows, or use my method. As you've gathered by now, I'm into simplicity. Being a visual learner, the first time I needed to make a correction, I took four garden stakes and a tape measure out to my gardens. I then measured out one hundred square feet (length times width) and put stakes at the corners. Next I grabbed a bag of elemental sulfur (in my case I needed to lower pH), an empty coffee can and my bathroom scale. I put the can on the scale and poured sulfur into it until I hit the necessary poundage per one hundred square feet. I then donned pharmaceutical gloves and cast the sulfur by hand as evenly as I could inside the staked area. Once I saw how the particles covered the space I could replicate this on other beds. Not terribly scientific, but it works. This technique works with many granular fertilizers as well. I am always cautious to err on the side of under-applying versus over-applying. Please do the same.

~ Lime and sulfur (especially sulfur) are slow moving agents in soil. You cannot race out the following week to retest your pH after an application. Patience is a virtue. You need to wait a minimum of three, preferably six months before retesting. You don't want to risk overcorrecting and causing yourself more problems.

~ A great time to test your soil's pH is in fall after cutting back the garden. There are two advantages. If a correction is needed you can do it then and the adjustment wll begin. Retest later in then spring. Secondly, it is easier to apply sulfur or lime after foliage has been cut back so it's out of the way.

photo courtesy of Gardener's Supply Company

~ If you don't have lime or sulfur handy, you can use the following substitutes:

ALTERNATIVES TO LIME AND SULFUR

To raise pH
Woodash
Sweet peet
Chopped maple leaves

To lower pH
Peat moss
Coffee grinds or used tea bags
Chopped oak leaves
Pine needles

~ It is best not to make more than a one point correction per year, otherwise plants may become shocked.

~ A commonly asked question is how to deal with acid-loving shrubs planted near non acid-loving neighbors. No problem. Both lime and sulfur move vertically in the soil, not horizontally. You can scratch in sulfur around the base of shrubs and the plants nearby won't 'feel a thing'. And to all of you Miracid fans, this pendulum-swinging fertilizing practice is not good for your plants, plus it is a poor substitute for a correction made be incorporating minerals directly into the soil.

Top Ten Tips for Jump-Starting Perennial Gardens in Spring

I expect a lot from my gardens. I practice tough love, refusing to pamper 'prima donnas' and you should too. By taking some simple steps in spring, I can have healthier, better-behaved gardens the rest of the year. Here are some of my tried-and-proven tricks for jump-starting beautiful gardens.

✤ In late March or April, after the snow has melted, cast 5-5-5, 5-10-5, 5-10-10 or 10-10-10 granular fertilizer on gardens before, or immediately after, the foliage starts to emerge. This will encourage strong root growth and development. Apply it at the rate of approximately 2 pounds per 100 square feet. Everything in my yard, except the lawn, gets this treat: perennials; spring, summer and fall blooming bulbs; climbing vines; roses; shrubs and groundcovers. Be aware that granular fertilizer will burn foliage so by applying it before plants emerge, you reduce this risk and save time. If foliage is already up and at'em by the time you have a chance to do this, make sure to wash off any fertilizer that landed on the leaves. Easier yet, wait to apply the fertilizer right before it's supposed to rain.

✤ In late winter cut back ornamental grasses. Larger varieties can be whacked with electric or manual hedge clippers. To reduce the mess, first tie twine, bungee cord or duct tape around the grass to hold it together, then cut it down to approximately 4" to 6". Weed whackers come in handy for smaller grasses. Some folks swear by chain saws but even I draw the line at certain power tools in the garden. Use gloves and caution when dealing with some of the larger grasses that have razor-sharp blades. For really beautiful grasses, after cutting them back, burn the remaining brown stubble to the ground. This will permit new blades to emerge without obstruction. Smaller grasses like Blue Fescue, Carex, and Blue Oat Grass (Helictotrichon) can be cleaned by simply hand pulling brown grass blades from within the clump.

✤ Prune most roses in late winter or early spring except for those that only bloom once in spring or early summer. Many antique roses fall into this category and should be pruned immediately after blooming. For all other roses, watch for green leaf buds to break from stems and prune canes right above outward facing buds. I prune shrub roses back by one-half their height to maintain compact plants. This may seem drastic but it works. My roses are covered with flowers each summer. If pruning makes you nervous, wait until you've had a bad day at work, with the kids, or in traffic and then grab pruners. Remove dead or broken canes as well as those that rub against each other. In general, when you see the Forsythia in bloom, let the games begin. Also pull back soil or compost mounds from around rose trunks at this time.

 Apply a time-released fertilizer like organic Plant-Tone (5-3-3) or synthetic Osmo-cote (14-14-14) five to six weeks after you applied a granular fertilizer. I don't use time-released fertilizers on every plant in the garden; only on heavy-feeding perennials that quickly deplete nutrients from the soil. Plants that 'wolf down their food' benefit from a slow, steady release of fertilizer over three to four months. Follow directions for the application rate, scratch it into the soil around the plant, and water in. Perennials that benefit from this extra serving of fertilizer include Delphinium, Clematis, Astilbe, bulbs in the Lilium family and ever-blooming roses.

 Mulch gardens to reduce weeding. This also helps conserve moisture, supply nutrients and make gardens look nicer. Don't make the mistake of mulching too early. You need to allow the soil to warm up and dry out. Timing will vary depending on your hardiness zone and if you have sandy or clay soil. My 'green flag' for swinging the mulch shovel is when many of my perennials are about 4" tall. For perennial gardens I recommend nutrient rich, organic mulches such as aged compost, manures and shredded leaves. Spread mulch approximately three inches thick around plants, being careful not to build it up against perennial stems. Remember that three inches will settle to about two inches. Heavier bark and wood mulches are best applied around trees and shrubs. Rubber mulches are not recommended. Research now shows there are toxicity issues with these plus if they catch on fire, they are harder to extinguish than wood chips given their petroleum make-up. And crushed glass mulches? I guess one positive attribute is their ability to keep animals out of the garden.

 If your garden is plagued by chomping slugs and snails, now is the time to squash their rebellion. Check out my Top Ten ways to win the battle against these slimers.

 Beat nasty powdery mildew that strikes Bee Balm, Phlox, Lilac and False Sunflowers in summer by taking action in May. There are two homemade organic recipes that do the trick: baking soda and water (one teaspoon of baking soda to one quart of water) or milk and water (one cup milk to a quart of water). To either mix, add 3 to 4 drops of liquid dish detergent, Murphy's Oil Soap or vegetable oil as an 'adhesive'. Shake well and spray away. Make sure to hit both upper and lower leaf surfaces. Spray once every two weeks through mid-July. Either method will 'wash that gray away'; something my son has been asking me to do with my hair. I keep telling him that silver hair (not gray) is a mark of distinction and a sign of wisdom. He's not buying it.

᭰ Thinning can be done to reduce mildew on Garden Phlox, Bee Balm, Asters, Heliopsis and Delphinium. Remove approximately one out of three stems by pinching them at soil level. You may feel misgivings about this, thinking you'll have less color with fewer flowers. In reality, even though there will be fewer flowers, they'll be larger, shower and healthier.

᭰ Start dividing summer and fall blooming plants when shoots are 3" to 4" tall. Hosta can be divided just as the pips (stem tips) are coming through the ground. This is an ideal time for those that have intimated you by their size. You are a lot bigger than they are at this point. Go for it.

᭰ Cut back Lavender, Caryopteris (Blue Mist Shrub), Montauk Daisy, Russian Sage, Mums and Butterfly Bush in April.

Top Ten Summer Tips for Beautiful Perennial Gardens

Remember not to deadhead biennials (Foxglove, Forget-Me-Not, Sweet William, Hollyhock, Money Plant, English Button Daisy, Wallflower) if you want seedlings next year. Many biennials actually germinate later the same summer they were seeded. But if you prefer a biennial to behave like a short-lived perennial (hopefully living three or four years) then cut flower stalks off before they go t0 seed.

In early to mid-June pinch back summer blooming plants that you want to keep shorter and bushier. Good candidates include Bee Balm, Clara Curtis Mum, Black-Eyed Susan, False Sunflower (Heliopsis), Tall Garden Phlox and Malva. In early July pinch back fall blooming perennials: Chrysanthemums, Sedums, Asters, Yellow Waxbells (Kirenge-shoma) and Boltonia. I like to be creative and only pinch the front half of some plants so these sections bloom later than the rest of the plant. When the second flush of flowers appear in late summer, I simply cut off the taller, spent earlier blooming stems.

Deadhead, deadhead, deadhead! Many gardens in the Northeast peak in June and July which means there are lots of plants requiring deadheading as flowers finish blooming. Consistent deadheading extends the blooming season of many perennials. Perennials that demand frequent deadheading or they quickly go to seed are Broad-Leaf Coreopsis such as 'Early Sunrise', Balloon Flower and Bellflowers. Needless to say, you will see few, if any, of these time mongers in my gardens. When deadheading, pinch flowers off just above a set of leaves, not right at the base of a flower. If you're desperate for time and the majority of flowers have already gone by, then reach for a hedge trimmer or grass clipper to quickly shear the whole plant.

Summer is when Japanese beetles arrive in force. GRRRRRRRRR. Rather than using toxic chemicals you can hand pick and toss the 'monsters' into soapy water. Or, if it has been a bad day, squish 'em and drop them in the garden. The scent of squished colleagues dissuades others from visiting. If it has been a really bad day, some gardeners enjoy collecting a bunch and tossing them into a blender with water; blending on medium and then sprinkling this puree around plants bothered by beetles. A bit too heavy handed for my tastes. Organic products that contain neem or pyrethrin (a natural derivative of chrysanthemum flowers) can also be effective. Surround at Home is another organic option for battling Japanese beetles. This mineral-based film has kaolin clay in it. Kaolin clay is also found in aspirin and toothpaste. When you spray the substance on plants munched by Japanese beetles, the material 'globs' the beetle's mouth parts and puts the bug on a permanent diet. It has been used on crops such as apples and pears as well as in greenhouses for years but is now finding its way into home gardens. The only downsides are when it dries there is a white film on the leaves plus it washes off in rain, requiring additional applications. Surround at Home is sold by Gardens Alive (www.gardensalive.com). Catmint, Chives and Garlic are also noted for repelling Japanese beetles around roses and other beetle-attracting plants. Finally, traps get mixed reviews. Many times they attract more Japanese beetles than they kill. If you are going to use these, place them far away from your garden or give them as gifts to your neighbors.

✿ If after your Peony has bloomed, the foliage is taking up too much space or blocking the view of nearby flowering perennials, give it a haircut. Prune back the foliage to the height and shape you want so it becomes a nice backdrop for its neighbors. This may include pruning off some of the outer stems to within a few inches of the ground to allow more space for adjacent flowering plants. You can also do this type of aggressive pruning with other spring blooming perennials that hog too much summer space. These include False Blue Indigo (Baptisia), Carolina Lupine (Thermopsis), Bleeding Hearts and Lemon Daylily.

✿ Prune back spring blooming perennials that get ratty looking foliage after flowering. Oriental poppies and old fashioned Bleeding Hearts are a few. By early July they become eyesores as they go dormant for summer months. Why not give them a helping hand and reduce your stress level at the same time? Whack back the foliage to within 3" - 4" of the ground. Fill the cavity with some colorful annuals or plant perennials nearby with foliage or flowers that will expand into this space. Some good companion perennials include Baby's Breath, Daylilies, Crambe, Astilbes and Hosta. Perennial Batchelor Button (Centaurea montana) can also get ratty in early July. Shear it back to within a few inches of the ground to stimulate new growth and flowering in August. Now is also the time to divide your Bleeding Heart if it has outgrown its spot.

✿ Buy spring blooming perennials and shrubs that are on sale. You will likely find terrific deals on plants that are past their prime. Prices are slashed to move them out to create more room for summer and fall blooming perennials. They may look a bit scrappy but don't let that scare you. Get them into good soil, give them some loving care, and you will be rewarded with beautiful flowers next spring. A little dollop of rock phosphate (0-4-0) in the planting hole will also help. Delayed gratification is the name of the game.

Mid-July can be when some early summer bloomers start to sputter. Delphiniums are one of these. Prune down spent flowering stems to encourage a second flush of flowers. Cut the stems off at their base. If you did not give Delphiniums a time-released fertilizer in spring, give them some Plant-Tone or apply 5-5-5 or 10-10-10 granular fertilizer now. This is also the time to shear back Catmint (Nepeta), Silvermound (Artemisia), perennial Salvia and Spiderwort (Tradescantia). Cut back plants by ½ to 2/3 their height. Then stand back and be delighted with how tidy they look plus a second bloom later that summer. Silvermound will not bloom but it will regain its neat mounded appearance.

If you notice your gardens are starting to look a little worn and blasé as summer progresses, add some late summer blooming perennial show-offs. For sun to part sun, check out: late blooming Daylilies such as 'Chicago Apache' (Bright Red); Helenium (Helen's Flower); Oriental Lilies; Chelone (Turtlehead); Allium 'Ozawa'; Russian Sage; Shrub Hibiscus; Joe Pye Weed and of course ornamental grasses. For shade to part shade try later blooming Astilbes such as 'Finale' and chinensis 'Pumila'; Yellow Waxbells (Kirengeshoma); Cimicifuga 'Brunette' and Hillside Black Beauty'; Toad Lilies and Eupatorium 'Chocolate'. A great way to discover some great winners is to visit public gardens and field grown perennial nurseries in late summer to see what is in bloom.

Summer is when most perennial gardens are in full bloom and demand a lot of our time. This is an ideal opportunity to consider replacing some needier perennials with low-maintenance flowering shrubs. As I have matured as a gardener, and in years, I've placed a lot more value on flowering shrubs. There are great choices for the front, mid and back border. Shrubs need less maintenance (deadheading, watering, dividing) and provide winter interest. Most flowering shrubs are also welcomed food and shelter sources for wildlife. For more on flowering shrubs and some great picks, check out the Top Ten flowering shrubs lists.

Top Ten Fall Tips for
Beautiful Perennial Gardens

❧ Cut all perennial foliage down to 2" to 3" inches except Lavender, ornamental grasses, Russian Sage, Montauk Daisy and Mums. Also leave roses and Butterfly Bushes alone. You may choose to leave some perennials for winter interest and feed for the birds such as Sedums, Coneflowers, Black-Eyed Susans, Astilbes and Globe Thistle. To cut back foliage use a hedge trimmer, weed whacker, pruning shears, hand pruners or even a lawn mower (raise the blade height). Remove all foliage from the garden and compost. Do not put diseased foliage in the compost pile, especially leaves infected by mildew or aphids.

❧ Put your roses to bed for the winter. Do not keep deadheading roses into fall. Allow blooms to develop rose hips to help them go dormant. I primarily garden with rugosas, hardy shrub roses and floribundas grown on their own root. Hybrid teas are beautiful but they're just too much work for me. Here are the steps I take to protect roses:

* Mound soil or compost 6" to 10" deep around the base of the rose. Do this after several hard frosts and the ground is cooling down, usually in late November. You can also 'box' in roses with stakes and burlap, in addition to the mounding, for extra protection.
* For climbers, mound soil around their bases as above plus spray the canes with an anti-desiccant like Wilt-Pruf in mid-November. For added protection in windy areas, also place several layers of burlap over the canes and tie in place.
* Old Garden Roses and tall shrub roses also benefit from twine roped around their middles to cinch them in for the winter. This protects tall canes from being whipped around by winter winds and possibly snapped.

❧ Winter care for flowering shrubs.

* Keep flowering shrubs properly watered in fall. They need to be well hydrated before the ground freezes and shuts off their water supply. This is especially important for spring flowering shrubs that have set flower buds. If the plant is 'parched' going into winter, the buds are compromised and could lead to poor spring flowering.
* In November place chicken wire around shrubs that are targets for winterkill, stress or frozen flower buds. Pack the interior of the hooped cage with raked leaves. Shrubs that benefit from this protective measure include Hydrangeas that bloom on old wood and Butterfly Bush.
* In late November or early December spray anti-dessicant (Wilt-Pruf) on broad leaved evergreens like Rhododendron, Holly, Boxwood and Pieris (Andromeda).

- Protect temperamental shrubs in windy areas with 'burlap screens' using wooden stakes and burlap. These can include bud-ladden spring flowering shrubs or those that are borderline for your zone. I use wind screens in front of the thread-leaf Japanese maples and 'Carol Mackie' Daphnes.
- Planting spring, summer and fall blooming bulbs. Most people only plant spring blooming bulbs in fall but don't stop there. Hand dig or drill (using a bulb auger) summer and fall bloomers too for three seasons of color. Check out the Top Ten flowering bulbs list for choice bulbs and planting tips.

∾ Preserve tender bulbs, tropicals and annuals.
- Tender plants need to be dug and stored. These include Tuberous Begonias, Dahlias, Gladiolas, Callas and Caladiums. Wait until right after the first frost, dig, cut back foliage, remove soil from bulbs, allow to air dry for a few days and store in a cool, dry place. They can be stored in peat moss, vermiculite, newspaper, brown bags or onion bags.
- Containers of tropicals like Banana trees, Shield plants (Alocasia), Elephant Ears (Colocasia) and Agapanthus can be brought inside and grown as a houseplant or allowed to go dormant in a cool, dry place like the basement. If these tender plants are in your perennial beds, then dig them up and either place them in a decoratve container as a houseplant or allow them to go dormant in pots.
- For annuals you want to carry over to the next year, take stem or root cuttings. You can also move annuals inside as houseplants. Make sure to wash off leaves with an insecticidal soap or soapy water to kill bugs.

∾ Do a soil pH test if you haven't done so for several years. Fall is a great time to apply lime or sulfur after foliage has been cut back.

∾ Fall is the recommended planting time for Peonies, Oriental Poppies and German Bearded Iris.

∾ To save a bundle of money, purchase marked-down perennials in containers and overwinter for next year's use. Be sure to keep the potted plants consistently watered while they are still in active growth. In late October, cut back the plants in their pots. In late November give all pots a good drink of water and then cover with small squared chicken wire. This keeps voracious wildlife like chipmunks, voles and squirrels from eating the roots. If you want to further protect the plants, place mice bait between some pots. After securing the chicken wire, cover everything with tarp. Uncover in early April, depending on weather. If you have an unheated garage, shed or barn, then winter them over there and skip the tarp step.

❧ If your soil needs improvement, apply nutrient-rich mulch such as compost or aged manures around the plants after cutting them back. This will start breaking down and enrich the soil through fall, winter and spring.

❧ Many upright Arborvitaes, especially 'Green Emerald', benefit from 'cinching' to reduce damage from snow and ice storms. In November circle twine around Arborvitae, winding it from the base to the top, and tie off.

Top Ten Perennial Division Tips

Dividing plants is good for them, despite how stressful it may look or feel to you. Division stimulates new root growth. Younger roots are more efficient at their job than older ones. Plus dividing perennials yields more plants (especially valuable for perennials that don't come true from seed), opens up space between plants, reduces disease and insect problems, and allows more nutrients per plant from less root competition.

Many perennials benefit from divisions every two to four years depending on how vigorous the plant is. Some signs of a plant crying out for division include:

❋ smaller or fewer flowers
❋ there is a 'hole' in the center of the plant
❋ the plants gets too tall and leggy
❋ the whole clump looks messy

Here are some tips for dividing perennials for the greatest success and minimal stress.

❧ General protocol for perennial divisions calls for dividing spring bloomers in fall; summer and fall bloomers in spring. This needs to be slightly modified for cold climate gardeners. Given our shorter growing season and erratic fall weather, it is best to divide spring bloomers right after they finish flowering. This way they have a whole season to recover and set new roots before the ground freezes. Dividing them after they finish blooming is also a more efficient use of your time. You are whacking back the spent flowers anyway, why not whack the roots while you're there? Exceptions to this rule are Peonies, Oriental Poppies and German Bearded Iris that are best divided in late summer.

❧ Don't divide perennials when they are in flower or bud. If you have to divide the perennial 'in this delicate condition', you may need to cut off some, or all, of the flowers if the plant shows signs of stress after the procedure. Flowers and buds consume a lot of a plant's energy. By removing flowers you redirect resources to recovering roots. Once the roots are happily settled, then the plant's focus will be redirected to top growth.

❧ Divide perennials on a cool, cloudy day or in the cool of the morning or early evening. A light rain or mist are good too.

❧ Recommended steps for dividing perennials:
◆ water the garden the day before so the soil is easier to work.
◆ if there is a lot of foliage, cut back some for easier handling and to be able to see the roots better.
◆ insert the spade straight down and dig a circle around the plant at a distance of four to six inches from the outer stems.

- lift the plant from soil, shake some soil from the roots and place the clump on its side. If the perennial is too big to lift in one clump, create 'subdivisions' by carving sections right in the ground with a spade or knife and then give these the old heave ho.
- work soil away from roots with your fingers or use a strong spray of water to blast soil free so you can see the roots.
- divide by either 1) slicing with a spade or knife, 2) pulling sections apart with your hands or 3) breaking off newer outer growth. The double fork method is frequently mentioned but you need two people to do this and the process is overrated.
- discard any old woody sections.
- if you are replanting a division where the original plant was, you will need to add additional soil to make up for the loss of mass. While you are at it, add a dollop of organic matter like compost or aged manure.
- set the division in the hole, pour in about a cup of diluted liquid fertilizer such as Neptune's Harvest Fish Fertilizer, back fill with soil and water in with 'plain' water. Make sure the plant's crown, where the stems meet the roots, is level with the soil. Not too deep, not too high, but just right.

Another division technique is to cut pieces from the side of the plant without lifting it from the soil. Hosta and Daylilies are great for this. Simply use a sharp knife or spade to cut a pie-shaped wedge from the back of the plant. Refill the resulting cavity with fresh soil, 'fluff up' the leaves and you can hardly tell it underwent reduction surgery.

Most plants can be divided as noted except for those that resent divisions or have tap roots. These plants are usually propagated by seed, stem or root cuttings. Perennials in this category include Baby's Breath, Sea Lavender, Perennial Flax, Lupines, Oriental Poppy, Balloon Flower and Gas Plant.

Divide ephemerals (woodland plants that go dormant by early summer) and other spring blooming perennials that take 'summer siestas', right after they bloom. These include Virginia Bluebells, Leopard's Bane, Trillium and Bleeding Heart.

To reduce the need to divide fast spreading perennials as often, sink them in large pots. Make sure the sides of the pot are at least 5" deep. This will slow down their advance. You will still need to 'dig' them every three or four years to refresh the soil in the pot but this is still less work than annually dividing out spreading roots.

If you have done a lot of divisions in fall, apply a winter mulch as a protective 'blankie' their first winter. Straw (not hay that has seeds in it), pine boughs and shredded leaves are possible mulches. Do not put the mulch down until after the ground has frozen. This might not be until sometime in December, if we are lucky. The whole point of winter mulch is to keep the ground evenly frozen. Winter temperature swings that cause the soil to freeze and thaw is what does so much damage to perennials. And the damage is even greater in winters with little insulating snow cover.

A great way to save money is to divide two and three gallon containers of perennials. Simply remove the plant from the pot, place it on its side, divide or quarter as size permits, and plant. Be sure the plant is not rootbound before dividing. A rootbound plant has densely matted roots and usually some that are coiling around the base. This makes it difficult for the plant to absorb nutrients and inhibits the plant's roots from spreading out into surrounding soil. The plant is 'strangling' itself. If the plant is rootbound, first rough up the surface with your hands or a knife before dividing into pieces. The whole point of this 'harsh treatment' is to get the roots to head out to fresh soil and not stay tight together in the shape of the pot.

Most plants don't require large amounts of fertilizer. Some are very sensitive (read as, can overdose and die) to overly rich conditions. Many silver leaved perennials are in this category.

Just for clarification, since the topic of fertilizer can cause our minds to swim, the primary purpose of a fertilizer is to provide nutrients to plants while soil amendments like compost or manure, do more for a soil's structure (the way the soil particles fit together). Most soil amendments also contribute nutrients but just not at the same level as fertilizers. For example, if you compare a synthetic liquid fertilizer, Miracle-Gro Bloom Booster (15-30-15) to horse manure, the phosphorus (middle number) is 30% by weight in Miracle-Gro versus 0.55% in manure. So why wouldn't any flower-hungry gardener go for the fertilizer with the higher number? Ahhh, good question.

Working with organic fertilizers requires a reboot of how we typically think about fertilizers. Allow me to use the turtle and the hare children's story as a teaching tool. The turtle is the organic contestant that steadily runs the course while the hare takes off, burning up all his energy up front and is left the loser in the long run. Most chemical fertilizers are fast release and short term. Probably the best known product in this category is Miracle-Gro. Miracle-Gro recommends 'blue watering' your plants every 7 to 14 days. I refuse to create 'plant junkies' that require routine chemical hits to perform well. To make matters worse, I become the 'drug runner' who administers the goods. Miracle-Gro travels quickly off the leaves and past the roots resulting in very little being actually utilized by the plant. That is part of the reason that you need to reapply it every 7 to 14 days. So where does the rest of the fertilizer disappear to? Our water tables and storm drains to name a couple. In contrast, many organic fertilizers are slow-release, requiring microorganisms to gradually break them down, improving not only the soil's fertility, but even more so, its structure. An added benefit is that many of these organic fertilizers are recycled materials themselves, such as horse and cow manures, compost, leaf mold, fish emulsion and seaweed.

Thankfully, there has been an explosion in organic fertilizers. Good choices include products made by Bradfield Organics (www.bradfieldorganics.com), TerraCycle (www.terracycle.net), Espoma (www.espoma.com), Coast of Maine Organic Products (www.coastofmaine.com) and Gardener's Supply Company (www.gardeners.com). These companies are committed to offering exceptional products for lush lawns and gardens that are not at the environment's expense.

Before giving my top ten instructional list for using fertilizers, let's do a quick review of what the numbers mean. There are three numbers. The first is for nitrogen (N), the second is for phosphorus (P) and the third is for potassium (K) also called Potash. Simply said, nitrogen is for leaves and stems; phosphorus is for roots, flowers, and fruits; and potassium is for hardiness, disease resistance, root growth, and overall plant health.

❧ A simple way to fertilize gardens is with a nutrient-rich mulch that conditions the soil, provides nutrients to plants and reduces weeds. Aged cow, horse, sheep, pig, rabbit, chicken and alpaca are solid mulch dispensers. Finished composted manures should have an earthy smell, not one that makes your nose crinkle. For years I've mulched my gardens with composted cow manure and the results are spectacular. Last fall I spread a couple inches of screened horse manure over the entire lawn and raked it in. You could almost hear the grass blades smacking their lips.

❧ Other great nutrient-rich mulch materials include compost, aged leaves, cocoa bean hulls and seaweed (washed of salt). You can also use composted bio-solids (sludge) but this is not recommended around edibles. Many are familiar with the popular product, Milorganite. This contains sludge, as one whiff of the bag's contents will attest.

❧ Four footed creatures aren't the only source for 'Black Gold'. Red worms are worthy producers. Worm farms are sold at many garden centers as well as by mail-order. Red worms quickly convert kitchen and garden waste into vermicast (worm poop). A pound of worms, about 1,000 wigglers, will run you in the neighborhood of $20 – $30. A few bins filled with selected garbage and you've got action. Indoor and outdoor worm bins come in various sizes. Why not think outside the box and place a worm bin in the family room for endless entertainment? For more about worm bins and their value, check out Down to Earth Worm Farm of Vermont (http://www.downtoearthwormfarmvt.com). If you'd rather skip the farming part, TerraCycle (www.terracycle.com) sells both liquefied and granulized poop. And talk about a passion for minimizing one's carbon footprint, TerraCycle also packages their products in recycled soda bottles and milk containers.

❧ Old-fashioned compost tea, made from finished compost steeped in water, is another way to fertilize lawns and gardens. You can make this yourself by simply scooping a shovel of compost into some cheesecloth or burlap and then letting it 'steep' in a large bucket of water for several days. Stir it a few times daily to oxygenate the water. When the brew is earthy brown, remove the bag, straining it as you would a tea bag. The finished tea is ready to be 'served'. This method works best for small areas. For larger lawns and gardens, you might want to contact an organic lawn care company that uses efficient sprayers and large tanks.

❧ The Espoma Company (www.espoma.com) manufactures many organic fertilizers. As I am into simplicity and a tightwad, rather than buy a lot of different fertilizers, I primarily buy Plant-Tone for use on perennials, shrubs, annuals, vines and evergreens.

It's the same approach with our family dinner. I cook one meal, serve it to everyone, and they can eat it or not.

❧ Blood meal (dried blood from cows that have been 'processed' for meat) is high in nitrogen and super around perennials primarily grown for foliage, like Hosta. Blood meal is also effective at keeping bunnies at bay, although you do have to reapply after it rains.

❧ Broadly speaking, there are three types of fertilizers: liquid (water-soluble), granular, and time (or slow)-released.
- Liquid fertilizers like Miracle-Gro, fish emulsion, and manure tea are quickly available to the plant; absorbed primarily through the leaves. These usually are effective for up to two weeks.
- Granular fertilizers such as 5-5-5, 5-10-5 and 10-10-10 are applied to the soil with the nutrients released to the roots. If you get granules on the leaves, you may burn the plants. These fertilizers are usually effective for about five to six weeks.
- Time (or slow)-released fertilizers like Plant-Tone, Holly-Tone and Osmocote are also applied to the soil but release nutrients over three to four months.

❧ Apply liquid fertilizers in early morning, late afternoon or on a cloudy day. Plants close their leaf pores on hot days to reduce water loss. Fertilizing on a hot day can also burn plants.

❧ Stop fertilizing perennials and flowering shrubs after August 1. You do not want to keep pushing new growth and flowers. It is time to let plants start slowing down for the winter ahead and redirecting energy to roots.

❧ If you use Miracid on your acid-loving, flowering shrubs, please stop. Miracid is high in nitrogen and is recommended as a liquid application every few weeks resulting in a plant's 'jumpstarts and crashes'. A better option is to adjust the soil pH if needed with sulfur and then apply Plant-Tone organic time-released fertilizer. Or you can use Holly-Tone that contains acidifying agents.

❧ If you still get overwhelmed with all the different fertilizer choices, one of the safest bets is to pick a balanced fertilizer where all three numbers are the same. Ideally is should also be organic.

Top Ten Tips for Preparing New Perennial Beds

How many times did I hear my Mom say, do it right the first time. But all I seemed to hear was the "Wa, Wa, Wa, Wa" noise made by Charlie Brown's teacher.

Granted, it is a lot more fun to buy plants than to prepare garden soil. I hate to be the party pooper but poor soil is one of the main reasons gardeners are frustrated by their sad looking gardens. There is a saying among professional gardeners. It is better to buy a $1 plant and put it in a $5 hole than buy a $5 plant and put it in a $1 hole. Allow me to save you the mistakes I made and help you do it right the first time. Mom would be proud of me.

Before letting the old shovel fly to prepare a new garden, it is important to have some idea about your soil's 'complexion'. Let's start with your soil type. Soil particles are defined by their size. Sand is the largest particle; next in size is silt, and the smallest is clay. Your soil is made up of all three, along with air, water, organic matter and living organisms. The percentage of each particle will determine your soil type. Borrowing from a popular fairy tale: sandy soils are "too big" (composed of mostly larger particles that drain too quickly and lose nutrients); clay soils are "too little" (with smaller particles that pack together tightly resulting in poor drainage and little air space); but loam is 'just right'. Most experts consider great garden loam to consist of at least 5% organic matter and be approximately 40% sand, 40% silt, and 20% clay or an equal mix of all three. Okay, that was a really simple soil 101. To know which soil type you have, do one of the simple soil tests provided or take a sample to your cooperative extension office and they will test it for you.

KISS (Keep It Simple, Silly) SOIL TESTS

Watch what happens after a steady rain. If your soil drains fast and hardly looks like it was even watered, hello sand. If water puddles quickly on the surface or runs off, bring in the potter's wheel (clay). If it drains nicely but the soil remains slightly moist to the touch after it has been watered, halleluiah loam.

The ball test. Take a small amount of soil in the palm of your hand and moisten it. Squeeze your hand into a fist and then open it up. If the sample never holds a shape, you have sandy soil. If it forms a mound that gently falls apart, loam. And if it remains in a tight little ball, clay.

The Mayonnaise jar test. Put a cup of soil in a clear quart jar, fill with water from the sink, and shake, shake, shake (put the top on first). Let the jar sit for at least 24 hours. The soil will settle into layers. Sand will be at the bottom, topped by silt, then clay. You can now estimate the percentage of each in your soil by measuring the depth in inches of each layer. If you get ¼ inch sand, ¼ inch silt, and ½ inch clay then you have clay soil. Actually if you have more than ¼ inch (25%) clay, you still fall into the clay category. If there is 50% or more sand, you have sandy soil.

Having done a soil test, you are a winner if the 'soil wheel of fortune' landed on loam. But what if you fall into the sand or clay category? Join the gang. Most of us are not blessed with rich, crumbly loam from the get-go. We will need to apply some oomph to transform our good-for-nothing 'dirt' into loam. How? The magic ingredient is organic matter. Humus is just another name for finished, decomposed organic material that is usually dark brown or black and smells 'earthy'. 'Earthy' is a hard term to describe, but what it is not is a rotten, sour, reeking or ammonia-like aroma.

Whatever amendment you add to your soil, it should accomplish two things. One, it should increase the fertility of the soil, providing nourishment for plants with the addition of nitrogen, phosphorus, potassium and other nutrients. Just like people, the better nourished your plants, the healthier and better they will perform. Secondly, it should improve the soil's structure, the way the soil particles fit together. The goal is for sandy soils to retain water and nutrients better, while clay soils should drain faster and have more air space between particles. The chart includes some recommended organic soil amendments. Some may be more readily available and less expensive than others depending on where you live. And brace yourself. You should add organic matter every year since it continually breaks down. The good news is this is easily done by applying it as a mulch around your plants.

ORGANIC SOIL AMENDMENTS

Compost (decayed leaves, grass, other yard wastes)
Composted animal manure
Mushroom compost
Peat moss
Biosolids (treated sewage)
Leaf mold (decomposed leaves)
Grass clippings (untreated and composted)

Two cautions about organic soil amendments. Many people mistakenly believe peat moss is the preferred amendment. Actually, peat moss only contributes one of the two qualities we want from amendments. It is a super soil conditioner but it contains almost zero nutrients. Its claim to glory is its ability to hold water, like a huge sponge. This is a desirable asset for sandy soils, but a detriment to their clay counterparts. Plus peat moss is quite acidic, which can negatively affect your soil's pH. Those with sandier soils should absolutely add peat moss to your soil, but always along with another amendment such as manure or compost. And please stop putting peat moss in planting holes for shrubs and trees. This used to be the recommended protocol but has now been refuted as it may actually wick moisture away from tree roots. My second caution is short and 'sweet'. You cannot use cat or dog droppings in your gardens. These may contain bacteria and organisms that can cause disease.

❧ Make sure to prepare the soil deep enough when readying your perennial garden. You only get a chance to do this once, versus annual or vegetable beds that are turned over every year. Loosen the soil to at least 8" deep and up to 12" for clay soil. Do this before adding amendments. As you dig, work backwards so you don't step on dug soil. Use flat boards to step on if necessary.

❧ When digging a new bed, you cannot just rototill grass under and think bye-bye. These clumps and chunks will come back to haunt you as they sprout new shoots. You need to kill grass and weeds before turning them under. Some choices for accomplishing this include:

- BurnOut II (organic) and Round Up (chemical) are post-emergents weed killers that kill anything they are sprayed on. Be careful to follow label directions. Once the grass has browned, it can be turned under and worked into the soil.
- Solarization is a method where you 'steam' the grass to death in sunnier spots. Water down the area well and then place a thick clear plastic sheet over it and pin down with rocks, landscape staples, logs or anything else that is handy. Allow this to steam for 4 to 6 weeks and then turn under (take the plastic off first.)
- 'Smotherization' is my term for doing the same in shady areas but with this approach you starve the grass and weeds of light and water. Cover the area with black plastic and pin down as above. Keep it covered for 4 to 6 weeks and presto, you should have killed most everything beneath. I say almost, because there are some incredibly persistent plants like Bishop's Weed (Aegopodium) that can survive pretty tough situations. If it does raise its ugly head, pull it quickly, even if you do not get the whole root. Because of its already stressed state, that should be the final blow needed.

❧ 'Top spading' is another way to clear grass. Use a flat edged spade and slice under the grass about 2" to 3" deep. You can peel it back and throw the pieces in the compost pile or use them to patch other lawn areas. Start from the back of the bed and work your way to the front so you do not step on already cleared ground. Looking for an easier solution? Rent a sod cutter that makes quick work of the job. Many rental centers have these. After removing the grass, then prepare the soil at least 8" deep as noted above. Remember that since you removed 2" to 3" of root mass and soil, you will need to add additional soil to the area so the garden is not a 'sunken pit'.

❧ If you don't mind waiting a bit longer to install the garden, you can simply cover the grass with newspaper (6 to 8 pages thick with no colored, glossy ad pages), cardboard or rolls of landscape paper, and then top this with 3" to 4" of topsoil enriched with some organic matter. In about 6 to 8 weeks you can dig right through the paper easily to install plants. If you are impatient, you can lay the paper down, cut X's or circles through it with a sharp knife, install the plants, water the whole area well, and then apply 3" of mulch on top of the paper and around the plants. Ta Da! My only word of caution on this 'express' method (paper over grass and plant) is to those with poorly draining or clay soil. These soils really needed to be amended more deeply for long term, sensational results versus just a 'surface fix'.

After loosening the soil to a depth of at least 8", then add organic matter. See the chart of some acceptable goodies. Depending on how deeply you dug the soil, add up to 1/3 of that depth in inches of organic matter. For example, if you prepared the bed to 12", then add 3" to 4" of matter. Then use a landscape rake to smooth out the bed. Make sure the soil level is a few inches higher than you ideally want, as the soil will settle.

To accelerate great root development in a new bed, when preparing the soil work in a time-released organic fertilizer such as Plant-Tone (follow package directions for amount). This will provide nutrients over a three to four month period. Or, you can use 10-10-10 granular fertilizer that is effective for between 4 and 6 weeks. You can also fertilize existing flower beds with these fertilizers. Simply scratch the fertilizer into the soil around plants and water in. Apply this to your soil before putting down mulch or pull back mulch, apply, and then reset mulch.

Do a pH test, or better yet, a more thorough soil testing including nutrient analysis, after mixing all ingredients together. Make any correction(s) needed to the soil before planting.

After preparing the bed, water and allow the soil to settle for a week before planting. If you are the impatient sort (finger pointing at me) you can plant right away by using my 'tap dance' technique. Grab a big piece of plywood and set it on the prepared soil. The step on the plywood and gently tap dance to lightly compact the soil. If done right, the soil will not be too fluffy, nor too compact, but just right for planting. Move the plywood along the bed, starting with the deepest part of the bed first and moving forward. Be careful not to step on the soil. If you need to use a plank or another piece of plywood to reach the deeper sections of the bed, do so.

I find gardens that are slightly mounded to be more eye pleasing. The slight elevation sets off and frames the garden better. To get this effect, make sure to allow for additional height when prepping the bed so when the soil settles, it is still higher than the surrounding area.

❦ Raised beds are especially good for problem areas and ease of accessibility. They don't demand as much bending and great soil can simply be placed into the prepared 'cavity' and then planted.

CHAPTER 9

Pest Patrol

Top Ten Deer Resistant Perennials

Before I get to the list, let me start by pointing out the word resistant. One can resist but eventually succumb. Plus deer vary in what they find delectable from one area to another. There are never any guarantees in life (except that my teenage son will leave his dirty dishes in the sink).

In general, perennials that are lower on Bambi's browse list have fragrant or textured leaves. Of course poisonous plants also fare well. I have not included poisonous plants on this list, they have their own. By the way, it is not cold-hearted to use poisonous plants. Deer and rabbits are far too smart to ingest these to the point of a lethal injection. One little nibble and they turn away.

There is also a list for the Top Ten ways to protect your plants from ravaging deer and rabbits. I feel like a rep from Allstate – you're in good hands. I've got you covered.

Siberian Iris (Iris siberica) 28" - 42" Sun to Part Sun. Spring bloomer. White, yellow and white, pink, lavender, blue and purple flowers. After flowering, remove the flowers and stalks for a neater appearance. If the clump becomes unruly in summer, give it a hard haircut, removing 1/3 to ½ the folaige. Zone 3

Peony (Paeonia) 15" - 5' Sun to Part Sun. Spring bloomer. White, pink, red, purple, lavender, yellow and apricot flowers. All peonies: herbaceous, fern-leaf (tenufolia), tree (suffruticos) and intersectional (cross between herbaceous and tree) are snubbed by deer. Zone 3

Astilbe (Astilbe) 8" - 4' Sun to Part Shade. Summer bloomer. White, pinks, red, lavender and purple flowers. Plant Early (mid-June through early July), Mid (July) and Late blooming (mid-July through mid-August) varieties for six to eight weeks of color. Astilbes are heavy feeders. To encourage impressive plumes, work some slow-release fertilizer such as Plant-Tone or Osmocote (14-14-14) into the soil once a year in early May. Zone 3

Gas Plant (Dictamnus) 24" - 3' Sun to Part Sun. Early summer bloomer. White, pink, and rosy-purple flowers. Both the leaves and flowers have a lemony fragrance. The plant gets its common name because the flowers emit a flammable gas. If a match is lit near the bloom on a still day, a blue spark results. Gas Plant is a handsome plant all around. Dark green shiny leaves, splendid flowers, nice seed pots and stiff stems. But with its exquisite beauty comes a cost. It is extremely slow growing and hates to be divided. Translation: buy the largest container you can get your hands on. Zone 3

Gay Feather (Liatris) 12" - 4' Sun to Part Sun. Summer bloomer. White, violet-lavender and lavender-pink flowers. Gay Feathers are striking plants that add nice vertical interest to a garden. They start flowering from the top of the spike down so you can prune off spent sections and have attractive flowers for weeks. Great for flower arrangements. I like 'Kobold' the best with its stiff 12" - 15" purple spikes. Zone 3

Balloon Flower (Platycodon) 6" - 30" Sun to Part Sun. Summer bloomer. White, pink or blue flowers. Balloon Flowers make great conversation pieces. The buds look like puffed up balloons and then the burst open to cup-shaped flowers. There is even a variety that never opens and stays inflated. Flowers can be single or double petaled. There are dwarf cultivars like 'Sentimental Blue' (blue, 6" - 8") and taller ones such as 'Fuji Blue' (blue, 25"). Balloon Flowers should have a 'Do Not Disturb' sign next to them. They resent being divided, moved and are very late 'waking up' in the spring. Zone 3

Coral Bell (Heuchera) 6" - 20" Sun to Shade. Summer bloomer. White, cream, pink and red flowers. There are dozens of Coral Bells. Some have solid colored leaves while others can be bicolor or tricolor. Those with brilliant red flowers are 'Firefly' (green leaves), 'Splendens' (green leaves), 'Hercules' (green and white leaves) and 'Ruby Bells' (green leaves). Rich pink flowers decorate 'Snow Angel' (green and white leaves), 'Rave On' (greenish-purple leaves), 'Dolce Mocha Mint' (silvery-purple leaves) and 'Tango' (silvery-purple leaves). 'June Bride' has impressive sprays of white flowers above medium green foliage. Zone 3

Lady's Mantle (Alchemilla) 6" - 18" Sun to Shade. Early summer bloomer. Chartreuse flowers. Lady's Mantle is a must for cottage gardens. Its frothy greenish-yellow flowers foam above crisp, scalloped leaves. To keep it looking pretty into fall, prune off older leaves with brown edges to reveal new leaves below. Most cultivars grow 12" to 18" but erythropoda only gets 6" - 8" tall. A. alpina is the same size as erythropoda but has silvery leaf edges. Zone 3

Black-Eyed Susan (Rudbeckia) 24" - 6' Sun to Part Sun. Summer, fall bloomer. Yellow flowers with dark brown center cones. Black-Eyed Susans are no-fuss plants. Some spread more quickly than others but the color they provide for six weeks or more is hard to resist. 'Goldsturm', a favorite of many, has dark leaves and large orange-yellow flowers. 'Henry Eilers' is a head turner. Its wide spaced, narrow flower petals make it look like a 3' to 6' tall pinwheel. Be wary of triloba with its cute button-like flowers. It reseeds heavily due to its biennial nature. Zone 3

Statice, Sea Lavender (Limonium) 10" - 24" Sun. Summer bloomer. Lavender and lavender-blue flowers. Statice has dark green leaves that lay flat on the ground and sprays of flowers that are famous for drying. Annual Statice offers more flower colors but the perennial version is less work. All Statice require fast draining soil. Zone 4

Globe Thistle (Echinops) 30" - 40" Sun. Summer bloomer. Blue or white flowers. I love Globe Thistle's prickly globes that dance above textured leaves. No wonder they are not bothered by 'Bambi' or 'Thumper' but thirsty butterflies swarm them. These sun worshipers need room, they can get 3' across. 'Veitch's Blue' is the shortest blue variety with slightly taller options being 'Blue Globe' and 'Blue Glow'. If you want to try something different plant 'Artic Glow' that has glowing white spheres and a silvery cast to its leaves. Zone 3

Ornamental Grasses Please see the separate list for these.

drought tolerant   deer resistant

Rabbits (I refuse to call them bunnies or I'm afraid I'll get emotionally involved) are keenly interested in our perennials' tender new spring growth. This is when they become 'mulching mowers' in our gardens. Unfortunately rabbits have a much more diverse menu than deer. Thankfully there are some plants they wrinkle their noses at. Rabbits are not trespassers to be dealt with lightly. Consider the fact that they breed February through October (they take November through January off for the holidays); have a gestation period of only 30 days, and produce five to eight bouncing, gnawing babies per litter, that adds up to a lot of mouths to feed. You can almost empathize with Elmer Fudd.

In addition to smart plant picks, there are other strategies for outsmarting Bugs Bunny. Fencing is always effective. Surround the garden with a 2' to 4' high chicken wire fence with a 1" mesh. To sabotage burrowing rabbits make sure the wire extends into the ground at least 6" or make the wire L-shaped at the bottom so it is flush with the ground. You can also use taste and smell repellants such as Bobbex-R, Ro-pel, Plantskydd and Liquid Fence but these should be varied from time to time so rabbits don't get used to them. Most need to be reapplied after heavy rains or at periodic intervals. Be especially diligent about this in spring when tender new growth is most attractive to rabbits. Blood meal is another option. The smell of dried blood is not very comforting to them. Predator urines, such as fox and coyote, also wave a warning flag, as does the scent of dogs. Trapping is extremely effective if you can get them to enter the trap. I have tried many times with no success. Garlic clips work. You can buy these in bags of 25 or 50. Also a dash of red cayenne pepper is good. It almost sounds like a soup recipe. Farther off the beaten trail is used cat litter, ideally from a cat that is a good hunter of wildlife. To offset the used cat litter fragrance, plant Lavender and Catmint (Nepeta) with foliage that smells awful to rabbits. Personally, I'm going to try casting Rabbit's Foot good luck charms around the garden and see how those work.

The list below highlights perennials they are most likely to hop by. As with the deer list, poisonous plants are on a separate list.

Daylily (Hemerocallis) 8" - 5' Sun to Part Shade. Summer, fall bloomers. All colors except blue. Please see my Top Ten list for Daylilies. Zone 3

Columbine (Aquilegia) 6" - 3' Sun to Part Shade. Spring, early summer bloomers. Pink, red, white, blue, yellow, purple, violet and bicolor blooms. Columbines come in many different heights and flower shapes. Some flowers are spurless (no long 'tails' at the base of the flower), long spurred, short spurred, double petaled, downward facing or upward facing. The foliage can be green, chartreuse, blue-green and variegated gold and green. "Gee Toto. I don't think we're in Kansas anymore." All Columbines add grace to spring gardens. Although short-lived perennials, many will seed where happy. 'Little Lanterns' (red and yellow, 8" tall) and canadensis (red and yellow, 2' - 3' tall) are generous reseeders. Chrysantha 'Yellow Queen' has to be the longest blooming Columbine I have ever grown. It reaches 2' - 3' and blooms June through July. All Columbines are prone to attack by leafminers. Their calling cards are squiggly white lines on leaves. These lines are actually caused by moth larvae tunneling and feeding inside the leaves, not on the surface. They will not kill the plants, just disfigure them. The best way to deal with leafminers is to trim off infected foliage and dispose of it, but not in the compost pile. If the whole plant is infected, prune it back to within a few inches of the ground. The new foliage almost always remains clean. Zone 3

Stonecrop (Sedum) 3" - 30" Sun. Summer, fall bloomer. Pink, white, yellow and burgundy flowers. Double your pleasure with Sedums, you get great flowers and foliage. Creeping Sedums bloom earlier than taller varieties. Creeping Sedums come in many foliage colors including red, bronze, yellow, blues, various shades of green as well as bicolor and tricolors. Taller Sedums benefit from pinching stems in early July resulting in heavier flowering, compact plants. If you are looking for some unusual upright Sedums, check out 'Hab Gray' (sulfur yellow flowers, blue-green foliage), 'Diamond Edge' (creamy yellow and green leaves, burgundy red stems and rose flowers) and 'Red Cauli' (bright pink dense clusters, burgundy red stems and purple-tinged leaves). Zone 3

Stokes Aster (Stokesia) 8" - 24" Sun. Summer bloomer. Purple, lavender, white and yellow flowers. Huge, disk-shaped flowers cover dark green foliage. Some dazzlers are 'Purple Parasols' (purple, 18"), 'Blue Danube' (lavender-blue, 15") and 'Color Wheel' (white, lavender and purple, 24"). Deadheading helps to prolong blooms. It's easy to grow as long as it is not in a wet spot. Zone 5

Catmint (Nepeta) 8" - 4' Sun. Summer bloomer. White, pink and shades of lavender-blue flowers. Catmint can be petite and well mannered like 'Little Titch' that tops out at 10" and has mat-forming silvery-green leaves. On the other hand, 'Wild Cat' can reach 48" with lavender flowers. 'Dawn to Dusk' is the first to have pink flowers. There is also a white flowering variety, 'Snowflake'. Some Catmints reseed more than others. I find those in the subsessilis group to be very generous with their offspring. Gardeners are not the only ones to enjoy Catmint. So do cats. They like to nibble the leaves. I'm okay with that, but not so happy when Sylvester rolls on it (although this won't kill the plant, only reshape it). Zone 3

Sea Holly (Eryngium) 6" - 3' Sun. Summer bloomer. Steely blue, dark blue or white flowers. Sea Holly has mounded seed heads that sit on 'plates' (bracts) of finely cut leaves in July and August. 'Jade Frost' is the first variegated Sea Holly with showy pink, white and green leaves. 'Mrs. Wilmott's Ghost' has bewitching white flowers. It is considered a biennial or short-lived perennial so it's important to allow the plant to seed for more in future years. Folklore has it that Mrs. Willmott, a British gardener, kept these seeds in her pocket and tossed them in people's gardens so they would pop up a year later like a ghost. Zone 4

✢**Lungwort** (Pulmonaria) 8" - 15" Part Shade to Shade. Spring bloomer. Pink, blue and white flowers. Flowers are delicate beauties that 'drip' from the stems. Leaves can be solid green, spotted, silver or green with white margins. 'Redstart' is the earliest to bloom in spring. 'Majeste' has totally silver leaves. 'David Ward' has minty green leaves with white margins. Lungwort does have a bad habit of getting yucky looking leaves from powdery mildew after flowering. Fix the problem by cutting back foliage to within 2 inches of the ground. The new leaves will look great. Zone 3

✢**Windflower** (Japanese Anemone) 18" - 4' Sun to Part Shade. Late summer, fall bloomer. White or pink flowers. Windflowers add grace to late summer gardens. The flowers balance on long stems that wave above neat mounds of foliage. Anemone multifida. 'Rubra' is one of the shortest windflowers at 18". It has ferny foliage and blooms in summer. I have not had the greatest luck in getting these to winter, even though they are rated for Zone 5. Windflowers can have single or double petaled blooms. One of my favorites is 'Whirlwind', a white double at 3'- 4'. I have it on the west side of an island bed where it is exposed to blustery winter winds and it has done grand for years. The only Windflower I caution folks on is 'Robustissima'. It can be thuggish. Zone 3

✢**Hardy Geranium** (Geranium) 8" - 30" Sun to Part Sun. Late spring, summer bloomer. White, pink, magenta, violet and purple flowers. There are so many wonderful Geraniums to choose from. 'Rozanne' is the flower marathon winner with its violet-blue flowers June through October. There are also some fetching foliage cultivars. 'Midnight Reiter', 'Dark Reiter' and 'Espresso' have dark, chocolate foliage; 'Phillippe Vapelle' has gray-green, fuzzy leaves while 'Ann Folkard' and 'Anne Thomson' display yellowish-green leaves with magenta flowers. I tried growing 'Ann Folkard' but eventually got rid of it when I kept getting that Pepto Bismal feeling. Bright yellow and pink will do that to me. Another Geranium I actually escorted out of my garden was phaeum 'Samobor'. I like the darker markings on its green leaves but I found it reseeded more than I liked. Zone 3

✿✢**Perennial Salvia** (Salvia) 8" - 30" Sun. Summer bloomer. Violet, purple, white and pink flowers. Salvias are very forgiving plants. After the first flush of flowers in early summer you can shear them down to within three inches of the ground and new stems will generate another round of flowers. Some unusual looking Salvias include 'Plumosa' (18") with thick, purple plumes and 'Purple Rain' (24") with arching, smoky-purple flowers. Zone 3

Top Ten Deer Repellents and Strategies

Do you ever feel like someone's watching you but you cannot see them? It's an eerie, uncomfortable feeling, even ominous. That's how many garden plants 'feel', especially in spring. Bambi and friends are eyeballing tender new foliage, plump tulip buds and the unfurling leaves of your prized Hosta. It's almost as if a green checkered flag is waved and the food frenzy begins. I can deal with my teenage son and his friends raiding my refrigerator but the gardens are off limits. And yours should be too.

First of all, understand your opponent. Deer are very habitual. They tend to move in the same browsing patterns. The goal is to not have your property on their dining route. One way to accomplish this is by giving them an unpleasant experience right from their first nibble. Once they associate your gardens with a yucky taste or sensation, you're headed in the right direction, and they are hopefully heading in your neighbor's direction. That doesn't mean they won't be back. Deer will eat almost anything if very hungry. Ditto teenage boys. Here are some ways to create 'do not touch' boundaries.

๔ Commercial taste and smell repellents. Olfactory products work best in warmer weather; taste in colder temperatures. The most effective line of defense is a combination of both. Bobbex (www.bobbex.com), Tree Guard (www.treeguard.com), Plantskydd (www.plantskydd.com), Hinder (www.hinder.com) and Invisible Fence (www.invisiblefence.com) have received praises from many gardeners. Hinder is one of the few sprays that can also be used on edibles. Not Tonight Deer (www.nottonightdeer.com) has a great name but questionable results....on deer. Spray your weapon of choice on foliage and flowers per label recommendations. Even though most applications last four to six weeks, spray more frequently in spring. Voracious deer, coupled with rapidly growing plants and untreated foliage, equal trouble. Switch products periodically during the season to confuse your opponent and keep deer from becoming desensitized to your defensive tactics. Plantskydd (www.plantskydd.com), with bloodmeal as its main ingredient, is reportedly very effective in winter when other odor repellants can be compromised due to cold temperatures. It seems the unnerving message of shed blood is not easily missed.

๔ Fencing is still one of the best ways to keep deer away. A 6' to 8' wall or fence is best. Even though deer could still jump this, they are less likely to do so when they can't see where they're landing. Double fencing, 3' apart, is very effective. Electric fencing has also been used but could be considered unfriendly in developments. A more feasible option is an individual, battery-operated, scent-charged electric post that gives tender noses a zap when they are attracted to the scent emitter. Black polypropylene mesh fencing is great. It's virtually invisible from 20'. Many gardeners also swear by surrounding gardens with fishline at a height of 1' and 3' from the ground.

ᏺ Home-made concoctions. If you are a Julia Childs or Rachel Rae at heart, whip up your own nose-turning formula. Rotten eggs are always pleasant. Two eggs whipped into two cups of water and allowed to 'brew' a few days will do the trick. If this is too strong for your stomach, use one quart of water. Cayenne pepper and Tabasco sauce stirred into water and gently shaken also produces nice results. Add a few drops of vegetable oil or Murphy's Oil Soap to these mixtures so they stick longer to leaves. Fill a mister bottle with your favorite recipe and spray away. A garnish of hair or fur is the finishing touch. Dog, cat or human hair sprinkled liberally after spraying provides added protection. If hair is in short demand at your home, then shavings of Irish Spring soap will do.

ᏺ Recycled waste is always environmentally responsible. Dollops of Milorganite strategically placed around gardens works like a charm. Milorganite is treated human sewage. Although it initially has a sharp sewer smell, the vapors soon become imperceptible to the human nose but are still 'enjoyed' by four-footed marauders. Milorganite also works as a fertilizer but given its source, should not be used around edibles. On a similar note, one of my girlfriends swears she gets the same results from using teenage clothing left undisturbed in gym lockers or a dorm room for a semester.

ᏺ Predatory urine is prized by many at their wits end with munching deer and rabbits. I've found 'yellow gold' to also be effective against chipmunks and squirrels. Popular 'dispensers' include wolves, bobcats, fox and coyotes. You can purchase this deterrent in a liquid, granular or powder form. A dab or shake will do around plants you wish to protect; not on plants. Leg Up Enterprises is one popular manufacturer.

ᏺ Human urine. Yuck you say. Well, it works. We are at the top of the predator pyramid. Some imaginative gardeners have engaged the help of their husbands in marking gardens under the cover of darkness, although I doubt Emily Post would ever endorse such behavior. One of my friends routinely sends her husband out after he has polished down a few sodas or beers. They live in a rural area with a yard edged by woods. Unfortunately this approach is less appealing in my neighborhood where houses are close together. I can just see my husband 'walking' around our yard in the evening, greeting our neighbors as he 'goes'.

ᏺ Deerbusters systemic tablets are another option, although pricier than others. Non-toxic tablets are simply placed in planting holes, or dug in around existing plants. The material is then absorbed by roots and distributed by the plant's vascular system. Allow four to six weeks for the plant to be fully 'inoculated'. Nibblers are rewarded with a bitter taste. You can use tablets to protect bulbs, perennials, annuals and shrubs for two to three years. Just don't place them around edibles designated for the dining room table. If you are adventurous, try planting some of the above-mentioned, ripened teenage laundry around at-risk plants, although the results may be lethal to both plant and browser.

❧ Smart plant selection. Choose plants that are rarely browsed by deer or are poisonous. Smart plant selection is probably the easiest way to keep your blood pressure down. Steer clear of Bambi magnets like Daylilies, Tulips, Roses, Hosta, Asiatic and Oriental Lilies, Yews and Arborvitae. Build in distasteful perennials such as Siberian Iris, Russian Sage, Herbs, Coreopsis, Salvias, Catmint, Astilbe, Globe Thistle, Dianthus, Coneflowers, Lady's Mantle and ornamental grasses. See my Top Ten deer resistant perennials list for others. Most scented or silver leaved plants are also Bambi turnoffs. To further protect plants at risk, 'barricade' them with borders of yucky tasting ones. Safe to plant shrubs include Dogwoods (many also have colorful stems for winter interest), Boxwood, Clethra (wonderfully fragrant summer flowers), Spirea, Lilac, Potentilla, Tree Peony and Butterfly Bush. Poisonous perennials like Monkshood, Foxglove, Hellebores, Colchicum, Lobelia and Daffodils are always foolproof. One little nibble and deer are off to the next plant. No harm done to the plant or Bambi. Of course, if you are mean-spirited, or insanely desperate, you could always give deer 'bon-bon' plants to your neighbors as gifts. Just don't overdo it or they might get suspicious. Rooftop gardens are another thought.

photo courtesy of Gardener's Supply Company

❧ Garlic clips. Garlic loaded clips attach to plant stems to turn nibblers away. Clips are effective for up to eight months and are usually sold in packages of 25. You can also get garlic sachets if you're looking for a more fashionable look.

❧ Scare tactics. Motion detectors capture silently advancing deer. The element of surprise caused by spraying water, music (I bet rap works best), dogs, clanging aluminum pans dangling from strings, and ultrasonic devises are all possibilities. Then there is one product, Predator Eyes, that is supposed to look like the red eyes of predators at night. Backyard Deer Deterrents (www.backyarddeer.com) has lots of interesting tactics.

Top Ten Mole and Vole Deterrents

Okay, let's not blame moles for everything. I'm not a mole lobbyist but it seems whenever there is any 'trafficking' going on underground, moles get blamed. Voles, chipmunks and squirrels are quick to point the furry finger. Unfortunately, moles are so ugly, they are easy scapegoats.

I'm here to set the record straight. Moles are carnivorous. They eat grubs, beetles and earthworms. Actually, earthworms are almost 70% of their diet. Moles are not eating your plants. Yes, they tunnel, or should I say swim, through the ground with their big, clawed appendages but as they go they aerate the soil. Moles create two types of tunnels. Those close to the surface are used for feeding and the deeper ones are used to connect the feeder tunnels. A soil mound at the surface is created from excavating the deeper tunnels. Moles are very solitary creatures. Cornell Cooperative Extension states it is rare that more than one or two moles will reside in a half acre property. The only time moles gather is to reproduce and it is not pretty. Males are extremely aggressive and can fight for mating rights even unto death. Males….

Voles are field mice. Nasty little, voracious creatures that can rapidly reproduce and create a hungry, destructive army. Fertile little things, they can reproduce almost 50 babies in a year. To complicate matters, they do not hibernate in winter. They just keep munching on roots and bark. Voles create slightly smaller holes and tunnels than moles and the tunnels are closer to the surface. Voles can also 'tunnel' (chew) through taller grass. Above ground, they will also gnaw on bark and damage or kill trees. Wrap hardwire cloth around the base of susceptible trees in fall to protect in winter. Remember to allow for snow and adjust for this additional height.

Chipmunks are not much better. Cuter, yes. They create tunnels and will chew on plants and bulbs. If you have stone walls or stone ledges on your property, chipmunks will come. You could be out in the middle of nowhere and they will find you. Eerie. Sadly, voles and chipmunks can use mole tunnels to access and nosh on plant roots giving moles a bad rap.

❧ Havahart traps can be used to capture critters without harm. The problem is what to do then. In many states, including New York, you cannot transport wildlife off your property.

❧ Mouse traps work well for voles. Simply bait the trap with peanut butter or go gourmet with Quaker Oats and peanut butter hors d'oeuvres balls. Place traps near the varmint's holes or grass 'tunnels'. To prevent cats, children or others from stepping into a trap, place it under a box with a 'Ben and Jerry' mouse door cut in the side. You can also put a large pot from a prior plant purchase over the hole and trap.

❧ Rat traps work the same for chipmunks. I know I am not making friends writing this but many gardeners have told me how this approach dramatically reduced chipmunk infestations. To each his own. One word of advice trappers shared was to bait the trap but leave it unset for the first three or four times. Then set it. Chipmunks are smarter and more cautious than mice, but eventually the stomach wins out.

☙ Predatory urines can be dissuasive. Coyote, fox and bobcat fragrances are top sellers. You can get these in liquid as well as granular form. Just shake, shake, shake around where critters have been munching. I put drops of liquid coyote urine on cotton 'grenade' balls and 'launch' them into rock wall cavities where I see signs of feasting (nut shell pieces). Works like a charm.

☙ Hungry cats are an option. Unfortunately most cats are 'fat and happy' and not looking for snacks between meals. One of my neighbor's cats is a super hunter. Even though I hate cats using my garden as their little box, at least one of the six felines is making 'other' contributions.

☙ Depending on your position, mice poison is effective. d-CON is one of the most popular brands. Of course you need to be extremely careful using this around children, pets and other wildlife. I find a concoction of peanut butter and mice poison stuffed down a nosher's hole is a targeted approach.

☙ Castor oil has received high marks for repelling moles. Molemax, manufactured by Bonide, is a spray used on lawns where mole activity has been sighted. In tests by Michigan State University, it was effective 26 out of 27 times. It is also supposed to shoo voles as well. Bonide also sells Mole and Vole Repellent that is a granular, time-released castor oil product that protects lawns for up to two months.

☙ I was amused to read about a gadget, MoleMover, that sends out chatter replicating a mole's alarm and distress call to warn each other of danger. It won't kill the mole, just relocate it to your neighbor's yard. If you are curious or just want to have it as a conversation piece in your yard, check out www.exhart.com. They also sell Go Pher-It that 'communicates' with voles and gophers. Who thinks of these things?

☙ For those of you with an adventurous spirit, you can always try one of the following rumored remedies:
- Sticking little windmills in the holes to create annoying vibrations
- Stuffing mothballs or chewed bubblegum down holes
- Moistening cotton balls with spearmint oil and stuffing them down holes
- Feeding a garden hose into the hole and flushing the varmint out another opening
- Blowing fire extinguishers into holes
- Directing car exhaust into holes with the help of plastic piping.
- Dumping used cat litter dumped down holes
- Chunks of chocolate in holes (hey, it's poisonous to dogs)
- And one woman simply sends her children out with beach shovels to scoop dog poop and pat it into holes.

Top Ten Solutions to Slugs and Snails

Slugs are gross. At least snails discreetly cover part of their slimy figures with shells. But both are beauty queens compared to iris borers.

Slugs and snails enjoy partying at night. They come out under the cover of darkness and chew holes in leaves. Hosta is one of their favorite diners. They can also act like paper shredders and wreck havoc on foliage with less substance. Another calling card of slugs and snails is their slimy mucus trail they leave behind. It's almost like a sci-fi movie. Thankfully the slime is good for something. It seems the mucus is a natural anesthetic. If you lick a slug long enough, your tongue will go numb. Years ago some Native Americans would 'swish' slugs in their mouths when they had a toothache. We're just not as creative anymore. Except for little boys……

If luck were on our side, the deer mowing down our Hosta could engulf slugs as they go. I think the deer spit them out. So how can we naturally wage war on these slimers? There are a number of ways to get the upper foot.

❧ Diatomaceous Earth can be cast on the ground around vulnerable plants. DE is the sharp-edged skeletal remains of microscopic creatures. Sharp is not an attribute well received by these soft-bodied creatures. Concern is one of the popular brands available. This Diatomaceous Earth is not the same as that used in swimming pools.

❧ Iron phosphate is very effective on slugs and snails. Sluggo or Escar-Go are two popular products but you can usually find less expensive brands. Just make sure iron phosphate is the active ingredient on the label. Iron phosphate granules are a safe deterrent that won't harm children, pets or wildlife plus any that are not ingested will breakdown into your soil and fertilize your plants. Everyone wins except you know who.

❧ Beer traps are always a saucy solution. Pour stale beer into bowls and set them into the ground with the lip of the bowl just at soil level. Slugs slip into the brine and drown. Of course this approach assumes that you drink beer and that you don't 'drink to the last drop'. Personally, I can't stand sharing my beer with slugs.

❧ Copper stripping and bands are exciting. When the slimers start over the copper, they receive an electrostatic shock. You can enclose a garden bed with strips of copper set upright in the ground, or nail copper along the top edge of raised beds, or use copper tubing and circle individual plants.

❧ Flat boards are wonderful retreats for slugs. The board offers protection and a cool setting during the day and a launching point to slip out for their evening feed. Every few days pick up the board and remove the 'treasures' underneath. Another angle is using halved grapefruits or oranges. After enjoying your citrus, take the remains out to the garden and place the fruit face down on the soil near 'attacked' plants. The slugs and snails will be drawn to this nutritious snack. After a few days, you'll have a bowl full of slimers than can be set out for foraging birds to enjoy.

❧ Save those egg shells. Crush them and place around plants at risk. The shells will break down into the soil adding calcium, a little nitrogen and some trace minerals.

❧ Hand pick slugs and snails off leaves in the evening or early morning before they scurry off to their daytime hideout. Depending on how desperate my son is for cash, I have paid him an agreed upon amount per slimer or Japanese Beetle collected. The problem is counting.

❧ Hosta with thicker leaves are less interesting to slimers. The heavier substance leaves are more work for them to chew. What 'slugs'. Most blue Hosta, as well as those with heavy puckering in their leaves, fall into this ignored group.

❧ Don't water at night. You are just making it easier for them to slip over wet leaves. Make them work for their food.

❧ Ammonia and water will clean up the problem. Use household ammonia and mix it with water. Some say at a rate of one part ammonia to seven parts water. Others go as strong as one to four. I recommend using the more diluted mixture first to spray on leaves before inching up the strength of 'Mr. Clean'.

❧ Are you a coffee drinker? Coffee grinds have shown to be effective when spread around vulnerable plants. A combo of 80% coffee grinds and 20% chewing tobacco (unchewed) has received even higher reviews.

Top Ten Natural Insect Repellents

It seems many people have a bug up their sleeve with bugs. Insects are a part of our garden's ecosystem. The good, the bad and the ugly. Our goal should not be to blow away all of the 'bad' bugs, but rather to establish a healthy balance between these and beneficial insects without using chemicals. One easy way to address insect damage is to grow healthier plants. The 'fitter' your plants, the less problems they will have. It's the weakened or diseased plants that suffer first.

Some of the most common chewing and sucking insects are aphids, leafhoppers, spittlebugs, leafminers, spider mites, Japanese beetles, slugs, snails, and grasshoppers. There are many environmentally-friendly ways to control these. Chemicals are not one of them.

❧ Reach for non-chemical sprays like insecticidal soaps, horticultural oils, garlic or hot pepper sprays, and products that contain neem or pyrethrin. Neem is a renewable resource and is harvested from the seeds of neem trees native to India, Africa and other tropical regions. This amazing oil has been shown to be effective on many bugs that munch vegetables as well as on Japanese beetles, aphids, leafminers and cutworms. Safer products (www.saferbrand.com), Gardens Alive (www.gardensalive.com) and Gardener's Supply Company (www.gardeners.com) are all superior sources for organic products. When buying organic products, look for the label OMRI. This stands for Organic Materials Research Institute. Companies can submit their products to this nonprofit organization to become certified as organic if they meet OMRI's strict perimeters.

❧ Maintain healthy gardening practices including allowing plenty of airflow around plants and watering properly. The closer and more congested a plant's living space, the more attractive it is for insects that thrive in low light and 'stuffy' spaces. When watering plants, encourage deeper, healthier roots by watering less often but for longer intervals. Never water at night. Wet leaves on humid nights is only inviting problems.

❧ Make your gardens attractive to birds, frogs and toads that eat insects. Did you notice I did not say snakes? Put out welcome mats for these helpers by incorporating bird baths, bushes with edible berries and toad houses. I'm always amazed by how putting in a little water feature draws frogs from out of nowhere. Or you can purchase a Grow-A-Frog kit, a hands-on teaching tool sold for children of all ages. You can put it next to your red worm farm or ant farm.

❧ Plant a variety of flowers that provide diversity in pollens and nectars to attract different insects. This is healthy for both plants and insects.

photo courtesy of Gardener's Supply Company

꿈 Incorporate plants that draw beneficial insects (the 'good' guys) that feed on the 'bad' guys. Sweet Alyssum, Dill, Yarrow, Tansy, Fennel and Golden Marguerite (Anthemis) are seductive plants. Conversely, plant others that repel 'bad' insects like Garlic, Chives, Marigold and white Geraniums.

꿈 Purchase beneficial insect phermones, lures that attract targeted species. These work something like Japanese beetle traps but they don't actually capture the insects. They just draw them in. The mating drive is a strong one. For some, colognes and perfumes can be categorized as phermones.

꿈 Go straight to the source and buy containers of beneficial insects. Popular insects for sale are Lady Bugs, Green Lacewings, Hover-Flies and Praying Mantis. Sometimes insects are sold as adults and other times as eggs. These can be purchased at many garden centers as well as online. One concern raised among gardeners is how many purchased insects actually stick around after being released. Rest assured that a few may wander but most will remain faithful to you. It also helps to release bugs after it has rained or early in the morning when there is a lot of dew. Once released, these beneficial insects are in search of water and many more will stay in your yard if a water source is right there.

꿈 Buy *The Truth about Organic Gardening* by Jeff Gillman. This book was reprinted in 2008 and is a fabulous resource.

꿈 A mixture of mineral oil and water works great for controlling many insect and fungal problems. This is a homemade version of commercial Horticultural Oils that use more refined petroleum products. Homemade recipes vary but one tablespoon of mineral oil to a quart of water is a popular one.

꿈 Bounce dryer sheets. Why not? There are 101 uses for them. Why not 102? Many gardeners swear they repel mosquitoes and other bugs. Why not toss sheets throughout the gardens and see what happens. Use lavender or rose scented sheets for an added return on your money.

꿈 And while we are on the subject of pesky insects, how about deer flies? You know, those little buzzing pests that just can't leave you alone. I'm talking about deer flies, not my teenage son and his buddies angling for a favor. Here is a humorous, but effective, way to deal with these annoying flies. Deer fly defense patches. You place these sticky, adhesive strips on the back of your gardening hat and when a deer fly buzzes too close to the patch, zlotch! You will set a whole new fashion statement in the neighborhood. Check them out at Gardens Alive (www.gardensalive.com).

CHAPTER 10
Money-Saving Tips

Top Ten Money-Saving Gardening Tips

Let's start by admitting we have a 'problem'. Go ahead and say it. We are gardenaholics. But that is okay. We bring beauty to our neighborhood and enjoyment to many who admire our gardens and benefit from their bounty. Plus, we hopefully have healthier bodies and minds as a result of our efforts.

But such pleasures come at a cost: our expenditures at the oh-too-many garden centers and online companies. Cost-saving measures are vital to keeping sanity, especially during tough economic times. The following are some ways I 'stretch' my dollar. My contribution to helping you save is to provide twenty-five tips for the 'price' of ten.

❧ Buy two and three-gallon perennials and then divide the plants.

❧ Buy garden mulch in bulk (by the cubic yard) instead of by the bag. Check out these figures. One cubic yard of aged compost, manure or finely shredded wood may run around $25, plus delivery if you cannot pick it up yourself. One cubic yard will cover 100 square feet (10' X 10' area) just under 3" thick which is the recommended depth of mulch for perennial gardens. In comparison, one bag of garden mulch typically sells for around $4. Now visualize how many bags you would need to buy if you laid them side by side (they are about 3" thick when laid like this), on the same 100 square foot area. You decide which is more economical. As far as bulk garden mulches, check with your regional cooperative extension office for sources of weed free material. Also see if your local municipality offers mulch for free or at greatly reduced prices. You can also save a lot of money by making your own compost.

❧ When potting up containers, window boxes and hanging baskets, replace some annuals with perennials. At the end of the season, replant the perennials in the ground to overwinter and divide for more inventory the next spring.

❧ Watch for plant society sales (i.e., Iris Society, Hosta Society, Daylily Society), garden club fundraisers, and garage sales. When shopping at garage and garden club sales, be cautious of potential thugs that may take over your garden. While shopping, also take advantage of purchasing used tools, rakes, and other curb-side specials.

❧ Purchase perennials and shrubs that may be borderline for your zone from mail order catalogs. Many companies offer better guarantee policies than can be found at local garden centers.

❧ Shop with a friend for nursery specials that feature sales such as buy two, get one free. Combine mail orders for plants with a friend for bonus plants or discounts given for larger purchases. You can also split the shipping charges. Also swap divisions, seeds, bulbs and cuttings with friends.

෨ᓚ Don't fill containers with potting soil. Fill 2/3 of the space with 'fillers' (packing peanuts, bubble wrap, pine cones and styrofoam chunks).

෨ᓚ If a plant is borderline for your area, try the species first before buying cultivars. Allow me to explain. When you look at a plant's name, the genus (family) is the first word and it's capitalized. The next word is the species. This is usually in italics and in lower case. The third word (if there is one) is the cultivar. This is capitalized and in single quotation marks. This is the 'cultivated variety' or cultivar for short. The good ole species is usually hardier than its crosses.

෨ᓚ When shopping at garden centers in spring, keep a lookout for containers that were wintered over from the prior season. They will not look as pretty as the fresh pots coming off the delivery trucks but their roots will be almost twice as big. In other words, you will be getting a two-year old plant for the cost of a one year plant. Once these are planted in your garden, fertilized and watered, you will see big dividends.

෨ᓚ Spend less money on fertilizer, insecticides, fungicides, and plant replacements by using nutrient-rich mulch to enrich the soil and improve its structure; watering properly, and following good maintenance practices.

෨ᓚ Save on water bills by watering correctly (once or twice a week if needed); buying drought tolerant plants; and mulching the garden to reduce evaporation.

෨ᓚ Buy plants that are hardy for your zone, better yet, buy one zone colder. This will save you replacement costs and as well as the expense for winter mulch 'blankie'. Site borderline plants and broadleaf evergreens, like Rhododendrons and Hollies that can get damaged by winter winds, in sheltered locations.

෨ᓚ Grow perennials and annuals from seed. If you have the patience and room inside to start seedlings, this saves a lot of money.

෨ᓚ Share the rental of larger tools and equipment with friends. Possible tools could be a lawn aerator, sod cutter, power edger, dethatcher, hedge trimmer, Bobcat, and a jackhammer.

෨ᓚ Save money on short-lived perennials. Buy them in 4" pots, not gallon containers. Ideally, purchase these in the fall when they are on sale. Then either repot them in gallon pots or plant them in your don't-know-what-to-do-with-it-yet bed. Then when one of your short-lived perennials dies in the garden, replace it with your inexpensive backup. See the Top Ten list for short-lived perennials for more thoughts and a plant list.

🌿 Buy first year biennials in 4" pots. These will flower the following year. Biennials have a two year life-cycle. First year leaves (this is why so many are left on the sale tables in fall because most people buy containers in bloom); second year flowers, third year dead. Biennials include Forget-Me-Not, many Hollyhocks, Foxglove, Money Plant (Lunaria), Sweet William, and English Button Daisy (Bellis Perennis).

🌿 Buy 5-5-5, 5-10-5, or 5-10-10 fertilizer in the fall when it goes on sale for next spring's 'jump-start your gardens' application.

🌿 Buy a bulb auger (if you do not already have one) that fits most power drills. This makes planting bulbs quick and easy. Wait until bulbs are marked down at great clearance prices before purchasing them and then drill away.

🌿 Buy perennials and shrubs on sale in the fall. Dig into the ground for the winter or store under chicken wire and tarp until they can be planted next spring. If you have space, store them in an unheated garage or other building. If pots are under a protective roof, they will not need to be tarped. Still cover them with chicken wire to protect against foraging chipmunks, squirrels, mice and voles. I keep grabbing plants on sale until mid to late October. The only plants I stop purchasing as of October 1st are broad leaved evergreens like Rhododendrons and Holly bushes.

🌿 Buy annuals that live two years. I know that sounds like an oxymoron but there are some annuals, like many single-petaled Dianthus and Snapdragons, that can make it through one winter and bloom the next year.

🌿 Buy annuals that self seed easily to carry inventory over year after year. Cosmos, Verbena bonariensis, Snapdragons, Portulaca, Alyssum and Cleome are prolific choices.

🌿 Shop at field grown garden centers in spring. Look for summer and fall blooming perennials that have not yet been divided. Many field grown centers divide these in late spring. The smaller divisions are then replanted and sold for a fair price when they go into flower later that season. By shopping early, you get bigger plants that you can then divide when you get home.

🌿 Check for plant and seed swap groups in your region or online. Just google plant or seed swaps and see what your options are.

🌿 Don't assume that 'big name' products are better than others less advertised. For example, Sluggo (organic slug and snail bait) sells for around $14.95 in my area. I can get the same size container manufactured by Slug Magic for $8.95.

🌿 Participate in 'preferred customer' clubs sponsored by garden centers where you get either a free plant or dollar value after so many purchases.

Top Ten Tips for Buying from Mail-Order Companies

In the middle of bitter Northeastern winters, I open my mailbox and it's jammed with gardening catalogs just waiting for me to devour. Like chocolate, alluring photographs of lush, bloom-covered plants, tempt us into overindulging. We usually end up buying more than our pocketbooks or gardens can accommodate. Or, we find our choices are really 'empty calories' that end up in unwanted places such as the compost pile, although thankfully not our waistline. Long, cold winters can warp our gardening sanity. Allow me to bring you to your senses with a blast of reality before placing an order.

Certainly there are advantages to shopping by mail-order. The primary benefits being:

* Time and labor-saving conveniences. You can do all your shopping from home plus have the plants delivered to your doorstep.
* Greater selection. Many catalogs offer a more extensive plant selection than available at local nurseries, especially when it comes to recently introduced or hard-to-find varieties.
* Bargain prices. Prices can vary dramatically by catalog and these don't always correlate to plant size. You also need to factor in shipping and handling charges to a plant's overall cost. More often than not, bargain prices are offered when a number of the same plant variety is purchased.
* Good cultural information but this varies by catalog. Many of the better catalogs do a nice job describing the plant's growth habits and requirements as well as recommending companion plantings. Larger companies usually have toll free numbers staffed by people trained to help answer questions about plants. This valuable information is sometimes lacking at busy local nurseries where a staff person's knowledge of perennials may be spotty.
* Plant replacement policy can be exceptional. Replacement policies vary by company but frequently are better than you will find at local nurseries. Some will guarantee a plant for your personal lifespan; for a year; to the end of the current growing season or simply gurantee plants will arrive in good shape.
* Planned garden designs. Many catalogs offer complete garden plans and the plants at bargain prices, which saves you money if you had to pay for the plants separately and for a design service.

Most mail-order catalogs are national in scope and sell plants for many hardiness zones. When creating your list, make sure the plants are for your zone and also match your light and soil conditions.

🌿 Find out the size of the plants being shipped if the catalog doesn't clearly state this. The smaller the plants, the more attention they will need from you to grow into mature specimens. Time is money. Most container plants come in 2 ¼" to 4" pots.

🌿 Check the ratings of a company by going to The Garden Watchdog that reviews over 7,000 mail-order companies based on the feedback of thousands of customers. Visit www.davesgarden.com/products/gwd

🌿 Order early for better availability. You may want to call first to confirm the plants you want are in stock. Be sure to note if you don't want substitutes if your original request can't be met.

🌿 If possible, specify your order's arrival date. Plan for plants to arrive on a Thursday or Friday if your intentions are to get them in the ground over the weekend. It is also preferable that they arrive at a time when you are home so they don't sit on a hot porch all day. If you can't get a specific delivery date, then ask for the anticipated week. Most nurseries can give you an approximate date. Have your garden ready for planting before the plants arrive.

🌿 Double check a glowing catalog's description of a particular plant with several plant references to confirm it's really as noteworthy as described. Some catalogs have greatly 'enhanced' color photos. What you see is not necessarily what you get. Is the flower really that blue? If a special looks or sounds too good to be true, it usually is. Be wary.

🌿 If you are expecting an order during the hotter part of the summer, elect for the quickest shipping option to reduce the stress on the plants, even though it is more expensive.

🌿 Open and examine your plants immediately upon arrival. If there are problems, call right away to voice concern so there is no lag time noting your complaint.

🌿 If you haven't used a company before, start with a small order to check out the quality and size of the plants and their arrival state.

🌿 Many nurseries have a minimum shipping fee and a sliding scale for shipping charges. You can usually save money by getting some of your friends to combine orders with you.

Top Ten Tips for Buying the Best Plants at Garden Centers

When recruiting plants for your garden team, don't nickel and dime. Buy from reputable garden centers that sell healthy plants, properly watered and cared for while they sit one the benches. When you bring these first string players home, they'll perform like All Stars in your garden.

Once you get to the garden center, it's time to squeeze the melons and smell the cantaloupes, so to speak. As savvy shoppers, you want the very best plants in your shopping cart.

 Don't buy the plant with the most flowers; it is likely to stress out when transplanted. Select one that is well shaped and budded; this will make the adjustment easier and provide longer bloom in your garden.

 Pass over plants that have a space between the potting soil and the side of the container. This is a sign of irregular or poor watering. Ditto with plants that have soggy soil.

 When purchasing variegated plants, check to make sure none of the leaves have reverted back to a solid color. This 'retreat' is not uncommon. You need to stop the insurgence quickly by pruning off stems of solid colored leaves or the whole plant will quickly follow.

 Needless to say, leaves with bugs, brown and black spots, powdery mildew or that are curled and discolored are a no-no. Also, just because the runt of the litter is the only pot left for sale doesn't mean you have to take it home.

 Buy plants with healthy roots. Borrowing from a popular children's fairy tale, you don't want roots too 'big' (rootbound); too little (a four inch plug that was just potted in a gallon pot); but just right (fine white roots netting throughout the potting medium). To see what is happening you can gently turn the pot to slip the plant out a bit. Remember the quality of the roots is more important than top growth.

 Keep your eyes open for striking foliage plants, not just ones with pretty flowers. When you find a terrific plant at a great price, don't struggle with a decision to buy it. Just do it. And, when plants look weak or poor, don't talk yourself into buying them. Walk away.

~ Plan to be at garden centers earlier in the season, instead of later, to get the best selections. If possible avoid weekends. Usually mornings are less crowded and staff are more available to address questions. If possible, find out what day of the week new plant deliveries usually arrive. The early bird gets the worm.

~ Field grown garden centers are great resources. Perennials are grown in the ground and usually benefit from more stable growing conditions. If a perennial can overwinter in a field near you, it will most likely do fine in your garden as well. The size of clumps can vary. Some of the best buys are early in the season before larger, overwintered clumps have been divided. Finally, most field grown garden centers have a mature display plant in each bed. This can be very helpful for better understanding the height and width a plant will get in your garden.

~ When buying flowering shrubs and trees, don't just look at the flowers. Check out the trunk's shape and overall branching. You don't want to buy misshapen specimens.

~ Keep your ears open for smaller businesses who don't put a lot of money into advertising, but who offer exceptional plants. These places are usually discovered by word-of-mouth and are wonderful treasures. Try to support sellers that grow their own plants, which isn't that common these days due to the overhead. This is truly a labor of love. Many times these 'mom and pop' operations feature plants that are well cared for and the owners are truly interested in sharing their love of gardening with you.

CHAPTER 11

Well, You Don't Say…

Top Ten Stories Heard Down the Garden Path

Gardeners are interesting and amusing people. One of my great joys is meeting hundreds of gardeners every year through my business. As fellow hobbyists, we love to share special garden tricks or stories. Here are just a few of the thigh-slappers I've been privy to.

❧ At one of my garden talks a question was raised as to which manure was best on perennial gardens. There were many suggestions given by the audience including horse, cow, chicken, pig, sheep, rabbit and assorted other manufacturers. But one woman silenced everyone when she said they were all thinking too small. Elephant dung was her prized poop. She would travel to county fairs, armed with a shovel and hefty bags, and search out the elephant tent. She would then drag back the goodies to her station wagon and waiting gardens.

❧ One of my patrons experienced an unusual 'side effect' of using stale beer to eliminate slugs in her garden. She said it reduced the slug population but now squirrels were a problem. It turned out squirrels were knocking back the beer and stumbling around drunk in her yard. I suggested non-alcoholic beer.

❧ One new gardener was confused about applying lime to her garden. She called her local cooperative extension office and asked how many limes to add per 100 square feet.

❧ At a home garden consultation, my client told me she and her neighbor were having a friendly competition to see who could get beautiful blue flowers on their hydrangeas first. They both had the challenging bigleaf variety that blooms on old wood. One day she looked over and saw mounds of large blue flowers covering her neighbor's bush. Green with envy, she snuck over to take a closer peek. To her surprise, she saw the most realistic silk flowers wired to the stems.

❧ A gentleman in one of my lectures responded to a woman's question on how to get her dwarf crabapple to bloom. He had great success getting his fruit trees to bloom by taking a padded mallot and walloping the lower trunk several times. It seemed to 'scare' the **&^%#$^^ out of the tree, causing it to cough up flowers.

❧ One mother was desperate to find her young children something fun to do in the yard. Then she came up with an idea. She loaded plastic squirt guns with salt water and had them go on a safari hunt for slugs. Once they found these prehistoric looking creatures, they would spray the slugs and delight in how they 'magically' shriveled and disappeared (slug bodies have a high percentage of water and the salt extracts it quickly).

According to research done by Ben Miller at the Department of Horticulture at Cornell University, if paperwhite narcissus are given a nip of diluted alcohol it stunts the stem growth so they don't get tall and floppy. Gin, vodka and whiskey all will do fine. Save your money on the top shelf stuff. You might want to try giving some of your perennials shots to see if this works better than pinching. One for them and one for you and one for them, ...

I was giving a lecture at a very formal garden club meeting and I told the story of my friend's method for keeping deer out of her gardens. When her husband, Ted, got home from work, he would enjoy a soda or beer and then head outdoors with a full bladder to 'mark' their rural property. It worked like a charm. I also mentioned how another gardener said she did essentially the same thing by collecting her urine in a spray bottle and misting her plants. After my talk, an older woman dressed to the nines marched over to speak to me. I realized I'd probably made a big mistake telling the Ted story to this audience. To my absolute surprise she said "You know, you don't have to use straight urine. I dilute mine by half with water and it works great. I just didn't want to mention this in front of the others." And then she slipped off.

As a college prank, one of my friends put several Japanese Beetle Bags insides her friend's car and rolled down all of the windows.

In an effort to keep male dogs from peeing on my perennials and shrubs, I shook hot cayenne pepper on and around their 'targets'. It worked great and also gave me a chuckle. When a dog approached a treated area, he would sniff around as usual before adding 'his two cents'. But upon sniffing, the pepper would get into his nose and cause him to snort and shake his head, much to the wonderment of his owner. Mission accomplished and no real harm done. I later found red pepper flakes last longer than the powder. This method also works for squirrels but they hop too.

Top Ten Gardening Questions

There will never be a lack of gardening questions, or at least I hope not or I will be out of a job. In this book I've tried to address topics related to questions I've received over the years. The following Questions and Answers were published in garden columns I've writen and either expand on, or address new, conundrums.

Question: How do I get rid of Bishop's Weed in my garden? It is mixed in among my perennials.

Answer: I know some like Bishop's Weed (Aegopodium) but as far as I'm concerned the plant should be outlawed. It is an invasive thug to the 10th degree. There are a number of ways to tackle this headache-giver. You can use a post-emergent weed killer. Burnout II and Nature's Avenger are two organic choices. Roundup is a chemical option. Post-emergent weed killers are sprayed on the leaves. Be careful not to use post-emergents on breezy days; they will annihilate anything they touch. To kill plants in a tight spot where it is difficult to spray, put on rubber or plastic gloves, then wear cotton gloves over these and dip your hand into the solution. Simply touch the leaves and say bye-bye. You can also 'paint' the liquid on with a small paintbrush. Another option is hand pulling. Tiresome and frustrating I know, since Bishop's Weed has long white roots that twist through the soil. But the good news is if you keep pulling at the new top growth as it appears, eventually the plant will die when it uses all the food stored in its roots. If the thug has weaved itself into the center of a perennial, the best way to get at it is to dig the perennial up, shake the soil from the roots, pull out the Bishop's Weed, and then replant the perennial. Even though this takes more time and effort, it is really the only safe way to get at the trespasser hiding in stems of other perennials.

Question: How can I keep my neighbor's cat from using my garden as its litter box?

Answer: Get a dog. Just joking. Flower gardens seem to be irresistible portapotties for many cats. They enjoy a huge litter box with privacy screens. You really can't blame them. But this doesn't ease the frustration one feels when we hit one of their buried treasures. There are smell repellants you can apply to send them away in disgust. Bonide makes a granular product called Shot-Gun Dog and Cat Repellant that has an obnoxious odor to four-footed friends. Shake-Away is a product that works the same way but it contains fox and coyote urine. You simply scatter granules on the soil to dissuade visitors. Pepper and garlic sprays also work when applied to plants. Rue graveolens is an attractive herb that smells disgusting to cats. Rue is a perennial hardy to Zone 5 with showy bluish-green leaves and yellow flowers. It grows about 2' to 3' tall in full sun and well-drained soil. It looks pretty in my beds and works as an invisible cat fence. Cats also dislike the smell of citrus. Scatter orange and lemon peels around areas that show signs of a cat's calling card. Cat Scat is an interesting product. It looks like a bed of one-inch nails but it is a brown mat with plastic spikes that effectively discourages cats. Or to save money, make your own version by using thorny rose canes or brambly branches. Needless to say, trapping is out.

Question: Many garden centers start selling perennials in April. With our erratic spring weather that can include April 'snow showers', is it safe to put plants in the ground that early or should I wait until later in spring when the weather is consistently warm?

Answer: In April many gardeners fall prey to 'the call of the garden center' and a primeval urge to buy anything with a flower on it. Those who start flowers and vegetables indoors from seed know the importance of hardening off seedlings before plunking them outside on their own. This same process applies to greenhouse-grown perennials or bedding plants. These young neophytes have only known the pampered conditions of a closely monitored environment. The real world, without their plastic-insulated jackets, can be shocking and very stressful. To harden off plants simply put containers outside in a shaded area or indirect light for a few hours a day for the first few days. Then keep increasing the number of hours each day. After about a week of this adjustment, the plants are ready to be dug in and can hold their own. When shopping at nurseries in early spring, if perennials and bedding plants are still on sale tables inside the nursery, it is safe to assume they haven't had to "muscle-up" yet. That is your job as the new trainer. For those plants just moved to outside displays, it would be wise to ask garden staff the status of these plants. Even though they've made this next 'developmental step' to the outdoors, they may still get covered at night with protective clothes. So when getting a jump-start on your plant shopping in April, don't assume the plants are ready to be popped into your garden when you get home. Better to wait than be sorry.

Question: What is the difference between compost and mulch? I heard a speaker at a garden show say that compost was good to use as a mulch. I thought compost was what you turned into your soil. I'm confused.

Answer: Don't feel alone. Many people have asked me the same question. Basically, when someone says they mulched their garden, all this means is they shoveled some material on top of their soil, around plants, to reduce weeds, conserve moisture and to make the garden look nice. There is quite a range of materials that you can use for mulching beds. Compost is one of these. Compost is typically a combination of decomposed leaves and grass. Additional compostable items include kitchen waste such as vegetable and fruit peels, egg shells, coffee and tea grounds. Do not add meat and dairy products. Compost is a super mulch for perennial gardens because it breaks down more quickly than wood products, releasing valuable nutrients to your plants. Other materials that can be used for mulch include aged manures, cocoa hulls, straw, finely shredded wood, aged grass clippings (only if they are not treated with chemicals), shredded newspaper, and pine needles (these do not change pH as quickly as people think). Some folks even use recycled rubber, stone and crushed glass as mulch. A word of caution concerning cocoa hulls. Many dogs find these chocolate-tasting morsels irresistible. Unfortunately, chocolate is toxic to them and ingestion may cause a very upset stomach or worse, death.

Question: I have a wooded area in my backyard and want to create a woodland garden. What plants do you recommend?

Answer: Woodland gardening is becoming more and more popular. It is a very low maintenance, natural form of gardening and a great way to use native plants that are quite tough, disease and critter resistant. Winning points all the way around. When working with woodland plants, be aware that many are spring and early summer bloomers that go dormant once hotter summer months arrive. They like a rich organic soil in a cooler setting that gets at least partial shade. Deciduous woods are better settings than under heavier evergreen canopies. To kick off the spring show, I suggest the following bulbs: Trout Lilies (Erythronium), Winter Aconite (Eranthis), Striped Squill (Puschkinia Scilloides) and naturalizing Narcissi. In addition to these bulbs, tuck in some pink, burgundy, white or yellow Trilliums. Their delicate three-petal flowers just scream woodland garden. Wild Bleeding Heart (Dicentra cucullaria) is another forest hallmark with its feathery foliage and white or pink flowers. Wild Columbine (Aquilegia Canadensis) adds great color with its delicate red and yellow flowers that combine nicely with the rich blue flowers of Virginia Bluebells (Mertensia virginica). And how could you not plant ferns, Wild Ginger (Asarum), Woodland Phlox (Phlox stolonifera), Hepaticas, Foam Flowers (Tiarella), Hosta, Solomon's Seal (Polygonatum) and Bugbane (Cimicifuga)? A combination of any of these will give you a strong jumpstart to creating a charming woodland garden for fairies to visit. And remember, some woodland plants are protected wildflowers. It is important that you do not dig these from the wild or buy them from people who do. Purchase them from reputable nurseries that propagate these legally.

Question: I am tired of setting up wooden tents to protect shrubs from falling snow around the foundation of my house. Can you suggest plants I can use that can handle this beating?

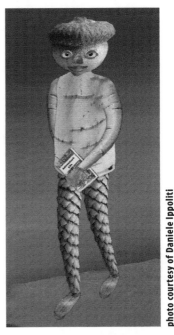

Answer: There are a number of 'big boy' perennials that provide the weight and scale of shrubs but duck below the ground (go dormant) before the snow starts flying. A nice pick for the sunnier side of your home includes False Blue Indigo (Baptisia). It reaches 3' - 4' and has attractive leaves with June flowers that are either blue, smokey-purple, yellow, or white depending on the cultivar. Ornamental grasses are another choice. Of course, a benefit of most grasses is that they provide winter beauty to landscapes but if they do get pounded by snow, it won't kill them. A few other sun-loving 'shrub-alikes' include Joe Pye Weed (4' - 6', mauve flowers in fall); chocolate-leaved Bugbanes (4' - 5', incredibly fragrant flowers in August); Thalictrum 'Lavender Mist' (6' - 8', lavender flowers in summer) and Thalictrum flavum glaucum (4'- 5', sulfur-yellow blooms in late June-July). Shade choices include large Hosta. And by large I am referring to those reaching three or more feet (with an equal or greater width) and sporting massive leaves. 'Frances Williams', 'Sum and Substance', 'Krossa Regal', sieboldian 'Elegans', 'Blue Angel' and 'Big Daddy' all fit this bill. Another candidate is Astilboides that looks like it is from another planet. A Zone 5 dweller, it has monstrous leaves that can measure over 2' across, spreads to 3' - 5', and gets about 3' tall. White, astilbe-like flowers decorate it in July. It prefers partial shade with evenly moist soil. Moving on to Astilbes, 'Purple Candles' (purple-rose flowers); 'Cattleya' (rosy-pink plumes), and taquetii 'Superba' (lilac plumes) all stretch to almost 4' and bloom in midsummer. As with all Astilbe, they do well in spots that get some sun, not deep shade. So give some of these plants a whirl and stop wrestling with as many heavy shrub protectors.

Question: I've heard my friend talking about reblooming Daylilies. How are they different from other Daylilies and where can I buy them?

Answer: Reblooming Daylilies are the rage. They are also commonly referred to as twice blooming or repeat blooming daylilies. Most Daylilies only bloom for three to four weeks. Rebloomers persevere for six weeks or longer. The one that many people are familiar with is Stella D'Oro; an 18" golden yellow daylily. In my opinion, it has been greatly overused. There are so many other rebloomers on the market these days. Some of my favorites are 'Custard Candy' (soft yellow with maroon band, 24"); 'Happy Returns' (medium yellow, 18"); 'Sunday Gloves' (white, 27"); 'Fairy Tale Pink' (light pink; 24"); 'South Seas' (coral-tangerine, 30"); 'Bama Music' (pink, 28"); and 'Little Business' (red, 18"). To keep repeat bloomers flowering their best, cut off each long stem (scape) right to its base after all the flowers have bloomed on it. This will encourage the plant to send up additional scapes with more buds. If you don't do this, the plant will put its energy into producing seed pods (those swollen knobby looking things that trick you into thinking they are buds). You can also treat your Daylilies to a time-released fertilizer such as Plant-Tone that will slowly fertilize them over three to four months. Repeat blooming Daylilies are usually more expensive than others but they are well worth the expense with their glorious extended blooming season.

Question: My 'Nikko Blue' Hydrangea stopped blooming a few years ago. Now it is just a big, leafy bush. Why isn't it flowering?

Answer: There could be a number of reasons for your flowerless Hydrangea. 'Nikko Blue' is one of the mophead, bigleaf Hydrangeas (macrophylla). To bloom best it needs sun to part sun. I find that many times people have it in too shady a spot where it only receives a couple of hours of direct sun. Sometimes the reason is due to using the wrong fertilizer, namely one that contains too much nitrogen (the first of the three numbers on the fertilizer bag). Excessive nitrogen will encourage leaves at the expense of flowers. If your Hydrangea is surrounded by, or alongside the lawn, your lawn fertilizer (high in nitrogen) could be leaching to it and may be part of the problem. Fertilize your Hydrangeas with a balanced fertilizer such as 10-10-10. Proper pruning is also important for good flowering. The best time to prune is right after they finish flowering in late summer. Most mopheads set their flower buds on the prior year's wood. This makes them susceptible to bud freeze over our long, cold winters, resulting in few if any flowers the following year. 'Endless Summer' is an introduction that blooms on both old and new wood and is hardy to Zone 4 (the majority of mophead Hydrangeas are only hardy to Zone 5). Because 'Endless Summer' blooms on new wood, the danger of bud freeze is greatly reduced. 'Endless Summer' will flower either pink or blue depending on if you have sweet soil (raising the pH with lime) or acid soil (lowering the pH with sulfur).

Question: My gardens always seem to look so washed out in August. What perennials can I plant to add late summer color and interest?

Answer: You are not alone in your frustration over the lack of color in late summer gardens. Many times this is caused by the simple fact that most gardeners like to buy plants in bloom. After our long winters, most of the perennials we buy during our spring shopping sprees are already in bloom, resulting in colorful gardens in spring and early summer. Few, if any, of our purchases were pots of leaves with tags promising late summer flowers. By adding some of the following later flowering perennials to your beds, you will give your garden a standing ovation instead of pulling the curtain on it. Terrific choices for sun to part sun are Helen's Flower (Helenium); Russian Sage; later blooming Daylilies such as 'Chicago Apache' or any of the repeat blooming varieties; ornamental grasses; Turtlehead (Chelone); Blue Plumbago (Ceratostigma); Asters; Japanese Anemone and Boltonia. Since most shade plants bloom in the spring and early summer before trees leaf out, there is not as large a selection for low light. Some nice picks include Toad Lily (Tricyrtis); Bugbane (Cimicifuga); Yellow Waxbells (Kirengeshoma); Monkshood and Eupatorium r. 'Chocolate'. Striking foliage plants also play a key role in contributing to a shade garden's overall beauty, especially as summer progresses. A few well placed shade-loving annuals like Impatiens, Wax Begonias, Browallia and Tuberous Begonias will add the finishing touch.

Question: Can you tell me something about Knockout roses? My neighbor raves about them.

Answer: And well she should. Knockout roses are incredible. They radically changed the way I thought about roses. I used to shun roses; having no patience for their general lack of hardiness in our area, susceptibility to black spot and other diseases, and overall need for attention. I am now a huge fan of any roses in the Knockout line, including the climbing red rose called 'Ramblin' Red'. 'Knockout' (cherry red), 'Pink Knockout' (fuchsia), 'Sunny Knockout' (yellow), 'Rainbow Knockout' (soft pink with yellow centers), 'Blushing Knockout' (light pink), and 'Whiteout' (white) are single petaled; 'Double Knockout' (red), 'Double Pink Knockout (pink) and 'Ramblin' Red' are double petaled. All are fragrant and bloom from June through October; are resistant to black spot; have showy blue-green leaves; are drought tolerant; flourish in full to part sun (growers are boasting that they will even do well in light shade); and hardy to Zone 4. You can now say wow. In addition to being super additions to flower beds and foundation plantings, they also make striking hedges. Their only bad rose habit is their attractiveness to Japanese beetles. But I must say they are not nearly the beetle magnets as other roses I've grown.

CHAPTER 12

Monthly Gardening Calendar

Before you scan these monthly lists and start hyperventilating, let me say that it is not realistic, or even sane, for you to do every single thing. I simply tried to write down the garden projects I've done over the years sorted by season. This doesn't mean that I do every one of these every year. I'm not crazy, nor are you. Some of these will have been mentioned earlier in the book but repition can be a good thing. Except when your three-year old whines "Mommy", "Mommy", 'Mommy" (keep repeating for another nineteen times).

Each monthly list starts with those items I feel are most important for having beautiful, healthy, low-maintenance perennial gardens. You can do as many, or as few, of these recommendations as you wish. I'm not looking over your shoulder.

photo courtesy of Daniele Ippoliti

૭ When we get dreaded ice storms, do not go out and whack the snow off the tree branches. You will probably do more harm than good, snapping branches in the process. Allow the ice to melt off. As it is melting, this is the time to gently try to dislodge some of the ice on the more weighted branches. If the weight of the ice has the limbs dangerously close to breaking, try to prop up the limbs with a stake or shovel. After snow storms, make sure to sweep or shovel off snow that has piled up on evergreens such as yews, Arborvitae, Junipers and Hollies. You do not want the weight of the snow to disfigure these. Use the pile of removed snow to build a snowman.

૭ Take time to daydream and think outside the 'garden box' about what you might want to do differently in your gardens this year. January is perfect for musing. The rush of the holidays is over and the onslaught of gardening catalogs hasn't jammed mailboxes yet. I get many ideas from great gardening magazines like Fine Gardening, Garden Gate, Country Gardens, Garden Design and Horticulture. Each year I pick a design element I want to address on my property. These have included: replacing some perennials with flowering shrubs; adding focal points; adding seating areas; creating more winter interest, and hardscaping hard to grow areas.

૭ Do not use rock salt on sidewalks and driveways. This will cause damage to nearby trees, shrubs and perennials as salt leaches into the ground. Substitutes include sand, products with urea and kitty litter. You have no control over what your local municipality is using for ice control, so for roadside gardens plant salt tolerant perennials such as Sea Holly, Sea Thrift, Sea Lavender, Daylilies and Black-Eyed Susan.

૭ Consider switching some of the needier plants in your landscape to natives. This will save you time, money and you'll be environmentally-responsible. So what's the big deal about natives? Native plants have evolved so they are in synch with other plants and wildlife in a region. They are important to a region's lifecycle, supporting its wildlife and pollinators. Flowers are food sources for birds, insects, bats and other small mammals while foliage serves as protective cover. In exchange these creatures benefit the plants by aiding with pollination, flowering and fruiting. A beautifully orchestrated pattern. Native plants are also hardier and require less assistance from you (watering and fertilizing) compared to man-manipulated cultivars. The American Beauties collection makes buying natives simple. This plant series was introduced in 2006 by two renown plant growers: Prides Corner Farms in Connecticut and North Creek Nurseries in Pennsylvania. The series features four theme collections: those for birds, dry shade, wet areas and butterflies. American Beauties does a superb job packaging and teaching homeowners about working with natives. Plant tags are well marked, stating which collection the plant is in, its bloom time, height, hardiness zone and water requirements. The American Beauties web site, www.abnatives.com, is a superior resource. Some of the categories you can sort by include foliage color, bloom time, alkaline or clay soil, salt tolerant and the ever-popular – plants that are less desirable to deer and rabbits.

❧ If the winter sun has melted snow from the base of roses, grab your shovel and start hurling. Snow is a great insulator. Mound up a good 12" of snow around each rose. I do not use styrofoam cones on roses. Instead, I simply toss soil around their trunks in late fall. Secondly, I'm not into the artificial igloo look in the winter landscape; my son's snow forts are much more interesting.

❧ On a similar note, if warm weather has melted snow away on the southern or western side of your home's foundation, then first aid may be needed. The exposed soil is subject to extreme temperature shifts. This can result in a see-saw action as the soil expands and contracts. This shifting harms sleeping perennial roots and heaves some unsuspecting plants right out of the ground. Shelter gardens at risk from this freezing and thawing action with a 'winter umbrella'. Evergreen boughs placed in early winter work nicely. You always know the gardeners in the neighborhood when you see bundled up figures scurrying down the road dragging discarded Christmas trees and kissing balls.

❧ Treat yourself. Get a manicure. Many gardeners welcome winter as a siesta from three seasons of maintenance. Our hands usually show the brunt of it. It's a treat not hiding them in our pockets to cover up rough skin, scratches or lingering dirt under the remaining good nail, I mean nails.

 # February

❧ The bitter winter months can take a toll on evergreens. Winds suck moisture from foliage that continues to transpire water even though it cannot be replenished by roots locked in the frozen ground. Shrubs on the west and northwest side of your home are most vulnerable. Couple this dehydration with winter sun burn (yes, scorching occurs and is exasperated by reflecting snow), and plants take a beating. Apply an anti-dessicant to foliage when the temperature is above 40 degrees. Hopefully this is the second application; the first having been in December. If not, better late than never! Do not spray blue-needled evergreens. They actually have their own waxy substance that protects the needles and spraying will do more harm than good.

❧ Check on tender bulbs you may have stored in a cool dark place for the winter. These might include Dahlias, Tuberous Begonias, Caladiums, Cannas and Gladiolas. Peek in on them to make sure there is no nonsense going on such as mold, rot or other no-no's. Some shriveled specimens may need a light misting to rejuvenate them.

꧁ Gardening catalogs will start arriving daily. These are a great way to get your gardening 'fix' as long as you don't lose all common sense while leafing through pages. Review my list for the Top Ten ways to get the most from mail-order sources. If plant descriptions sound irresistible and too good to be true (they should if the brochure designer has done his or her job), double check the plant's profile on some good web resources. PerennialResource.com, Perry's Perennial Pages (based out of Burlington, VT, http://www.uvm.edu/~pass/perry/) and Dave's Garden (www.davesgarden.com) are reliable sites.

꧁ Visit some of the great flower and garden shows in your region. These are jammed with fabulous floral displays, garden products, gardening seminars and more. The National Gardening Association's web site, www.garden.org, has an outstanding calendar that covers events across the country plus they also have other useful pages including a Public Garden Directory, how-to videos and seed swaps.

꧁ If you are into starting flowers and vegetables by seed, this is the month that the games begin. Unfortunately this is not my expertise but there are many resources available to help you step-by-step, including the above-mentioned web site, www.garden.org .

March

꧁ Force some colorful spring flowering shrubs to get a jump-start on spring. Probably the most popular choices are pussy willow and Forsythia. Other great picks are Serviceberry, Crabapple, Flowering Quince, Mock Orange, Bridal Wreath, Redbud and Fothergilla. Simply cut branches, about 1' to 2' in length, and bring inside. When selecting branches be careful not to take all of them from one spot or your shrub will look lopsided as a result. You want to make it look like nothing is amiss; sort of like how my son tries to sneak fresh baked cookies from the cooling rack. Place the branches in a bucket of warm water overnight (if you can totally submerge them, all the better); re-cut the ends the next day at an angle, and make additional slits at the base of the stems to increase water absorption. There is no need to smash the ends with a hammer as commonly recommended unless you've had a tough day. Place branches in a vase in a cool spot out of direct light until you see buds starting to break. Remember to change the water occasionally or you will soon have that distinct smell of swamp water. The branches would also benefit from an occasional misting if you feel so inclined. It will take anywhere from one to three weeks for branches to burst into flower. Staring at them won't help. Once the branches start doing their 'glorious thing', move the vase to a sunny spot in the center of your home so all can oohh and ahhh in anticipation of spring.

꧁ In late March or April cast 5-10-5, 5-10-10 or 10-10-10 granular fertilizer (ideally organic) on your gardens before, or immediately after, the foliage starts to emerge. This will encourage strong root growth and development. Follow the application rate on the label. I generally apply it at 2 pounds per 100 square feet. Everything in my yard, except the lawn, gets this treat: perennials; spring, summer and fall blooming bulbs; climbing vines; roses; shrubs and groundcovers. Granular fertilizer will burn foliage so by applying it before plants emerge you save time. If foliage is already up when you finally get to this, then apply the fertilizer right before it's supposed to rain.

🌀 Cut back ornamental grasses. Refer to Top Ten list for ornamental grasses.

🌀 Don't wait until the gardening season is in full gear to buy fertilizer, garden tools, stakes, twine and other necessities on your shopping list. Do it now while the gardening pace is slower. Remember to think organic and stop using harsh chemicals. The environment, kids and pets will thank you!

🌀 Watch for heaving plants (not the same as heaving children). As the soil warms in the spring, some plants are pushed out of the ground, exposing their roots to drying air. Not good. Gently press them down into the soil or gently step on them if you've had a bad day. Either way works. Perennials prone to heaving are Coral Bells, Heucherellas, German Bearded Iris and Foamflowers.

🌀 Now is the time to prune many summer and fall flowering shrubs or trees that bloom on new wood (wood that hasn't gone through a winter). The plants haven't leafed out yet so it is easy to see the frame and prune as needed. Prune out any broken branches or those that rub against each other. Prune to maintain the desired height and width as well as for a pleasing shape. Refer to my Top Tens for pruning flowering shrubs for more details.

April

🌀 Prune roses in early to mid-April except those that only bloom once in late spring or early summer. Many antique roses fall into this category. These should be pruned right after they bloom. For reblooming roses watch for green leaf buds to break forth from stems and prune back canes right above outward facing buds. Generally speaking, when you see Forsythia in bloom, let the games begin. I prune my shrub roses and floribundas back by one-half to two-thirds their height to maintain compact plants. Prune dead or broken canes and those that rub against each other. Prune climbing roses as well. Remove dead, broken or diseased canes plus, for older climbers, remove one of the oldest canes and train a new, younger one to take its place. Make sure climbing canes are tied to their support so they are not growing straight up. You want a curve to the cane so that more roses are produced by the smaller branches growing from the canes. If the canes are allowed to be mostly vertical, you will primarily get blooms only at the top of the canes. A different way to curve the canes is to tie small weights (like a metal washer) to the tip with fishing line and let gravity do the work for you. Some folks even create 'rose arches' by hooping the longest canes and pinning the tips to the ground with a garden staple.

✤ Pull chicken wire and burlap from around protected shrubs in early to mid-April. It's time to wake up the little darlings from their long winter nap. Up and at'em.

✤ Pull back compost, shredded leaves or soil that you mounded around the trunks of roses in fall. Wait until next month to give them breakfast; a nice healthy serving of slow release, organic fertilizer.

✤ If you applied a winter mulch such as straw or pine boughs, remove it in late March or the early part of April. I recommend pulling it off in two stages: first take off about two-thirds of the mulch and lighten up the remaining cover. About one or two weeks later remove the rest. Personally I refuse to put 'winter blankies' down on my perennial beds. If a plant cannot make it past Old Man Winter, I will find one that can. Tough love. It works! Also rake off debris such as leaves, branches, twigs and lost baseballs to make way for emerging perennials. Remember to watch for spring blooming bulbs that are just breaking through the ground. If you snap these tips you can say bye-bye to this year's flowers.

✤ Start watering potted perennials purchased at last fall's super clearance sales or that were divided from your own garden. If you stored them in an unheated garage, move them out into the sunlight and water. If they wintered over outside under a tarp, uncover the pots and water. Then sit back and feel smug about how much money you saved. You now have two-year old plants that normally sell in two or three-gallon containers for half the average cost of a gallon pot.

✤ If you're like me, you probably bought some spring blooming perennials while enjoying spring flower shows or shopping at the supermarket. Primroses are very popular sellers and quite irresistible. Make sure you give them tender care while they are on 'vacation' inside your home. Keep them watered and in the right light based on their requirements. Deadhead spent flowers and pinch off tattered or sad looking leaves. You can fertilize them with half strength fertilizer every week. Once the weather has warmed up in late April or early May, send them packing to the garden.

✤ Gardeners get antsy in April, our fingers are itchin' to get in the dirt. Hold yourself back until the ground has dried out. Depending on your zone and soil you may be able to start 'playing in the dirt' in mid to late April. Do not work soil when it is wet. Other than making the job harder than it needs to be, you're damaging to the soil's structure (the way the soil particles fit together). Walking on wet soil is just as bad. If you absolutely need to get somewhere in the garden and the soil is still wet, then use a piece of plywood to get where you need to go. At least this will distribute your weight.

❧ Get a jumpstart on weeding but be sure you know it's a weed before yanking. If you are not sure, leave it alone and it will show 'its hand' soon enough. Gardens should be weed-free…okay, at least less weedy….before applying mulch. Be careful if you decide to use a pre-emergent weed killer like corn gluten meal (organic) or Preen (chemical). These are usually non-selective so you may also lose perennials, biennials and annuals that have self-seeded.

❧ If you have not done a soil pH test for several years (or ever) now is the time. Simply said, the soil's pH affects a plant's ability to utilize nutrients. Most perennials, trees and shrubs in the northeast like a pH in the 6.0 to 7.0 range. Acid-loving shrubs such as Rhododendrons, Azaleas, Hollies, Mountain Laurel and Blueberries like acidic soils with a pH between 5.0 - 5.5. Lower pH with sulfur, peat moss, coffee grinds or chopped oak leaves. If you need to raise pH, use lime or wood ashes. For more on soil pH, refer to the Top Ten soil pH list.

❧ Clean tools that were not properly put away in the fall. Wash dirt off shovels, spades and hoes. Sharpen pruners, spades, hoes, lawn mower blades and other cutting tools with a whetstone or file. Or find a local business that sharpens tools. After sharpening tools, make sure to wipe them down with a light, penetrating oil. Also apply oil to moving parts and hinges. This is also a time to consider buying new tools that are more efficient. Check out the powergear hand pruners by Fiskars that are lightweight and ergonomic, making pruning easier on hands. Felco and Corona also make super garden tools.

❧ If your Peonies were infected with botrytis last year, start spraying newly emerging foliage with a fungicide that treats this disease. Symptoms include blackening of foliage and buds, buds that form but never open, and a gray mold on leaves and stems. This disease is caused by fungal spores in the soil. Old fashioned Bordeaux Mix (a finely powdered copper mixture) is a popular treatment for botrytis. Bonide Copper Spray or Dust is a modern version of this old remedy. Apply the spray as directed until the flowers bloom. To help prevent future problems, make sure to prune off infected leaves and buds. Do not put these in your compost pile. Also cut back Peony stems every fall, right to the ground, or better yet, just below ground level. Once again, do not put these in your compost pile. You can use the same fungicide spray on your Hollyhocks if they are troubled by rust (brownish-red spots).

❧ Put a post-it note to yourself to prune back spring flowering shrubs right after they've bloomed. These include Lilac, Forsythia, Fothergilla, Rhododendrons, Azaleas, Mountain Laurel, Flowering Quince and Daphne.

꙳ April is the time to cut back perennials that prefered to be left alone in fall. These include Lavender, Mums, Russian Sage, Montauk Daisy, 'Powis Castle' Artemisia, ornamental grasses and Butterfly Bush. Many gardeners are too gingerly with the old pruners. This only leads to frustration later in summer when plants become overgrown and a scraggly mess. If you are a hesitant pruner, wait until you've had a rough day at the office, with the kids, battling traffic, whatever…and then grab the pruners and go for it. You'll feel a lot better and the plant will look fuller and compact. Everybody wins!

꙳ If you've ordered plants from mail-order catalogs, keep an eye out for little brown boxes arriving at your front door labeled 'LIVE PLANTS'. Give potted plants a good drink of water after opening the box. If you cannot plant right away, place pots in a shady spot and make sure to keep them watered. You can 'heel-in' bare-roots in a trench in the ground, or pot them up, as a temporary way to hold them until they can go in their permanent home. Soak bare-roots in tepid water for at least two hours before planting. If there are any problems with shipped plants, call the nursery right away to voice your concern. Don't delay. Most nurseries are great about replacing plants or allowing you to use the credit towards others.

꙳ Cut off dead or weather-beaten foliage on perennials. Some perennials that benefit from 'deadleafing' are Asarum (Ginger), Bergenia (Pigsqueak), Helleborus (Lenton Rose), Heuchera (Coral Bell), Pulmonaria (Lungwort) and Epimedium (Barrenwort).

May

꙳ Apply a time-released fertilizer like organic Plant-Tone (5-3-3) or synthetic Osmocote (14-14-14) five to six weeks after you applied the earlier spring fertilizer. I don't use time-released fertilizers on every plant in the garden; only on heavy-feeding perennials that quickly deplete soil nutrients. Plants that 'wolf down their food' benefit from a slow, steady release of food over three to four months. Follow directions for the application rate, scratch it into the soil around the plant, and water in. Perennials that benefit from this extra serving of fertilizer include Delphiniums, Clematis, Astilbe, Lilium bulbs such as Oriental, Asiatic, Trumpet and Orienpet Lilies as well as ever-blooming roses.

꙳ Mulch your gardens. Don't make the mistake of putting mulch down too early. You need to allow the soil to warm up and dry out. The timing of this will vary depending on if you have sandy or clay soil. My 'green flag' for swinging the mulch shovel is when many perennials are about 4" tall. For perennial gardens, I recommend some type of nutrient rich, organic mulch such as composted grass and leaves, aged manures, biosolids (yup, sludge – but not where you have edibles) and shredded leaves. Be careful of using sweet peet if your soil already tends to be alkaline. Sweet peet is an organic product harvested from farms and usually includes materials such as manure, wood and vegetative products, alfafa or straw. Its pH is around 7.5. When applying these mulches put them down approximately 3" thick. Be sure not to build it up around perennial stems, shrubs or trees. Remember that 3" will settle to about 2". Heavier bark and wood mulches are best applied around trees and shrubs.

❧ Start dividing summer and fall blooming perennials. As soon as the foliage is approximately 3" to 4" above ground, grab your shovel and giddy up. By dividing plants early you won't wrestle with a lot of foliage or disturb the flowering cycle. This is especially a good time to divide monstrous Hosta that have bullied you into doing nothing. You can attack these as soon as the stem tips are only 1" to 2" above the soil. At this point you are a lot bigger than they are.

❧ If your garden is plagued by chomping slugs and snails, now is the time to take action. Review the Top Ten list for 'squashing' slugs and snail problems.

❧ Fresh, tender spring growth is a welcome mat for nibbling wildlife. Review the Top Ten lists for dealing with deer, rabbits, voles and other trespassers.

❧ Watch for powdery mildew. This white, powdery-looking stuff usually appears on leaves starting in July. The most commonly hit plants are Phlox, Bee Balm, Heliopsis, Zinnias and Lilacs. Powdery mildew thrives in locations where there is poor air flow, overhead watering (especially inconsistent watering) and hot weather. Powdery mildew will rarely kill your plants but it will make them look yucky. Strip off infected leaves and get rid of them. Do not put them in your compost pile. If the plant is a real mess, cut the whole thing down to within 3" to 5" of the ground. New growth is typically not infected. To reduce 'PM' in your gardens, open up space around your plants by divisions or weeding; water from below with soaker hoses; water in the morning so leaves are dry by nightfall if using overhead sprinklers; and buy mildew-resistant plants. You can also spray leaves of mildew-prone plants before you see any signs of trouble. Starting in early May, and then every two weeks, spray one of the following two solutions on the upper and lower surfaces of the leaves: Baking soda and water - one teaspoon of baking soda to one quart of water. Milk and water - one part milk to four parts water. To both recipes also add 3 or 4 drops of liquid dish detergent, Murphy's Oil Soap or vegetable oil as an adhesive. Shake well and apply.

❧ When buying perennials in smaller pots (2 ½" or 3" are common mail-order sizes), give them a boost by first potting them up in a 6" or quart-sized container. Let them grow on in these before planting them in the garden. It's also a good idea to pinch young plants back by 1/2 when transplanting to encourage fuller growth.

❧ Save time, energy and sore wrists by using a power drill and bulb auger to plant annuals in your garden. First water annuals in their trays if they are not already moist. Then simply drill a hole in the ground, toss in an annual plug, drizzle a little time-released fertilizer in the hole around the roots, backfill with soil, tamp down and move to the next hole. Be sure to water in the annuals well after planting. It's almost too easy....

✿ May is the month when plant shopping is at its peak. We swarm garden centers, snatching up more plants than we generally have room for in our gardens. When scooping inventory, look for plants with clean leaves (free of 'crawly things' or fungal diseases); that are compact, nicely shaped, and not scraggly; that are not loaded with flowers (these tend to stress more when transplanted); and that are not rootbound (roots pushing thought the base of the pot or coiling around inside the pot).

✿ Plant, plant, plant! Set out perennials, herbs, shrubs, and trees and start diggin'. The cooler spring weather makes transplanting less stressful. Make sure to dig holes large enough so that you are not cramming roots into it. When planting perennials and flowering shrubs, amend the planting hole soil with compost or manure and a little rock phosphate (0-4-0). Place the plant into the prepared hole, spread the roots out evenly and give them a splash of liquid fertilizer like fish emulsion, backfill with amended soil, tamp down gently and water-in with 'plain' water. Contrary to popular belief, do not add amendments to planting holes for trees. This only lures the tree's roots to stay where the food is a'plenty and easy gettin'. This encourages roots to circle within a smaller area instead of spreading out to new territory to better anchor the tree.

✿ Now is the time to place hoops and other supports (stakes, twigs), to provide assistance to floppy foliage. It is much easier to do this now when there is less foliage to fight with.

✿ Remember to allow foliage of spring-blooming bulbs to ripen (look brown and yucky) before you cut it off. If you remove the foliage before it dies back, the plants may not flower well, or at all, next year. The chlorophyll in the foliage is needed for photosynthesis that produces the food stored in the bulb for next year's flower. Do not braid or rubber band the foliage. You want as much surface area exposed to sunlight as possible. If you cannot stand how long it takes for foliage to call it quits, plant bulb varieties that grow 10" or shorter. Their foliage ripens quickly.

✿ Later this month, plant your containers and window boxes. Look for time-saving annuals that do not need deadheading such as Salvia Farincea, Vinca, Coleus, Portulaca, Browallia, Impatiens, Wave Petunias, Million Bells, Zinnia Profusion series, Lantana and Verbena. Use time-released fertilizer such as Plant-Tone or Osmocote in your potting soil (if the mix does not already include this) to save on fertilizing the pots through summer. A time-released fertilizer feeds your plants for three to four months saving you many trips with 'blue water fertilizer'. By the way, these annuals are also great to plant in the gardens for extra pops of color, especially where spring blooming bulbs or early blooming Asiatic lilies reside.

❧ Spring is a good time to propagate many perennials by stem cuttings. Look for fresh, new growth that does not have buds on it. Cut stem pieces 4" to 6" in length and place them in a container of water or a moistened paper towel inside a plastic baggy until you can plant them in potting medium. Use soil-less mixes such as perlite or vermiculite. Re-cut the stems to 3"- 4" with a sharp knife and remove lower leaves so there is 1" of bare stem to insert into the soil-less medium. Leave a few leaves for photosynthesis. Use a pencil to make a hole in the medium, dip the stem into a rooting hormone, insert it into the hole, and gently press the medium around the stem's base. Water well and place in a warm spot out of direct sunlight. Check the cuttings every day and mist the soil when dry. Depending on the perennial, roots should form within 4 to 5 weeks. Repot them to larger pots to allow them to grow on before putting them in the garden with the 'big guys'.

❧ Consider renting larger tools that are only used occasionally from your local rental service center. Why spend a lot of money for bigger ticket items when you can rent them for a day? Better yet, go in with a neighbor, split the rental fee and each of you can enjoy a half day of 'fun' using a machine. Some time-saving tools to consider renting include a dethatcher, aerator, overseeder, roto tiller, lawn roller, spreader, chipper, stump cutter, hedge trimmer, sod cutter and believe it or not, a jackhammer. We used a jackhammer to break through hard-pan, compacted clay soil one year. I should have captured this on film.

❧ Be careful of late-emerging perennials and shrubs that trick you into thinking they are dead. Some great actors are Butterfly Weed, Balloon Flower, Hardy Ageratum, Lead-wort (Ceratostigma Plumbago) and Hibiscus.

June

❧ Continue to remove spent foliage from spring flowering bulbs. After flowers fade, cut off stems but don't touch the leaves. They need to ripen (turn yucky brown) before removing. Ideally you should be able to simply pull the leaves from the soil when they are ripened. Daffodils keep their foliage for a long time. I usually can't stand the messy foliage any more by early July and I whack it back to a 6" tall clump.

❧ Compost weeds, garden and grass clippings, leaves, fruit and vegetable scraps. Composting is a great way to recycle and create 'black gold' for your gardens. To learn more about the how-to's of composting, contact your local cooperative extension office or click on http://cwmi.css.cornell.edu/smallscalecomposting.htm for a gold mine of resources and useful links.

❧ Pinch back selected summer and fall bloomers to make them shorter and compact, reduce the need for staking, and to extend the blooming season. Simply prune each stem by about 1/3 to ½ its total length in early June. Make sure to cut the stems just above where a leaf enters the stem. As a result, the perennial will not grow as tall and it will have more flowers. Pinching usually delays bloom by 1 ½ to 2 weeks but you will still get the same length of bloom, only later into the season. A fun, creative way to prune is to only pinch the front half of the plant. The back will bloom when it usually does but the front will kick in as the back is starting to fade. Plants that I aim my pinching fingers or hand pruners at are Phlox, Bee Balm, Heliopsis, Asters, Rudbeckias, Malva, Clara Curtis Mum, Shasta Daisies, Veronica, Sedums and Chelone. Some plants that should not be pinched are Foxglove, Delphinium, Gayfeather and Hollyhock.

❧ Divide spring bloomers that go dormant in summer. Many early blooming woodland flowers do this. Perennials in this category include Bleeding Hearts (Dicentra Spectabilis), Leopards Bane (Doronicum), Virginia Bluebells (Mertensia), Trillium and Shooting Stars (Dodecatheon).

❧ And while we are on the subject of dividing, also tackle those spring-blooming bulbs that have outgrown their designated areas. As the foliage begins to ripen and brown, simply dig up the clump, pull apart the bulbs and replant immediately. Make sure to water them in well.

❧ Buy annuals that go on sale later this month. I always stock up on some as 'reinforcements'. I use them around spring or early summer blooming perennials that die back or around perennials that I shear back after blooming due to their ratty foliage. Plants that cry our for 'annual camouflages' are spring-blooming Bleeding Hearts and Oriental Poppies; Asiatic Lilies (after their stems turn brown and I cut them down) and spring-blooming, woodland ephemerals. Shade-loving annuals also add a needed color jolt in late summer when few shade perennials are in bloom.

❧ Keep on top of watering gardens, especially if there is not a lot of rainfall in June. This is a month when many perennials have major growth spurts and they need their 'eight glasses of water a day' to grow big and strong. What I mean by that is not watering your gardens every day but instead deep watering your gardens up to two (clay soil) or three (sandy soil) times a week if needed. The general rule of thumb is to apply one inch of water per week, taking into account natural rainfall. Newly planted gardens will need shorter, more frequent watering the first few weeks until their roots get established.

❧ Prune spring blooming shrubs shortly after they've flowered. They get down to business fast and start setting their buds in early July for next year's flowers. If you wait too long to prune you will be eliminating, or certainly detracting from the show. Spring blooming shrubs include Forsythia, Lilacs, Weigela, Rhododendrons, Fothergilla, Azalea, Mountain Laurel, Deutzia, Flowering Quince, Daphne and Mock Orange. Pruning helps control the shrub's size, shape and stimulates growth and better flowering.

❧ Thin and stake Delphiniums. Before I tell you how I handle Delphiniums, let me first say that these gorgeous plants have a bad habit. They tend to die on you. Please don't think that you are to blame, well, maybe in some cases. Delphinium are categorized as short-lived perennials. If you get three years out of them, give yourself a big pat on the back. Having said this, by their second year they can get pretty big if they are happy. I thin out about one third of the stems right to ground level in early June. This allows better air circulation; less problems with fungal diseases; larger, showier flowers on the remaining stalks, and fewer stalks for me to have to painstakingly stake. Place bamboo or plastic stakes into the ground a few inches from the stem to be staked. Make sure the length of the stake is about six inches shorter than the flower will eventually reach. Or, if you have a lot of time, you can start with shorter stakes and then change the length of the stakes as the plant grows. Tie the stem to the stake at approximately one foot intervals. I use plastic-coated twisty ties and make 'figure eights' so that a loop goes around the stem and another loop around the stake. This allows the stalk a little 'wiggle room'. Keeping on top of tying stalks to stakes as plants grow is a drag, but seeing the flowers smashed down after a heavy rain or wind is an even bigger drag.

❧ Shear back spring blooming perennials after flowering for nicer looking plants the remainder of the season. Do heavy pruning on Arabis (Rockcress), Aubrietia (Purple Rockcress), Iberis (Candytuft), Dianthus, Phlox Divaricata (Woods Phlox), Phlox Subulata (Creeping Phlox), Aurinia Saxatilis (Basket-Of-Gold), Pulmonaria (Lungwort) and Cerastium Tomentosum (Snow-in-Summer). You'll be rewarded with fresh new foliage that pleases the eye. And don't let those Oriental Poppies sneak by with their ratty foliage. Yes, they get oohs and ahhs when they are in bloom but their foliage gets ughs after the flowers go by and the plant starts to go dormant. Prune foliage down within 3" to 4" of the ground when the leaves start to look yellow and messy. They will look better; you will feel better. If there is a gapping hole left, fill it with bright colored annuals that can be pulled out at the end of the season. Fun, eye-catching containers will also do the trick.

❧ Deadhead perennials to encourage more blossoms. Many gardens in zones 3, 4 and 5 peak in late June and July which means lots of plants that need our attention. Consistent deadheading extends the blooming season of many perennials. Perennials that demand frequent deadheading or they quickly go to seed are broad-leaf Coreopsis like 'Early Sunrise', Balloon Flower and Campanulas (Bellflowers). Not all plants will continue to send up more flowers when deadheaded but many will reward you with a longer bloom season if you simply get your pinching fingers (or pruners) moving. When deadheading, be sure to pinch off the spent flower just above where a leaf enters the stem, not directly beneath the base of the flower. The plant's growth hormones (auxins) are concentrated at the point where leaves and stems meet. By pinching there you will encourage more growth and buds.

 Consider adding some fun statuary, colorful pottery, or other entertaining features to your gardens for greater interest and to give the eye a place to rest when taking in all the flowers. Use your imagination. I've tucked in birdbaths, stone bunnies (the only kind I allow in my gardens), old chairs with seats filled with annuals, old work boots and hiking shoes and mischievous fairies. You can also use reflecting globes, urns, moss-covered rocks, water features and more. My son's unique contributions include soccer balls, baseballs, tennis balls and an occasional basketball.

July

 Remember not to deadhead biennials (Foxglove, Forget-Me-Nots, Sweet William, most Hollyhock, Money Plant, Wallflower) if you want seedlings next year. But if you want the biennial to behave like a short-lived perennial, cut flower stalks off before they go to seed.

 When purchasing a shrub, carefully inspect its overall shape, branching and the trunk's straightness. Buy plants that will mature to the space allotted instead of constantly pruning to keep it in check. Match the shrub to the site's light conditions and, if the soil tends to be very sandy or clayey, install plants that can handle these extreme conditions. When digging in plants around the foundation, be sure to plant it at a distance of half the shrub's mature width plus add another foot for air circulation.

 This is the month that Japanese beetles arrive in force. Rather than using toxic chemicals you can hand pick and toss the 'monsters' into soapy water. Or, if it has been a bad day, squish 'em. Organic products that contain neem or pyrethrin work as well, as some insecticidal soaps.

 If your Peony's foliage takes up too much space after blooming or blocks the view of nearby flowering perennials, give it a haircut. Prune back the foliage to the height and shape you want so that it becomes a nice backdrop for its neighbors. This may include pruning back some of the outer stems to within a few inches of the ground to allow more space for nearby flowering plants.

 At this point your Oriental Poppies and old fashioned Bleeding Hearts (Dicentra spectabilis) are probably looking really ratty, eyesores not associated with pretty perennial gardens. Whack back the foliage within 3" to 4" of the ground. The plant is going dormant for the summer. You are just giving it a helping hand. You can fill the resulting cavity with some colorful annuals or plant perennials nearby that have foliage or flowers that expand into this space. Companion perennials include Baby's Breath, Daylilies, Crambe, Astilbes and Hostas. Now is also the time to divide your Bleeding Heart if it has outgrown its spot.

❧ Early July is a good time to give some fall blooming perennials another pinch to encourage more heavily flowering, compact plants. Some plants to aim your 'pinchers' at are Mums, Sedums, taller varieties of Asters, Kirengeshoma and Boltonia.

❧ Later this month prune down spent Delphinium stems to encourage a second flush in late summer. Cut the stems right at their base. This is also the time to shear back Nepetas (Catmint), Centaurea montana (perennial Batchelor Button), perennial Salvias and Tradescantia (Spiderwort) that look scraggly. Cut back the entire plant by ½ to 2/3. You can also shear Silvermound (Artemisia) to its base if it has gotten floppy. It will fluff up and look nice again by September.

❧ Buy spring-blooming perennials on sale now. Prices usually have been slashed to move them out so there is more room for summer and fall perennials. They may look scrappy but don't let that scare you. Plant them in good soil and give them some loving care. You will be rewarded with beautiful flowers next spring.

August

❧ If you don't have Sweet Autumn Clematis (Clematis paniculata), please get one. You will love it. Airy white flowers cover this vine in August and September. And if that's not impressive enough, the flowers smell heavenly. Sweet Autumn Clematis can be pruned in late fall or early spring (it blooms on new wood) within 1' of the ground to keep it in check. It prefers full sun but tackles part sun just fine.

❧ Remember to water gardens, especially during the hot, steamy days of August. Water in the morning and be sure to give them a long, deep drink. You want to wet the soil a good 6" to 8" down for sandy soils, 4" to 5" for clayey loam.

❧ Use the space between stepping stones to plant tough, showy perennials. They will choke out weeds and soften edges. Some good picks for sun to part sun are Thyme, Creeping Yellow Jenny, Veronica 'Sunshine', Creeping Phlox and creeping sedums such as 'Angelina'. Those that can handle part shade to shade include Sweet Woodruff, Ajuga, Lamium and Irish Moss.

❧ Consider spray painting your dried astilbes and alliums bright colors. Go ahead and walk on the wild side. Alliums are particularly fun to work with as they have hollow stems. You can remove the ball-topped stalks from the ground (they detach easily from the bulbs) and insert a stake into the hollow stem. Then place these sturdy, spray painted balls around the gardens.

ᴄᴄ Monarch butterflies will soon start arriving in the gardens, a seasonal treat I always look forward to. Butterflies are truly 'art in motion' and we should do all we can to attract these lovely creatures. Some perennials that will draw them include Bee Balm, Sedum 'Autumn Joy' and 'Matrona', Asters, Joe Pye Weed, Butterfly Weed, Butterfly Bush, Yarrow, Catmint, Black-Eyed Susan, Globe Thistle and Coneflowers.

ᴄᴄ If you are 'getting out of Dodge' for an August vacation, be considerate of your flowers and make plans to have a friend water your gardens and containers while you're away. Perhaps they will even pull a weed or two.

ᴄᴄ Visit local field-grown garden centers in your area to check out what is in bloom or bud. Field-grown plants haven't been pampered in greenhouses. What you see, is what you get, when you get it in your region. Catalog pictures can be deceiving and the bloom time can vary by region.

ᴄᴄ Later this month is a good time to start dividing overgrown Peonies and German Bearded Irises. This will give them time to settle in before the ground freezes. Prune back the foliage, dig, divide and reset in planting holes amended with organic matter, and water in well. Remember to leave about half of the German Bearded Iris's rhizome above ground. Don't bury it or cover with mulch.

ᴄᴄ Order spring blooming bulbs now for a tidal wave of color next year. Walk on the wild side as you shop. Don't just purchase Tulips, Daffodils and Crocus. Tuck in some Alliums (great purple, raspberry pink, blue and white balls), Fritillaries, Eranthus (winter aconite) and Erythronium pagoda (dog-tooth violet).

ᴄᴄ Consider adding a splash of fall color with shrubs and trees with showy fall berries or brilliant leaves. Plants brimming with colorful berries include Cotoneaster, Viburnum, Holly, Winterberry and Dogwoods. Super shrubs for stunning leaf color include Fothergilla, Oakleaf Hydrangea, Sargent Viburnums, Witch Hazel, Clethra, many Spireas, Serviceberry and of course, sugar maples.

ᴄᴄ Plant fall blooming Colchicums and Crocuses for fall color. Many garden centers have these for sale starting this month. These fun-looking plants will surprise you as they show off their flowers on short stems without leaves. The leaves emerge in spring and go dormant in summer. An added bonus is Colchicums are not bothered by critters like chipmunks, voles and squirrels. The bulbs are poisonous.

ᴄᴄ Stop fertilizing your gardens, trees and shrubs. Time to let them rest and store their energy for the long winter ahead.

September

❧ For bigleaf (mophead) Hydrangeas near the foundation of older homes, scratch a little elemental sulfur or coffee grinds into the soil around the roots for rich blue blooms next year. Water in well. This will help compensate for lime that continually leaches from the foundation. Lime raises soil pH and pushes blooms towards the pink range.

❧ Buy bags of 5-5-5, 5-10-10, or 10-10-10 granular fertilizer to store in your garage or garden shed for next spring's application. It is hard to find these products in early spring when it's time to apply it to dormant gardens.

❧ Fall is a good time to prep new gardens for planting next year. Soil is generally lighter and easier to work now than in the spring after snowy, wet winters. Roughly till or spade the soil and then work in shredded leaves that will slowly decay over the fall and winter. Other organic amendments that can be added include aged manures, compost or other organic soil amendments available in your area.

❧ Buy some Pansies for a splash of fall color. Next spring they will usher in a new gardening season with another floral display. Pansies are mighty little plants that can surprise you with the degree of snow and frosts they handle. Since they are small in stature (but big in spirit) place them near entranceways so you can easily spot their shining faces greeting you when everything else in the garden may look bleak.

❧ Even though you may feel like looking the other way when it comes to the garden at this point of the year, you still need to keep on top of weeding. Allowing weeds and fast, self-seeding perennials to get the best of you in this cooler weather will only haunt you next year.

❧ Plant new shrubs. The cool evenings and warm days reduce transplanting stress plus encourage strong root development. Most deciduous shrubs and younger trees can safely be planted through October in 4 and 5; through September in zone 3. Of course you greatly increase the odds of how these survive Old Man Winter's attacks with proper planting and good watering. Before planting, water the container well. When digging the hole, make sure it is at least twice the width of the container and a depth that is the same height of the container. If you are feeling generous, you can add a dallop of compost or manure to the planting hole, mix it into the existing soil and set the plant at the same depth it was in the pot. Water the root ball well, backfill the hole with soil, tamp down and water again. Continue watering the new plant regularly until the ground freezes. I am hesitant to plant any evergreens after mid-October in zone 4 and 5; mid-September in zone 3 . Evergreens are more vulnerable to winterkill because they continue to transpire water through their foliage in winter. Unfortunately evergreens cannot replenish water loss from frozen ground. This can be extremely stressful to a plant, even fatal, if it hasn't rooted out well after transplanting. Finally, the healthier a plant is before you dig it in, the better its odds of surviving the winter. If the plant already looks stressed in the pot because it was not properly cared for at the garden center, then it is already behind the eight ball. Leave it there.

❧ Watch for frost warnings and take in tender perennials and annuals you want to save from Old Man Winter. You can winter them either as dormant tubers, corms or bulbs in your basement or treat them as houseplants. If you choose the later method, make sure to spray the leaves with insecticidal spray to kill any bugs hiding on leaves. Don't be surprised if plants initially set back a bit as they get adjusted to the new environment.

❧ September is still a great time to move and divide Peonies and German Bearded Irises or buy them at fall sales.

❧ If you don't already have a Tree Peony, consider buying one and planting it this fall for a spectacular show in the years ahead. It may take a year to settle in before really taking off. Remember, patience is a virtue. You'll get your reward. Tree Peonies are especially good choices for those who don't have full sun. They actually like part sun or even filtered shade.

❧ Another special Peony is Peony tenuifolia, a delicate, ferny leaved Peony that only gets 15" to 20" tall and has single, cherry red or pink flowers in May. It's an eye-popper at an eye-popping price. It can run between $35 - $50. But it is worth every hard earned penny.

❧ Start planting spring blooming bulbs. Make sure bulbs are disease-free, firm and a good size. The general rule of thumb for planting bulbs is to plant them at a depth of approximately three times their bulb height and two to three times their bulb width apart. For more on spring blooming bulbs and planting tips see the Top Ten flowering bulbs list.

❧ If you did not do so earlier in the year, divide spring and summer blooming perennials in early September. The only summer blooming perennial I do not divide now are Astibles. These have woody centers and take a while to set out new roots, perhaps too long, and Old Man Winter could get the upper hand. When dividing perennials cut back the foliage, dig up, divide with a sharp knife or spade, and replant. Stop dividing all perennials by mid-September to be on the safe side.

❧ Don't throw out leaves you've worked so hard raking. Chop leaves up by running a lawn mower over them or 'puree' them in a garbage can with a weed whacker. Spread this wonderful mulch around your perennials. This organic matter will slowly breakdown into the soil over fall and winter. Remember that oak leaves are acidic so check your soil's pH every few years to see if a correction is needed. You should do a pH test every few years anyway, oak leaves or not.

🌱 Take advantage of super clearance sales at garden centers. Keep your eyes open for great perennials, shrubs, statuary, containers, fertilizer and other goodies.

🌱 Collect seeds from your favorite annuals and perennials to plant next year and give as gifts. Collect seeds that are fully ripened (many times you can hear them rattling in the seed pod) and air dry for a few days on paper. Store them in a paper envelope, glass or tin jar in a dry, cool place out of sunlight. Remember to label the container with the name of the seeds.

October

🌱 Cut back gardens for the winter any time from mid-October on. Leave about 3" of foliage above ground, everything else takes a hike. Do not cut back these perennials: ornamental grasses, Montauk Daisy, Russian Sage, Artemisa 'Powis Castle', Lavender and Mums. Prune these in spring.

🌱 When cutting back perennials, remember to leave some for winter interest and bird food. See the Top Ten winter interest list.

🌱 Cut back perennials in pots you either picked up at fall sales or divided out of your garden and potted up. Continue to keep these watered until the final 'lockdown'.

🌱 Remember to deep water your gardens in fall. Perennials, shrubs and trees with well hydrated roots do better making it through the winter than those with dry, brittle roots.

🌱 Don't cut back roses in fall. Allow rose hips to set that help roses harden off for the winter ahead. The time to prune most roses is early spring. For roses with very long canes, tie canes together with twine so they don't whip around in winter winds. The only winter protection I give shrub roses is soil or compost mounded around their trunks. I put this down in late October or by mid-November depending on the weather. The roses should have dropped all of their leaves and be going dormant plus the soil should be starting to freeze. I do the same mounding technique for climbing roses but I also spray their canes with an anti-dessicant (Wilt-Pruf) for further insurance against damaging winter winds. To really coddle climbing roses in windy spots, cover their canes with burlap as well.

🌱 Rake fallen rose leaves from around roses, especially if they had mildew or black spot. Removing this debris reduces the chance of having these diseases back next year. The spores overwinter in the soil, transported there by infected leaves.

ꙮ The season of deer damage is fast approaching and I am not talking about hunting season. It's time to come up with a plan to outsmart Bambi this winter so he doesn't ravage your landscape. Check out the Top Ten deer deterrents list.

ꙮ Clean containers and window boxes and tuck them away for the winter.

November

ꙮ Water potted sale perennials or divisions one last time and either 1) move pots inside an unheated garage or shed or 2) group them together outside, ideally on the east side of a structure away from winter winds. Cover the pots (inside or out) with small holed chicken wire to keep feasting critters (voles, chipmunks, squirrels) from dining on the roots. Finally, for outdoor pots, cover the chicken wire with tarp and seal the edges with rocks or other heavy objects. That's it. Walk away until spring.

ꙮ If you want more flowers on your bigleaf (mophead) Hydrangeas that bloom on old wood (such as Nikko Blue) give them winter protection in November. Most bigleaf varieties set their flower buds in late summer for next year's show. Protect these buds from winter damage by giving then a burlap 'jacket' or encircling the bush with a chicken wire 'corset' and stuffing chopped leaves inside the cage. For added protection, first spray the bare stems with an anti-dessicant like Wilt-Pruf and then wrap them up with burlap or chicken wire. 'Endless Summer' and 'Blushing Bride' are two bigleaf varieties that don't need this coddling. They form flower buds on old and new wood. They are tough and beautiful. So if you are in the market to purchase additional hydrangeas, dare I need to say which ones you should get?

ꙮ Butterfly Bushes have a hard time getting through Zone 5 winters. Zones 3 and 4 are usually totally out of the question. To bump the odds of Butterfly Bushes making it, protect these the same way as mophead hydrangeas that bloom on old wood. Wrap them with chicken wire and chopped leaves. Do not cut these back in fall. Prune them hard in spring after uncovering them.

ꙮ For flowering shrubs and small ornamental trees susceptible to winter wind damage, shield them with a burlap wall. I use wooden stakes, a power stapler and burlap. Many times I don't totally surround the plant. I just put one or two panels in the direction the wind comes from. I like to use two or three layers of burlap for added protection. Some 'woodies' that I protect are thread leaf Japanese maples, Oakleaf Hydrangea and Daphne. You could also use this approach for keeping deer from eating 'shrub candy' like Arborvitaes, Yews and Rhododendrons. Make sure to block all sides of attack.

ꙮ Set-up wooden tents over shrubs to protect from crashing snow. If you want to make it easier on yourself, replace some foundation shrubs requiring protection with 'full bodied' perennials that provide the visual 'weight' of shrubs but disappear under ground with the onset of winter. Some possibilities are Peonies, Baptisia (False Blue Indigo), Thalictrum (Meadow Rue), variegated Fallopia, Cimicifuga (Bugbane), Ligularia, large Hosta, Rodgersia and Ostrich or Cinnamon ferns.

Many upright Arborvitaes, especially 'Green Emerald', benefit from being 'cinched' to reduce damage from snow and ice storms. In November circle twine around the Arborvitae, working it from the base to the top and tie off.

I do not use protective winter mulches on my gardens. After whacking the gardens, I turn my back and wave farewell until spring. Established gardens do not need to be mulched if the right plants are used and the garden has been maintained so plants are healthy. Having said this, there are two reasons I would apply straw (not hay that is filled with seeds) or pine boughs: if I have done a lot of fall divisions or to protect tender perennials (not that I have these in my low-maintenance gardens). Do not apply mulch until after the ground is frozen. This could be sometime in December depending on your zone. Pine boughs are also good 'sun umbrellas' for areas that tend to thaw during mid-winter warm spells.

I love Hydrangea's dried flower heads for winter interest but for younger tree Hydrangeas I remove some, or all, of the flowers before snow arrives. I don't want the weight of snow and ice to tear or break slender branches. As the trees mature, the branches will become stronger and more able to withstand this stress.

December

For broadleaf evergreens that get wind or sun burned in winter, apply the first application of anit-dessicant on a day when the temperature is above 40 degrees. Rhododendron, Holly, Mt. Laurel, Boxwood and Pieris benefit from this kindness.

Gift-giving is the theme this month. There are so many cool gardening gifts for blessing family and friends. Some interesting choices include gardening magazine subscriptions; memberships to arboretums or plant societies; power tools and gift certificates to unique mail-order nurseries and bulb companies.

Start forcing bulbs to bloom during the holidays and cold winter months. The two easiest and most often forced are Paperwhites (Narcissus) and Amaryllis. Paperwhites usually flower in two to three weeks while Amaryllis take up to 6 to 8 weeks. By staggering the potting time, you can have an ever-blooming indoor garden. One word of caution about Paperwhites. The fragrance will either be heavenly or strongly unpleasant depending on the sniffer's perception.

Kick back, relax and enjoy great times with family and friends.

Index

A

Achillea 14, 69, 75, 109
Aconitum 25, 50
Actinidia 83
Agastache 45
Ajuga 65, 75, 77, 118
Akebia 83
Alcea 43, 101
Alchemilla 11, 74, 189
Allium 17, 29, 94-95, 112
Alpine Clematis 47
Amsonia 10, 109
Anemone 11, 16-17, 29, 193
Angelica 36, 108
Annuals 97-100
Antennaria 116
Anthemis 27
Anti-Dessicant 173, 224, 240-241
Aquilegia 191, 216
Aralia 49
Aristolochia 83
Artemisia 33, 70, 115, 136, 172, 229, 236
Artic Kiwi 83
Aruncus 11
Asclepias tuberose 69
Asiatic Lily 95
Aster 16, 44, 169-170, 233, 236-237
Astilbe 21, 23, 66, 71, 77, 125, 143-145, 171-173, 188, 217, 236
Astilboides 107, 217
Astrantia 13
Athyrium niponicum 23, 122
Autumn Crocus 51
Azalea 86, 164, 228, 234

B

Baby's Breath 68, 70
Balloon Flower 34, 170, 177, 189, 232, 234
Baptisia 11, 68, 171, 217, 242

Bare-root 110, 158, 229
Barrenwort 18, 65, 76, 127, 229
Batchelor Button 28, 114, 153, 158, 171, 236
Beard Tongue 118
Bees 45-46
Bee Balm 32, 39, 43, 137, 158, 168-169, 228, 233, 237
Begonia 98, 174, 219, 224
Belamacanda 27
Bellflower 23, 31, 34, 53, 77, 130
Bellis perennis 101
Beneficial Insects 201-202
Bergenia 67, 229
Biennials 28, 89-90, 101-102, 170, 206
Big Root Geranium 66, 74, 76
Bigleaf Hydrangea 89, 218
Blackberry Lily 27
Black-Eyed Susan 74, 145, 170, 173, 189, 223, 237
Blanket Flower 27, 35
Bleeding Heart 18, 22, 110-111, 113, 128, 143, 158, 171, 216, 233, 235
Blood Meal 181, 191
Blue Fescue 104-105, 167
Blue Oat Grass 105, 167
Blue Star Flower 10-11, 109, 129, 132, 143
Boltonia 16, 170, 236
Bolton's Aster 16
Botrytis 228
Bottlebrush Shrub 86, 150-151
Broadleaf Tickseed 27
Browallia 98, 131, 141, 219, 231
Brunnera 18, 53, 66
Buddleia 43
Bugbane 24, 40, 45, 118, 127, 144, 142
Bugleweed 65, 75, 77, 118
Bulb Auger 161, 174, 206, 230
Bulbs 93-96, 136, 174, 206, 216, 224,

231-232, 237, 239
Burnet 17
Burnout II 154, 184, 214
Bush Clover 91
Bush Honeysuckle 92
Butterbur 107
Butterflies 17, 42-44, 190, 223, 237
Butterfly Bush 43, 91, 169, 173, 196, 229, 237, 241
Butterfly Weed 69, 232, 237

C

Calamagrotis 106
Calibrachoa 98
Callirhoe 68
Camassia 95
Campanula 23, 31, 34, 53, 77, 102, 234
Campsis radicans 84
Canterbury Bells 102
Cardinal Flower 21, 43, 72, 158
Carnation 10, 111, 153
Carolina Lupine 11, 171
Catmint 29, 41, 44, 46, 152, 171, 191-192, 196, 236
Centaurea Montana 28, 114, 153, 158, 171, 236
Centranthus 41
Cerastium 74, 116, 234
Ceratostigma 25, 219, 232
Cercis canandensis 88, 145
Chameleon Plant 32, 123
Chasmanthium 30, 106
Checkered Lily 94, 136
Cheiranthus 102
Chelone 22, 71, 172, 219, 233
Chinese Lanterns 32, 51
Chipmunks 175, 197-198, 206, 237, 241
Chives 29, 112, 171, 202
Chocolate Vine 83
Christmas Fern 67

Cimicifuga 24, 40, 45, 118, 138, 172, 216, 219

Clematis 41, 47, 79-82, 137, 164, 236

Clethra 90, 196, 237

Climbing Hydrangea 79-80, 83, 131, 137, 145

Colchicum 51, 94, 96, 136, 143, 237

Coleus 97-99, 141, 131

Columbine 191-192, 216

Comfrey 48

Compost 28, 54, 64, 68, 76, 97, 156-157, 168, 173, 179-180, 183, 204, 215

Coneflower 29, 58-59, 74, 126, 144-145, 158, 237

Containers 64, 81, 97-99, 137-138, 140-142, 174, 204-205, 231

Convallaria 50

Coral Bell 22, 44, 56-57, 113, 117, 122, 136, 144, 189, 226

Coreopsis 13, 27, 34, 58, 109, 143, 152, 170

Corn Gluten 28, 155, 228

Corydalis 22, 29

Cotinus 90, 148

Crambe 36, 107, 147, 171, 236

Cranesbill 29, 118

Creeping Sedum 16, 74, 77, 192, 236

Crocus 51, 96, 136, 237

Culver's Root 137, 144

Cushion Spurge 11, 68, 122, 129

Cypripedium 47

D

Daffodil 93-94, 136, 196, 232, 237

Dame's Rocket 102

Daphne 86, 145, 150, 174, 228, 241

Daylily 14, 35, 40, 54-55, 69, 75, 121, 131-132, 143-144, 191, 218

Dead Nettle 20, 116

Deadheading 34, 97, 140-141, 170, 234

Deer 22, 60, 145, 188, 194-196

Deer Repellants 194-196, 213, 224, 241

Delphinium 26, 35, 52, 153, 162, 168-169, 172, 233-234, 236

Dianthus 10, 102, 111, 136, 153

Diatomaceous Earth 199

Dicentra 18, 22, 110-111, 113, 216, 233, 235

Dictamnus 188

Diervilla 92

Digitalis 51, 102

Diphylleia cymosa 49

Dodecatheon 20, 233

Dogtooth Violet 94

Donkey Tail Spurge 112

Dryopteris 67

Dunce's Cap 37

Dutchman's Pipe 83

Dwarf Crested Iris 19

E

Eastern Redbud 88

Echinacea 29, 58-59, 74

Echinops 190

Edelweiss 116

Edging 31, 137, 159

Elderberry 91, 129, 148

Elephant's Ear 47

English Bluebells 95

English Button Daisy 101, 170, 206

Ephemerals 20, 47, 52, 177, 233

Epimedium 18, 65, 76, 229

Eryngium 46, 68, 122, 192

Erythronium 76, 94, 216, 237

Eupatorium 17, 25, 45-46, 73, 172, 219

Euphorbia 11, 112, 122

Evening Primrose 32, 158

F

Fairy Wings 18, 65, 76

Fall Blooming Crocus 96

False Hydrangea Vine 83

False Indigo 11, 127

False Sunflower 14, 35, 120, 130, 144, 168, 170

Feather Reed Grass 106

Fernleaf Peony 36, 110, 128

Fern-leaved Bleeding Heart 22, 110-111, 143

Fertilizer 54, 64, 66, 76, 97, 141-142, 167-168, 177, 179-181

Festuca 105, 111

Feverfew 30, 39, 158

Filipendula 72, 113

Fiveleaf Akebia 83

Flax 26, 52, 109, 177

Fleece Flower 14, 126, 143

Flowering Shrubs 86-92, 145-146, 150-151, 172-173, 181, 223, 225-226, 241

Foamflower 19, 121, 138, 226

Foamy Bells 67, 119-120, 128

Foliage 103-123, 147-148

Forget-Me-Nots 101, 132, 170, 235

Forsythia 86-87, 150-151, 225-226

Fothergilla 86, 150-151, 225, 228, 234

Fountain Grass 105, 145

Foxglove 51, 102, 170, 196, 206

Fritillaria 94, 237

G

Gaillardia 27, 35

Galium odoratum 77

Garden Centers 204-206, 209-210

Garden Heliotrope 40

Garden Phlox 13, 44, 120, 169-170

Gas Plant 39, 177, 188

Gaura 44, 109

Gayfeather 43, 233